Black Cultural Traffic

BLACK CULTURAL TRAFFIC

Crossroads in Global Performance and Popular Culture

EDITED BY

Harry J. Elam, Jr., AND Kennell Jackson

The University of Michigan Press

Ann Arbor

A CIP catalog record for this book is available from the British Library.

Library of Congress Cataloging-in-Publication Data

Black cultural traffic : crossroads in global performance and popular culture / edited by
Harry J. Elam, Jr., and Kennell Jackson.
   p.   cm.
   ISBN-13: 978-0-472-09840-8 (cloth : alk. paper)
   ISBN-10: 0-472-09840-3 (cloth : alk. paper)
   ISBN-13: 978-0-472-06840-1 (pbk. : alk. paper)
   ISBN-10: 0-472-06840-7 (pbk. : alk paper)
   1. African Americans—Race identity.   2. Blacks—Race identity.   3. African
Americans—Intellectual life.   4. Blacks—Intellectual life.   5. Popular culture—United
States.   6. Popular culture.   7. African American arts.   8. Arts, Black.   9. Performing
arts—Social aspects—United States.   10. Performing arts—Social aspects.   I. Elam,
Harry Justin.   II. Jackson, Kennell A.
E185.625.B555   2005
305.896'073'09051—dc22   2005012544

ACKNOWLEDGMENTS

The editors would like to acknowledge and thank all the participants in the international
symposium "Making the Spirit of the 20th and 21st Century Culture," held at Stanford
University in 1999 and sponsored by the Committee on Black Performing Arts and the
Black Popular Culture Workshop at Stanford. The event inspired this collection and
spurred us on to collect the additional articles on black performance and popular culture
it contains. We would also like to thank Elena Becks and Kim Fowler for all their work in
making this book possible, including organizing and conducting the interviews with the
artists. Matthew Daube, Micaela Díaz-Sánchez, Shawn Kairschner, and Arden Thomas
provided valuable assistance in proofreading and preparing the volume for publication.
Jisha Menon, Micaela Díaz-Sánchez, and Ebony E. A. Coletu were instrumental in secur-
ing rights for the images included. Hal Brands and Tory Penzi were valuable research assistants to Kennell Jackson. Harry Elam thanks Michele Elam for all her constructive input
and invaluable intellectual contribution. We both would also like to thank LeAnn Fields,
senior executive editor at the University of Michigan Press, for her commitment to this
project.
   "Continental Riffs: Praisesingers in Transnational Contexts," by Paulla A. Ebron, first
appeared in *African Identities* 2, no. 2 (2004). Reprinted with permission from Routledge.
   Portions of "When Is African Theater 'Black'?" appeared in *Ghana's Concert Party Theatre* by Catherine M. Cole (Indiana University Press, 2001). Reprinted by permission of
Indiana University Press.

   Cover illustration: *A3 Blackface #21*, by iona rozeal brown. The subject, a corked-up
geisha with afro-puffs, was influenced by the phenomenon of *ganguro*, in which Japanese
youth darken their skin and pay to have their hair permed into afros.

Contents

TRICIA ROSE

Foreword

The traffic in black culture to which this volume is dedicated is tethered to the traffic in black bodies on which these cultural exchanges are based. They share several disheartening characteristics: similar trade routes, unequal forms of exchange, and, often, a soulless focus on capital gain. These respective black traffics also share powerful traditions of possibility, such as strategies of refusal, revision, generative exchanges across policed boundaries, style and innovation as life-saving devices and unexpected alternative routes (a paved road isn't always the most traveled one). Despite the troubled ground on which these traffic patterns are set, a good deal of black culture emphasizes sacrifice for the larger good and a steadfast commitment to affirmation and confirmation against relentlessly long odds.

Racial ideologies undergirding the historical trade of bodies on which black cultural traffics are based have ensnared interpreters of black cultures in an endless paradox: black culture has been both an enduring symbol of unchanging purity, in full and complete opposition to white, western normalcy and yet a highly celebrated example of cutting-edge change, dynamism, and innovation. Forever "new," "exotic," and yet "always black," black culture must always be *recognized as black* for its daily bread (as in *familiar in its blackness*) and yet must also be *newly black* (as in pure and untainted by "outside forces") for the same ration. Always a key player in the world of racialized cultural exchange in the modern world, black cultures are playing an increasingly visible and complex role in this latest stage of globalization, a stage fueled primarily by the export of cultural products as Trojan horses of neo-imperialism.

This collection is part of a productive direction in the field, an effort that has found a way to move beyond the paralyzing nature of this inherited paradox. Previous efforts to explore black cultures sometimes unwittingly adopted the binary oppositional thinking about race that produced this fixed/always new black paradox in the first place. Much ink has been spilled in the service of defending both the presumed fixity of blackness and the immovable parameters of black cultural boundaries. Others have countered that blackness itself didn't exist because it could not be definitively identified and did not represent all black people.

This volume adopts a fruitful both/and position: sustaining the category "black culture" does not require the denial of incorporation, hybridity, transformation and exchange. One need not adopt the fiction of "absolute difference" under which black people have had to labor in order to recognize blackness as a reality. Alternately, to acknowledge incorporation, transformation, change and hybridity in black culture does not bring an end to the category "black culture" or black people, for that matter.

We do not invest in cultures randomly; cultural exchanges, desires, appropriations, and affinities always speak to already existing relationships, conscious and otherwise—those we want to reinforce, transform, deny, embrace. The cultural traffic in blackness is part and parcel of a legacy of race, even as myriad, dynamic, and hopeful new paths are being forged. No matter how lightly we hope to travel, we've always got baggage of some sort or another, from trips past.

Sorting through the meanings of black cultural expressions and traffics in light of this lingering paradox and in our vastly interconnected and complexly mediated world is more difficult and also more promising than ever before. Market forces, myriad forms of hybrid invention and re-appropriation, performances of blackness as a means of survival, cynical uses of black cultural symbols for profit, generational conflicts, new community formations and sympathetic exchanges all conspire to turn black cultural traffic into the proverbial parking lot.

This dynamic and generative collection breaks through this intellectual gridlock. Rather than steering away from these complexities, these scholars and artists embrace the details, the multiple locations, contradictions, exclusions, contexts, forms and styles themselves. The seemingly impossible juxtapositions produced by these trade routes and traffics are not what happens when you get lost—they constitute the journey itself.

DONALD BYRD

Twenty Questions

1. Today when we say "black popular culture" do we really mean American popular culture?

2. I used to believe that popular culture was a barometer of the attitudes and values of a society. Should I be afraid of what today's black popular culture signifies?

3. Is today's popular culture an authentic signifier? An artificial construct? A capitalist invention (a way of selling records, movies, baggy pants, images, etc.)? Or is it an organic, holistic ecosystem that has developed out of a natural mixing of dynamic cultural entities?

4. Does black contemporary popular culture really speak to the common values of most African American people? Should it? Is it supposed to?

5. Is there a singular black culture or a singular black popular culture?

6. Which black are we talking about? Black American, black Caribbean, black African, black European . . . black . . . black black . . . black?

7. Can people of African descent be the only ones to contribute to black culture? Would it still be black if nonblacks contributed?

8. Can white people play jazz? Should they?

9. Can black people dance ballet? Should they?

10. Is basketball a black sport?

11. Is rap music really black music or ghetto music?

12. Is ghetto black or just ghetto? When we say ghetto do we really mean "the projects"? Are black middle-class people being nostalgic for the ghetto when they respond to rap and hip-hop culture? Is it like plantation memory? Missing the "ol' folks at home?"

13. Why do white people listen to rap and dress like inner-city black boys? Is it penis envy, guilt, or performance? Is it black performance?

14. Do black youth think they are supposed to like rap—that it expresses who they are in definitive terms? Is rap, like fifties rock and roll, the music of rebellious and alienated youth—only now the "youth" are black instead of white?

15. I was sitting in the lobby of the Bel Age Hotel in West Hollywood and noticing a lot of well-dressed, baggy-pant-and-too-old-to-be-wearing-that-shit black music artists, wondering and asking myself: are they serious? Who is this show for? When did it start? Is this life or the theater? Can I be in the "gimme some of that money" show?

16. When I moved from New York to Los Angeles, and was stopped by the cops for walking instead of driving, or for having dreadlocks, or for being in the wrong neighborhood, was what I did to avoid arrest performance?

17. Are black people in America always performing? For themselves? For white people? For the world? Do we always feel like we are being watched? Are we being watched? Are we watching?

18. For black Americans, is performance linked to survival? Is performance a survival reflex? Is performance a result of genetics, like sickle-cell anemia? You have one gene and you are resistant to malaria or cops? Two genes and you become a dancing and singing coon?

19. Can we all sing and dance? Do we all have rhythm? Are we all God's chillen?

20. Is being black in America a cosmic performance? A comedy for the gods? A tragedy of Olympian proportions? Or just a sorry show?

KENNELL JACKSON

Introduction
Traveling While Black

In 1849, William Wells Brown set off for a journey to France and England. He was being sent to the Paris peace congress as a member of an American delegation. The thirty-five-year-old Brown was surely a most distinctive delegate. Fifteen years earlier, he had escaped from Missouri slavery, first into Ohio and later into New York. He exemplified what he called "self-culture,"[1] having taught himself to read and write extraordinarily well. He had made himself extremely well informed on political matters, an excellent conversationalist, and a stylish man. The year before the peace conference, his slave narrative had been a best-seller in America, and he had achieved first-rank status as a speaker on the American abolitionist circuit.[2] It was inevitable that he would become much sought after in Paris and in England.

Once overseas, he stayed in England for five years, partly to avoid being captured and returned to slavery, a prospect he faced if he went back to America. In 1855, Brown recounted his overseas experiences in *The American Fugitive in Europe: Sketches of Places and People Abroad*. Brown's book is rarely read these days, but it should be, for it is an early record of a free black man participating in a considerable black cultural traffic. In fact, he understood that he was performing as a traveler, his book being "the first production of a Fugitive Slave as a history of travels" (iii). Existing at the time was a small, but consequential and growing, movement—a traffic— of black speakers and performers within the northern, free American states and across the Atlantic to Europe.

Brown had already represented enslaved blacks and black runaways in America, mostly in New York and New England antislavery gatherings. Now he was stepping onto a larger stage, an international one, in Europe, where he was to become a performer in the fast-growing American-European black cultural traffic of the mid–nineteenth century. His experiences are a good entry point to the theme of this collection of essays. On the title page Brown wished his book to find a place in the future: "Go, little book, from this my solitude . . . The world will find thee after many days." It has found that place, in this new effort.

By 1850, northern America and parts of Europe had a well-developed black cultural traffic devoted to the eradication of slavery.[3] It consisted of a transatlantic lecture circuit, but also more:[4] rallies, meetings, marches, speeches, manifestos, newspapers, even songs and memorabilia. It engaged impressive numbers of people, especially women and women's clubs, and by the time of Brown's arrival in Europe, it was rapidly becoming a mass or popular culture arrayed against slavery. In large measure, this culture's authenticity depended on one luminous moment, when former slaves testified about their trauma in slavery, detailed their brave escapes, and in turn excited an optimistic hope for a future world free of slavery. This was, in cultural anthropologist Johannes Fabian's expression, one of the "moments of freedom" for former slaves.[5] But it was simultaneously highly problematic.

Every black person standing before the largely white antislavery audience—often called "friends of the Negro," Brown reported (216)—became a performer who had to negotiate perceptions of slave blackness. Balancing a black presenter's sense of self with an audience's need for a particular black type was tricky. Abolitionist campaigners sometimes desired a plantation vernacular from speakers fully capable of formal English. Still, within this problematic moment, a cultural exchange between blacks and others was going on. This cultural traffic contained many noble political possibilities and many cultural anxieties—what one might call a rich Ellisonian mixture, one that still surrounds contemporary black cultural performance.

For his part, Brown rose to the occasion. He performed deftly on the international stage of the 1850s.[6] He helped advance the view that blacks had great intellectual capacities. Antislavery gatherings at which he gave speeches—"more than one thousand public meetings" by his own count (32)—were his primary performance venue. Other stages appeared when he met and was feted by the great, including Victor Hugo, Alexis de Tocqueville, Tennyson, and Harriet Martineau. Other venues of his performances were his visits with farmers, among the working class, and meetings with London's free blacks.[7] On these tiny stages, he strove to demonstrate his sincerity as a populist.[8] At other times, he showed himself a tireless, high-minded tourist, visiting cathedrals, famous authors' houses, and museums. Brown's reaction to London's famous Crystal Palace exhibit in 1851 revealed what future world his speeches were intended to generate. Its throngs were an "amalgamation of rank," containing "a goodly sprinkling" of "colored men and women—well dressed and moving about with their fairer brethren" (195–96).

Proslavery Americans traveling overseas were one problem for Brown, with their confrontational, sneering remarks. He also faced a possible rivalry, for Frederick Douglass's stentorian magic, spun around England five years before Brown's visit, might have challenged Brown's status as an orator. However, probably the biggest threat to Brown's impeccable stage-craft was the arrival, in 1852, of the sensational *Uncle Tom's Cabin*, suggesting an image of blacks as dependent, long-suffering, and in need of paternalism.[9] It was the fictional Uncle Tom—a character doted on by the English reader—who really threatened to overtake the persona Brown had so painstakingly constructed. No dependent black, Brown took as his core value "independence of feeling" (80). A few London newspapers came to his defense against Stowe's treacly book, urging readers to put it down and pay attention to Brown, a "real fugitive slave" speaking in his own voice (318).

Was Brown conscious of participating in a cultural traffic? Brown wrote, in an understated way, of negotiating the rapids of mid-nineteenth-century blackness. However, his volume's twenty-eighth chapter, "Joseph Jenkins: African Genius," the only chapter devoted to one person, is very revealing. Here, Brown recounts his encounters with a free black Londoner from the Sudan, a man of "many characters" (272), who was as much a trafficker, as skilled in the commerce in blackness and black culture, as Brown was. At a lower level of society, Joseph Jenkins was also moving from stage to stage. Brown encountered him first as a working-class man handing out handbills. Next, he saw him daily cleaning an intersection. Much later, Brown found Jenkins playing Othello in a small theater "to deafening approbation" (270). A year later, he discovered him in a pulpit preaching. When Brown finally spoke with Jenkins, he found out that Jenkins led a musical group, too. It could be argued that Brown wrote so much about Jenkins because he recognized himself in the man—a person moving from one venue to another, each time assuming a slightly different posture. Brown called him "the greatest genius I had met in Europe" (275).

Brown's Legacy of Cultural Traffic

Remote as it might appear at first glance, Brown's odyssey in the 1850s highlights three core issues within the larger concept of black cultural traffic. First, it tells us this traffic—in performances, images, impressions—is old. The modern era, the twentieth and twenty-first centuries, with its technology dispersing black performances so widely and so quickly, does not have a monopoly. From the 1840s on, this traffic was dynamic. In that decade the John Luca family troupe was touring in the nonslave sections of America. By the 1870s, the Bohee brothers troupe was teaching banjo and dancing to European royalty.[10] One can find evidence of black cultural traffic as early as the seventeenth century. In the eighteenth century, "Negro jigs" and dances were being absorbed by whites on American plantations.[11] When we speak of black cultural traffic, therefore, it pays to consider it a historically layered phenomenon reaching back in time.

Because of this layering, few public spaces occupied by a black performance or a black performer are entirely free. Few tabula rasa spaces exist, empty of previous black content. Spike Lee's film *Bamboozled* (2000) is a devastating inquiry into the imprisoning impact of past racism on contemporary black performance.[12] But it is not only layers from the past that surround performances. As Brown found out in England, contemporary notions about blacks and blackness also crowd the performance space. Not all of these notions are entirely harmful. In fact, this thick layering of past and present notions of blackness is partly responsible for the public's intense interest in black presentations. Simply put, the density of ideas about blacks pulls people in, even though they often bring along a jumble of troublesome notions of blackness. For centuries, therefore, performances within black cultural traffic have been highly charged and greatly magnetic.

Brown's experiences provide a second insight into black cultural traffic. His account reveals that performance is a key element in such traffic. Public performance is what Brown and Jenkins engaged in—they were maestros of public spaces, of the spaces allotted to blacks, spaces that they powerfully reinvented. The performance moment is key because it is the instance in which some representation of blacks, black cultural material, or blackness is offered. That representation need not be well articulated. In fact, these performances seem to work best at projecting their representations when they are broadly suggestive about blacks and black culture, when they allow the audience to insert its own ideas into the performance.

A good analogy, as art critic E. A. Gombrich tells us, is the difference in visual impact between a simple line drawing of a human figure and a detailed one.[13] The former tells us it is a human and allows us to add our own interpretations, whereas the detailed drawing restricts us to imagining a particular person. Brown always drew a big picture of the "America enslaving nearly four millions" of his "brethren" (29).[14] A century and a half later, we find in the film *Kings of Comedy* the comedians drawing a similarly broad picture of blacks—this time a black essence—as a prop for their jokes.[15] "Oh, you know us," says Steve Harvey. D. L. Hughley is blunter: "we do shit different," and "we are different." Cedric the Entertainer says, "White people live by a different creed, and black people live by a whole different creed." Never is the quality they allude to exactly defined. By making this essence broad, the Kings allow the audience to see themselves in this black folk-geist. Each time they cite this black essence, the audiences get excited. It is like talking about a very public secret.

Third and very important, Brown's account tells us that black cultural performances and representations of blacks can travel far and wide. Performances and representations derived from black cultural material have shown enormous mobility. They can end up in unlikely places, in contradictory alliances, can take on new and unintended forms, and can synthesize radically disparate materials. Think of how jazz sprouted in New Orleans and Chicago in the first two decades of the twentieth century and went through countless American transformations until the 1960s, all the while spreading in Europe, South Africa, the Soviet Union, and Japan.[16] Traveling black culture is like eighteenth- and nineteenth-century runaways from slavery who, against the odds, managed to travel vast distances, avoiding being ensnared. "Artful" was the word a slaveholder's advertisement might use to describe his runaway. From his perspective, the runaway was deceitful. From the runaway's view, being "artful" was being "ingenious." Runaways often slipped the noose of their pursuers by turning into thespians. When possible, they took on accents, pretended to be free, and stole clothing, becoming new characters. Likewise, a force keeping black cultural traffic moving along—allowing it to spread widely—is its ability to reshape itself, to adjust to different circumstances—to be "artful" like the runaway.[17] Reconstituting and reenergizing has been fundamental to the black cultural travel. In South Africa, in congested, mostly poor black townships, for example, American jazz of the 1920s and 1930s took on its own tonal character, gave women singers a greater role as club singers, and incorporated Zulu musical formulas. The new jazz was called *marabi* music. All the while, these new jazz producers believed in its kinship with American jazz, imitated the showiness of black bands, and were likewise initially rejected by the black middle class.[18]

Extending Black Cultural Traffic: Concepts and Examples

The essays in *Black Cultural Traffic* come into being in the midst of today's dizzying black cultural movement. We are in the midst of another version of globalization, a differently inflected dispersion of cultural forms. The ubiquity of black cultural elements in national cultures and in global culture calls for chroniclers, analysts, and commentators. Yet our view of this mobility is not celebratory: beholding the sweep of black culture is not the posture of these writers. There is no triumphalism here, acclaiming the dominance of black cultural traffic.

The main goal of this volume's contributors is the analysis of the fluidity of black mass or popular culture, its capacity to move within black communities but crucially outside of black communities, too. Usually, black cultural performance is analyzed within a particular situation or context. For instance, black gospel music is commonly explained by way of its historical origin, from its Pentecostal church roots and its evolution through its principal composers, Charles Albert Tinsley, Lucie E. Campbell, and Thomas Dorsey.[19] By contrast, essays in this volume take a different approach to black music, specifically gospel. They start with the assumption of a mobile black music: it can travel, settle, and flourish in niches beyond its point of origin. It can be broken apart, with elements inserted and reimagined in another form, much in the way that West African weavers in the nineteenth century purchased foreign fabrics only to break them up and reuse the imported strands to achieve a new color palette and texture for established local designs.[20] The essays in this volume analyze a wide variety of black cultural traffics, in music, film, television, language, and definitions of individual and collective self. Regardless of where we look at black cultural presentations, we track them in travel, observing what happens to material as it crosses boundaries, moving on to new destinations.

The general concept of cultural mobility has been gaining ground in today's cultural commentary. Several factors account for this: the rise of the view that culture is a system of communications; the growing interest in culture as commodity or consisting of commodities; and a broader, more flexible view of the phenomenon of "influence." In 1990 the literary critic Stephen Greenblatt wrote of "cultural mobility," arguing that "this mobility is not the expression of random mobility but of exchange."[21] He went on to add that "a culture is a particular network of negotiations for . . . exchange."[22] His stress on mobility and exchange is appropriate for this collection of essays. Greenblatt might have been prompted in his embrace of cultural mobility by Roger Chartier, whose influential 1987 writing on the culture of printed texts in sixteenth- and seventeenth-century France stressed the circulation of cultural artifacts across social boundaries, and the fact that both elite and common people constantly imitated and borrowed each other's cultural forms.[23]

Greenblatt's definition and Chartier's model are helpful, but the most seminal work promoting black cultural traffic as a concept is Paul Gilroy's *The Black Atlantic* (1993),[24] which traces both black intellectuals' nationalist ideas as they traveled to and fro across the Atlantic and the travels of popular culture, specifically black music. Gilroy's chapter "Jewels from Bondage: Black Music and the Politics of Authenticity" is one to heed in building the case for these essays; in it Gilroy offers a highly kinetic model for the routes in the movement of black music. He makes the significant point that today's black music travels in much the same way it did in the first breakout of black music into the world's popular culture in the late nineteenth century. This is a point that we have already stressed in our reading of Brown's travelogue. Gilroy refers to present and past black music movements as "circulatory systems."[25]

To amplify his points, he chooses the little-known example of the Fisk Jubilee Singers and their singing tour of England, Ireland, Wales, and Scotland in the early 1870s—the first time "African-American folk forms" passed into "the emergent popular cultural industries of the overdeveloped countries." Once again, however, the public space the Fisk Jubilee Singers occupied was not a tabula rasa. Fifty years of blackface performance in England nearly undermined their appeal. What would real blacks offer as songsters that was different from the singing of minstrels? That was the raging question. English blacks themselves worried about the singers' presentation of serious, morally upright spirituals before white audiences who had grown used to the gimmicks of minstrelsy. In the end, as we know, the singers succeeded on their new stages, creating new constituencies for black music among both working people and elites.[26] Gilroy's full analysis of the Fisk Jubilee Singers' moment achieves great insight because he is not daunted by the complexity of black cultural traffic.

So far, I have used the phrase *cultural traffic* in an operational sense, as a way to describe actual movements of black cultural material from place to place, rather than in a conceptual sense. This has been a helpful approach because it is important to establish first that such movements can and do occur. Bringing together our previous discussion with the remarks by Greenblatt and Gilroy, we can now codify this volume's notion of cultural traffic.[27]

Even using the few examples offered thus far, it is obvious that cultural traffic can take many forms, but it always presupposes the movement of cultural matter. Even more importantly, cultural traffic involves some system of exchange or commerce. Between black performances and the viewers looking in on those performances, there occurs trade in ideas, styles, impressions, body language, and gestures. Let's look at one quite recent example. When Missy Elliott and Madonna were choreographed together in a Gap advertisement (summer 2003), connoisseurs of these performers avidly consumed every tilt of their tams, position of scarves, swift foot moves, and their womanly toughness. Many connoisseurs of black culture noted the quiet elevation of Missy Elliott to Madonna's stature, and Madonna's reliance on Missy Elliott's hip-hop heft to revitalize her public image. In that very summer of 2003, in which medical science was busily separating many Siamese twins,[28] Gap was headed in the opposite direction, trying to make a twinship of Missy Elliott and Madonna. *Joined at the hip culturally* was the Gap message. (At one point, they even turn their monogrammed derrieres toward one another, virtually touching.) Of course, the concept of cultural traffic is more complex than this deconstruction of an ad can illustrate. But the ad does suggest the trade aspect of cultural traffic, the ideas emanating from even a short primetime television performance involving one of today's major black animators of public spaces.

The everyday wordage and metaphors surrounding *traffic* give us a clue as to the complexity of the general issue of cultural traffic. One associates *intersections, nodes, crossroads, side roads*, and *freeways* with traffic, as well as *congestion, being stuck in traffic, gridlock, traffic jam, merging traffic*, and *on-ramp*. Few of these words might actually be useful in designing a vocabulary for analyzing cultural traffic, but intersections, nodes, and crossroads already have a history in cultural analysis. In fact, *intersection* has been emptied of much of its valuable analytical content from overuse. In a place like California, with its intense car culture, traffic vocabulary can achieve arcane dimensions: *mixmasters, traffic particles*, and *traffic citings*. Listing these words helps us to picture the many possible paths or routes that cultural material can move along.

Crossroads is the word we have borrowed for this volume's subtitle because we are anxious to stress a fascinating reality of recent black cultural traffic. That reality is this: we are approaching a time when the relationship between black cultures and performance by blacks is becoming highly problematic. Eminem comes to mind here, because he has become a very successful rapper or hip-hopper, but as his detractors will quickly say, he is a white man who should be considered an intruder in the field. At the same time, he cannot be easily dismissed as a cultural bandit favored by antiblack popular media happy to have a white rhymester—another Great White Hope—for hip-hop. Labeled by the *Village Voice* in 2002 a "Trailer Park White Boy: Crossover Dream,"[29] he has become a recognized wordsmith within hip-hop circles, to a degree other whites who performed an assumed black art form never achieved.

The assumed organic relationship between black cultures and black performers or performances has always been open to question. But today, this relationship shows new ruptures. Our current condition is not one to disparage but to treat as an interesting state of affairs that can enrich future black cultural analysis. In fact, the *Crossroads* subtitle can suggest a place where new, even magical, things can happen. It is a space full of possibility, but newness always begets new issues. Art critic Thelma Golden may have been trying to address the erosion of an organic relationship through her idea that the black artistic world is increasingly "postblack," meaning that artists do not engage in previous representations of blacks but are going into new spaces. According to Golden, they "embrace the dichotomies of high and low, inside and outside, tradition and innovation with a great ease."[30] Although steeped in black cultural material, their work does not come clearly imprinted as "black." It is more oblique in its reference to black culture, subtly shifting from previous artistic approaches to black subjects and at the same time, foregrounding new cultural material that carries black import. This represents not so much a jettisoning as a reworking of black cultural materials. Suggestiveness, ricocheting meanings, and a lot of plain old signifying are taking over. At the same time, directly black figurative painting continues to lay claim to public attention, but it too is undergoing dramatic changes. For example, the great art of the statuesque from the 1960s and 1970s, such as Barkley Hendrick's,[31] can be seen in Kehinde Wiley's recent presentations of young black males dressed in lavish velvets with gold brocade, posed against backgrounds suited for the ruling houses of Renaissance Florence.[32] These new modalities in art tell us that the performance of black cultural material is not to be expected to be predictable.

One cannot leave behind the wordage and metaphors of cultural traffic without mentioning one of its most fundamental definitions, that of the buying and selling of goods for profit and the bargaining that goes into traffic in goods. The economic or financial transactional life of cultural traffic has to be of great concern in an analysis, and especially in connection with black cultural traffic, where, to put it plainly, so much capital has been generated through marketing black culture. Tom Fletcher's highly informative and anecdote-rich *100 Years of the Negro in Show Business* (1954) is first of all an insider's history of black entertainers from the 1840s forward.[33] But Fletcher's prominent subtext is the struggle by blacks to gain primacy in the performances where black culture was being represented. They wanted to make the money from the presentation of black material. One can see the imprint of money in all the examples offered so far in this introduction; an economic infrastructure surrounds these cultural moments as well. Brown insisted that he not be seen as on "a begging mission, for some society or for themselves" as were many "colored men who have visited Great Britain from the United States" (30). Positioning himself in this way, he acknowledges that finances were often key to the transatlantic black traffic before the Civil War. In the Jubilee Singers' tour, the purpose was the collection of funds for Fisk University. In South African jazz, there was the expense of creating and sustaining bands and the vibrant marketing of illicit liquor in the *shebeens* where the bands performed. In *Bamboozled,* money is both a centerpiece of the film and important in determining Lee's options in making the film itself. The Gap ad is unashamedly an act of commodity commerce. While enthralling viewers with street moves, it screams: buy our clothes!

One of the more fascinating aspects of writing on black culture is how little of it notes that trafficking is important to the culture's vitality. Moreover, it is interesting how difficult the traffic has been to define. Even a writer as agile as Gilroy produces a chapter on music that creaks under the weight of the vocabulary he deploys to represent the movement of black cultural material. The high quality of his analysis stems from his relentless search for an imaginative vocabulary that mirrors the convolutions of black cultural traffic. At one point, he writes of "loops" and "fractals."[34] W. T. Lhamon's outstanding *Raising Cain: Blackface Performance from Jim Crow to Hip-Hop* (1998)[35] tracks the elusive blackening trope—from black plantation culture and nineteenth-century New York City black culture to the blackface of urban theater and bar performances. His analysis succeeds because he abandons the idea of linearity in the movement he details.

It is essential to loosen our views of the pathways of black popular matter, even within black societies, to open a full, new field of black cultural material's passages. This is no mere scholarly urge. It is essential because the material demands it. When we speak of the traffic in black cultural material, we often refer to fragments of cultural complexes that break loose and assume a life of their own. In addition, there is often no performance that transmits this material, no person on a stage—though a performance is being suggested, just as a stick figure drawing can suggest a whole human being.

Take, for instance, the strange careers of the recent idea of "bling bling" at one end of the spectrum and of African dress and fashion at the other. "Bling bling" was still just bubbling up in usage in the mid-1990s. When New Orleans rapper B.G. in 1999 created the anthemic hit single "Bling Bling," it began its wild journey.[36] For some time, it remained within black youth circles, but by 2001, the idea appeared increasingly in the regular print media, even in mainstream venues such as the *New York Times*.[37] It was used more frequently in television pop culture show commentary such as *Inside Hollywood* and *Entertainment Tonight*. In the fall of 2002, London's *Financial Times* column "How to Spend It" noticed the renewed preference for jewelry and, in particular, the new craving among established elites for platinum, no doubt due to the hyping of "ice" bling bling by hip-hoppers. Topping this off was the inclusion, in 2003, of *bling bling* in standard dictionaries.[38] Who could have predicted this zigzagging pathway for the concept, from the benjamin-rich youngster's platinum ring bought from B & A Jewelry on New York City's Canal Street to the platinum- and diamond-dazzling fingers of the tony classes of London. When B.G. said, "my pinky ring is platinum plus,"[39] who knew that he would be creating the desires of Europe and America's rich? Who could have guessed that, in the summer of 2003, a *New York Observer* reporter would call Princess Diana's royal jewels "Diana's bling-bling?"[40]

In the case of African dress and fashion, the passage is similar and just as complicated. African fabrics and clothes began coming into America and Europe in a major way through immigrants in the 1970s. Within black urban America and in places like black London and black Paris, these clothes achieved a popularity, mostly through smallish shops with colorful signs, because they fitted in with various 1970s black power and Afrocentric movements and niche cultures. Eventually, though, they began to become a part of middle-class dress, particularly through the dispersion of on-the-spot tailoring that was typical of African marketplaces. As the 1960s and 1970s evolved, African dress became an integral part of black fashion tours featuring mostly women and in fact was a way that black models, mostly women, asserted their independence from "white notions of beauty." In recent years, African dress has turned another page, becoming a major theme in haute couture collections, most recently in Dior's John Galliano's runway shows.[41] Again, there is no one pass play that put African fashion into contact with these radically disparate elements, 1970s black power and Afrocentric communities; black middle-class fashion extravaganzas; black models leveraging their physical assets against a monopolistic white beauty standard;[42] and finally, the haute couture houses of Paris. Black cultural material in these instances acts like Velcro, sticking to all manner of surfaces where it finds sufficient texture.

Advancing a metaphor like "cultural Velcro" might suggest that black cultural material is indiscriminate in its pathways and comes to settle in random places. Undoubtedly, black communities worldwide have been net cultural exporters for almost two centuries, radically so in the twentieth century. With such voluminous outflows of cultural material, there are bound to be seemingly random alliances, and many amusing ones. But the evidence shows that even unusual traffic has a certain functionality. One of the biggest areas of recent black cultural export has been in the field of linguistic invention. Rick Ayers, the editor of the *Berkeley High School Slang Dictionary* (2000)[43] wrote recently, "Most of the new words entering American English . . . come from the African American community and African American experience."[44] His word "entering" suggests moving from a side road onto a larger artery, a case of merging traffic.

Here are two interesting examples of this merging. After World War II, "funk" became prominent in black and hipster slang. It meant "troublesome," "stinky," "obnoxious." In the 1950s, "funky" was quite popular in jazz circles and in song titles, and meant "basic" and "bluesy." It then began to take on the shading of "soulful" and "down-home," as a quality expressed in black music.[45] In the 1970s it took on meanings from George Clinton's Parliament popular music, with its multiple overlapping rhythms. Now it has moved on to describe personal and national mood, suggesting a dense, foggy experience, a depression in which it is hard to find one's way, and more specifically, as a description of American economic downturns. A second Clinton, Bill Clinton, took part in cultural traffic when, in 1995, he used *funk* as part of his political vocabulary. He had remarked that an important feature of his job was "trying to get people out of their funk."[46] Now such expressions as "The economy is in a funk" and "The stock market is going through a funky patch" have become part of the lingo of financial news anchors on television. Continuing on another road is funk as "down-home."[47]

Now, take the word *dissing,* that is, "showing disrespect." It has been used to describe rhetorical battles between George W. Bush and Saddam Hussein prior to the Iraq War. Most of the black cultural material that travels and settles in different or new territory is there for a purpose. Developing a more systematic discussion of black cultural traffic depends on identifying, of course, the paths this traffic uses but also deciphering why this particular cultural material fits so well in particular niches. *Funk* and *dissing* were adopted because they provided concepts—not mere words, but ideas—that commentators needed to make their reports more understandable, more immediate. They completed people's mental sentences. Audiences could grasp what actually was happening in human terms. Use of *dissing* said that world leaders are only people, maybe people in a large neighborhood, but still neighborhood powers. As in neighborhood conflicts, they resort to rhetorical jousts, defaming their adversaries. Street wars and world wars both use "dissing," verbal dishonoring.

A major moment in the travels of *diss* came more recently. During NBC's *Meet the Press* on September 7, 2003, Tim Russert, while questioning Secretary of State Colin Powell on the plan to get United Nations help in Iraq, used *diss,* this time in a higher realm of discussion than trash-talking between warring leaders. This time, the word was used in a prime time conversation between television's leading political reporter and the most famous foreign policy executive in the world. Russert said that the French and the Germans were not ready to join America in postwar Iraq. "You called us 'Old Europe,'" said Russert, making reference to the Secretary of Defense Donald Rumsfield's remark prior to the war. "You dissed us," continued Russert. Showing his comprehension of the term, Powell immediately tried to counter Russert's assertion. Now, though *diss* proved its utility in this instance, Russert's using it highlighted the complications of the traveling of black cultural material.[48] Was he attempting to appear au courant, or was he suggesting that his was a language Powell would understand? Was he "dissing" Powell by lowering his status through the use of vernacular? Or has the term become so common in elite conversational circles that no one bothers to check if it is carrying a proper passport for radical crossings of racial and class borders? Is *diss* on its way to joining elite language traffic? Black culture and language have taken stranger journeys.

Bumps in the Road: Resistances to Black Cultural Traffic

Black cultural material often moves with purpose and nests in suitable places as it travels outside of black cultural zones. This does not mean that it moves without resistance. It is possible to get caught up in a master narrative of black culture traffic as an uncongested freeway, where the way ahead is guaranteed, the only problem being the position of a particular item in the on-ramp queue. In real life, however, getting on freeways does not always mean easy movement.

In the 1950s, white Americans, particularly the older generations, resisted the incursion of the new black rhythm and blues into their new suburbias,[49] seeing it as subversive to their children's moral upbringing. However, they were unable to get their children to reject the siren calls of Johnny Ace's "Pledging my Love" (1955), or Little Willie John's "Talk to Me" (1958), or LaVern Baker's "Jim Dandy" (1957) or Frankie Lymon's "Why Do Fools Fall in Love" (1956). Parental resistance was probably one cause of the proliferation of 1950s crossover sites, a place where black cultural content or a black performer was remasked or reconfigured as culturally white. Pat Boone's renderings of Little Richard's "Tutti Frutti" (1956) and Fats Domino's "Blueberry Hill" (1956) are perfect examples of this blanching process. Gone were Little Richard's hoops and hollers, his radical stand-up piano virtuosity, his pompadour hairstyle, his eye-rolling and dazzlingly inviting smiles, and his hints of eyeliner—all markers of black wildness, and androgyny to boot, together overtaxing the earnest visual purity of television of the 1950s and making a space for a tamer, domesticating mediator to appear. Pat Boone also got rid of Fats Domino's rotund black body, his shiny conk, his gold tooth, and honeyed lyrics suggesting "thrills on Blueberry Hill."[50]

In the 1950s, Dick Clark's *American Bandstand,* with its primarily white dance crowd and its aversion to showing black youngsters on camera, became another safe site for trafficking in black cultural material. Black entertainers were necessary for *Bandstand*'s media success, but beyond that, they were almost expendable. By now, *American Bandstand*'s Cotton Club–like exclusion of blacks is almost forgotten.[51] Many more instances of white resistance to traveling black cultural material could be cited, because it has been a prevalent theme in the history of black cultural traffic. But this has not been the only resistance of importance.

Certain black cultural performances have not been embraced by black communities. Historical revisionism has allowed us, for example, to see the rise of jazz as an assured ascendancy. But in its early years, influential voices in the black middle classes spoke against it,[52] and in the early twenties jazz had not yet won broad support from the black intelligentsia, opinion makers of many types, who would later cluster around it, endorsing and explaining jazz's performance values. Another example of black communities' resistance to importing black cultural material: in Africa, the postindependence intelligentsia of the 1960s and 1970s was often a critical force opposed to the adoption of African American cultural exports. The much-touted Afro hairstyle of the 1960s met consistent resistance in West Africa by local writers, who saw it as inconsistent with African body presentation traditions—a truth rarely mentioned in today's histories of the Afro.[53] In 1970s East Africa, the late writer Okot p'Bitek, a critical and creative powerhouse, dissented from African youth's cultural "apemanship" in absorbing black cultural material from the West. He wanted a reversal of cultural traffic, asking, "When will the youths of Africa influence the youths of the world?"[54]

One of the most poignant examples of resistance by blacks to black cultural material comes from a poem by Chicago-based Margaret Danner, who recalls black-middle class resistance to African art. "The Convert" explains that she first disliked greatly an African nude sculpture brought by the African art-lover and famous actress Etta Moten to Danner's Chicago Art Study Group tea. The year was 1937, a time by which one might expect that the value of African art was established among the literary and artistic black urban middle classes. Danner explains that when Moten, "Parisian-poised and as smart as a chrome toned page / from Harper's Bazaar, gave / my shocked / guests this hideous African nude, I could have cried." Every feature of this black body, encoded in an aesthetic of exaggeration, horrified Danner. The "tea" devoted to "art study" had been upset. But, as "the turn of calendar pages" occurred, Danner's "eyes would skim / the figure . . . / until, finally, I saw on its / ebony face . . . a radiance." She was on her way to a conversion to a new aesthetic.[55] Danner's poem is a confessional: it gives us an invaluable insight into the hesitancies marking the African American approach to African artistic performance, a reality often overlooked in the Pan-Africanist cultural agenda of recent years.

The larger point that these examples of resistance make is that black cultural material has a conflicted history as it has passed within black communities. It is such an important point that another example is necessary to help drive it home. Contemporary appraisers of black cultural history are often astonished that writer Langston Hughes's poems about the little people of Harlem, as in *Weary Blues* (1926),[56] were greatly criticized by black critics when they first appeared because their subject matter was too democratic. He dared to traffic in the dramas of everyday Harlem, the rough, intimate world of black work and leisure. A year later, middle-class critics in black newspapers and magazines treated his *Fine Clothes to the Jew* (1927)[57] even more harshly for its depiction of lower-class blacks, especially in the blues poems. His portraits in "Gypsy Man," "Po' Boy Blues," and "Ruby Brown"[58] brought the reader close to the wayward folk of black life. His skillful juxtaposition of a "Gin on Saturday, Church on Sunday" black life was new and upsetting. Few books of American verse have been more harshly reviewed. He was called a "sewer dweller" and "the Poet Low-rate of Harlem."[59] Hughes encountered cultural resistance because he allowed new material into the traffic flows. He might have seen himself like the jazz band in his poem "Jazz Band in a Parisian Cabaret," which acted to disperse black music to the wider world. Just like Hughes, the musicians were traffickers: "Play that thing, Jazz Band! / Play it for the Lords and Ladies / For the dukes and counts / for the whores and gigolos / For the American millionaires / And the school teachers out for a spree."[60]

Disruptions of smooth traffic flows, as in the case of Hughes, are a critical, instructive part of the total story of the travel of black cultural material. It is vital for us to understand these disruptions, especially when class figures as an important element, as the case of Hughes suggests. Automobile traffic today is filled with incredible snafus. Television and radio "traffic pulse reports" remind us endlessly of disruptions. Somehow motorists get through, often only after overcoming tremendous impediments. Commentaries on black cultural traffic should not ignore the fact that blacks themselves often have initially resisted the very cultural innovations that black intelligentsia later have proclaimed as noble, as theirs and theirs alone.

Another Traffic Complexity: Cosmopolitanism in the Local

There is another complexity—actually a paradox—important to under-standing black cultural flows. Again, it has not been sufficiently addressed. Again, once addressed, it enhances our inquiry. Carl E. Schorske, the distinguished cultural historian of late-nineteenth- and early-twentieth-century Europe, has reminded us that in assessing cultural traffic it is important to take account of the way cosmopolitanism feeds localism. In his study of Basel, he asserted that the Swiss city "learned to live by a paradoxical combination of cosmopolitanism and narrow localism."[61] With some modification, his idea can be applied profitably to the formation of black cultural material. Much has been made in this introduction of blacks and black communities as net exporters of cultural material to others. But there is an important corollary to this premise: blacks have been remark-able importers of cultural elements from other groups and cultural traditions. Though black cultural products appear highly local and group-specific in origin, they have relied on a vigorous cosmopolitanism in their formation.

Cosmopolitan traffic has fed the formation of black cultural material. In the Americas, this consumption of others' cultural material has been proceeding at least since the onset of slavery, from the late sixteenth century. In Africa, this has been happening since at least the early seventeenth century with the beginnings of trade with outsiders,[62] and during colonialism in Africa from the 1870s to the 1960s.[63] For as long as black enclaves have existed in Britain, France, Portugal, and Holland, cultural inflows have been occurring.[64] Even within Africa itself prior to great contact with outsiders, cultural transactions were constant. The idea of pure "tribal cultures" has no reality in African cultural history. Therefore, the cultural material that we call "black" is often significant core cultural elements supplemented by many streams of incoming cultural traffic, coming from outside of black cultural notions. Blacks and black communities reconstitute these materials over time, and bring to them new arrangements. Force and violence and segregation have often been behind these cultural inflows, but those vicious forces have rarely had the final say in the outcomes of traffic. Maybe the real genius of black cultural production has been the ability to reorganize a welter of cultural materials into innovative, arresting new arrangements.[65]

Instances of this incoming cultural traffic come in large, medium, and small episodes. A large episode: jazz emerged from New Orleans in the early twentieth century, where African, Cuban, American, Afro-American, Parisian, Martinican, and Iberian musical influences were rampant. New Orleans was a sonic carnival of the likes rarely seen before in human history. When Louis Armstrong made his first highly original recordings of 1925–28, he drew unconsciously on this vast musical corpus, while adding trumpet experiments, scat singing, casual delivery, unique solo accenting, and of course, his exuberance.[66] A medium-range episode: Rastafarian ideology has brought together varied elements from a pan-black world—Garveyist pro-African idealism, Ethiopian history and imperial hagiography, marooned or runaway Jamaican community histories—reworking this material to achieve its current spiritual and political prominence. To this has been added exceptional linguistic invention, biblical templates, and a new spiritual philosophy for the uplifting of the black body.[67]

A small-scale episode: in places as disparate as West Africa, Uganda, and central Africa, postcolonial female garb for special occasions often blended many local dress styles and Victorian English dresses, creating Afro-Victorian as a dress genre, bustles and all. In central Africa such skirts were called *misisi*.[68] Often these Afro-Victorian dress styles became the source of great pride as "distinctive national dress" in the years following independence when traditional cultural revival was a nationalist goal.

All these intricate comings-together tell us how limited is the idea of "hybridity," recently so popular in academic circles. (Hybridity is a metaphor borrowed from philology and biology, though the more accessible biological origin of the concept has overshadowed its philological aspect).[69] How much easier would be the task of explaining the formation and traveling of black culture if we could rely on only two cultural elements fusing, as biological "hybridization" would suggest. Hybridity is too mechanical and predictable and is, thus, but a way station where we can rest and catch our breath, before proceeding to the frontier of more complex black cultural traffics, where the real action is.

Bringing all these complications to bear on our discussion of black cultural traffic seems to destabilize the concept of "black culture." Anyone who has ever seen a Robert Farris Thompson lecture on black art and black performance in the New World—with his drumming, asides in many different languages, his terpsichorean maneuvers—realizes that as Thompson traces the building of New World black cultural material and performance, he also undermines the idea of a solid, seamless, highly integrated black culture. Before our very eyes, Thompson brings into being complex cultural edifices, informed mightily by cultural traffics with many vectors, and simultaneously dissolves the archetype of "black culture" as an entity. "Black culture" or "black cultures" is at best shorthand for a profound process of cultural formation, inflows, and outflows. Such cultural formation has resulted in a highly distinctive expressivity for black communities as a part of their being in the world. For our purposes, therefore, it is important to stress that black culture is a highly variegated entity at any historical moment or in any one historical situation. Black cultures have arisen from the action of vast historical forces. Cultural material has emerged from black communities established across many times and across many geographies. They range from the slave communities of the New World to the rural niches of precolonial Africa; from the urban black neighborhoods to the urban native quarters and reserves of colonial Africa; and from the post-1960s black urban centers in places like Soweto, Oakland, Nairobi, Kingston, Accra, London, Amsterdam, and the Belleville section of Paris.[70] Hence, when we speak of black cultural traffic, we are always implying the traveling not of whole cultures, but elements— even microelements—from these variegated formations. In his thousands of antislavery lectures in England and Scotland, William Wells Brown was bringing together a composite from a large cultural material, performing that portrayal, and in the process, promoting further black cultural traffic.

Yet Another Complexity: The Desire for Black Cultural Material

The penultimate issue for this introduction is what motivates a desire for black cultural material that has brought into being this enormously intricate and fascinating traffic. In a rarely noticed 1966 essay tracing black cultural traffic of a literary nature, "Harlem and Its Negritude: The Twenties,"[71] Langston Hughes emphasizes "the voltage"[72] behind "the Renaissance connections": "the voltage in one way or another came through to all of us." "Us" in this case refers to the black literati and cultural intelligentsia of the 1920s and writers running all the way to Richard Wright and Ralph Ellison, but also and just as crucially, to the African writers in Paris and "in far-away South Africa." Hughes points out that South Africa's "Peter Abrahams wrote in his autobiography *Tell Freedom,* how as a teenager at the Bantu Men's Social Center in Johannesburgh [*sic*], he discovered the Harlem writers of the Twenties."[73] Hughes was pointing out two traffics, one moving within the American black community of writers and cultural performers, and a second, jumping across the Atlantic to Europe's young African and Caribbean writers in Paris, who had come from France's sprawling empire. Hughes is onto something when he speaks of voltage, for cultural traffic requires energy and demand. What, then, is it about black cultural material, performances, and representations that puts them in such demand?

It is impossible to answer definitively. But one obvious mistake in seeking an answer would be to ignore differences in the level of demand for black cultural material over the last two centuries. Another obvious error would be to see the circulation of material among blacks and among outsiders as entirely the same. A caveat has to be added immediately to this last statement: it is surprising to some that marginality plays a role in black cultural traffic among both blacks and outsiders. Black cultural material coming from niche cultures, such as that of early jazz musicians or early rhythm and blues, was desired and reviled by many, regardless of racial territory, because it was seen as coming from the lower depths of black experience—occasionally, even from a primitivity. In fact, black musicians often playfully engaged this notion, "junglefying" their club, early film, and recording appearances.

History can be helpful here. The demand for black cultural material— generating Hughes's voltage—has not been constant, and certain periods have witnessed more traffic than others. The first of these runs from the 1840s to the 1880s.[74] This was probably the first era in which black cultural performances gained audiences outside of plantations and villages.[75] This occurred primarily in America and England, where the performances were usually of the abolitionist mass culture type, such as those in which William Wells Brown engaged. Beyond abolitionist mass culture, a few black musical entertainers became popular in northern cities and in Europe.[76] However, all-white performances projecting a faux black culture of the minstrel variety greatly outpaced black entertainment. For many audiences, minstrelsy *was* black life. After slavery ended in 1865, black entertainment challenged the hegemony of white minstrelsy, by often "corking-up," too, and following minstrel themes.

Intense cultural traffic began again in the 1890s–1920s, though the backdrop for the traffic is violence and repression in both the New World and Old World black communities. Tom Fletcher, the entertainer cum black performance historian, argues that this is a period of great expansion, with some African American singing groups even touring South Africa. In this period, black stage performers edged closer to creating their own voice, emancipating themselves slowly from plantation show formulas. African flows into the cultural traffic were restricted by the tight grip of colonialism across the continent, yet a few performers make their way to the colonial metropoles, but mostly as participants in exhibits in colonial expositions and fairs. One of the most significant flows of African cultural material into the world was assisted by colonialism, by colonials collecting vast caches of African art objects for marketing, often in curio shops and museums in Europe. This traffic did not involve directly African performers at all, but art pieces that inspired, around 1905, the beginnings of a variety of European and American cubisms, which later included many black American painters and sculptors. Writer and avant-garde cultural promoter Gertrude Stein called this infusion of African art "a veritable cataclysm."[77] It was cataclysmic because African art altered the paradigm for the representation of the human body in many arts in the West.

The next expansion arrived shortly after the end of World War I. After a few years of gestation, this burgeoned into the Harlem Renaissance, which, we need to be reminded, was only one of multiple black renaissances in places like Havana, Paris, London, Germany, Accra, Lagos, and South Africa.[78] One of the principal reasons black cultural material broke out into greater streams was the advent of recorded music. In 1923, Bessie Smith made her first recording, "Gulf Coast Blues" and "Downhearted Blues," which sold 750,000 copies.[79] In 1926, Zanzibar's popular songstress Siti binti Saad issued her first recording, and it went on to sell 75,000 copies along the East African coast and the Indian ocean rim.[80] It was during this period that one finds African cultural performers traveling. For example, Asadata DaFora, the Sierra Leonean who taught dance in Berlin and Dresden, formed a touring company that performed in Europe, Canada, and the United States before settling in New York City.[81] Black cultural productivity was so vast during the 1920s that one sometimes overlooks the place of black renaissances within wider cultural upsurges in places like Vienna, Prague, Moscow, London, Paris, and Berlin. Black cultural traffic was advanced by, and influenced, the voltage behind a worldwide attempt to reshape culture after the disastrous European war.[82] A war-weary world yearned for cultural revivification.

Within the last two centuries, the period from the 1940s to the end of the millennium is easily the most crowded with traffic. It should be divided into two subperiods, one running from the 1940s, that is, during World War II, to the mid-1960s. Pumping the traffic during this time is the tremendous unleashing of the forces of political change throughout the black world. It is a time when blacks, nearly everywhere and of all ideological stripes, were caught up in the sense of a new historical destiny for their part of the world. Regardless of how this period's ethos was subverted by both events and retrospective revaluations, it was a time marked by historical optimism, and that optimism brought to culture-making work a sense of challenge and expansiveness. Okwui Enwezor's large 2001 museum exhibit of art, photographs, and music "The Short Century" makes this point clearly.[83] Making an alternative cultural modernity to match the political upsurge was a major goal of black writers, artists, and performers across the world. Taking one small corner of this attempt at a cultural world shift, one need only look at the West African state known as the Gold Coast and later Ghana. From the 1940s through Ghana's independence in 1957 and into the early 1960s, Ghana was one of the centers of cultural and political traffic in the black world. Ideas and cultural material coming from Ghana entered the world, not just the black world, in particular the European liberal lefts and the Asian decolonizers, with astonishing alacrity, and a diverse parade of foreign visitors, of which many were blacks from the diaspora, went to Ghana to see a new black destiny emerging in microcosm.[84]

While citing Ghana as a state that became a focal point of cultural comings and goings, it is also important in viewing the period from the 1940s to the 1960s to recognize that black cultural traffic defied national, regional, and linguistic groupings and was not unidirectional, that is, not from visitors to Africans. We can see this specifically in some of the jazz produced during this era, by such musicians as Randy Weston, Mongo Santamaria, in Ghanaian E. T. Mensah's *Ghana Freedom* album, and in the township music of South Africa. The driving conception behind this jazz was a cross-traffic of techniques, instrumentations, and sounds, and its aim was to create a music greater than the sum of its parts, more than the contributors' backgrounds and past music orientations.[85] It was to be a music aspiring to capture this unprecedented moment of black quests for freedom.

For this period of the 1940s through the 1960s, we can also see in the photographs of Mali's youth and young adults in and around the capital city of Bamako made by the West African Malick Sidibé other ways in which black cultural traffic defied previous boundaries. His party photographs show young Africans dancing to Chubby Checker and James Brown in the early 1960s and preening in the dress and hairstyles of the era.[86] Yet commentators such as Manthia Diawara, who first brought these photographs into clear view, have insisted that this was not a simple appropriation by Malian youth.[87] Youth in their bell-bottoms, with their manicured Afros, and with their album covers prominently displayed at dances were using the music and the dress styles as a way of renegotiating the heavy French colonial influence that remained after independence, of trying to set a new cultural trajectory for themselves and their country. In fact, they were also probably gently spurning the new African government's revival of African music, song, and dance. The youth were assembling a new cultural presentation of self, partly African American and partly new Malian. In dress in the party photographs, they retain both high African dress styles and streamlined or minimalist French suits and dress styles. Their new cultural personas created a space for their new country, one that began with youth but could radiate outwards to the whole country, a space that was beyond the previous polarities of Malian and French, former colony and colonial overlord, African and European, *noir* and *blanche*.[88] Could this be achieved through dress, music, dancing, and partying? Not really, but these performances could suggest the possibility, itself a launching toward the future. Both of these cases from the middle decades of the twentieth century tell us how vital they were in generating new modes of black performances that crossed old boundaries. By the mid-1960s, the traffic takes another turn as black power ideologies swirl through Africa, Europe, and the New World. This black power period is the one Gilroy has been adept in illuminating.

The last surge in black cultural traffic is the one we currently inhabit, which began in the mid-1970s and for a quarter century has run exceedingly strong. In fact, it could be conjectured that one of the main reasons "popular culture" has become a category for inquiry has been the enormous success of hip-hop culture and its component performance domains, rapping, graffiti writing, break dancing, emceeing, and deejaying. A huge intelligentsia—scholars, television and newspaper journalists, museum curators, a wide range of artists, hip-hop magazine cultural critics, and filmmakers—has been seduced by hip-hop's growth and vitality. Hip-hop has played a role in establishing the field of black mass cultural studies. It has taught us much about what the "popular" in "black popular culture" can possibly mean. Hip-hop has traveled to new places on a scale unimaginable for earlier black cultural material. Still, from the time in the 1970s that Kool DJ Herc (Clive Campbell) set up his mammoth speakers in

South Bronx parks, mixing classic soul grooves, Latino music, blaxploitation soundtracks, Caribbean dance hits, forming the sound foundation of
hip-hop, this popular music has surged forward.[89]

These bold hip-hop wanderings are the main context in which black
cultural commentators work today. But it would be wrong to limit the
travels of black cultural material and performance from the 1970s on to the
mobility of hip-hop. Hip-hop-centric studies can do a great deal of harm
to black popular culture studies because they focus us largely on African
American cultural products and because they may cause us to overlook
other forms of black cultural dispersion. For example, a powerful issue for
Africa has been the use of black mass cultural material as a populist
weaponry in contests with the state. Kenyan writer Ngugi wa Thiong'o's
experience of trying to mount theatrical productions containing political
commentary in 1977 caused him to realize that popular theater material
enters an arena where "enactments of power" take place.[90] For him, the
Kenyan colonial and postcolonial state saw "the entire territory as its performance area . . . the nation-state performs its own being relentlessly."[91]
Therefore, when he launched his Kamiriithu People's Theater in Kenya, an
open air theater built by locals, and put on *I Will Marry When I Want,*
thousands of people sought out the theater, and after ten performances,
the Kenya government shut it down. What the government also destroyed
was the concerted work of village women, as theater builders and actors,
for they were a principal ally of Ngugi's.[92] Popular culture in Africa, even
the popular culture of Africa that can be seen abroad, often has a politically
and socially critical edge, particularly around the issues of gender.

Even a film like *Faat Kine* (2000),[93] one of Senegalese filmmaker Sembene Ousmane's least overtly political films and one that incorporates
many popular culture elements, carries an incisive political and gender critique. This film, widely seen outside of Africa owing to its melodramatic
plot and its high production values, is unable to become simply entertainment. It visits the issues of women's independence, intergenerational
conflicts, male accountability, and subtly, through the medium of painting
as domestic decoration, it addresses (by not denying) an African middle
class's continuing pursuit of African nationalism.

In Africa, when black cultural forms critique power and social status,
this critique often contributes "voltage" to its mobility. Karin Barber's
work on Nigerian popular theater and its critique of "petro-naira," the vast
sums of money that flooded the country during its late 1970s oil boom
days, tells a similar story.[94] In this case, cultural material circulated not so

much as leverage against the state as commentary on a new moneyed class. The theater addressing this theme drew large audiences—"not elite but farmers, workers, petty traders, minor public servants, drivers, school-children"[95]—because it skillfully dissected the impact this new money had on the traditional conception of the path to wealth. As these examples suggest, the importance of looking outside the hip-hop frame of reference is that we are reminded that the critiquing power of popular culture can be a source of its momentum and mobility. For many, hip-hop does much the same critical job, of critiquing power, and does it well. But since the late 1990s, it is not as much a purpose of hip-hop as in its rowdy, more anti-establishment earlier days. Searching outside of today's American black cultural context helps shatter the preference for looking at black cultural performance as mostly entertainment, while retaining the idea that a compelling style of cultural performance is essential in carrying, in supporting, cultural critique. Ngugi's play was able to draw people into its critique of the postcolonial Kenya state because of its rich overlay of language, story-telling, and well-characterized personalities. It was the styling of cultural elements that supported his message.

In a very recent example, Charlie Gillett's music compilation "World 2003"[96] contains a number of African performers who advance a pro-African, critical, populist message through a captivating blend of syncopa-tion, sampling, and original spirited vocals. One such song is by the Sene-galese musician Daara J., whose haunting "ParisDakar" speaks to youth who travel to Paris. Daara J. urges them not to forget Dakar because of Paris, and urges them to ponder the reality that Africa, even in France, is still in their soul. This song is the ultimate example of black cultural traffic with several layers of mobility: the song itself is traveling outward to world music listeners; it represents a performer who has appeared abroad, has picked up hip-hop elements; and it is a critique of the possible cultural subversions embedded in Senegalese youth going to Paris.

The Volume's Essays: Exploring Specific Traffics

The seventeen essays in this collection were inspiration for this introduc-tion. In addition, four artists' conversations add excitement to the mix, derived from the real-life experiences of cultural performers and cultural producers. The essays and the conversations can be thought of as analyti-cal riffs, pieces that are the core of the book, but also play off of each other and the introduction. Like riffs in jazz, they give more amplitude to the subject of black cultural traffic.

The essays cover a wide range of specific instances, itself proof of the fertility of the book's basic theme. Donald Byrd's "Twenty Questions" is an exciting and provocative querying of the themes surrounding the category called black culture, its performative aspects, and its mobility. He causes us to worry over the problematics of defining black culture, black performance, and cultural movement. After his swift, take-no-prisoners questioning of black culture, almost as if it were in the dock in a courtroom, the essays move along many lines. Collecting papers over a wide range of specific instances was our deliberate strategy. Our purpose is to show a variety of cultural mobility and traffics, but also to present a range of analytical approaches, to show how different scholars and commentators approach the subject. Another purpose of this breadth is that the essays provide a test of the possibilities of analyzing cultural traffics in general, whether labeled black or not. The last trait these essays have in common is that they extend the meaning—sometimes questioning the usefulness—of some of the conventional categories of cultural studies: authenticity, appropriation, hybridity, cultural tradition, commodity, borrowing, as well as others.

Aptly, the four parts of the book are defined by deploying the language of traffic. Part 1 is "Crossroads and Intersections in Black Performance and Black Popular Culture." Its papers cover the phenomenon of black cultural material's encounter with new contexts. This material has come to a cultural intersection where it is joined by other cultural agendas. What we find in these crossroad encounters is that *blackness* and *black* are not useful labels for the resultant cultural products. They appear to be "black" cultural products, but their distance from an archetypal "black" cultural experience is sufficiently great to show us the flaw in using race as a broad cultural label. Catherine M. Cole's "When Is African Theater 'Black'?" is a perfect illustration of this problem. Cole explores Ghana's popular concert party performances, a kind of theater where blackface is practiced without the overtones of minstrelsy. Even when pressed in interviews, the practitioners of the concert party were reluctant to put themselves within a hard black-white polarity. E. Patrick Johnson's "Performing Blackness Down Under: Gospel Music in Australia" is an ethnographic account of an all-white, atheist, a cappella gospel group in Sydney and their adoption of gospel music. Like Cole, Johnson brings fascinating interviews with the performers into the interpretation of their work. Using a variety of theoretical assists, Johnson brings into view how they see their affiliation to black gospel. Danzy Senna uses autobiography in "Passing and the Problematic of Multiracial Pride (or, Why One Mixed Girl Still Answers to Black)" to get at the intersection of a biracial family history with the outside world's shifting definitions of "being black." Growing up within this shifting landscape of race markers gives Senna a vantage point from which to question the credibility of Afrocentric worldviews and *black* as a label. Kennell Jackson's "The Shadows of Texts: Will Black Music and Singers Sell Everything on Television?" is a look at the incorporation of black music into television commercials, and the resultant racialization of television marketing. The importance of this essay lies in its excavation of a largely subliminal black cultural material.

Part 2, "Stop Signs and Signposts: Stabilities and Instabilities in Black Performance and Black Popular Culture," recapitulates some of the questioning and unease of the first papers, but takes a different tack. The four commentators present four cases of the instabilities in definitions of blackness and the complications that appear often in the path of traveling black culture material. W. T. Lhamon, Jr., presents in "Optic Black: Naturalizing the Refusal to Fit" a subtle discussion of the fascination with blackness from the 1830s on that became fundamental in the North Atlantic cultural commerce. He comes forward in time to the hip-hop performer Big Pun, a prominent Latin emcee of the late 1990s. Lhamon's idea is that blackness has been a treasure trove for peoples and individuals seeking alternative identities, from early Irish male immigrants to America straight through to the Chris Rocks of today. His essay unsettles both the definition of black and black performance as well as whiteness. Kobena Mercer has written a wide-ranging essay, "Diaspora Aesthetics and Visual Culture," that looks at the issue of visual representations by blacks, some examples coming from new black artists such as the British Yinka Shonibare. He illuminates why it has been so difficult for black visual artists to gain visibility for their subjects and for themselves. His essay drives home an important point about the nature of black visibility and invisibility, and draws in materials from Ellison and Fanon plus an important revisionist interpretation of the idea of the mask in twentieth-century black cultural history. Tim'm T. West follows with a telling essay on the fear of homosexuality within hip-hop culture and the overdetermined policing of boundaries to contain the potential menace. Hip-hop has proved that it can travel around the world, but it is forbidden to engage the homoerotic world, and has had anxiety attacks over the homoerotic in its midst. West's "Keeping It Real:

Disidentification and Its Discontents" is one of a very few essays that tackles hip-hop's hypermasculinity and representational strategies that exclude queer identities. Caroline Streeter looks at another race instability in "Faking the Funk? Mariah Carey, Alicia Keys, and (Hybrid) Black Celebrity." This is a challenging subject, and Streeter explores the ins and outs of contemporary mulatto figures in black popular culture in a skillful way, handling the complexities that these figures and their media lives present. Her essay is both a query on "faking the funk" by mulatto performers and a delicate understanding of their dilemma-ridden public personas. Part 2's essays show traveling black cultural material, but with real obstacles and uncommon turns along the way. It is not all green lights and open highways.

From this intellectual position, the collection in part 3 moves to consider more vivid examples of world travel for black cultural material. Tyler Stovall in "Black Community, Black Spectacle: Performance and Race in Transatlantic Perspective," explores bell hooks's argument that black performance has two faces—that of community creation and voyeuristic spectacle. What emerges from his questioning is a distinctive look at how these faces are bound together, Janus-like, in this early example of the quest for black modernity in 1920s–early 1930s Paris. Manthia Diawara's "The 1960s in Bamako: Malick Sidibé and James Brown," looks at the south Atlantic transfer of black cultural material in the form of James Brown and the African performer Ali Farka Toure into the youth and young adult culture of Bamako, Mali, where it was recorded by the nearly all-seeing camera of Malick Sidibé. Diawara's essay rediscovers this cultural episode and advances a theory about the maintenance of African culture in New World slavery versus under European colonialism in Africa. Halifu Osumare's essay "Global Hip-Hop and the African Diaspora" brings us another vital perspective on the dispersion of hip-hop and reminds us that even though hip-hop is a commercial enterprise these days, it holds within it the promise of creating solidarities among the poor and dispossessed youth of the black diaspora, in particular in Cuba and Brazil. She is interested in what are termed "connective marginalities" of global hip-hop. She concludes with the powerful statement that "hip-hop in the African Diaspora continues a powerful legacy of accessing the Africanist aesthetic . . . to reveal and critique the world's extant social inequalities." Paulla Ebron's "Continental Riffs: Praisesingers in Transnational Contexts" brings into view a famous West African performer, the *jali* or oral historian. In many West African communities, as in Gambia from which Ebron's song examples derive, the *jali* are celebrated for their performative memory of culture and history. Giving listenings to three recorded songs, Ebron tracks the *jali*'s performance outside of Africa as it engages transnational encounters, showing how the praisesinger's songs translate to different audiences.

The last section, part 4, examines "Trafficking in Black Visual Images: Television, Film, and New Media." As we enter a period in which critics of television networks talk about the absence of black shows and black performers on prime television, Herman Gray looks at whether television, as a medium, can represent blackness as cultural identity. Is today's television the appropriate venue for pursuing this ideal? Given that today's shows are often broadcast to audiences with little or no historical experience with America's ethnic representation, what is the value of their projections? Gray takes on these major questions. Nicole R. Fleetwood's "Hip-Hop Fashion, Masculine Anxiety, and the Discourse of Americana" handles one of the most pervasive influences of black youth on today's culture—as fashion-shapers, up and down the social hierarchy and across new geographies. She uncovers an alliance—an unholy alliance for some—between hip-hop fashion and Americana, producing a type of style nationalism, particularly in young male fashion. Her essay effectively deepens our knowledge of the impact of hip-hop fashion by penetrating to its recent ideology. Harry Elam, Jr.'s "Spike Lee's *Bamboozled*" considers a much-debated film that raises the question of whether black performance is in fact little more than updated versions of minstrelsy. There are many twists and turns in Lee's film, and Elam unlocks the separate subplots that give the film its dense set of meanings and questions. It is a film that demands a commentary, for near its end, it moves swiftly through a montage that traverses a large part of black performance in film and television. For such an ambitious, pressurized presentation, Elam's critique is helpful. A similar response could be made for Jennifer Devere Brody's "Moving Violations: Globalization and Feminism in *Set It Off*." It is a rigorous scrutiny of this 1996 film, with a sense of its similarities with and differences from 1970s black exploitation films and its fit in the current issues of black women's history. Brody brings the film to life owing to her critical acumen and constant reference to a broader theoretical literature. What she accomplishes is going beneath the easy shibboleth of globalization to interpret specific states inhabited by the film's women characters. Practically no aspect of the film goes unexamined, including the emancipatory trajectory allowed one of its characters.

This anthology contains a unique feature, an Artist Interlude section. It features interview comments from hip-hop performer Michael Franti, performance artist Rhodessa Jones, theater artist Keith Antar Mason, jazz musician Christian McBride, choreographer Robert Moses, theater director Chike Nwoffiah, filmmaker Euzahn Palcy, and hip-hop theater artist Will Power. The interviews were conducted individually, and they are put here to extend the conversation of the essays. Many of the issues discussed as evidences of cultural traffic are taken up by the artists. They provide the informed and invested perspective of practicing artists. Thus, the inclusion of this section as an interlude between the scholarly essays allows for the purposeful interplay of theory and practice.

Present Heirs to Brown

When William Wells Brown traveled to England in 1849, he was pioneering a new geography of cultural import for blacks. He arrived there, having been created by vast forces, the Atlantic slave trade and the empire of slavery that still dominated the Americas. It is understandable, therefore, that for all his discipline, just under his exterior, he was a person marked by history's vicissitudes: his runaway status, mixed race heritage, his hard-won literacy, his hardscrabble existence in his early years as a free person and no less important, his assumed middle and last names. (Until his escape, he only had a single name, "William," a practice in slavery.) Brown enacted a cultural traffic and, simultaneously, was the creation of the traffic in human beings that slavery had generated. And yet he aimed to put his personal stamp on even the small details of his life. It is impossible to read *The American Fugitive in Europe* without sensing a modern or postmodern character in him. And so, as we move forward to our own times, in discussing black cultural traffics, it is important to keep in mind always how past black traffics mirror our own cultural exchanges. Brown was a black culture-naut, foreshadowing many of the features of today's cultural travels and travelers.

It is appropriate therefore to close by looking briefly at two contemporary cultural traffickers. The first is Kwame Kwei-Armah, a newly prominent black British celebrity, playwright, and public advocate. Looking at him, we can see how black cultural traffic has changed and how it mirrors past traffics. Kwei-Armah is a most captivating figure. Originally, he hails from west London, where his family from Grenada settled and where, in

1967, he was born and named Ian Roberts. In 1979, he had a transformative experience of watching Alex Haley's greatly popular television miniseries *Roots:* finally, he saw a portrayal of Africans not as savages, "with bones through their noses," but as people of capability.[97] At this point, he tells his parents of his desire to change his name. "Carrying a European name supports the notion of western superiority and I won't have that." He chose a new name, his personal name taken from Kwame Nkrumah, the first prime minister of independent Ghana. He first came to public notice through the BBC's *Celebrity Fame Academy,* an entertainer competition show, where he sang sentimental songs such as "Try a Little Tenderness," and where he was spotted on camera praying for a favorable competition result. He lost, but went on to become an affectionate public celebrity in the tabloid press and in a television role on BBC's hospital soap *Casualty.* From this varied composite of cultural influences and performances, Kwei-Armah has emerged as a black cultural trafficker of considerable consequence.

Two triumphs have occurred. He has written a successful, tough play for the National Theatre—*Elmina's Kitchen,* set in a poor West Indian diner in east London. The title is an obvious historical reference to the Gold Coast (later Ghana) slave depot, Elmina Castle, a fortification from which West Africans were shipped to the New World. This play, actually his second (the first being the prize-winning *Bitter Herb*), focuses on the bleak prospects facing young blacks in Britain, to whom Kwei-Armah is deeply committed. The play drew more blacks into the National Theatre than had its other offerings. The other triumph is his alliance with Christian Aid, which convinced him to go to Senegal to see firsthand the economic ruin being created among Senegal's food producers because of subsidized food imports from the West that undercut local prices. He reported back on what he found. Rather than choose an abstract way of telling this story of Senegalese difficulties, he seized on narrating the fact that one of Senegal's national dishes, *thieboudienne,* was these days made more cheaply by buying rice from the United States, onions from Holland, tomatoes from Italy, and oil from Europe. The quality of the fish ingredient has been reduced because the foreign fleets offshore net the best fish, leaving what local chefs call poetically "the dust of the sea." Kwei-Armah finds himself using his composite personal history, performance fame, and plays to inspire young blacks and to tackle the straitjacketing trade assumptions of the World Bank, the International Monetary Fund, and the World Trade Organization. A latter-day black cultural trafficker finds his métier. William Wells Brown would have understood.

His understanding would have extended to another fascinating performer who has recently emerged as yet another promoter of black cultural mobility, the singer Angelique Kidjo. Kidjo comes from one of the most powerful cultural origin points in the black diaspora, Benin in West Africa, the source of a diversity of inputs into the New World. It is no coincidence that Melville Herskovits in his classic study of New World black culture, *The Myth of the Negro Past* (1941),[98] returned again and again to Benin. From Benin came slaves who became plantation labor, their singing patterns, the highly dramatic vodun religious system, and several artistic practices, in particular cloth appliqué techniques that became central to the Americas' quilting traditions. It is natural for Kidjo to blend a variety of black music and black music techniques, given her variegated Benin cultural background.

Her 2004 album *Oyaya* is a cross-pollination of West African musical traditions with funk/jazz plus Caribbean music. The term *oyaya* is, according to Kidjo, "joy" in Yoruba. When speaking of her work, Kidjo can barely restrain her excitement over finding this informal empire of black music that covers thousands of miles and hundreds of cultures. She samples thirteen Caribbean musical styles in the album, including salsa, calypso, and ska, and speaks with passion about using bata drums brought to the Caribbean by slaves from Nigeria. She, though, is no mere enthusiast. Part of her musical work today is researching and reviving old forms (such as Benin's ancient tradition of animal horn-blowing) and the work of slightly remembered performers, such as Henri Salvador, the French Caribbean jazz singer.[99] She has become a singer with a commitment to music scholarship, on the new frontiers of black cultural traffic, dispersing an ambitious performance style that does justice to the complicated traveling history of past and contemporary black culture.

NOTES

1. William Wells Brown, *The American Fugitive in Europe: Sketches of Places and People Abroad* (Boston, 1855), 229. Subsequent page references are given in the text. Speaking of himself in the third person in the preface, he writes, "the education he has acquired was by his own exertions, he never having had a day's schooling in his life" (iv).

2. Brown begins *American Fugitive* with a "Memoir of the Author" (9–34), a narrative containing the major facts of his life.

3. Karen Halbersleben's *Women's Participation in the British Anti-slavery Movement: 1824–1865* (Lewiston, N.Y.: E. Mellen Press, 1993) confirms the spread of aboli-

tionism, the movement in which Brown was a participant. Cf. also William Andrews, *To Tell a Free Story* (Urbana: University of Illinois Press, 1986), 1–15; Adam Hochschild, *Bury the Chairs: Prophets and Rebels in the Fight to Free an Empires Slaves* (Boston: Houghton Mifflin, 2005), for a new popular history of British abolition movement that caused the cessation of the British slave trade in 1807 and the freeing of Britain's colonies in 1838; and Sterling Lecater Bland, Jr., *African American Slave Narratives* (Westport, Conn.: Greenwood Press, 2001), 11–12.

4. Audrey A. Fisch, *American Slaves in Victorian England* (Cambridge: Cambridge University Press, 2000), 73.

5. Johannes Fabian, *Moments of Freedom: Anthropology and Popular Culture* (Charlottesville: University Press of Virginia, 1998), 139. Fabian elaborates the idea on pp. 20–21.

6. Andrews, *Free Story*, 107–8. Andrews writes explicitly of the "stage" and "performative" aspects of the public presentation of slave autobiography. A detailed biography of Brown is William Edward Farrison, *William Wells Brown: Author and Reformer* (Chicago: University of Chicago Press, 1969).

7. Important studies of blacks in eighteenth- and nineteenth-century Britain are Paul Edwards and James Walvin, *Black Personalities in the Era of the Slave Trade* (Baton Rouge: Louisiana State University Press, 1983); and Paul Edwards and David Dabydeen, eds., *Black Writers in Britain, 1760–1890* (Edinburgh: Edinburgh University Press, 1991).

8. As it turns out, once returned to America, Brown wrote a play, *The Escape; or, A Leap to Freedom,* in 1858 that dramatized the slave narrative genre and in which he played a part. Perhaps speaking on the abolitionist circuit heightened his theatrical understanding and ambition. Cf. Harry Elam, Jr., "The Black Performer and the Performance of Blackness: *The Escape or a Leap to Freedom* by William Wells Brown and *No Place to Be Somebody* by Charles Gordone," in *African American Performance and Theater History: A Critical Reader,* ed. Harry J. Elam, Jr., and David Krasner (New York: Oxford University Press, 2000), 288–305.

9. Clare Midgley, *Women against Slavery: The British Campaigns, 1780–1870* (London: Routledge, 1992), 145–46, "The Influence of Uncle Tom's Cabin." The cover sheet of Harriet Beecher Stowe's book in England shows a tall woman, white, in flowing robes that partially wrap around three small black children. Her soft eyes are cast down on them. The drawing constitutes an iconography for *Uncle Tom's Cabin*'s public presentation.

10. James Weldon Johnson, *Black Manhattan* (New York: Knopf, 1930), 93. Chapters 7–11 are an excellent account of black performers of the nineteenth and early twentieth centuries, a reminder of the overlooked riches of this volume.

11. Katrina Hazzard-Gordon, *Jookin': The Rise of Social Dance Formations in African American Culture* (Philadelphia: Temple University Press, 1990), 51, has collected reports of several eighteenth-century plantation dance episodes and of whites in attendance. Cf. also Albert Murray, *Stomping the Blues* (New York: Vintage, 1976), 62–66; and Josephine Wright, "Early African Musicians in Britain," in *Under the Imperial Carpet: Essays in Black History, 1780–1950*, ed. Rainer Lotz and Ian Pegg (Crawley, Eng.: Rabbit Press, 1986), 14–24.

12. Spike Lee, dir., *Bamboozled*, 2000.

13. E. H. Gombrich, *Art and Illusion,* 2nd ed. (London: Phaidon, 1962), 90–98.

14. Brown's speech at the 1851 London meeting of fugitive slaves was a masterpiece, delicately shaded with emotion and poetic language, that broadly depicted the forces of enslavement (219).

15. *The Original Kings of Comedy*, dir. Spike Lee, filmed in 1998–99, and released in 2000.

16. Many studies exist on the movement of jazz and jazz overseas, especially in the Soviet Union. See especially S. Frederick Starr, *Red and Hot: The Fate of Jazz in the Soviet Union, 1917–1980* (New York: Oxford University Press, 1983); and William Minor, *Unzipped Souls: A Jazz Journey through the Soviet Union* (Philadelphia: Temple University Press, 1995).

17. In 1769, Thomas Jefferson's Sandy, a runaway slave, was advertised as one whose "behavior is artful and knavish." Cited in Leon Higginbotham, *In the Matter of Color: The Colonial Period* (New York: Oxford University Press, 1978), 447–48. "A runaway lived a thespian's life" is a quote from Kennell Jackson, *America Is Me* (New York: HarperCollins, 1996), 100, where this phenomenon is documented. Runaways used many performance techniques: acquiring new clothes; appearing humble; passing for white if possible; and interestingly, traveling with a white friend or lover, pretending to be his or her slave. See also Freddie Parker, *Running for Freedom: Slave Runaways in North Carolina, 1775–1840* (New York: Garland, 1993).

18. Christopher Valentine, *Marabi Nights: Early South African Jazz and Vaudeville* (Johannesburg: Ravan Press, 1993), ii–xii, plus the introductory chapter, 1–15. Thorough analysis is illuminated by a tape of selections.

19. Bernice Reagan, *We'll Understand It Better By and By: Pioneering African American Gospel Composers* (Washington, D.C.: Smithsonian Institution Press, 1992) is the best rendering of gospel's unfolding and foreshadows possible new departures.

20. Peter Adler and Nicholas Barnard, *African Majesty: The Textile Art of the Ashanti and Ewe* (London: Thames and Hudson, 1992), 67–68.

21. Stephen Greenblatt, "Culture," in *Critical Terms for Literary Study*, ed. Frank Lentricchia and Thomas McLaughlin (Chicago: University of Chicago Press, 1990), 229.

22. Greenblatt, "Culture," 229.

23. Roger Chartier, *The Cultural Uses of Print in Early Modern France* (Princeton: Princeton University Press, 1987), 5–21.

24. Paul Gilroy, *The Black Atlantic: Modernity and Double Consciousness* (Cambridge: Harvard University Press, 1993).

25. Gilroy, *The Black Atlantic*, 88.

26. Doug Seroff, "The Fisk Jubilee Singers in England," in Wright, *Under the Imperial Carpet*, 42–54.

27. Often, in the late 1990s, the idea—and language—of black cultural mobility nested in contemporary art exhibits. In 1997, "Transforming the Crown" brought together African, Caribbean, and Asian artists' work to identify "the routes of national (British) culture." See Mora J. Beauchamp-Byrd et al., *Transforming the Crown: African, Asian, and Caribbean Artists in Britain* (New York: Franklin H. Williams Caribbean Cultural Center/African Diaspora Institute, 1997), 16–41. In 1999, the National Gallery of Canada put on "Crossings," featuring a Yinka Shonibare installation. *Parachute*, July–September, 1999, 44–45.

28. Joshua Davis, "Till Death Do Us Part," *Wired*, October 2003, 110–20.

29. R. J. Smith, "Trailer Park White Boy: Crossover Dream," *Village Voice,* November 6–12, 2002, 34–37.

30. Thelma Golden, introduction to *Freestyle* (New York: Studio Museum in Harlem, 2001), 15.

31. Studio Museum in Harlem, *Black Romantic: The Figurative Impulse in Contemporary African-American Art* (New York, 2002), 12. One of the great figurative paintings of the 1970s by a black artist of a black subject was Barkley Hendrick's *Lawdy Mama* (1979). It endures as a classic owing to its power to communicate aesthetics at several levels.

32. Malik Gaines, "Kehinde Wiley: Pieces of a Man," *Iconic,* Artists in Residence, July 10–September 22, 2002, Studio Museum of Harlem (New York, 2002), unnumbered pages. *Passing/Posing #1* and *Easter Realness, 2002* are examples of his representations.

33. Tom Fletcher, *100 Years of the Negro in Show Business* (New York: Burdge, 1954), 29–117.

34. Gilroy, *The Black Atlantic, 76.*

35. W. T. Lhamon, Jr., *Raising Cain: Blackface Performance from Jim Crow to Hip-Hop* (Cambridge: Harvard University Press, 1998).

36. B.G.'s hit appeared on the album *Chopper City in the Ghetto,* released in April 1999.

37. More than seventy articles in the *New York Times* over the past ten years have used "bling bling." Twenty-five references appeared between June 2002 and November 2003, illustrating the alacrity with which an elite paper was sampling hip-hop argot. A similar look at the *Washington Post* shows twenty-five articles in a year beginning in November 2002.

38. Della Summers, director, *Longman Dictionary of Contemporary English* (New York, 2003) described bling bling as the wearing of expensive items such as jewelry in a way that is easy to notice.

39. Verse 1 of "Bling Bling." The song is actually a catalog of expensive items necessary to the blinging life. It also explains bling bling in the relations between men and women.

40. Philip Weiss, "Hail Tony Blair!" *New York Observer,* August 4, 2003, 1.

41. Suzy Menkes, "Celebrating Fashion's African Themes," *New York Times,* April 6, 1997. Cf. also *The Global Circulation of African Fashion* (New York: Berg, 2002).

42. Kennell Jackson, "What is *Really* Happening Here?: Black Hair Among African Americans and in American Culture," in *Hair* in *African Art and Culture,* ed. Roy Sieber and Frank Herreman (New York: Museum for African Art, 2000), 179–80.

43. Rick Ayers, *Berkeley High School Slang Dictionary* (Communication Arts & Sciences, Berkeley High School/North Atlantic Books: Distributed by Publishers Group West, 2004).

44. Rick Ayers, "Bling Bling in His Grill? That's Hecka Ill," *San Francisco Chronicle,* August 10, 2003, A5.

45. Max Decharme, *Straight from the Fridge, Dad: A Dictionary of Hipster Slang* (Harpenden, Eng.: No Exit, 2000), 64–65. Cf. listings in Clarence Major, ed., *Juba to Jive: A Dictionary of African-American Slang* (New York: Penguin, 1994), 187–88.

46. "Grand Funk," *Washington Post,* September 28, 1995, A28. Clinton's remarks brought out the lexicographers among journalists, as illustrated by John Farrell, "Pres-

ident Backs Away from Remark," *Boston Globe,* September 26, 1995, 3. Sadly, the journalists pursued "funk" in *Webster's New World Dictionary.*

47. On December 9, 2003, Colin Powell, at a dinner celebrating the year's Kennedy Center winners, appointed the performer James Brown to the position of "secretary of soul and foreign minister of funk." "Powell 'Appoints' Soul Legend James Brown to New Diplomatic Post" (Agence France-Presse).

48. *XXL* magazine has reported that *CNN Headline News* "is getting all gully with its bad self " by using "phat turns of phrase such as 'jimmy hat,' 'fly' and 'ill' " (December 2002, 54). An internal *Headline News* memo, captured by *New York Daily News,* urged newscasters to use hip-hop lingo in the scrolling text boxes that run during the news hour: "in an effort to be sure we are as cutting-edge as possible, please refer to this slang dictionary when looking for just the right phrase. . . . All you homeys and honeys add a new flava to your tickers."

49. See Craig Werner, *A Change Is Gonna Come: Music, Race, and the Soul of America* (New York: Plume, 1998), 33–100; and Brian Ward, *Just My Soul Responding: Rhythm and Blues, Black Consciousness, and Race Relations* (Berkeley and Los Angeles: University of California Press, 1998) for discussions of the dispersion of rhythm and blues and impediments in its path.

50. A decade after Pat Boone was domesticating black rhythm and blues for white consumption, Mick Jagger was studying black dance steps to augment his bad boy image, a detail reported by British singer Tom Jones, *Fresh Air,* National Public Radio, December 11, 2003.

51. John A. Johnson, *American Bandstand: Dick Clark and the Making of a Rock 'n Roll Empire* (New York: Oxford University Press, 1997), 56–57, describes the decision to make sure that blacks and whites were not shown dancing together because it would have sunk advertising revenue.

52. Pianist and band leader Dave Peyton's "The Musical Bunch" from the *Chicago Defender,* 1928, is presented as "A Black Journalist Criticizes Jazz," in *Keeping Time: Readings in Jazz History,* ed. Robert Walser (New York: Oxford University Press, 1999), 57–59. Robert W. S. Mendl, a British critic, published the first book about jazz in Great Britain, *The Appeal of Jazz* (London: P. Allan, 1927), remarking, "Jazz has secured and still retains a more widespread vogue among its contemporary listeners than any other form of music ever known" (80).

53. Nina Darnton, "Lagos Hairstyles Reflect African History (and the Afro Is a Put-on Wig)," *New York Times,* January 6, 1977, 1–3.

54. Okot p'Bitek, "Pop Music, Bishops, and Judges," in *Africa's Cultural Revolution* (Nairobi: Macmillan Books for Africa, 1973), 5. His worries appear to be realized, as reported by Paul Redfern, "Anglophone Youths Now Adopt a Global Culture," *Daily Nation* (Nairobi), November 1, 1999.

55. Margaret Danner, "The Convert," in *A Broadside Treasury,* ed. Gwendolyn Brooks (Detroit: Broadside Press, 1971), 40–42. Cf. also her "Her Small Bells of Benin," 39, and "Etta Moten Barnett's Attic," 39.

56. Langston Hughes, *Weary Blues* (New York: Knopf, 1926).

57. Langston Hughes, *Fine Clothes to the Jew* (New York: Knopf, 1927).

58. Hughes, *Fine Clothes,* 22, 23, 30.

59. I am indebted to Arnold Rampersad, the Hughes biographer, for the information on Hughes' reception among black critics.

60. Hughes, *Fine Clothes,* 74.

61. Carl E. Schorske, *Thinking with History* (Princeton: Princeton University Press, 1998), 57 .

62. For some hints of the incorporation of outside elements in African cultural life, see William Fagg, *Afro-Portuguese Ivories* (London: Batchworth Press, 1959) for sculpture, and Lalage Brown, *Two Centuries of African English: A Survey and Anthology of Non-fictional English Prose by African Writers since 1769* (London: Heinemann, 1973), particularly 24–25, citing a coastal Nigerian trader in 1786 who kept his records in English.

63. A remark by Aminata Dramane Traore sums up this historical situation: "There is nothing new about cosmopolitanism in Africa." "African Fashion: A Message," in *The Art of African Fashion,* ed. Els van der Plas and Marlous Willemsen (The Hague: Africa World Press, 1998), 20.

64. Cf. Allison Blakley, *Blacks in the Dutch World* (Bloomington: Indiana University Press, 1993), 78–170, 225–75; and Peter Fryer, *Staying Power: The History of Black People in Britain* (London: Pluto Press, 1984).

65. Stuart Hall, "What Is this 'Black' in Black Popular Culture?" in *Black Popular Culture,* ed. Gina Dent (Seattle: Bay Press, 1992), 27.

66. *Louis Armstrong in His Own Words,* ed. Thomas Brothers (New York: Oxford University Press, 1999), 82–110, contains his writings, often detailing his musical contexts, from 1918 to 1931. An excellent view of Armstrong's synthesis of vast musical material and its extension through his own powerful will to innovate is presented by Laurence Bergreen, *Louis Armstrong: An Extravagant Life* (New York: Broadway Books, 1997), 143–235.

67. Ennis Edmonds, *Rastafari: From Outcasts to Culture Bearers* (New York: Oxford University Press, 2003) for an exceptional analysis of the coming together of disparate parts to make the Rastafarian community.

68. David Kerr, *Dance, Media-Entertainment, and Popular Performance in South East Africa* (Bayreuth: E. Breitinger, 1998), 31.

69. Sabine Mabardi, "Encounters of a Heterogeneous Kind: Hybridity in Cultural Theory," in *Unforeseeable Americas: Questioning Cultural Hybridity in the Americas,* ed. Rita de Grandis and Zila Bernd (Amsterdam: Rodopi, 2000), 2.

70. Bennetta Jules-Rosette, *Black Paris: The African Writers' Landscape* (Urbana: University of Illinois Press, 1998), 147–75.

71. Langston Hughes, "Harlem and Its Negritude: The Twenties," Schomburg Library, New York, "Sent to AMSAC—for the African Forum, 1–18–66."

72. Hughes, "Harlem and Its Negritude," 2.

73. Hughes, "Harlem and Its Negritude," 12.

74. Michael A. Gomez, *Exchanging Our Country Marks: The Transformation of African Identities in the Colonial and Antebellum South* (Chapel Hill: University of North Carolina Press, 1998) records the time before the 1840s in which African customs and cultural practices were brought to the Americas by Africans caught in the Atlantic trade in humans. Under "Festivities and Pastimes," A. C. Saunders's *Social History of Black Slaves and Freedmen in Portugal: 1441–1555* (New York: Cambridge University Press, 1982) writes of dances (one called the *guineo,* no doubt after West Africa's Guinea coast) and singing by blacks as well as comments on their drumming and flute playing at public festivals. Blacks also held parties of their own, one the *festa*

dos negros where they elected a king. All black gatherings were outlawed in Lisbon in 1559.

75. Hazzard-Gordon, *Jookin'*, 42–43, presents data on the free black festivals in New England surrounding the election of a "Negro governor." From 1740s to 1850s, these were public performances, communicating black cultural material.

76. To this add the performances of black boxers, many of them Americans, who competed in Britain to great fanfare, beginning with Bill Richmond, "The Black Terror" in 1804–18. For their profiles, see Nat Fleischer, *Black Dynamite: Story of the Negro in the Prize Ring from 1782–1938*, vol. 1 (New York: C. J. O'Brien, 1938), 21–122. All of them bore signal-sending monikers, for example "The Virginia Slave," "The Black Wonder," "The Liverpool Darkey."

77. Gertrude Stein, *Picasso* (Paris: Floury, 1938), 64.

78. Abiola Irele, "Negritude or Black Cultural Nationalism," *Journal of Modern African Studies* 3, no. 3 (1965): 321–48, especially 330–38 on multiple renaissances. The companion essay, also pioneering, is Abiola Irele, "Negritude-Ideology and Literature," *Journal of Modern African Studies* 3, no. 4 (1965): 499–526.

79. Lawrence Cohn, *Nothing but the Blues: The Music and the Musicians* (New York: Abbeville Press, 1993), 90–91.

80. Laura Fair, *Pastimes and Politics: Culture, Community, and Identity in Postabolition Urban Zanzibar, 1890–1945* (Athens: Ohio University Press; Oxford: J. Currey, 2001), 3.

81. Bruce Kellner, *The Harlem Renaissance: A Historical Dictionary for the Era* (New York: Methuen, 1984), 93–94.

82. Alfred Appel, Jr., *Jazz Modernism: From Ellington and Armstrong to Matisse and Joyce* (New York: Knopf, 2002), 7–84.

83. Okwui Enwezor, ed., *The Short Century: Independence and Liberation Movements in Africa, 1945–1994* (New York: Prestel, 2001), 3–32. Probably most evocative of 1960s Africa are the photographs from the time, pp. 180–216.

84. Two of the latest entrants in the story of Ghana's magnetism are Gerald Horne, *Race Woman: The Lives of Shirley Graham DuBois* (New York: New York University Press, 2000); and Doran H. Ross, ed. *Wrapped in Pride: Ghanaian Kente and African American Identity* (Los Angeles: UCLA Fowler Museum of Cultural History, 1998).

85. Robin D. G. Kelley, "Jazz Folk Here and There: A Transatlantic Conversation," St. Clair Drake Memorial Lecture, Stanford University, May 23, 2003.

86. André Magnin, *Malick Sidibé* (New York: Scalo, 1998); Michelle Lamunière, *You Look Beautiful Like That: The Portrait Photographs of Seydou Keïta and Malick Sidibé* (Cambridge: Harvard University Art Museums, distributed by Yale University Press, 2001).

87. Manthia Diawara, *In Search of Africa* (Cambridge: Harvard University Press, 1998), 86–119.

88. Diawara, *In Search of Africa,* 101, where Diawara discusses how the speaking of English by Malian youth was an innovation in a "Francophone country, where one acquired subjecthood through Francité—that is, thinking via French grammar and logic." Diawara spoke English to a traveling African American musician in Junior Wells's band and became an overnight sensation in Bamako. The youth dream then had been to "be as adept at Francite as Senghor, who spoke French better than the French."

89. "What Are Some Landmarks in the History of Rap Music and Hip-hop Culture?" in Jackson, *America Is Me,* 382–84.

90. Ngugi wa Thiong'o, "Enactments of Power: The Politics of Performance Space," *Dance Review* 41 (fall 1997): 11–30.

91. Thiong'o, "Enactments of Power," 13.

92. Ngugi wa Thiong'o, "Women in Cultural Work: The Fate of the Kamiruthu People's Theater in Kenya," in *Readings in African Popular Culture,* ed. Karin Barber (Bloomington: Indiana University Press, 1997), 131–37.

93. Sembene Ousmane, dir., *Faat Kine,* 2000.

94. Karin Barber, "Popular Reactions to the Petro-Naira," in Barber, *Readings,* 91–98.

95. Barber, "Popular Reactions," 92.

96. Charlie Gillett, "World 2003" (2003).

97. John-Paul Flintoff, "Lunch with the FT: Kwame Kwei-Armah, Free Trade's Celebrity Opponent," *Financial Times,* August 16/17, 2003, W3.

98. Melvin Herskovits, *The Myth of the Negro Past* (New York: Harper and Brothers, 1941).

99. Angelique Kidjo, interview, National Public Radio, May 4, 2004.

PART ONE

Crossroads and Intersections in Black Performance and Black Popular Culture

CATHERINE M. COLE

When Is African Theater "Black"?

At the psychic center of black popular culture is Africa: at once the source, the motherland, the wellspring of humankind, the site of slavery's original trauma, and the locus of anticipated healing. The continent's silhouette emblazoned on clothing, its name soulfully invoked in song lyrics, Africa looms large. Yet Africa's current realities are more dimly seen. Kobena Mercer has argued that the image of Africa animating black popular culture may bear little resemblance to Africa as it is.[1] The gulf between the imagined and lived realities of Africa is not so much my focus here as it is my point of departure. I enter this discussion as a scholar of African theater and performance, West African popular theater in particular. As I try to address the themes of this book, I find myself asking whether African theater belongs in a volume on black popular culture at all. Is it popular? And, perhaps more provocatively, is it black? Yes, most theater in sub-Saharan Africa is created by and for black Africans. Whether these artists identify and affiliate with a transnational notion of blackness is another matter entirely.

Theater in Africa takes many forms: from Soyinka's poetic literary masterpieces written in English to improvised, nonscripted shows in indigenous languages; from traveling melodramas to community-based skits promoting literacy; from internationally successful South African productions like *Woza Albert!* to Ngũgĩ wa Thiong'o's grassroots Kamiriithu theater in Kenya. Much African theater uses proscenium-style staging with a bicameral separation between audience and spectators. This spatial configuration has roots in colonial schools that used European theater and its realist trappings to inculcate students with the ways of "civilization." But African cultures had rich performance traditions long before the arrival of Europeans. Theater as it is known in the West represents just one segment of a large spectrum of performance modes. As much as one can generalize about such an enormous and diverse continent, one can say that indigenous African performance genres (meaning those with roots that predate colonialism) tend to use fluid spatial dynamics. For instance, masquerade performers at festivals or annual rites may move through a town with audiences constantly converging and dispersing as they go. Storytellers may perform in an impromptu theater-in-the-round with spectators encroaching on the performance space as the dramatic tension builds.

Spatial dynamics have both a literal and figurative significance when one views African theater through the lens of black popular culture. African performance deploys a tremendous range of styles and genres. But it is primarily in theater as it is defined by the West—that is, scripted, literary dramas in European languages that utilize proscenium-style staging—that the transnational signifier of "black" takes on substance and weight. Blackness is a term of contrast that gains meaning through its antithesis, whiteness. South Africa is a country whose obsession with race and institutionalized racism during the apartheid regime ensured that the terms *black, white,* and *coloured* permeated every aspect of life, from the profound to the most mundane. Though apartheid officially ended in the mid-1990s, its heritage cannot be readily legislated away. Of South Africa's past and present, one can quite reasonably ask, "What is the relationship between the black performer and the black community?" Such questions have long been part of the critical analysis of township musicals as they moved into white-dominated urban venues and, eventually, overseas to Broadway houses. With the end of official apartheid, theater practitioners have had to engage in an even more thoroughgoing analysis of what black theater is about, what communities it will serve, and how these will be defined. Will the dismantling of a racist social structure in South Africa necessitate the suppression of an explicit discourse on race, a discourse in which terms like *the black community* are meaningful? Gross inequities in the distribution of wealth in new South Africa continue to be so clearly racialized that one can argue it is highly problematic *not* to speak of race.

Yet in parts of Africa where whites have never represented a statistically large proportion of the population, either in the colonial or postcolonial eras, notions of black and white may not be of sufficient significance to be the subject, subtext, or organizing feature of theatrical production. For instance, the practitioners of the concert party theater in Ghana are indeed black, yet they do not describe their art as "black." Kobena Mercer speaks of the "burden of representation" for black artists, the expectation that one must speak on behalf of the black community.[2] The Ghanaian concert party is multilingual and multiethnic, interweaving different aspects of Akan culture—such as Asante and Fante—while at the same time incorporating allusions to neighboring languages and ethnicities such as Ewe, Ga, and Hausa.[3] Yet rarely does this theater assume the transnational identity of blackness, nor does it speak for, to, or on behalf of subjects explicitly identified as black. Who is the black community from the point of view of concert party spectators and performers?

A time-based art form dependent upon embodied enactment, theater in the form of touring performances travels beyond Africa only rarely. Published play scripts, theater reviews, or production videos may circulate in the global marketplace along with other elements of black popular culture such as CDs or Afropop music tours, yet African theater outside the continent is, by any measure, obscure. In America, for instance, far more people would recognize the name of Ladysmith Black Mambazo, the South African choral group featured on Paul Simon's *Graceland* album, than that of Wole Soyinka, the Nobel Prize–winning playwright from Nigeria. Few indeed have heard of the Kumapim Royals, one of Ghana's most popular touring theater and music groups. The closest African theater has come to global popularity was the film adaptation of the South African musical *Sarafina* starring Whoopi Goldberg, a film so embarrassingly and ineptly executed that few African theater practitioners or scholars would wish to be associated with it.

While African theater is largely unknown in the United States, quite the opposite is true in Africa. In the absence of widespread local video or cinema production prior to the 1990s, theater long served as a primary medium for telling stories that expressed themes of local relevance. African theater has engaged in the boisterous process that has preoccupied much of African culture in the twentieth century: combining "tradition" with more recent imports and innovations while retaining cultural integrity. A vibrant and adaptive form, African popular theater continues to attract intensely engaged audiences, from farmers to lawyers, taxi drivers to teachers, entrepreneurial business owners to wage-laborers. This theater is popular both because it draws large audiences and because it is perceived to be an expression by and for the people.

Because popular theater is so widespread throughout Africa and also because of its complex negotiation of colonial and postcolonial social conditions, it has been the subject of a growing body of scholarly literature. David Kerr's encyclopedic *African Popular Theatre* (1995) is an excellent, if cursory, introduction to the subject. The number of monographs on West

African popular theater alone attest to the richness of this cultural form. Among the most notable studies are *Come to Laugh* (1981) by Kwabena Bame, *L'Invention du Théâtre* by Alain Ricard (1986), *The Yoruba Popular Travelling Theatre of Nigeria* (1984) by Biodun Jeyifo, *Yorùbá Popular Theatre* edited by Karin Barber and Báyo Ògúndíjo (1994), and *West African Popular Theatre* by Karin Barber, John Collins, and Alain Ricard (1997). The most recent additions to this field are Karin Barber's *The Generation of Plays* (2000) and my own *Ghana's Concert Party Theatre* (2001), with an accompanying videotape, *Stage-Shakers! Ghana's Concert Party Theatre* by Kwame Braun (2001). The annual *African Theatre,* published by Indiana University Press, attests to the continued vibrancy and diversity of African theater.

What emerges from these studies is a clearer picture of transnational patterns of African theater. For instance, popular theater in Nigeria, Togo, and Ghana often dramatizes the conflict between ill-gotten riches and those earned honestly, the plight of orphans, and the power of supernatural forces. One also sees the common themes of class divisions, inheritance disputes, and modern reinventions of tradition. West African popular theater rarely portrays or alludes to blackness as a concept of racial or cultural affiliation, whereas ethnicity, seniority, and gender relations are dominant concerns across national boundaries.

One apparent exception to this is the Ghanaian concert party, a popular theater form that was partly inspired by American blackface minstrelsy. I first encountered the Ghanaian concert party in the Northwestern University library in 1992. It was there I found Efua Sutherland's small booklet *The Original Bob,* a biography of the famous concert party actor Bob Johnson (1970). On the cover was a picture of Johnson in top hat and tails, wearing a plaid tie, his beaming smile broadly painted in white, his hands extended outward at his sides: a perfect evocation of Al Jolson singing "Mammy." This picture of Johnson, so suggestive of the controversial and racially charged American minstrel genre, raised questions about how blackface traveled all the way to West Africa. Why did Africans wear blackface? Did this makeup, clearly influenced by American and British minstrelsy, signify ideas about race circulating during British colonial rule?

Perhaps colonial Ghanaian performers were offering what Homi K. Bhabha calls a "revaluation of the assumption of colonial identity through the repetition of discriminatory identity effects."[4] Blackface performance practices might have been subversive strategies through which Africans disrupted racist colonial domination by turning "the gaze of the discriminated back upon the eye of power."[5] Yet as someone who strongly believes that postcolonial theory needs to be rooted in historical specificity, I question just how such an interpretation of the concert party's subversiveness could be supported with historical evidence. Would it require intentionality on the part of the performers? Or would audience reception be more important? Subversiveness may not be consciously articulated at all, for concert parties are comedies, and humor, as Freud has shown us, registers in regions of the human psyche often beyond the reach of rationality, inaccessible to the historian searching for evidence firm enough to move an argument beyond speculation and surmise.

Empirical methods demanding transparent sources must be suspended when considering performance practices forged, as blackface was, under conditions of exploitation and domination. However, despite what Paul Gilroy sees as the ultimate failure of empirical models in this context, I believe that a thorough immersion in evidentiary sources is especially crucial where conditions of domination prevail. Postcolonial theory asserts that colonial mimicry and stereotypes were ambivalent. But to speak of mimicry and colonial ambivalence ultimately does not tell us very much. What is much more revealing is to analyze in detail *how* specific valences were created, reproduced, and transformed through particular representations over time. What did blackface come to "mean" as it moved geographically from Boston to Hollywood, from London to Africa, and temporally from the late nineteenth through the twentieth centuries? Looking at the particular valences of ambivalent signs takes us much further into understanding the cultural maelstrom where colonialism and performance converge, the busy intersections of black cultural traffic.

During the course of my field research in Ghana from 1993 to 1995, I asked many people where blackface, or "tranting" as they call it, came from and what it meant.[6] I never met anyone, either among performers or spectators, who explicitly said blackface carried any notable ideological weight in terms of race. When I asked the leaders of the veteran company Jaguar Jokers why they painted their faces with black, they said, "Because it is attractive. In fact, it creates laughter too. When you wear the trant, it creates laughter."[7] Kwame Mbia Hammond said actors do it "just to crack jokes to the audience. If you don't make up your face and disguise yourself to the audience, you don't get laughs."[8] Blackface is part of a whole aesthetic of artifice in which actors use self-consciously presentational techniques to foreground the artifice of performance. Conventions such as female impersonation, nonnaturalistic staging, cartoonish characterizations, and a broad acting style create comic distance between the actors and their characters.

When I visited Ghana in 1993, the Concert Parties Union was preparing a proposal to perform at Ghana's 1994 Pan-African Historical Theatre Festival (Panafest). This semiannual event attracts participants from throughout the African diaspora, for it commemorates the devastation of the African slave trade and reunites African peoples whom slavery dispersed throughout the world. The Ghana Concert Parties Union members discussed their participation in Panafest not as an occasion to reflect upon diasporic issues, but as an opportunity to advance the Union's reputation.[9] Knowing that many Americans would come to Panafest, they decided to feature the American-derived aspects of their art form by doing an old-style show in which blackface featured prominently. The show was to be performed on a stage constructed within the Cape Coast Castle, the symbolic center of Panafest and site of the historic "Gate of No Return" through which Africans embarked on the Middle Passage. Union members seemed entirely innocent about how offensive blackface comedy performed in a former slave castle was likely to be for African Americans, especially those motivated to make a pilgrimage all the way to the motherland. Fortunately, this particular Panafest show never materialized, perhaps due to sluggish bureaucracy or a diplomatically astute festival organizer's intervention.

When I returned to Ghana in 1994, I asked performers more questions about blackface, but my inquiries led to blind alleys. Everyone said blacking up was done just to make people laugh—it meant nothing. Tranting was but one of the many techniques concert party actors use to transform themselves "for show." So I decided to give actors more information about why I was interested in this particular feature of their theater. On one occasion I gathered together six older actors for a reunion during which I showed them pictures of nineteenth-century American minstrelsy and early vaudeville. These performers, ranging in age from sixty-three to seventy-seven, were among the first and second generations of concert party practitioners.[10] These actors began their careers in an era when blackface was used in concert parties much more frequently than it is today. They also began acting at a time when African contact with British culture and the ideologies of colonialism was most intense. If blackface carried racial meanings in Ghana, I suspected this generation was most likely to be aware of it.

At the reunion, I showed the concert party elders a photograph taken in

1874 of American vaudeville actors Harrigan and Hart.[11] Everyone immediately explained, "Oh! They are Bob Johnson! Both of them are Bob Johnson!" recalling the pioneer of the Ghanaian concert party whose career
began in the late 1920s.[12] Rather than interpreting the photograph as evidence that Bob Johnson's wastrel attire and stage makeup came from
American precedents, these actors initially perceived Harrigan and Hart as
having copied Bob Johnson. After discussing the date of the photograph
further, the actors decided, "What she is showing to us simply means the
face painting aspect of the shows is not new. It has been there over the
years." Everyone readily perceived the continuities between the makeup
and costume styles used by Harrigan and Hart in the 1870s and those of
Ghanaian troupes in the 1930s and 1940s.

I then tried to explain what blackface means in America and why it is
now considered to be very offensive. Perhaps reacting to the seriousness
with which I conveyed this information, actor K. Acquaah Hammond
interpreted what I said to mean, "Today . . . if someone should paint his
face while staging a show [in America], one would be shot dead on the
stage. He will be shot dead immediately." During our conversation, there
were many misunderstandings, which suggested to me these older actors
were genuinely unaware of the history and ideological significance of
blackface as practiced outside of Ghana.

When I asked performers if they found blackface offensive, Y. B. Bampoe, leader of the Jaguar Jokers, offered his own interpretation. On previous occasions, Bampoe and I had talked extensively about blackface
because he would like to come perform in America someday and wanted
to know how his performance needed to be altered to appeal to U.S. audiences. At the reunion, Bampoe absented himself briefly from our discussion and returned wearing minstrel makeup fashioned impromptu from
cooking charcoal and blackboard chalk purchased at the local food market. Bampoe addressed his fellow performers, myself, and Kwame Braun,
my partner and videographer. He at times spoke in English rather than
Fante, knowing that by doing so on camera he was addressing a general
American audience:

> (In Fante) I want to give some explanation. The fact is some of our
> brothers elsewhere, we have been made to understand that if they see
> someone staging a show in Ghana or elsewhere with some paint applied
> to that actor's face, it means the actor is insulting them. I am referring
> to those who were sold into slavery. But that's not the idea. Here in

Fig. 1. The Akan Trio, ca. 1950. *Left to right:* J. E. Baidoe, Kobina Okai, and E. K. Nyame. (Courtesy of J. E. Baidoe.)

Ghana are many occasions when people apply paint to their bodies. When the Krobos are undergoing Dipo rituals, the body is smeared with some paint. The Nzemas apply some colors to their bodies during the Kundum festival. The Akuapem have a ritual known as *bragor* for young girls who have had their first menstrual period. The young girl and her intimate friends have some colors applied to their bodies. The Abiriws, Guans, perform the same rituals for young girls . . .

When therefore we apply colors to our bodies, nobody should think that he or she is being made fun of. It is customary. We normally paint our faces. Some people apply paints to their bodies before they attend some functions. We have the colors. We have all the colors: blue, green, red. . . . *(Switches to English)* Some people over the globe have different understandings or different interpretations that we are reminding them that they are slaves: is never true. It is completely out of gear. So nobody should think of that. We should all cooperate. When you see Africans painting their face, you should not be offended. It's for fun's sake.

(*Switches to Fante*) It is something we do, and people are happy about it. I would like to go to American in future. I have learned that the blacks in America don't like the idea [of blackface]. They should take it from me that there is no bad intention behind the scenes. . . . Our African priests practice [body painting] a lot, and at some of our festivals many people do it. . . . That's all I have to say.

What Bampoe sees in concert party blackface are connections not to American minstrelsy, but to Ghanaian puberty rites, annual festivals, and ritual practices performed by priests and priestesses of traditional religion. Body painting sets these occasions *and* concert parties apart from everyday life and highlights the liminal status of key performers. When I told Mr. Bampoe that not all types of body painting were problematic in America, just blackface painting, he said, "Oh, I see. Then it means when I come to America, I should paint my face green."

Bampoe's interpretation of blackface as being part of a tradition of ritual body painting was far from typical. In fact, he was the *only* Ghanaian I interviewed, either among practitioners or spectators, who expressed this particular reading. Bampoe's interpretation was also not categorical, for while he at one point disavowed racial connotations and emphasized reading blackface within a local, ethnically specific semiotic field, he later drew upon a much wider geographical frame, one with a distinct racial element. Bampoe asserted that in concert party blackface,

> there is a reason for using black and white: Dr. Aggrey used the keys of an organ to explain a point. He said that whites can't live happily without the blacks and the blacks also can't live happily without the whites. Furthermore, much of the raw materials they use are imported from Africa. After they've been used, they come back to us. We are, therefore, one people. If someone applies black and white to his face, it shows unity.

Bampoe alludes here to a piano metaphor associated with Dr. James Emman Kwegyir Aggrey, known through much of the world simply as "Aggrey of Africa."[13] Born in the Gold Coast in 1875, Aggrey came to the United States, earned degrees at Livingstone College and Columbia University, and then returned to Africa in the 1920s as part of the Phelps-Stokes Education Commission to Africa. This initiative was aimed at formulating new educational policies for Africa that would synthesize African

and European cultures. Aggrey was instrumental in founding Achimota
School in the Gold Coast, a school that remains today a flagship campus in
Ghana. A piano keyboard was the central image of Aggrey's philosophy of
education. He likened the cooperation between black and white races to
the harmony achieved through black and white keys on a piano keyboard,
and he advocated a school curriculum that would achieve such harmonic
synthesis.

Thus in our conversations about blackface, Mr. Bampoe first argued
that nothing about this theatrical convention is considered racially derogatory in Ghana because body painting is more readily associated with
African rituals than performance traditions propagated across the
Atlantic. But he simultaneously asserted that the colors used in concert
party blackface *do* indeed have racial connotations. Just as black and white
together on a keyboard symbolize unity, so a blackened face with whitened
lips signifies racial harmony. Adding a further layer of complexity to Bampoe's exegesis of concert party blackface, one must consider his desire to
tour professionally in North America and to make his performances accessible and palatable to audiences across the sea. His relationship with me
and interview on video provided what he saw as an opportunity to make
professional contacts for his desired tour abroad.

In the early years of the concert party, before Bampoe was even born,
blackface in colonial Ghana may well have carried racial connotations.
Newspapers of the 1920s and 1930s provide evidence that Africans were fascinated with black—or "Negro"—culture from America. Journalists
reported on African American achievements and the pervasiveness of
racism, and the African desire to emulate and connect with this larger
Negro world. This desire found expression on local stages in colonial
Ghana, when performers literally impersonated African American movie
stars. I have argued elsewhere that blackface minstrelsy did not carry in
colonial or postcolonial Ghana the same racist connotations it held in
Britain and America.[14] But while blackface in colonial Ghana was not
racist, it was on some level *about race* and racial affinity. The adoption of
this makeup expressed a burgeoning interest in black culture abroad.
Though in more recent periods, this connection has dropped away, with
practitioners seeing blackface as a local custom related to traditional religion, or alternatively as a symbol of racial harmony..

That so many different and ostensibly incompatible meanings can be
found in just one aspect of the Ghanaian concert party—the use of blackface—is entirely in keeping with larger patterns of cultural transmission in

the black diaspora. The circulation of performance cultures within the diaspora, as Paul Gilroy has argued, rarely follows any clearly defined or traceable trajectory. "Black performance . . . is a profane practice. It has been propagated by unpredictable means in non-linear patterns. Promiscuity is the key principle of its continuance."[15] Forged under conditions of domination, exploitation, and desire, black Atlantic cultures demand that we reconceptualize the whole problematic of origins. Scholars must dispense with evolutionary paradigms that impose a teleological model of development. Genealogical paradigms that imply notions of purity and legitimate lines of descent are similarly problematic. And positivist procedures that assume stable, unified meaning are utterly useless in this context. The challenge of African diaspora performance scholarship lies in representing and analyzing the multiple, contradictory perspectives found in the "behavioral vortex" of the circum-Atlantic, to use Joseph Roach's terminology.[16] We must identify the routes that were available to practitioners and spectators and ask why people followed particular trajectories through the busy intersection of cultures, and why they chose to stop at particular destinations along the way.

On the crowded highway connecting Accra, the coastal capital of Ghana, with Kumase, a market and cultural hub to the northwest, lies the town of Teacher Mante. A small market town comprised mostly of Akan people, Teacher Mante was an ideal location for a 1995 production of a classic play *Onipa Hia Moa (People Need Help)* by the concert troupe the Jaguar Jokers. For over forty years, this troupe has toured Ghana's cities, towns, and villages, bringing melodramas and rollicking, irreverent comedies to audiences in rural and urban venues. With theatrical careers bridging the colonial and postcolonial eras, the founders of the Jaguar Jokers command formidable expertise in the history of their art form. Y. B. Bampoe, the leader of the group, and his collaborator Acquaah Hammond grew up in the 1940s working as apprentices for the earliest commercial concert troupes: the Two Bobs and Their Carolina Girl, and the Axim Trio. Bampoe and Hammond were raised in Nsawam, a cocoa-trading town on the Kumase-Accra thoroughfare, just a few kilometers southeast of Teacher Mante. When I approached the Jaguar Jokers in 1995 about filming a performance for a documentary history of the concert party, Bampoe and Hammond chose Teacher Mante as a locale in part because they well knew the local tastes, gossip, leaders, and legends.

Concert troupes are famous for their skillful physical exploits, astute use of Akan proverbs, and incorporation of popular culture from everywhere. Concert performances of the early to middle twentieth century functioned as living magazines, forums for representation, contestation, and reformation of identities during a time of great social upheaval. Audiences looked to concert stages to see the current fashions, manners, and dances. Even as spectators appropriated ideas from plays, concert actors likewise exploited audiences, using local characters and their disputes as the basis for improvisational inventions. This dynamic interchange of ideas between audience and performers is at the very core of the concert party's vibrancy and dynamism. Concert parties use a proscenium-style stage with a thrust platform, thereby invoking the "fourth wall" and its realist pedigree. Yet this barrier between performers and spectators is constantly transgressed, with actors and spectators alike trading ideas across the footlights.

In the video documentary *Stageshakers! Ghana's Concert Party Theatre*,[17] the Jaguar Jokers prepare for their 1995 Teacher Mante show. The town crier announces the show's arrival, and actors create a performance space by converting an open-air compound house into a theater. As the day wanes, the actors light lanterns for the evening performance. Once darkness sets in, the house begins to fill with spectators. The camera takes us backstage, where the performers are getting in costume and putting on makeup. The show the Jaguar Jokers are to do this night, *Onipa Hia Moa*, is a classic piece. When first created in the 1960s by the JJ's, this show was performed by lantern light with acoustic instruments. This old-style performance contrasts with today's concerts, which are notable for their dependence upon rattling electric generators, blaring fluorescent lights, and explosively amplified dialogue. In the interests of giving historical perspective, the Jaguar Jokers perform *Onipa Hia Moa* in the older style of the 1960s; they present the concert party "unplugged," as it were.

Backstage, we see men dressing as women, since female impersonation has long been a standard feature of concert plays. The camera also reveals a man putting charcoal on his face and dabbing his lips with crushed white chalk. Later this actor, Acquaah Hammond, appears on stage with his partner Y. B. Bampoe, both in blackface makeup, black-and-white striped pants, and top hats. Looking like American Uncle Sams in a blackface minstrel show, Bampoe and Hammond dance and sing their opening chorus in English, using dance moves and a presentational style reminiscent of American vaudeville.

Interest in the racial significance of blackface motivated my first research trip to Ghana in 1993. However, not long into my research, concert performers let me know that although they were willing to discuss blackface, they did not consider it to be a particularly interesting or important dimension of their art form. From their point of view, I was yet one more American researcher viewing Africa through an overdetermined lens. Blackface has been a standard feature of the concert party for over eighty years. The practice has changed much in that time, as actors shifted from Jolson-style face painting to something more idiosyncratic and locally recognizable. For instance, one performer may appear with a white line painted down his nose, while another may have one eye rimmed with white and the other with black.

Onipa Hia Moa is a rough-and-tumble comedy in which our hero, Kofi Nyamekye, becomes seriously ill, loses his wife, and is ultimately saved by his loyal though self-centered friend, Opia. The Jokers and their Teacher Mante audience speak Twi. But near the conclusion of this Teacher Mante performance of *Onipa Hia Moa,* one character takes a remarkable linguistic digression. Opia, the friend of the protagonist Kofi, is onstage alone when Kofi's wife, Amma, returns from her wanderings. She had abandoned her husband in his hour of sickness and need, but she returns just after Kofi has been escorted to the hospital. Amma asks Opia in Twi, "Hey, Opia, where is Kofi Nyame Bekyere?" Opia replies, "Kofi Nyame Bekyere is dead. *(To audience)* Ladies and gentlemen, is not Kofi Nyame Bekyere dead?" Since Opia asked this question in Twi, the audience replies in Twi, "Wawu! [He is dead]." Opia then proceeds to ask the same question in five other languages:

Opia:	Kofi Nyame Bekyere egbeko lo? [Ga]
Audience:	Egbo.
Opia:	Kofi Nyame Bekyere maku a? [Ewe]
Audience:	Eku.
Opia:	Kofi Nyame Bekyere baamutu ba? [Hausa]
Audience:	Yaamutu.
Opia:	Kofi, abewuaa? [Kyerepon]
Amma:	Hey, Opia, I am asking you about Kofi Nyame Bekyere and what are you telling me?
Opia:	Kofi, ino die? [Pidgin English]
Audience:	Idie!!

As this exchange progresses, the humor and excitement escalate. How many languages does Opia speak? How many languages does the audience

FIG. 2. The Two Bobs and their Carolina Girl, ca. 1934. *Left to right*: J. B. Ansah, Charles B. Horton, and Bob Johnson. (Courtesy of C. K. Stevens.)

command? That both performer and audience are so versatile and accomplished is a source of great amusement. Each call-and-response segment makes Opia double over with delight in the audience and the opportunity to prolong Amma's embarrassment. Opia and the audience are conspiring in a lie. Kofi is not dead at all, merely ill, and he will soon get the treatment he needs. The performance revels in multilingual abilities, the rapid shifting from Twi, to Ga, Ewe, Hausa, Kyerepon, and Pidgin English. But which one of these languages is black? Pidgin English is probably the most likely candidate, for this is a coastal trade language that has been used for centuries to link *abibifoɔ* (people from Africa) with people from overseas, *aburofoɔ*.

Who is "the black community" in relation to African popular theater? For that matter, when is an African artist black? Only when he or she identifies as such? Or is skin pigment all that is required? Is blackness a cultural construct, and how can it be identified as such? African theater is so rich and diverse, it is hard to imagine its audiences fitting within the singularity implied by the phrase "the black community." African popular theater serves and represents many communities. Its levels and layers of significance are extremely fluid and dynamic. Just as the concert party utilizes and freely transgresses the fourth wall, so too does African theater utilize and dispense with various identities, of which blackness is only one. Opia and his audience in Teacher Mante speak Twi, yet their discourse ranges through a host of other languages. Is the concert party Akan? Is it Ghanaian? Or is it an archetypical African form? Whether we see African theater as being unified by race, ethnicity, language group, or nationality depends very much on one's vantage point. As is evident in South Africa, some African theater defines itself as black and exists within an environment where race is an inescapable factor of everyday life. Theater from elsewhere on the continent takes on "blackness" as a cultural construct at certain moments and dispenses, converts, and transforms it at such a dizzying pace, that one can never stop asking, "When exactly is African theater black?"

NOTES

1. Presentation at the conference "Making the Spirit of the 20th and 21st Century Culture," Stanford University, October 8–10, 1999.
2. Kobena Mercer, *Welcome to the Jungle: New Positions in Black Cultural Studies* (New York: Routledge, 1994), 240.

3. The Akan are Ghana's majority ethnic group.

4. Homi K. Bhabha, "Signs Taken for Wonders: Questions of Ambivalence and Authority under a Tree outside Delhi, May 1817," in *Race, Writing, and Difference,* ed. Henry Louis Gates, Jr. (Chicago: University of Chicago Press), 173.

5. Bhabha, "Signs Taken for Wonders," 173.

6. Kwame Mbia Hammond says the word *trant* came from a substance that was used in the colonial days to color school chalkboards. Actors would rub this black paste on their faces to create blackface.

7. Interview with Y. B. Bampoe and K. Acquaah Hammond, video recording, filmed by Nathan Kwame Braun, Adoagyiri, August 25, 1993.

8. Hammond, interview.

9. GCPU (Ghana Concert Parties Union), author's notes from Union meeting, August 26, 1993.

10. This group consisted of Bob S. Ansah of the Gold Coast Two Bobs, Jimmie Narkwa of the Dix Covian Jokers and the West End Trio, Joseph Emmanuel Baidoe of the West End Trio and the Axim Trio, and Y. B. Bampoe and K. Acquaah Hammond of the Jaguar Jokers.

11. Catherine M. Cole, *Ghana's Concert Party Theatre* (Bloomington: Indiana University Press, 2001), 44.

12. CPMR (Concert Party MpaninfoB Reunion), Reunion of concert party elders: Bob S. Ansah, Joseph Emmanuel Baidoe, Y. B. Bampoe, K. Acquaah Hammond, and James Kwaku Narkwa, convened by author and Nathan Kwame Braun, video recording, filmed by Nathan Kwame Braun, Sekondi, January 21, 1995; translated by K. Keelson.

13. Edwin W. Smith, *Aggrey of Africa: A Study in Black and White,* 8th ed. (London: Student Christian Movement, [1929] 1932).

14. Cole, *Ghana's Concert Party Theatre,* 17–52.

15. Paul Gilroy, "'. . . To Be Real': The Dissident Forms of Black Expressive Culture," in *Let's Get It On: The Politics of Black Performance,* ed. Catherine Ugwu (London: Institute of Contemporary Arts, 1995), 15–16.

16. Joseph Roach, *Cities of the Dead: Circum-Atlantic Performance* (New York: Columbia University Press, 1996).

17. Kwame Braun, *Stageshakers! Ghana's Concert Party Theatre,* video (Bloomington: Indiana University Press, 2001).

E. PATRICK JOHNSON

Performing Blackness Down Under
Gospel Music in Australia

I put it [a gospel record] on, and I just began to howl. I began
to weep. I just thought, this is extraordinary—the intensity, the
surrender, the joy, the yearning, everything that I could hear
in it.
  —Judy Backhouse

I've always sung music that comes from a black tradition. So, if
it's not soul, it's funk or reggae. So, I think African music
touches me in some way. I don't know why that is—a white
Jewish girl from Sydney, what can I say? Them's my roots.
  —Tracey Greenberg

In a black church, you know who you're singing to. They
believe every word you're going to say, and it's a fantastic
opportunity to get in touch with yourself. And also, because
they're far more responsive, as you know, it's like "whoa!"
  —Tony Backhouse

An all-white, mostly atheist, Australian gospel choir: at first it sounds contradictory. Yet when situated within the contested contexts of "blackness"
and "performance," white Australian, atheist gospel singers are no more
contradictory than black, gay Republicans. We live out the contradictions
of our lives, and an aversion to religion does not exclude persons from
making personally meaningful connections to gospel music that sometimes resemble, sometimes contradict, and sometimes supersede black
gospel music's functions in the United States. Once signs—or, in this case,
sounds—of "blackness" are "let loose" in the world, they become the site
at which cultures contest and struggle over meaning. Gospel music, as a
sign/sound of "blackness," has become one such contested site.

This essay examines the performance of black American gospel music in Australia. Focusing first on the formation and performances of the choir, the Café of the Gate of Salvation, and then moving to a general discussion of gospel performance in Australia, I examine the ways in which the medium of gospel facilitates a dialogic performance of "blackness." Given the racial, cultural, and religious composition of the Café and other Australian choirs, the essay also addresses the politics of appropriation by highlighting the ways in which Australians explain their interest in and performance of gospel music and the ironies that underlie their explanations.[1] The analysis, then, demonstrates the problematics of gospel performance in terms of cross-cultural appropriation, as well as the mutual benefits garnered when self and Other performatively engage one another via gospel music.

Initially, however, I wish to discuss the ways in which I construe "blackness" as a racial trope—as opposed to a biological essence—and its connection to authenticity and gospel performance. "Blackness" does not belong to any one individual or group. Rather, individuals or groups appropriate it in order to circumscribe its boundaries or to exclude others. When blackness is appropriated to the exclusion of others, identity becomes political. Because blackness has no essence, black authenticity is overdetermined—contingent on the historical, social, and political terms of its production. Moreover, "The notion of [black] authenticity implies the existence of its opposite, the fake, and this dichotomous construct is at the heart of what makes authenticity problematic."[2] Authenticity, then, is yet another trope manipulated for cultural capital. That said, I do not wish to place a value judgment on the notion of authenticity, for there are ways in which authenticating discourse enables marginalized people to counter oppressive representations of themselves. The key here is to be cognizant of the arbitrariness of authenticity, the ways in which it carries with it the danger of foreclosing the possibility of cultural exchange and understanding. As Henry Louis Gates, Jr., reminds us, "No human culture is inaccessible to someone who makes the effort to understand, to learn, to inhabit another world."[3]

And yet we must be aware of the reality of living within a racist, white supremacist, and capitalist society in which cultural appropriations have social, cultural, and political consequences. History demonstrates that cultural usurpation has been a common practice of whites and their relation to art forms not their own. In many instances, whites exoticize or fetishize blackness, what bell hooks calls "eating the other."[4] Thus, when white-identified subjects perform "black" signifiers—normative or otherwise—the effect is always already entangled in the discourse of Otherness; the historical weight of white skin privilege necessarily engenders a tense relationship with its "others."

This reality withstanding, human commingling necessarily entails syncretism whereby cultures assimilate and adopt aspects of the Other. Given that, all forms of cross-cultural appropriation are not instances of colonization and subjugation. Some of these appropriations are instances of genuine dialogic performance—instances that provide fertile ground upon which to formulate new epistemologies of self and Other.

Because gospel music is inextricably linked to black bodies and black culture in the United States, it necessarily registers as a signifier of "authentic" blackness. Accordingly, it is my contention that when Australians perform gospel music, they are engaging not only in the coproduction of the music, but also of blackness itself. Harry Elam suggests that "African American theater and performance have been and remain powerful sites for the creation, application, and even the subversion of notions of blackness and of concepts of African American identity."[5] Although Elam is referring specifically to theater written and performed by and about African Americans, I believe that black art forms performed by non-blacks extend the same creative and subversive possibilities of identity claims. Indeed, I argue that the Australians' performances of gospel are dialogic performances of blackness and thus "serve to reinforce the theory that blackness, specifically, and race, in general, are hybrid, fluid concepts whose meanings depend upon the social, cultural, and historical conditions of their use."[6]

"Couldn't Hear Nobody Pray": Discovering Gospel Down Under

I learned of the Café of the Gate of Salvation through Houston Spencer, a former classmate in graduate school. One of the things he and I share is a love of gospel music. Many of the letters he wrote to me from Australia included requests that I send him gospel tapes because they were hard to find in Australia. In the spring of 1992, he wrote to let me know that he had discovered a gospel choir in Sydney. This was not just any choir: it was an a cappella, predominately non-Christian or atheist gospel choir. I refused to believe him until he sent me a recording of the choir's self-titled compact disc. Three years later I secured a grant to travel to Sydney to conduct research, and in June 1996, I made my first trip to Australia.

Although I had heard their recording and had been amazed by the power of their voices, I still held a condescending attitude toward the choir when I arrived. As an African American raised in a black Southern Baptist church, I had my doubts about the abilities of an all-white Australian choir. My attitude changed, however, the first time I attended one of their rehearsals. If I had closed my eyes, I would have sworn I was back home at my church in western North Carolina. Not only had the choir accomplished a "black" sound, but they also had created the ethos of a black devotional service as they stood, hand-in-hand, in a circle singing "I Woke Up This Morning with My Mind Stayed on Freedom," an anthem from the civil rights movement of the 1960s. I was impressed.

During the three weeks of that first visit, I interviewed various choir members, all of whom were both willing to share their experiences in the choir and curious about my impressions of their performance. Specifically, they wanted to know if I thought they were "good" or if they sounded the way gospel "should" sound. My response was always encouraging but usually noncommittal. "I was really impressed," I often told them. Although I thought they had a great sound and, to some extent, had mastered the gospel idiom, I still felt something was missing. I realize now what I did not then: that I was essentializing gospel music based on my experience of growing up in the black church in the South. My initial response was one of admiration, coupled with skepticism as I dismissed the choir's performance as an approximation, but definitely not the "real" thing. I entered this ethnographic encounter with an "ax to grind rather than feeling for the organism."[7] Moreover, that first three-week visit was not long enough to get a sense of Australian cultures, day-to-day rituals, politics, and ways of being in the world. Later, I discuss how subsequent visits complicated my analysis of gospel performance in Australia. First, I provide a brief history of how the Café of the Gate of Salvation came into being.

"Blackness" in the Making

Tony Backhouse, a native New Zealander, formed the Café of the Gate of Salvation in 1986. His interest in gospel music began when he heard "You

Don't Know What the Lord Has Done for Me," a track on the album *Sorrow Come Pass Me Around* that was a part of the field recordings of David Evans, an ethnomusicologist at the University of Memphis. A record shop owner whose store was a few doors down from the Badde Manners Café that Tony managed gave the recording to the café's co-owner, Judy, Tony's wife at the time. When Judy played the song for Tony, both were powerfully affected. Tony recalls:

> The voices were so strange on it, and the feeling was just fantastic. To me, it was weird, like it was very exotic and, at the same time, kind of earthy and truthful. . . . [T]here was one strong singer, the alto, and then there was somebody else who sounded like someone's dying grandmother who was, sort of, seemingly, singing a soprano part or sort of set soprano tone, but she was actually singing lower than the alto in this kind of strange voice that was not always kind of hitting the same harmonies as someone else. And then there was a sort of bass voice that you could barely hear, so voices didn't blend, and half of it was inaudible, and that just added a fantastic character to it, and I just wanted to find out more about it.[8]

While this song piqued his interest in gospel music, he did not begin singing gospel right away.

Four years later, Tony "got a 'calling'" to found a choir. The idea came to him during a ten-day Buddhist meditation retreat. Soon after, he put up a sign in the café where he worked, in other cafés around Sydney, and in the Conservatory of Music. The sign read: "Singers Wanted for Gospel Choir. Buddhists Welcome." Forty people showed up at the first meeting in the living room of Tony and Judy's one-bedroom flat. "He had no idea what he was going to do really," Judy remembers. "He'd prepared one song, 'How I Got Over' (Aretha Franklin's version), and that was it—the choir was born."[9] The liner notes of the choir's first CD describe this meeting:

> The idea was to see if there was a bunch of singers around ready to go down a passionate, exhilarating spiritual, but culturally specific and little known byway; i.e., to form a choir inspired by the Afro-American religious singing tradition. When we started to rehearse in Tony and Judy's lounge room we had few expectations. It was an experiment that could have lasted 20 minutes or 20 years.[10]

Tony continued to learn more about gospel by obtaining records from Australian disc jockeys, through correspondence with white music scholars in the States, from articles on gospel, and by reading the liner notes of gospel recordings.

Regarding how the choir got its name, Tony remembers:

> I was reading a book on coffee at the time. It's [the Café of the Gate of Salvation] the name of an actual café out of Istanbul. It's been there since the thirteenth century or the sixteenth century. Just the ring of it sounds kind of nice. It's a terrible name. You can't fit it on any decent-sized poster. We should have called it "Punk" or something, a little bitty one-word [name] would have done a lot better.[11]

Nonetheless, the name stuck, and now, two recordings later, the choir enjoys a reputation as, arguably, the best gospel choir in Australia.[12]

In 1996, the choir had approximately thirty-five members. All but two were white: Cheryl, an African American woman from Detroit, whose hospital transferred her to Sydney, and William, a Maori from New Zealand.[13] Cheryl sang with the choir from 1993 to 1997 before leaving the group to star in musicals and form her own female singing group, Sisters. Until 1999, William sang in both the choir and Tony's quartet, the Heavenly Light Quartet. Other than Cheryl, no other African American has ever been a part of the choir. The choir is slightly more diverse in its religious affiliation and includes practicing Buddhists, Jews, and "spiritualists," as well as agnostics and atheists. Based on formal interviews and informal conversations with the members, it appears that most fall into the latter categories. Addressing this, Tony speculates, "I suppose you could say it's serving a therapeutic purpose, not necessarily a religious purpose, but . . . there has to be a place for non-specific spirituality, spirituality that doesn't necessarily attach itself to a label or a Messiah."[14] When I asked the obvious question of how one does that while singing about Jesus, Tony responded, "Well, I don't know. I mean there are Jews in the choir who have a little bit of trouble with the 'J' word, but they get around it by, I guess, making a mental flip in their mind—retranslating the word *Jesus* to mean 'my highest welfare,' or 'my highest good,' or 'mankind's highest good.'"[15] Comprised of working-class and middle-class people, heterosexuals, bisexuals, homosexuals, baby boomers, Generation Xers, leftists, hippies, and political activists, the choir is the site at which multiple identities converge.

Much of the gospel music aesthetic in the States is lost in the Australian translation. In addition to the absence of the call-and-response dynamic, other traditional features of the American gospel aesthetic are also lost.[16] Clapping, rocking, discipline in rehearsals, and dress—all extremely important in black American gospel performance—are not the Café's strongest suits. The choir seems a bit more casual about these aspects of the idiom. Unlike the billowing robes or "flashy" outfits donned by African American choirs, the Café's attire is eclectic—most of the time it's whatever they wish to wear. Even when they do enforce a dress code, they wear all-black costumes, accented with a colored sash or scarf. And while the Café, in general, has competent clappers and rockers, some of them are what I call "rock-and-clap challenged." I often teased members of the Café and those attending my workshops about their lack of rhythm. Often I found myself spending as much time teaching them how to rock and clap as I would teaching them songs. Judy Backhouse half-jokingly noted,

> We clap and rock, but we're not very good. We can't get that hard, solid clap. We can't get it. None of us have that sharp voice that cuts through, those sharp women's voices that sound like boy's voices. That's what a woman's voice should sound like in my book. There are some great solo singers in the choir, but they don't sound the same. We don't move in time. We don't clap in time. God knows what we're really doing really.[17]

Seemingly, Judy's commentary perpetuates the stereotype that all blacks can sing and have rhythm. However, her reflection also emphasizes differences in cultural valuation of rhythm. In other words, the valuation of rhythm in African American culture in various aspects of black cultural production—language, dance, music—makes it appear that having rhythm is an innate (authentic) quality of black folk. The fact that Australians can learn rhythm, however, dispels this myth.

For the most part, the choir does not try to replicate the sound of American gospel. They do not necessarily try to sound "black." In fact, this was never Tony's goal. According to him, gospel was a "starting point for developing our own musical language and our own nonspecific spiritual kind of music." However, as I detail later, some of the members' motivation for wanting to travel to the United States was to experience the "real" thing so that they could sound "better." While one might argue that this does not necessarily translate into trying to sound "black," it does register a desire on the part of some of the choir members to sound more "authentic."

When asked about what motivated them to sing gospel music, all but a few of the members cited the music's centrality in African American history. For example, Scot Morris stated:

> The whole thing about gospel is the release that it gives you . . . in terms of freeing your spirit, and the joy and sharing that goes on, is universal, even though it comes from those [slave] roots. . . . A lot of the songs are a metaphor for the freedom that people were longing for from the oppression that they found themselves in, and I think, part of the reason that we do a lot of the original sort of gospel numbers—and do them in a fairly traditional style—is out of respect [for] that tradition.[18]

It appears that the singers not only revere the music but also the history of the struggle out of which it comes. Moreover, they find a transcendent quality in the struggle of African Americans that allows them to generalize this experience to struggles over other various forms of oppression. The transcendence of struggle translates into a message of hope. Scot states, "There is a common thread in terms of recognizing the spirituality and the universality of the messages that gospel music brings and the joy." Similarly, Deborah Kerr explains:

> As I understand it, [gospel] came from the slave time and was what got them through those hard times, and I think a lot of people can relate to that because . . . people go—doesn't matter what race, religion, or color, whatever—everybody goes through their own constant, personal dramas, and [the meaning of] that music is, like, you can overcome. . . . I know you can overcome adversity, and you can overcome things, and the strength from the unity just makes you, just empowers you.[19]

The common thread that runs throughout these narratives is that gospel music is a universal language that transcends difference in order to help others overcome their own "personal dramas" and adversities. In fact, this focus on the history of gospel and the "empowerment" gleaned from that history was one of the factors that motivated the choir to organize a trip to the United States. According to Judy Backhouse, she and Tony wanted the choir to "see what they're representing and which tradition they're relating to. I don't think they really realize. We think they'd be really inspired, and it would make a huge difference in their singing, to their heart relationship to it." Eventually, the choir did travel to the United States, visiting churches in New York, Alabama, and New Orleans. As I discuss later, the trip did "change" them in ways that complicated how they had universalized gospel music.

Some of the choir members link their history as descendants of convicts to African Americans' history as descendants of slaves. For some Australian gospel singers, the music becomes the vehicle through which to express repressed sorrow and grief. Grant Odgers, a member of both the Honeybees and the Café states: "We do have the same history of cruelty and brutality [as African Americans], but we don't express it. I think that's why it's [gospel music] become so big, because we need the catharsis."[20] The "history of cruelty and brutality" to which Odgers refers is the "settlement" of Australia—then known as "Botany Bay"—by the British to contain their "criminal" population. In *The Fatal Shore,* Australian historian Robert Hughes chronicles the exportation of English convicted felons to what is now Australia. Hughes writes, "In the whole period of convict transportation, the Crown shipped more than 160,000 men, women and children (due to defects in the records, the true number will never be precisely known) in bondage to Australia. This was the largest forced exile of citizens at the behest of a European government in pre-modern history. Nothing in earlier penology compares with it."[21] The fact that these criminals were excommunicated by their "own" complicates further the already ambivalent feelings many Australians harbor toward Britain. "We know what it means to be treated like scum," one woman told me at a gospel music workshop I conducted. "Just like black Americans, we, too, have been put down because we're not of royal stock. We're the descendents of people who[m] the upper crust of England banished. So, in a way, we connect with black Americans and their fight to be legitimate. Singing gospel is the closest we come to making that happen."[22] According to Robert Hughes, this feeling of "illegitimacy" persisted until the 1960s, although, as evidenced in the woman's statement above, traces of it remain today. The reasons for these feelings are twofold: first, the English often reminded Australians of their criminal ancestry, and, second, the history of criminality in Australia forged a mythology around which working-class Australians could claim a history of oppression. Thus, English ridicule of Australians sent "upper-middle-class Australians into paroxysms of social embarrassment," while the working class created a stereotype of convict identity that said that "convicts were innocent victims of unjust laws, torn from their families and flung into exile on the world's periphery for offenses that would hardly earn a fine today."[23] These two stances—

denial/embarrassment and victim mythology—shape many Australians' current views of England and their relationship to British subjects. One result has been the creation of Australian nationalism. In the past few years, for instance, the Australian government has had heated debates about whether to break away from the monarchy and become a self-governing republic. Another result has been a longing to reconcile the past with the present. Gospel music, some singers argue, has helped bring about that reconciliation.

Romanticization or Identification? Universal Blackness

Although moved by the conviction with which members of the Café and other Australian singers expressed the joy and love for humankind that gospel music brings them, I kept wondering how they justified white Australia's treatment of Aborigines. Their romanticization of African American culture and history exists uneasily beside the virtual obliteration of Aboriginal culture. In fact, very few of the singers I interviewed discuss the white privilege they enjoy in relation to the subjugation of the Aboriginal community. As one storekeeper put it, "We don't have an Aboriginal problem because we don't talk about it."[24] This sentiment typifies the general attitude regarding the oppression of Aboriginal people. On the one hand, these gospel singers identify with an oppressed group thousands of miles away and condemn their oppressors. On the other hand, they fail to acknowledge the ways in which they participate in the subjugation of the "blacks" of their own country. Like many white Americans, many white Australians do not feel responsible for the past—at least in terms of acknowledging how they benefit, on a daily basis, from the subjugation of Australia's indigenous people. Thus, it was odd for me, as an African American, to have an Australian shake his or her head in disdain at what white Americans have "done to me." When I addressed the problem of racism in Australia with members of the choir or Australians in general, they seemed uncertain as to what to say.[25]

Australian singers universalizing the ethos of gospel music also do not acknowledge the specificity of African American history. African Americans who sing gospel do so from a place of struggle *and* faith. For them, the music functions not only as a testimony of their secular struggles of living in a white supremacist society, but also of their sacred faith in a God who has delivered them and continues to sustain them through those struggles.

Therefore, when Australian gospel singers state that they identify with African Americans who sing gospel, the comparison seems misplaced and inappropriate. Their rationale for singing gospel notwithstanding, they fail to recognize that the "struggle" they inherited as descendants of convicts is different from the struggle of African Americans from chattel slavery to freedom. In light of the white privilege they enjoy in their own country in relation to the Aborigines, their "struggles" seem decidedly different from African Americans. This is not to suggest that white Australians do not carry the pain of their criminal heritage. Rather, I believe that that history and its long-term material effects are distinct from and do not have the same impact as the history of oppression for either black Americans or black Australians. White Australians do not experience their bodies through the same racial lens as black Australians and black Americans, and to romantically dissolve the specificity of the history of "black" bodies remains problematic.

Nevertheless, the psychological wounds of convict heritage and second-class citizenship may allow these singers to connect to the African American experience. As much as spirituals and gospel music were a survivalist strategy to physically escape oppression, they also provided and provide a psychological escape from oppression. That psychological release stems from both the shared witnessing of joy and pain and the corresponding cathartic moment generated in gospel performance. Rhythm, syncopation, repetition, and call-and-response coalesce as a generative force that facilitates a psychological release. Among African Americans, that release is most often manifested physically. Whether through the waving of hands, dancing, rocking, crying, shouting, praying, or laying on of hands, the catharsis comes through bodily and verbal expression. Further, it is a communal act of experiencing this gestalt in the presence of others in that moment of mutual affirmation of faith and witnessing.

When members of the Café and other Australian singers talk about how gospel music makes them "feel better" and "picks them up," they, too, are naming the cathartic power of gospel. I argue, however, that their catharsis is brought on not by the universality of gospel "touching" them in the same way it does African Americans, but rather by the shedding of residual traces of British propriety. The physicality, emotionality, and self-display inherent in gospel performance does not accommodate self-consciousness, timidity, or taciturnity. Because Australian culture devalues self-display, when Australians sing gospel music, they cannot help but feel a release. It is as if they are discovering a hidden part of themselves for the first time. Therefore, what they are "connecting with" is not the oppression of African Americans but rather a part of themselves that had been underdeveloped or lying dormant and the generative and transformative power of the music itself. All of the testimonies chronicled earlier confirm that singing gospel brings about that transformative experience. Judy Backhouse believes singing the music is a way of empowering the self by singing with others. "There are very few ways in which people can authenticate themselves as singers or as artists of any kind," she said. "Usually, no one would come out and say, 'I'm a singer. I'm an artist,' even in this gospel community. But if they stand in a group and sing, they can sing without having to say anything about themselves. So it's a vehicle for their creativity and it's a vehicle for belonging, for joining."[26] The community that is created is, I maintain, based less on a superficial connection with African Americans than on the communal feeling stimulated when a group of people come together to share parts of themselves with one another.

Blackness and Dialogic Performance

There is no easy way to avoid the identity politics that arise when one group or culture appropriates another's art form, and members of the "indigenous" and appropriating cultures, as well as critics from both cultures, articulate conservationist or pluralistic arguments. Conservationists argue in essentialist ways that totalize and reduce black culture, most often in the name of black nationalism, while many pluralists explode the notion of any coherent organizing principal of blackness or black cultural production. There is, however, an alternative to either of these positions, particularly in reference to black music. Paul Gilroy writes:

> Black identity is not simply a social and political category to be used or abandoned according to the extent to which the rhetoric that supports and legitimizes it is persuasive or instantly powerful. Whatever the racial constructionists may say, it is lived as a coherent (if not always stable) experiential sense of self. Though it is often felt to be natural and spontaneous, it remains the outcome of practical activity: language, gesture, bodily significations, desires. These significations are condensed in musical performance, though it does not, of course, monopolize them. In this context, they produce the imaginary effect of an

internal racial core or essence by acting on the body through the specific mechanisms of identification and recognition that are produced in the intimate inter-action of performer and crowd. This reciprocal relationship serves as strategy and an ideal communicative situation even when the original makers of the music and its eventual consumers are separated in space and time.[27]

Key to Gilroy's demolition of the essentialist/antiessentialist binary is the primacy he places on the relationship between the body and discourse as a dynamic, intricate web of significations and meanings that are experienced as simultaneously both real and imaginatively produced. This view of "black" performance opens up new possibilities for interpreting the performance of gospel music by Australians. On the one hand, it calls attention to blackness as a visual marker of race and therefore experienced by "black" bodies as real. On the other hand, it points to the constructedness of blackness as a coproduced signifier that is socially, historically, and culturally determined.[28]

One way to view the Australians' performance of gospel is as an instance of cultural performance, wherein their performances provide a space for social and cultural reflection and critique. Although they are performing an Other's culture, their engagement with the music emerges from a cultural site specific to their own history as well: the legacy of British propriety and the secularity of contemporary Australian culture. Because their gospel performances are in striking contrast to socially and culturally sanctioned Australian cultural performances, they hold the potential of transgressing the strictures of hegemonic systems that sanction behaviors, beliefs, and attitudes. It is specifically the liminal space of performance that provides this occasion for cultural reflection and critique, this space where "the past is momentarily negated, suspended, or abrogated, and the future has not yet begun, an instant of pure potentiality when everything, as it were, trembles in the balance."[29] In this liminal state, "cultural performance holds the potential for negation, as well as affirmation," but nonetheless induces "self-knowledge, self-awareness, [and] plural reflexivity."[30] When, for instance, the members of the Café of the Gate of Salvation speak of the joy, love, and sense of belonging they experience when they perform, they are naming the process of self-knowledge and self-awareness facilitated by gospel. The fact that such self-awareness is induced by a cultural discourse (gospel) that transgresses the cultural milieu of Australia highlights the political nature of cultural performance. Accordingly, Turner suggests that cultural performances set in motion "a set of meta-languages whereby a group or community not merely expresses itself, but more actively, tries to understand itself in order to change itself."[31]

This change is facilitated by what Dwight Conquergood calls "dialogic" performance. Through dialogic performance, the performer comes to know himself or herself by performing the Other. According to Conquergood, dialogic performance

> resists closure and totalizing domination of a single viewpoint, unitary system of thought. The dialogical project counters the normative with the performative, the canonical with the carnivalesque, Apollonian rationality with Dionysian disorder. . . . Dialogicalism strives to bring as many different voices as possible into the human conversation, without any of them suppressing or silencing the other.[32]

The dialogic performance paradigm foregrounds the tensions between self and Other such that, despite evidence to the contrary, self and Other temporally and spatially come together and converse. This productive view of performance elides narrow, essentialist views of performance while, at the same time, acknowledging difference. Indeed, "dialogic performance celebrates the paradox of 'how the deeply different can be deeply known without becoming any less different.'"[33] Thus, dialogic performance makes possible the sharing of ideas, beliefs, and values across barriers of difference.

In "Performance, Personal Narratives, and the Politics of Possibility," D. Soyini Madison theorizes the politics, benefits, and limits of performance with regard to three subject positions that comprise dialogic performance: the audience, the performers, and the subjects being performed. For each of these subject positions, Madison highlights what she calls the "performance of possibilities" in order to articulate a politicized practice of dialogic performance. In what follows, I relate each of these three subject positions to Australian gospel performance.

For Madison, the audience's engagement with the performance is a critical component of political and social action:

> Action, particularly new action, requires new energy and new insight. In the *performance of possibilities,* when the audience member begins to witness degrees of tension and incongruity between the Subject's life-

world and those processes and systems that challenge and undermine that world, something more and new is learned about how power works. The question to what extent these life-worlds are threatened and, in turn, resist, is only partially captured in the space and time of performance; however, the audience, as involved citizens, both disturbed and inspired, may seek the answer long after the final curtain. This is a pursuit of possibility, a gift of indignation and inspiration, passed on from the Subject to the audience member. In the *performance of possibilities,* the expectation is for the audience member to continue, reaffirmed, or, to at least begin honing her skills toward "world travel." In the *performance of possibilities* both performers and audiences can be transformed. They can be themselves and more as they travel between worlds.[34]

Madison's notion of transformation here is important because it suggests emotional, psychological, and even political evolution on behalf of performers and audiences. For example, when members of the Café witness a gospel music performance on video or at live performances in Sydney or in the United States, they gain a glimpse into the lives and history of a geographically and racially distant Other. These possibilities of performance provide the space for transformation in social and political terms, in that this glimpse into the Other's history may motivate the performers to join in the Other's struggle for humanity and equality. For the Café, that transformative move is exemplified in the fact that all of the proceeds from their performances go to charity or are donated to black churches in the United States. Moreover, the Café's performance of gospel dramatizes the incongruity between the choir members' nonbelief and gospel music's theocracy, exemplifying gospel's "threat" to the choir members' lifeworld and their resistance to it. The result of this process is a group of people who, "long after the final curtain," see themselves differently—not only in relation to the racial Other, but to their own self. Thus, the ethos of gospel is reflected in the choir's close-knit community, its charitable contributions, and its desire to share a message of hope, love, and joy.

Self-reflexivity is one possible by-product of cultural performance, and therefore a possible outcome for the performer who performs the Other. In the meeting of self and Other in performance, Madison argues, the performer "is transported slowly, deliberately, and incrementally, at each rehearsal and at each encounter toward knowledges and life-world of the Subject" and, thus, "creatively and intellectually taking it all in[,] internalizing and receiving partial 'maps of meaning' that reflect the subject's consciousness and context."[35] If the performer "tak[es] it all in," then in many instances he or she may be transformed. "The process of being transported, or receiving meanings and generating meanings is a more intimate and, potentially, a more traumatic engagement for the performers than for the audience members, because the transportation is mentally and viscerally more intense."[36] The intimacy and visceral and mental intensity inherent in cross-cultural performance imply that an internal dialogue between self and Other is inevitable. This "felt-sensing"[37] experience energizes, inducing self-reflexivity, self-knowledge, and empowerment. For example, Judith Carson, an elderly woman who sings with the Honeybees, discovered her own singing voice again after having been discouraged from singing in her younger years. Now in her seventies, Judith is rediscovering that part of self which she thought she had lost—a rediscovery facilitated by her willingness to engage the Other. In an email to the author, she narrates the joy of her discovery:

> This is your most enthusiastic Sydney student. I am dotty about singing, as you probably realise. All my life it has been my dearest interest. Tragically for me, in 1952 I started having singing lessons. The teacher said, "Do it from the diaphragm," and "Lift your palate." Never, "Listen to that awful noise you are making." I broke my voice and could not sing at all for years. It was too important to me to give up, and I tried teacher after teacher. It has been disastrous.
>
> I love the power of your sweet voice, and the beauty of the music you made. Since you left, I have sung with your tapes, copying the sound and lilt of the music, and my body responds to the music I make and I am beginning to sing with my own voice. Perhaps you can imagine what this means to me? It's all a bit of a miracle. If you come to Sydney again soon I should enjoy very much singing with you again.[38]

Judith's testimony exemplifies Madison's call for the performer to be "committed—doing what must be done or going where one must go—to 'experience the felt-sensing dynamics' of the social world of the Other: its tone and color—the sights, sounds, smells, tastes, textures, rhythms—the visceral ethos of that world."[39] Although she was "copying the sound and lilt of the music," something in that process and in the music made Judith's body respond. When Judith placed those sights, sounds, and rhythms in her body, her body responded in ways that empowered her to find her own voice by singing with and through Others' voices. Her "transformation" was emotional, psychological, and physical. It was emotional in the sense that she was deeply moved by the music; psychological in the sense that her attitude toward singing changed from one of disquietude to confidence; physical because her voice became stronger and her body responded to the music. Her "broken" voice was "healed" through the "miracle" and power of gospel.

Judy Backhouse reports a similar self-discovery when she was persuaded to perform in New Orleans. In this instance, however, she and the subjects she performed mutually benefited from the performance, due, in part, to the space in which the performance occurred. Borrowing from Lawrence Grossberg's notion of "spatial territorialization," Madison argues that identities are "constituted by identification with certain cultural practices and connect to certain locales that are often ripe with struggle, conflict, and difference just as they are with creation, empowerment, and belonging."[40] In the following story, Judy Backhouse underscores the importance of place in relation to identity and dialogic performance:

It was one of the most harrowing nights of my life. . . . I was in this church. I made friends with this choir called John Lee and the Heralds of Christ in New Orleans. They said come to their church, they were giving a program, and I went along, and I was sitting in the audience. They were singing and everything was great: there was call and response, when, suddenly, John Lee said, "We have a good friend here from Australia, Ms. Judy Backhouse, and she's going to come up and sing." And I said, "Oh no! I'm not a soloist. I'm not a soloist, really." And he said, "Oh no, you're going to come up." And I said, "No, no, no." And I was very certain that I wasn't going to have to go up. I'm a strong person. No one's going to make me do what I don't want to do. However, I just couldn't not go up because it would have been an insult to everybody—everybody was wanting me to go up. And I had to go up. I was so scared, 'cause I thought, "I can't sing, they'll see that I can't sing. It will be the worst insult to them to sing badly in this great place where everybody is singing." Everything crossed my mind. I had to go up, I had to sing "Precious Lord." They said, "What do you want to sing?" And the only song I really love more than anything else in the world is "Precious Lord." Well, I've got a tape of this and it just sounds like someone on their deathbed, their last gasp, you know. But there they were, starting to encourage me: "All right," "Go on," "Do it." And that encouragement and that love they directed toward me, encouraged me really, it really emboldened me. By the end of the song, I was singing it, instead of just gasping it and panting it. I was singing it, and I just thought what it gives the performer, just makes you feel like you're in Heaven. And I wish we did that here in Australia. It will probably come in time.[41]

Judy's repeated emphasis on the place in which the performance occurred speaks to the fact that "identity is definable yet multiple, contested yet affirmed, contextual yet personal and a matter of difference and a matter of identification."[42] Her reluctance to perform was based on her own rigid notion of identity and performance, especially within the culturally pre-scribed space of the black church. She was in the Other's space and singing a song from the Other's culture, which made her briefly assume the stance that Conquergood calls the "Skeptic's Cop-out, in which the performer refuses to perform the Other because of empirical and biological differ-ence."[43] Quickly swept up in the centripetal energy of the church space, however, she moved to the center of dialogic performance. Once she began the performance, that liminal space where self and Other converse began to emerge, generating a powerful, dynamic transformative space. The encouragement of the audience whose art and cultural history was being performed helped Judy to "travel" in their world and, thus, provided her with a sense of belonging such that "by the end of the song, [she] was singing it, instead of just gasping it and panting it." Indeed, the supportive and generative force endemic to black church culture provided Judy the confidence to sing the song.

The words of the song that Judy sang were also crucial to the transfor-mative power of this performance. Thomas Dorsey's classic hymn exclaims: "Precious Lord, take my hand. Lead me on, let me stand. I am tired. I am weak, I am worn." Although Judy is a nonbeliever, through song she employs the aid of the black Christian folk myth of the anthropo-morphic God to take her hand and help her through the song, to "take her hand and lead her on." With the encouragement of the black Subjects in the church, and despite her status as non-Christian, Judy appropriated an Other's religious myth to empower herself to sing "in this great place where everybody is singing." The performed myth aided Judy in this moment of personal crisis. Conquergood writes, "It is through the liminal and transformative act of performance that myth and reality dissolve into a molten power that charges life with meaning and purpose."[44] Indeed, the liminal state of being, betwixt and between black church culture and Australian secular culture, created a tension that allowed Judy, through the immediacy and intensity of performance, to become self-reflexive about her own sense of identity. Ultimately, Judy sounding like "someone on their deathbed" was not the point. Rather, the fact that the Subjects sanctioned her performance of their culture is what transformed her relationship to and with the Other, what made her "feel like [she was] in Heaven."

The other members of the choir had an experience similar to Judy's when, in April 1999, the Café made its first journey to the United States. Many individuals from the Café had come to the States with Tony on one of his many "tours," but this was the first time that most of the choir's members together came to tour black churches in the United States. Traveling from New York City to Birmingham to New Orleans, the choir gave concerts, attended choir anniversary programs, rehearsals, and church services, and experienced the New Orleans Jazz Festival. I managed to arrange a trip to witness one of the choir's performances in New York. I was curious about how they would be received by African American churchgoers and how, in turn, the choir would react to that reception. I was especially anxious to experience the choir's performance in Harlem at the Baptist House of Prayer, an unlikely place, I thought, to invite a group of nonbelieving, white Australians to sing gospel music.

Located on 125th Street, the Baptist House of Prayer is a typical storefront church. It was Easter Sunday—the evening service—and an array of fuchsia, canary, and white wide-brimmed hats were sprinkled around the sanctuary. The crowd was small, but the pews gradually filled as the pre-program testimonies wore on. The devotional service continued for at least an hour and a half before the program officially began. Then the master of ceremony welcomed everyone to their Easter concert, featuring their special guests all the way from Australia: the Café of the Gate of Salvation. The choir gathered in front of the altar. All were dressed in black, but each member had added his or her own tie or scarf, a splash of brilliant color—red, purple, blue, yellow. A nervous energy filled the air as they stood before the church. No one, including the choir itself, knew quite what to expect.

The Café's director, Tony Backhouse, greeted the congregation with his consummate charm and graciousness, expressing the choir's gratitude for the invitation to sing. Their journey there had not been easy, he said, as they had to leave several singers behind due to family commitments or because they could not afford to make the trip. But one member, Deborah, had joined the tour despite her brother's death just days before the choir left Sydney. Deborah stepped forward and addressed the congregation. "He told me to come. 'Sing your heart out,' he said. Then he died the next day," she said tearfully, prompting cries of "Have mercy" and "Bless the Lord" from the congregation.

The choir lifted their voices to sing, and the congregation appreciated the first few numbers, but I had a sense that the choir was not really reaching them. Then something broke. The basses set an upbeat tempo, their heads bobbing in time and their faces lighting up. The tenors, altos, and sopranos joined the basses in harmony and rhythm. Soloist Tracey Greenberg stepped up to the microphone and launched into "You Brought the Sunshine," a song by the Clarke Sisters of Detroit that was popular in the early 1980s. The church pianist began to play, and there was uproar as the congregants rose to their feet and began to sing along: "You made my day / You paved my way / You heard me, every, every time I prayed. You brought the Sunshine (You brought the sunshine) In my life (You are the lifeline)." The choir beamed as the congregation's enthusiasm intensified, their shouts of "Hallelujah" and "Saaaaaannnng choir," syncopated clapping, rocking bodies, and stamping feet shaking the church's creaky wooden floorboards. At that moment, as the melodious voices lifted in the air, the Baptist House of Prayer fell under the spell of the spirit that moved the foundation of the church.

The performance of "You Brought the Sunshine" tapped into the Others' voice within experience, due in part to the Café's execution of and enjoyment of the song. This particular song registered with the congregation as "difficult"—even for members of its own choir—and the Café mastered it, demonstrating their commitment to, investment in, and reverence for gospel. The choir's competence as performers initiated genuine dialogue in that contested space where identities and subjectivities converse, commune, and contrast. During and after dialogic performance—and specifically within the "performance of possibilities"—performer, subject, and audience are transformed. Each comes away from the performance changed. They traverse the world of the Other, glimpsing its landscape, and this "sighting" leaves a lasting imprint on the consciousness of all who experience this symbolic journey. Indeed, they enter, "albeit symbolically and temporarily, in [the Others'] locations of voice within experience."[45] According to Madison, "performance becomes the vehicle by which we travel to the worlds of Subjects and enter domains of intersubjectivity that problematize how we categorize who is 'us' and who is 'them,' and how we see ourselves with 'other' and different eyes."[46] This blurring of subjectivities in the symbolic space of performance foregrounds the discursive nature of identity, such that during their performance in the Baptist House of Prayer, the Australian choir and the black listening audience participated in the coproduction of blackness vis-à-vis gospel music. Their performance inside the church and during this particular song foregrounded the arbitrariness of black signification as well as the possibilities created by means of performance. Indeed, the choir was engaging in what Richard Schechner calls "believed-in theatre": "At site-specific, event-specific, audience-specific performances, people gather as co-creators, participants, actors, spectators, witnesses, citizens, activists . . . doers. The occasions are frequently more social or personal or quasi-religious (ritual-like) than aesthetic. Sincerity and making an honest effort are appreciated."[47]

One should never underestimate the transformative power of dialogic performance. For the members of the Café of the Gate of Salvation, their experiences during their tour were life altering, collectively and individually. Four months after their tour, I traveled to Sydney to conduct more research and follow-up interviews after the choir's U.S. tour. What I found was a choir "transfixed"—to borrow Judy Backhouse's term—by the power of their intercultural exchange. Their relationship to one another and to the music had changed. For example, half an hour before their rehearsals, they held an optional meditation session to set the tone for the rehearsals. This newly introduced ritual was a version of devotional services and prayer meetings they attended while on tour. Despite their resistance to the spiritual ethos enlivened by gospel, the choir, through performance, came to realize, as Judy Backhouse had done already, that, like performance, the music "does something to you," or, as Tony Backhouse put it, "changes you for the better."

Conclusion

As a national and global commodity, black music has penetrated the boundaries between and among cultures around the world. As such, it becomes bound up in an intricately spun web of cultural, social, and political battles over origin, ownership, circulation, and performance. Until fairly recently, gospel music existed on the margins of this political minefield, due in part to its relatively limited circulation and popularity among mostly southern blacks. As it has found currency among a younger audience—a currency made possible due to a shift in how it is marketed and, more importantly, how it is produced—gospel music, like its musical sibling, rhythm and blues, has become more popular, both intra- and intercontinentally. It has, indeed, made its way over and "down under." Although black American culture is widely disseminated in Australia, gospel music's particular popularity in recent years may be due to the sense of community it encourages. Singing together in choirs provides an opportunity for an otherwise internationally diverse group of people to come together as Australians. Indeed, Judy Backhouse believes that the emergence of gospel singing groups in Australia represents the "first full community, the tribal thing, the group thing." This sense of group identity that gospel provides for Australians is not so unlike that which it provides for black Americans, though clearly for different purposes and aims.

Thus, the choir members' appropriation of blackness via gospel is both/and rather than either/or. Each time the choir performs gospel music they participate in what has become one of the most recognizable signifiers of black culture. Gospel, however, like other black cultural art forms, is enshrouded in identity politics. The fact that whites have appropriated other black musical forms such as R & B, blues, and rap, without paying homage or royalties to their progenitors, demonstrates the material reality of cultural usurpation in a racist and capitalist society. Gospel music is not beyond the reach of such appropriation, especially now that it has become more commercially viable.[48] The Café of the Gate of Salvation exemplifies how "messy" those politics may become. Their performance of their own and the Other's identity is never a static process, but one of flux and flow, of possibilities.

Negotiating any identity is a dangerous adventure, particularly in a postmodern world in which we have come to recognize that identities are made, not given. We also must realize that the postmodern push to theorize identity discursively must be balanced with theories of corporeality and materiality. In other words, "blackness" may exist as a floating signifier in various cultures, but the consequences of its signification vary materially, politically, socially, and culturally depending on the body upon which it settles.

NOTES

1. The research for this study occurred over a three-year period (1996–99) and four trips to Australia, each lasting from three to six weeks. In addition to Sydney, I

traveled to and conducted gospel music workshops in the following cities around Australia: Canberra, Wollongong, Newcastle, Melbourne, Adelaide, and Perth. I formally interviewed fifteen members of the Café and informally interviewed twenty-seven Australian singers at workshops. Because this research is part of a larger book-length project, many interviews are not included in this essay. The subjects interviewed all consented to using their real, full names, except where indicated.

2. Regina Bendix, *In Search of Authenticity: The Formation of Folklore Studies* (Madison: Wisconsin University Press, 1997), 7.

3. Henry Louis Gates, Jr., "'Authenticity,' or the Lesson of Little Tree," *New York Times Book Review,* November 24, 1991, 26.

4. bell hooks, *Black Looks: Race and Representation* (Boston: South End Press, 1992), 21–40.

5. Harry Elam, Jr., "The Device of Race: An Introduction," in *African American Performance and Theater History: A Critical Reader,* ed. Harry J. Elam, Jr., and David Krasner (New York: Oxford University Press, 2001), 6.

6. Elam, "The Device of Race," 5.

7. I credit Emily Toth with this phrase.

8. Tony Backhouse, interview by author, tape recording, Sydney, June 8, 1996. What Tony is describing here is called heterophony, a term used to describe singing that is not in harmony, but a mixture of voices singing in unison with one or two harmonizing in between. This style of singing is common in African American worship services, particularly in rural, southern churches.

9. Judy Backhouse, interview by author, tape recording, Sydney, January 10, 1998.

10. *The Café of the Gate of Salvation* (Sydney: Polygram, 1991), compact disc.

11. Tony Backhouse, interview.

12. The Café's second recording is entitled *A Window in Heaven.*

13. Cheryl and William wished to be identified only by their first names.

14. Tony Backhouse, interview.

15. Tony Backhouse, interview.

16. For more on the role of audience in African and African American performance see Oyin Ogunba, "Traditional African Festival Drama," in *Theatre in Africa,* ed. Oyin Ogunba and Abiola Irele (Ibadan, Nigeria: Ibadan University Press, 1978), 3–26.

17. Judy Backhouse, interview.

18. Scot Morris, interview by author, tape recording, Sydney, June 8, 1996.

19. Deborah Kerr, interview by author, tape recording, Sydney, June 10, 1996.

20. Quoted in Lauren Martin, "A Black and White Gospel," *Sydney Morning Herald,* September 13, 1999, A-399.

21. Robert Hughes, *The Fatal Shore* (New York: Knopf, 1987), 2.

22. Anonymous, interview by author, Sydney, August 24, 1999.

23. Hughes, *The Fatal Shore,* 158–59.

24. Anonymous, interview by author, Sydney, June 17, 1996.

25. I do not wish to imply that members of the Café are not concerned about or do not actively fight for Aborigines. I only make the observation that rarely was the plight of Aborigines a topic of conversation, and when it was, it was brief.

26. Judy Backhouse, interview.

27. Paul Gilroy, "Sounds Authentic: Black Music, Ethnicity, and the Challenge of

a Changing Same," in *Imagining Home: Class, Culture, and Nationalism in the Black Diaspora,* ed. Sidney Lemelle and Robin D. G. Kelley (New York: Verso, 1994), 108–9.

28. See Michael Omi and Howard Winant, *Racial Formation in the United States,* 2nd ed. (New York: Routledge, 1994).

29. Victor Turner, *From Ritual to Theatre: The Human Seriousness of Play* (New York: Performing Arts Journal Publications, 1982), 44.

30. Dwight Conquergood, "Performing Cultures: Ethnography, Epistemology, and Ethics," in *Miteinander Sprechen und Handelm: Festschrift für Hellmut Geissner,* ed. Edith Sembek (Frankfurt am Main: Scriptor, 1986), 59.

31. Quoted in Conquergood, "Performing Cultures," 66.

32. Dwight Conquergood, "Between Experience and Meaning: Performance as Paradigm for Meaningful Action," in *Renewal and Revision: The Future of Interpretation,* ed. Ted Colson (Denton: NB Omega, 1986), 47–48.

33. Dwight Conquergood, "Performing as a Moral Act: Ethical Dimensions of the Ethnography of Performance," *Literature in Performance* 5 (1985): 10.

34. Soyini Madison, "Performance, Personal Narratives, and Politics of Possibility," in *The Future of Performance Studies: The Next Millennium,* ed. Sheron J. Dailey (Annandale, Va.: National Communication Association, 1998), 285.

35. Madison, "Performance," 285.

36. Madison, "Performance," 283.

37. See Wallace Bacon, *The Art of Interpretation* (New York: Holt, Rinehart and Winston, 1979).

38. Judith Carson, email message to author, April 20, 1998.

39. Madison, "Performance," 284.

40. Madison, "Performance," 284.

41. Judy Backhouse, interview.

42. Madison, "Performance," 286.

43. See Conquergood, "Performing as Moral Act."

44. Dwight Conquergood, "Between Experience and Expression: The Performed Myth," presented to the convention of the Speech Communication Association, Chicago, November 1986, 2.

45. Madison, "Performance," 280.

46. Madison, "Performance," 282.

47. Richard Schechner, "Believed-in Theatre," *Performance Research* 2, no. 2 (1997): 89–90.

48. An example of how identity politics and appropriation has emerged in gospel music is the fact that in 1995, Angelo Petrucci and Veronica Torres, Italian and Latina, respectively, won "Best Contemporary Black Gospel Recorded Song" at the Dove Awards, an awards show for Christian music. See Lisa Jones, "Are Whites Taking Gospel Music," *Ebony,* July 1995, 30–34.

DANZY SENNA

Passing and the Problematic of Multiracial Pride
(or, Why One Mixed Girl Still Answers to Black)

I have never had the comfort zone of a given racial identity. My mother is a Bostonian white woman of WASP heritage. My father is a Louisiana black man of mixed African and Mexican heritage. Unlike people who are automatically classified as black or white, I have always been up for debate. I am forever having to explain to people why it is that I look so white for a black girl, why it is that my features don't reveal my heritage. It's not something I should have to explain, but in America, at least, people are obsessed with this dissonance between my face and my race. White Americans in particular have a difficult time understanding why somebody of my background would choose blackness. With Tiger Woods proclaiming himself a Cablinasian, multiracial activists demanding new categories, and *Newsweek* declaring it hip to be mixed, it strikes most people as odd that I would call myself a black girl.

But my racial identity developed when I was growing up in Boston in the 1970s, where there were only two choices for me: black and white. For my sister, a year older than me, with curly hair and more African features, there weren't even these choices. There was only black. And my parents, smitten with the black power politics of the time, taught my siblings and me, in no uncertain terms, that we were all black. They saw this identity as armor against the racism beyond our front door. They also knew that my sister didn't have a choice, and to define us differently would be damaging to us as a family unit. The fact that the world saw each of us as different (my sister as light-skinned black, my brother as Puerto Rican, and me as Italian) raised complications, but didn't change the fact that we were all one tribe.

Of course, we didn't always have an easy time in the black community. As philosopher Simone Weil once argued, when the weak get together, they mimic the actions of the formerly powerful. In the late 1970s, my sister and I attended an Afrocentric school, where I got teased—and on occasion roughed up—for looking so "light, bright, and damn near white." My sister, being bigger, braver, and more visibly black than me, became my protector. There I witnessed the hypocrisy of black nationalism. Although the school preached the Kwanzaa value of community, when it came time for the annual Christmas show—the black nativity—I was not invited to perform in it with the rest of my classmates. The reason was never stated, but I was old enough to know what was going on. I remember sitting in the auditorium on Christmas Eve, watching my sister, up on stage singing "Go Tell It On the Mountain" with the rest of my schoolmates, and feeling that I was inadequate. When my father and I went out into the world together, strangers, despite his "mixed features" and our clear familial resemblance to one another, often looked upon us with suspicion. I wondered more than once during my childhood if I had been switched at birth with somebody else; in my racial fantasia, I imagined myself a long lost Sicilian girl, the daughter of a Mafia kingpin. I envisioned a little black girl eating spaghetti somewhere in Boston's North End, while her family looked on in bewildered silence.

I faced a conundrum that many mixed people face: The black community of those heady times told me that I'd better identify as black, but that I would never be black enough. It was the ultimate double bind.

Needless to say, both my sister and I were relieved when my parents lost interest in negritude. We switched out of that Afrocentric school, and began to attend a school on a whiter side of town. But as I found out, the situation in "Caucasia," so to speak, was no better. There, my sister was the outcast; a group of Irish kids from the projects known as Whisky Point threw rocks and racial slurs at her on a regular basis. On our playground wall were the misspelled words: NIGERS GO HOME. I, on the other hand, had never been more popular. But my euphoria was short lived, as I quickly learned that acceptance in the white world came at a price.

The *American Heritage Dictionary* defines the word *pass* as (1) to move on or ahead, proceed. (2) to be accepted as being something one is not. (3) to cease to exist; to die.

In those situations where I was silent in the face of racism, where I "passed," I felt a part of me die. I was a witness to the things that white people say when they think they're alone. My school friends were forever talking about "niggers" and "spics," and then chummily patting me on the back and saying, "Don't worry, Danzy. We're not talking about you." For me not to assert myself as black in these situations was an act of betrayal against the people whom I loved the most. It was also a betrayal of myself.

So at a young age I made the decision that if the kids around me were going to call my sister a nigger, they had better call me one too. I feel now that this choice was not so much one between black and white, but one between speech and silence. It was how I learned to find my own voice, rather than letting my body speak for me.

I continue to identify myself as black. I don't see it in contradiction with my white and Mexican ancestry. Nor does it negate these other parts of myself. I have come to understand that my multiplicity is inherent in my blackness, not opposed to it. To be black, for me, is to contain all colors. The choice stems from my childhood decision not to define myself differently from my sister or my father. But it also grows out of my increasing understanding that race is not real, but rather is a social, political, and historical construct. Race has never been about blood, and it has never been about reason. Rather, it has to do with power and economics and history. One of my concerns about the multiracial movement is that it buys into the idea of race as a real, biological category. It seems to see race almost as chemistry: Mix black and Japanese, you get Blackanese, mix Caucasian, black, Indian, and Asian and you get Cablinasian. I wonder if it will work toward a deconstruction of race, or a further construction of it. When we look at societies that acknowledge racial mixture, such as Haiti, Brazil, and South Africa, it becomes clear that multiracial pride does not necessarily mean the end of racism. Even when we look at the history of our own country—blue vein societies, brown paper bag tests, and light-skinned privilege—it becomes clear that a multiracial identity can live happily with racism and white supremacy intact.

As it becomes more popular to identify one's self as mixed, and as the one-drop rule goes out of vogue, this black identity of mine is looked upon as more and more of an oddity by blacks, whites, and mixed people alike. At a black women's brunch group I attended in Los Angeles, I faced not hostility but bewilderment. It was as if none of these women—born after the civil rights movement—had a precedent for mixed people identifying as black. As I get less and less affirmation of this identity from the outside world, I begin to understand that my black identity is not about the way other people see or define me, nor is it about any one drop of black blood. It's something far more complex and mysterious, rooted in my personal history and my understanding of a larger shared history.

I believe that children of mixed marriages should be able to define themselves however they please. If Cablinasian works for you, so be it. I understand that my experience is specific to me, and cannot be imposed on other people. I think black people themselves bear some of the brunt of responsibility for defectors from the race, because of our inability at times to accept our own diversity.

But ultimately I'm not so fixated on what I call myself or anybody else calls himself or herself. I think that identity politics (and all questions of racial pride) can be a form of narcissism, and at their worst are a distraction from real questions of power. Why do we want a new category at all? Why is it we care so much about a census box or a school form? And why is it so important for many mixed people not to be defined as black? If the multiracial debate is about blackness, then let no mistake be made.

I used to go out of my way to tell people I was black. Around black people whom I didn't know, I craved acceptance. Around white people whom I didn't know, I avoided having to hear them make racist comments. I can now see that I was taking on the burden of other people's racial baggage. I was working hard to make other people comfortable. Today I allow for the discomfort. I go into black spaces and, knowing now that it is not my problem, feel strong enough to face that rejection, discomfort, and mistrust. I allow white people to embarrass themselves by making racist comments in front of me, feeling strong enough to respond to these comments after they have been spoken.

These days, when people ask me what I identify with, instead of giving them a simple one-word answer, I often turn the tables and ask them why they want to know. I interrogate their interest in my identity before answering. I ask them what each of my potential answers would mean to them. I want people to think more about what they are asking me. We have all become so lazy about race, just eating up the folklore that is shoveled our way: black equals athletic, poor, brown-skinned, left-wing, rap music; white equals intellectual, wealthy, pale-skinned, right-wing, rock music, and so on. We hold onto these archaic definitions despite a world that is increasingly blurred. I want to make people define the terms they so often use without thinking. Is the fact of my father erased by my skin? Are we all simply what we appear? I try to push people, and myself, to define the racial terms they are using. Once we begin to interrogate the language itself, things fall apart, and, as Yeats put it, "the centre cannot hold."

The world has changed since I was a little girl at the Afrocentric school, watching my sister on stage while I sat in the audience. There are more and more people like myself—children of interracial relationships—and more and more of them are defining themselves as mixed. I can only hope that as we celebrate this so-called New Race—the multiracial—we can begin to deconstruct and interrogate the very notion of race, rather than reinscribe it.

KENNELL JACKSON

The Shadows of Texts
Will Black Music and Singers Sell Everything on Television?

Turn the channel, there is Dinah Washington singing "Destination Moon" to sell Nike sneakers.
　　—Valerie Gladstone, arts critic, 1998

She [Erykah Badu] actually asked about appearing in the ad
because she does wear Levi's.
　　—Kojo Bentil, Kedar Entertainment, 1998

I really like it when I hear my songs in an elevator . . . I am a
big fan of elevator versions of my songs. It just strikes me that
it [my song] has penetrated the culture as far as it can get . . .
when it is background music in an elevator, it has reached
everybody.
　　—Paul Simon, singer, interview on *Weekend Edition*, June 12, 2004

For them [Run-D.M.C.], it [a Coke ad] meant they had
made it.
　　—Russell Simmons, hip-hop mogul

She was tiny and bubbly in the vintage manner of child stars. Though only
six years old, she was being billed as "the Pepsi spokesperson."[1] She was
white, but her costar was an African American woman. For over forty years,
this African American woman had sustained a most impressive singing
career, earning for herself the folk accolades of "the Queen of Soul" and
"Soul Sister No. 1." In 1986, she had had a cameo role in the film *Blues
Brothers*, but she was not known as a film star. The tiny girl also had been in
movies and charmed the hosts of late-night talk shows, but was not known
widely for her singing. In crucial ways, these two stars were different.

Maybe because of their differences, their cultural and status mismatch, they—Hallie Eisenberg and Aretha Franklin—were brought together to make one of the most discussed television commercials of recent years. Shown in 1999, the one-minute commercial debuted on Academy Awards night in March. Placement in such a highly visible spot revealed the ad creators' ambitions. Using a full minute of air time also revealed the dollars poured into the ad's making. The ad was warmly received, resulting in more air time.

In the ad's opening scene, Hallie is standing on a countertop in what appears to be a retro diner. Music is in full swing, and Hallie begins to dance. Suddenly, out comes a powerful voice, seemingly from her. The soaring voice moving through Hallie is lifting Pepsi's new anthem "The Joy of Cola." It can be easily recognized as Aretha's voice, with its characteristic clarity and range. One cannot help wondering, though: it is Aretha's voice, but where is she? To answer that question, the camera pulls back. Aretha is shown sitting in one of the diner's booths. She has witnessed Hallie's performance and she salutes her with "You go, girl." Here, as in African American social life, is a forward-urging statement of woman-to-woman solidarity. After a summation by Pepsi, the commercial ends.[2]

This essay uses the Pepsi ad as its launching point. It draws also on an insight from the French cultural critic Roland Barthes—a critic skilled at bringing to the surface subtextual communication. Barthes remarks, "There are those who want a text (art, painting) without a shadow . . . but this is to want a text without fecundity, without productivity, a sterile fact. The text needs its shadow."[3] Barthes urges us to look more carefully at what might be referred to as "background" for texts, in this case television commercials, to take the "shadow" more seriously, as more than an off-stage performance.

The main argument of this essay is that in the process of trafficking in black musical performances, television commercials have taken on an additional "fecundity," a fertility of ideas and cultural styles. This fecundity is double-sided: it is captivating to viewers and is a powerful assist to promoting traffic in goods; at the same time, it is problematic because of an aggressive stance with regard to black cultural material. Television ads incorporating black musical performances are a challenging cultural presentation to analyze because they have an undeniable seductive capacity, but they also represent a manipulation of black cultural material in ways that can be troubling. It is the same problem presented by the art gallery as a marketplace, as a bazaar for what has been idealized as noble art. In a gallery, a capitalist subsystem is purveying and maneuvering art. It is this bundle of forces—television capitalism and black musical material, often historically important material—that comes together in this little-recognized cultural traffic.

Television commercials are not often taken seriously as repositories of cultural possibility. They are at best considered the detritus from a deeply flawed image purveyor, television. Probably the most important reason for this dismissive attitude is that commercials are such tiny openings in programming, usually of sixty-, thirty-, or fifteen-second duration. But far from being trivial, within today's media, television ads based on black music have become a significant part of traffic in black cultural material. Every day, millions of people encounter black cultural expressivity through television commercials.[4] In a single week of November 2003, James Brown's "It's a Man's World" backed an ATT ad, Little Debbie's cakes used a group of kids singing the Temptations' standard "My Girl," and MCI invoked "Ain't Nothing Like the Real Thing." Included in this explosion was a parodic riff on the film *Eight Mile* in a Geico insurance advertisement in which a black club owner, flanked by two menacing younger blacks, auditions a bad white hip-hop performer. On some days in recent years, it has been impossible to keep up with the proliferation of such ads. Overseas, especially in Britain, more ads based on black music are also beginning to appear.[5] Viewing this cascade of ads, one is compelled to ask: are black music and the black singing voice going to deliver most of the pitches for wares on television?

The essay starts with a fuller discussion of the Pepsi advertisement, highlighting more issues while emphasizing the ad's success and its problematic content. A thumbnail history of black music and singers in television from the early 1980s to roughly 2002 follows. Next, the question of the concepts behind this commercial crafting is explored. Particular attention is given to the issue of what the black singing voice is imported to accomplish. This is a difficult, long-standing issue, which cannot be resolved here, but an essential one in understanding what the world thinks it hears in the black singing voice, and why it desires this voice. Closing the essay, we return to one of the issues raised by the Pepsi ad—that of black singers being presented mostly through their voices, as shadows of texts. Does the status as shadow foreshadow a partial erasure for black singers? Will they become in ads and generally in television and movies just disembodied voices traveling everywhere, heard beautifully and often in faraway places, but with their vessels—their bodies—rarely seen?

The Aretha-Hallie Ad: Context and Content

The Aretha-Hallie collaboration offers a fascinating glimpse into the relationship between black musicians and television advertising in the 1990s. The commercial was a cultural event—or, more aptly put, a microevent—of considerable significance. Partial proof of this significance can be found in the press notices it garnered. Days before the ad even appeared, *The Detroit News* blared, "Aretha to Sing for Pepsi."[6] Greater proof of its hold on the public mind can be found in subsequent cultural criticism. Three years later, the ad still attracts commentary, as in Leon Wynter's wide-ranging, too-celebratory *American Skin* (2002).[7] Wynter returns to it repeatedly because he believes it supports the thesis that America has transcended segmentary ethnic identities through a new transracial popular culture. Hallie singing in Aretha's voice is, for Wynter, an example of channeling across racial lines, with "the little white girl channeling Aretha Franklin."[8] Merit exists in Wynter's idea, for the ad plays on cross-racial channeling or ventriloquism. Present also is the larger issue of transracialism.

Beyond Wynter's view, there are other matters to be pointed out about the ad. The ad had an interesting historical context. The commercial came from a period in which black musical presence in television commercials had surged forward. A major black role in television advertising, limited at first, had been growing for nearly two decades. Not until the mid-1990s, though, did black musical backgrounds begin to be frequently used. The Aretha-Hallie ad appeared just as the influence of black singing voices in ads was cresting.

It was also the high point of television commercials using the voices of black singers of iconic stature, of legendary status. This marketing practice derives initially from the early 1980s. No matter what other new black musics—such as rap and hip-hop—enter television commercials, the classic performers have gained a steadily growing charisma. America now has a long-standing love affair with celebrity black singers' voices. This doting explains why ad makers have sought singers as varied as Johnny Mathis, Marvin Gaye, B. B. King, and Nina Simone to hawk their wares, even though some of these singers were unlikely participants in television commercials. Their unmistakable voices and lyrics have entered American sonic history.[9] Even though challenged by the 1990s' popular cultural generational divide, prompted by the rise of hip-hop, classic black singers and music still held their own. Aretha's ad showed the staying power of this classic elite. It also showed the resilience of nostalgia as a prompt for commercial uses of black music on television. Looked at historically, this borders on a kind of historical amnesia, a nation cozying up to what amounts to a musical version of comfort food from an earlier time, a black cultural material that has been smoothed of its original antagonistic, prickly assertions.

The Aretha-Hallie ad was seen by a nation of Academy Award movie fans. Pepsi planned the ad to capitalize on Hollywood's glitz and glamour. The Aretha-Hallie ad was created by BBDO's Ted Sann,[10] a highly touted ad-maker and a well-credentialed writer possessing a M.F.A. from the University of Iowa's writer's workshop.[11] When Pepsi's capital, a talented ad maker, and exposure through the Academy Awards are aligned for a commercial featuring the work of a black singer, it is not easy to miss the importance of the event.

All of this leads to some pertinent questions. One does not have to like television or television commercials to see that the ad was well crafted. Juxtaposing Hallie and Aretha, Aretha's dominant vocals, transferring Aretha's voice to Hallie, the Sophie Tucker–like performance by Hallie, even the concluding "You go girl!"—each detail was surprising and grand. Hallie's curly locks were unintentionally disruptive, perhaps transporting some viewers back to that other interracial performing duo, Shirley Temple and Bill Bojangles Robinson. Otherwise, the ad was successful as high artifice. Initially, the craft carried the day, resulting in the ad being counted as an homage to Aretha Franklin. But as it was replayed, it raised questions about the use of black music in commercials, particularly about the use of such a prominent, canonical black music performer as Aretha Franklin. Just as seriously, the question arose about whether she had been ever-so-gently sidelined. Should Aretha have been the main performer? Or would a duo of Aretha and Hallie have worked just as well, even though Pepsi aimed the commercial at the young? Was the synergy of a dynamic duo overlooked? It is impossible to answer definitively these questions, but it is good to keep them in mind.

Ultimately, however, television commercials are not in the business of maintaining the cultural categories of the intelligentsia. As mentioned before, this ad, and others like it, grafts the ambitions of television capitalism onto black musical art. In fact, the ad's makers saw themselves as creating a paean to Aretha Franklin's high rank. So, one could ask: is Aretha's location in the ad a permitted decentering, given the ad's great success? Did not the ad disperse her voice to a larger audience than any of her recordings had achieved? Did this not help Aretha Franklin's career in its later years? In 1998, she had two substantial successes. She had outdiva-ed three other divas on VH1's "Divas Live"[12] and issued a new album, *A Rose Is Still a Rose*. These two events were seen as a comeback effort. Was not the 1999 ad the crowning touch to that effort? Isn't it worth considering the question of whether television ad capitalism can give back to black music and black singers more than it takes away?[13]

Exploring Aretha's voice shadowing the Pepsi ad text reveals a Barthesian "fecundity," a collection of issues and questions. This is so even though the text was originally a mere sixty-second commercial, squeezed between Oscar awards and Whoopi Goldberg's jokes.

TV Commercials Based on Black Music in the 1980s and 1990s

In Charles Barkley's opinionated romp, *I May Be Wrong, but I Doubt It* (2002), he laments the absence of blacks on television: "How can CBS and NBC have no blacks on their shows . . . Thank God for the WB [Warner Brothers network] and UPN [United Paramount Network] or we just wouldn't be on television."[14] Since the NAACP's 1998 diversity-on-television campaign, this complaint has become minority leaders' mantra.[15] Barkley is mostly correct if one is counting visible actors. On the other hand, if one conducts a census of television commercials, blacks are often more than plentiful, occasionally as performers, but most certainly as voices, hovering just offstage.

In the 1970s, popular songs were rarely incorporated into commercials. Jingles were written for advertisements. According to Joe LuDuco, a veteran composer for television, "at one point [in the 1970s], it was considered selling out for a recording artist to license his music for advertising."[16] Gradually, this changed. One of the earliest incorporated popular tunes was the Carpenters' 1970 hit, "We Have Only Just Begun," which embroidered a bank ad. In 1974, the link between pop music and television advertising was accelerated when a Carly Simon soundalike sang her hit song "Anticipation" to promote Heinz ketchup.

Blacks' entry into this field began in a major way in the 1980s. It was limited for quite some time, until a few landmark ads proved the appeal of black musical material to television advertising companies. During the early 1980s, American television advertising conformed to the then-current national racial boundaries and cultural suppressions. Cultural independence was necessary from within advertising strategy teams for black musical materials to be deployed. That would not arrive until the years approaching the mid-1980s and early 1990s. Marvin Gaye and Tammi Terrell's "Ain't No Mountain High Enough" in 1984 for Lincoln-Mercury, claymation California raisins singing Marvin Gaye's "Heard It through the Grapevine" in 1987, Ben E. King's "Stand by Me" in 1987 for Levi's, Michael Jackson's Pepsi commercial in 1988—these were the first big steps for black music and black musicians into television advertising. All of these were successful. The singing California raisins slipped into popular consciousness without much controversy over the fact that their physical features (for example, their thick lips) were obvious caricatures of black doo-wop singing groups. Actual performers were optional; Play-Doh type figures would work fine. Obviously, they were stand-ins, down to their fancy footwork, for the Temptations or Four Tops.[17]

In 1991, Ray Charles scored a coup for black music in television commercials through a Diet Pepsi ad. Its chorus of "Uh-huh, uh-huh, you got the right one, baby" proved infectious beyond the wildest expectations of the ad's producers. At the time, Charles was regarded as a premier rhythm and blues artist. Since 1959, when he made the hit "What'd I Say," he had had a steady fan following, though by the 1990s, he was nearing sixty, and was counted as an elder statesman of music rather than a contemporary contender. The Pepsi commercial reintroduced Charles to the country. Surveys at the time concluded Charles's ad beat out the ever-popular, tireless Energizer Bunny in audience receptivity.[18]

It is possible to make too much of the centrality of this ad. Nevertheless, its results were there for all to see. Calculating advertising tacticians certainly took note. Ray Charles's performance was transformative for black music in television commercials in the same way that Michael Jackson's 1983 "Thriller" video had been for black artists on MTV. Advertisers saw that they could tap black music to sell commodities to the larger public, to the much-touted "mainstream." They could move beyond the constrictions of past racial and cultural compartmentalization. This experience taught them that black music could travel farther than had been imagined. Actually, it had already traveled farther, as evidenced by the participation of a wide variety of Americans and overseas citizens popularity of jazz, rhythm and blues, and soul music. Ad makers of the 1970s and 1980s stood separate from their own society's history of consumption of black music.

When the advertising teams began using black music, they were in fact catching up to, and exploiting, an already-existing appreciation of black music. To this day, television ad teams using black music insist that they are operating in a world where race and ethnicity no longer count much. Musical material is not identified as belonging to a race. This idea is rooted in the advertisers' experience with Ray Charles's swaying rhythms and the so-called "Uh-huh girls" of the early 1990s. It is important to note, too, that while targeting the mainstream, ad makers were sensitive to currying favor—through black-friendly ads—with African American consumers, who, by the mid-1990s, were growing ever more economically powerful.[19]

During the 1990s, black music entered into television commercials in a major way. What enabled this to occur so broadly was the existence of a treasure trove of black music. To the advertising business, black music offered a remarkable array of music styles, a seemingly endless gallery of performers, and many outstanding songs to which the label "classic" could be affixed. A 1991 media advertising survey on the arrival of black music in television commercials concluded that "The Real Golden Oldies Are Popular Again," as the title of an article in the *New York Times* put it.[20] Clips of Nat King Cole singing "Unforgettable" accompanied a Revlon fragrance commercial. Chanel No. 5 answered with an ad using the Ink Spots' silky "I Don't Want to Set the World on Fire." Louis Armstrong's "What a Wonderful World" was a favorite backdrop.[21] Once again, one of the most inventive 1990s ads used Aretha Franklin's voice from "Natural Woman." In an ad for Clairol, the voice of Aretha was sung through a twentyish white woman. Imitating a scene from the movie *Risky Business* (1983), the woman, wearing only a shirt, crooned in praise of Clairol's blonde hair coloring, "You make me feel like a natural woman." With her back to the camera, she shook her long blonde hair. The song endorsed Clairol's claim that a woman could change her hair color and still look—indeed feel—natural. She could be simultaneously false and real, unnatural and natural. Boldly, the Clairol ad was selling alchemy.[22] All of these television ads were also selling nostalgia and subliminality.[23]

Companies sold their products using black music. What did black musicians and singers get in return? It is hard to tell in exact dollar amounts, but the returns could be considerable. Making an ad with the original recorded music or an appearance by a performer commanded top dollar. Rerecording a song (commonly using a soundalike performer) or transposing it into the mouth of an animated figure or into the mouth of a child cut the price greatly, but still paid good money. Inclusion in a commercial also boosted one's profile, and music sales often increased from commercial exposure. So some black musicians got another stream of income through expansion into television commercials in the 1980s and 1990s. The on-the-shelf classics could be recycled into another money-making episode. It should be noted that this arrangement—a kind of collaboration between artist and television ad creators—gives "appropriation" a new twist. It reminds us that in late capitalism black cultural material often travels in commercial contexts with collusion of the makers of cultural products.

Before long, the love affair with black golden oldies began to wane slightly. A new competitor—the new music of rap—appeared on the scene. As early as 1990, some restless advertising strategists were attracted to rap music. As a *New York Times* report phrased it, "Madison Ave. Turns an Ear to Rap Music."[24] M. C. Hammer was signed for an athletic footwear company. Coca-Cola used rap groups to launch a Sprite summer promotion. Nevertheless, many television advertising teams still looked warily at rap.

Today, it looks as if the rise of rap and hip-hop in television commercials was always assured. However, it was not inevitable. Early in the 1990s resistance existed against this urban form. On the one hand, a few advertising experts proclaimed rap was the next new thing. John Gross, speaking for a New York agency, proclaimed, "Rap is the coming thing. We are working on a lot of demonstration tapes for advertisers that use rap."[25] Yet far more people were hesitant. Al Ries, the chairman of Trout and Ries, a strategic marketing consulting firm, voiced reservations: "Advertisers . . . using rap are gambling on the future. Rap has had a lot of trouble cleaning itself up, and there's still no guarantee that it will totally move into the mainstream."[26] Ries probably was referring to rap's reputation for explicit sexual lyrics and racial manifestoes.

Resistance to rap and, later, to hip-hop music for television commercials declined slowly. And then it suddenly collapsed in the quest for profits. Soaring sales of rap records and rising ratings for the *Yo! MTV Raps* cable show, which started in 1992, pointed the way. Specifically, *Yo! MTV Raps* was central in diffusing hip-hop beyond its origin points. It was a viewing site for youth outside the radius of hip-hop's urban homelands. Suburban youth, indeed all types of nonblack youth, were reached by this national broadcast. It came on for two hours daily and was first hosted by graffiti artist and rapper Fab Five Freddy. As a result of this and other dispersions or travelings, advertisers soon found that rap, and later hip-hop, could travel into that most-valued, most-elusive of consumer classes—

youth with lots of discretionary cash. Journalist Kim Flotz summed up this choice: "some advertisers and their agencies are obviously willing to take the chance." To William Katz, creator of some early rap-based commercials, the Pepsi "Cool Cans" ad, the choice was simple: "Young people have always had their own language, and this [advertising with hip-hop music] is a way to get them to pay attention. . . . We have to be on the leading edge."[27]

In 1996, *American Demographics*,[28] a consumer trends journal published by Dow Jones, ran an interesting article by Marc Spiegler entitled "Marketing Street Culture: Bringing Hip-Hop Style to the Mainstream" that confirmed just what Katz was saying. Spiegler attempts to decode the cultural language of hip-hop and to explain why it appeals to white youth. More importantly, his article serves as a primer on how to—and how not to—sell hip-hop goods, such as clothing, to a broad new hip-hop generation. Just about the time of Spiegler's article, the hip-hop generation was beginning to be a far-flung universe, embracing a variety of youth niches, many of whom were embracing the hip-hop style as an alternative identity. Television advertisers wanted to capitalize on this cultural moment. Ironically, while black urban youth themselves could not travel freely into the depths of suburbia without setting off alarms, their music and word-bending were full of stealthy possibilities for television advertising.

Once the resistance died away, and as rap and hip-hop ascended in popularity, the floodgates flew open. Soon ad executives such as Peter Foulds, Pepsi's director of advertising, saw rap as an excellent partner for their commercials: "Rap is perfectly tailored to television commercial's short form. . . . It is an easy way to tell a story."[29] Groups such as Two Live Crew, best known for their sexual boasting, and N.W.A., known for its gangsta rap, were not sought for commercials. But by late 1990s, nearly every one of note had been, including Kriss Kross, Mary J. Blige, Missy "Misdemeanor" Elliott, Fat Joe, Goodie Mob, Mack 10, Common, Busta Rhymes, and Eve. Sprite, for example, was most receptive to rap and hip-hop presence in their ads. Most of these ads showed on BET, MTV, VH1, and cable channels, sometimes on Fox, WB, and UPN TV. National network outlets in culturally diverse urban centers also showed them. Aimed primarily at the young consumer, they were generally assumed effective into the upper thirties age demographic.

Rappers and hip-hoppers were frequently featured in the ads, performing briefly. Just as often, though, their physical presence was considerably less important than the rhythms and lyrics they could bestow on a product. Alongside hip-hop, the perennial black standards returned to commercials in the late 1990s. However, the more they were used, the more their music was reduced to just voices. In the comeback, such songs as Sly and the Family Stone's "Everyday People" was used, as were the Isley Brothers' "It's Your Thing" and the Miracles' "The Love Machine." Undeniably, these voices alone can often be quite stunning additions to product marketing. For example, Apple Computer aired an ad in which the new pastel-colored I-Mac was rotated against a white background while sly Barry White vocals seemed to wrap themselves around the machine. Cool and hot were bound together. White's velvety voice was the packaging for a computer. No words were spoken, and none were needed. Nothing but a logo had to be added.[30]

Ultimately, it appears that black cultural input helped transform television commercials into a form of entertainment. This saved television ads from the dreary fifties and sixties version of the ad jingle. Ad agencies experimented with black music and, in turn, gained skills in the making of musical ads that quickly became a staple in the field. By the mid-1990s, everything in television ads had changed. Product marketing on television was elevated by a black popular cultural form. Many millions of dollars were made by using this world-famous music, by trafficking in black musical capability.

In the early years of the new millennium, the black musical voice was still performing, as a shadow, without the physical presence of black performers. It was as alluring as ever. In 2002, Chevrolet presented a comical ad showing two young men in their Monte Carlo; the driver used short, sharp taps on the brakes to upset the passenger's handheld drink. In the background was joyous hip-hop, full of fluid polyrhythms. Gap exhibited a captivating, happy Christmas ad backed by the 1970s hit "Love Train." Billy Preston's peppy "Nothing from Nothing"—another 1970s song— told viewers of no-interest GMAC car financing. Target had Stevie Wonder's distinctive voice wish everyone a cheerful holiday season. In 2003, Chevrolet Avalanche trucks began a campaign using a staccato blues melody. Honda Civic's new 2003 campaign was all about hip-hop: with a hip-hop voice background, a flotilla of cars moves unimpeded down an urban street, with the ad ending on a hip-hop signature—"Honda Represents." Television ad capitalism was going full speed ahead with a formula created in the eighties and nineties, pairing background black music and singing voices with product sales. The shadows were working their magic.

The Craft: Fusing Black Music with TV Ads

For nearly two years, Viagra ran a commercial advertising its sex-enhancing prescription drug. A thirtyish white man is shown upstairs in what is obviously a suburban house. He is dressing. A male voice is singing a blues background. The blues continues as the man puts on a tie, which he soon discards. Today, the man wants to be informal, younger, not the office-bound, uptight suburbanite. He wants to loosen up like the background blues music. He runs down the stairs, heads out the door, and gets into his car. The next and last scene has him in a doctor's outer office, where he obviously has an appointment to get Viagra. The blues voice has gotten louder, and suddenly, the words are more insistent. The blues voice says, "I am ready for you" and then, with a full growl, "I am ready for you, I hope you are ready for me." The name *Viagra* appears.[31] Pfizer pharmaceuticals must have been pleased with the ad, which presented a swift storyline. Its main message of sexual readiness—"ready for you . . . ready for me"—was delivered not so much by the visuals as by an offstage voice, by a shadow. No one could accuse the company of directly peddling a sex drug, yet the message could not have been more direct or sexually suggestive. In point of fact, the ad's "Ready for You" song is a rerecording of a song made popular by bluesman Muddy Waters. So, Waters's Delta blues has been married to Pfizer pharmaceuticals' sexual enabler drug. It might appear that this was solely a shotgun marriage, hastily arranged by the pressure to make money. Nevertheless, if one thinks about it, there is certain logic to this wedding. The blues, for many, are regarded as an aphrodisiacal music from steamy Mississippi Saturday nights in juke joints. The blues are also seen as direct, cutting to the chase, in the same way that Viagra is supposed to work. Readiness can be promised ("I am ready for you") and threatened ("I hope you are ready for me") because the drug guarantees results. Blues, Viagra, and suburban male sexual anxiety have been made into a triangle of image interactions.

The Viagra ad provides us with two important lessons about the state of the art of black music in television commercials. First, current ad makers possess a more-than-passable knowledge of black music. Someone in the Viagra ad team knew blues and maybe even Muddy Waters's repertoire. Only a few of the ad creators in major ad agencies are black, though this imbalance has been shifting, at a glacial pace, in the last half decade. Black-controlled ad teams were beginning to have impact on television ad design in 1999, the year of Aretha's Pepsi ad. Regardless of who created these commercials, they have a good grasp of black music. The reality of the cultural travel of black music is that people across the world—both black and non-black—have a deeper knowledge of black music.

It is often difficult for ad makers to explain why certain music segments are chosen to back products. Greg Johnson, in an ad survey, observed that "how songs get into spots remains more art than science." He added: "firms choose music that sets proper tone."[32] It sounds as if only intuition—a feel for music—guided the choice of black music segments. But, digging deeper into the very slim literature on black music in ad making, one finds a different picture of the process. Jonathan Takiff, writing on the linkage between pop music and Madison Avenue, says, "the creative departments at ad agencies are made up largely of young, artsy people who are themselves music fans." He goes on to say, "Maybe they even programmed a radio show when they were in college. So, they know a lot of artists [that] people haven't heard before and can rattle off obscure songs that fit a commercial perfectly."[33]

Taking this one step further, imagine television ad makers as possessing a reasonable mental database of songs, singers, and musical styles—a database brought to bear on ad projects. This agility has helped black music reinforce product identity.[34] Take, for example, the use of Jimi Hendrix's rebellious rendition of the national anthem for the sports clothing company Andı's commercial. Central to the ad also was an appearance by the very independent basketball star Latrell Sprewell. Together Hendrix's eccentric "Star Spangled Banner," a unique sports clothes brand, and bad boy Sprewell mutually reinforced one another. The clothing company got what it wanted.

Or take the use of Curtis Mayfield's superkinetic "Superfly" theme song as the backdrop for a Mitsubishi SUV plowing down a muddy back road. With the music line fading in and out, the car conquers the zigzagging forest road, performing as in a slalom race. The music and car movements are a duet. When this duet effect occurs, it is not far-fetched to claim, as critic Rick Lyon argues, that "commercials have finally become every bit as well-crafted as their feature-length counterparts."[35] Television ads can be like movies. Blacks, therefore, are providing the soundtracks to these tiny movies, furthering the future craft of television commercials.

Second, advertising creators are omnivorous, and they can be reckless, making bad pairings. This is the downside of their relentless incorporation of black musical material. They will use nearly any music that suits their purposes. Those who protest putting certain black musical segments in television commercials, who consider it is a sacrilege, miss the point of current advertising invention. For example, the use of black gospel choir backgrounds has generated criticism, as did a techno-pop remake of a Nat King Cole song as well as Minute Maid's combining Judith Jamison dancing with the song "Dem Bones." But none of this criticism has slowed television advertising's embrace of various black music and voice backgrounds.

The previous status of a specific black music segment—whether the music is a classic, a favorite beloved by fans, or derives from the black church—does not seem to hold much sway in advertising war rooms. For example, a spirited version of the old black religious standard "This Little Light of Mine" is seen as legitimate backdrop to a weight-loss chain ad for Curves. During the summer of 1999, a time of flood and storm disasters, Service Master, a home cleaning company, fused its ad to a black choir singing the lines "Sometimes, I am up. Sometimes, I am down. Oh yes Lord" from the Negro spiritual "Nobody Knows the Trouble I've Seen."

As these examples suggest, ad creators overreach. An ad selling Senokot, a laxative, for a long time used James Brown's "I Feel Good," complete with briefcase-toting professionals kicking up their heels to prove their returned liveliness. James Brown's music, voice, and vocal gestures have been a rich source for advertisers. But fusing this particular product with his music—actually, an impersonation of his voice—was a low point for the treatment of Brown's music. Here the product and the classic status of the singer and of his song collided. Yet the Senokot ad proved popular in advertising circles. Rick Lyon ranked the Senokot "knockoff" as his "current favorite" in 1996.[36]

In the late 1990s, Denny's restaurants hired New York's Loew and Partners to produce an ad promoting their All-Star Slam breakfast entrees. Denny's had just emerged from a class-action suit, which began in 1994, accusing the restaurant chain of racial discrimination. That did not deter them from using the Miracles 1976 disco anthem "Love Machine" as a backdrop. Jenifer Harmon, speaking for Denny's, said the song lent "positive energy to the brand."[37] Here, the black musical material clashed with the recent racial history of the company using it for ads.

What Do People Hear in the Black Shadows' Voices?

African American literary critic Farah Griffin, in the 2001 Radcliffe Dean's Lecture, spoke about her meditation on the public importance of black women's singing voices. Her investigation discovered more questions than answers. One of the questions, "what other American voice resonates in this way, mobilizes in this way. . . ?"[38] The question can be asked for black music in general and the black singing voice in particular. Why has it been the case that in most of the recent presidential inaugurations black singers—overwhelmingly women—sing the national anthem? What is behind this genealogy of black voicing of the nation's most significant official song? What was accomplished culturally by Whitney Houston's grand rendition of the national anthem at the Super Bowl during the Gulf War in 1991?

Television ad-makers also rely on black musical backgrounds to mobilize and to have resonance. But what do they desire specifically from this resource? Uppermost is capturing for their products the energy associated with black music. For a 2002–3 Pontiac campaign, the corporation wanted to show "that driving a Pontiac is an adrenaline pumping experience," and their ad team chose James Brown as their promoter. His music and singing was judged to provide "an explosive and soulful persona that can motivate even the weariest of viewers."[39] "Explosive" and "soulful" are energy measurements. At the other end of the spectrum is the pairing of Marvin Gaye's "Let's Get It On" with a Levi jeans advertisement. The song conferred a different energy, a love nest sensuality to the marketing of jeans. Yet energy comes from jazz music in television ads. Ad makers say jazz's "percussive quality, its energy, livens up anything connected with it." It "moves."[40] As historian Ann Douglas posits, black music, particularly jazz, gave New York a new dynamic sense of itself in the 1920s and early 1930s.[41] Black music is sought in ads because it quickens the pace.

Emotion is also desired from black music in ads, especially from the black songster. This is where Griffin's questions about the power of black women's voices to mobilize feeling become doubly important. Ad makers say that "music is the emotional bed we put the message on" and "music is emotional. It moves people and motivates them to think well of your brand."[42] To be specific, ad teams see the black singing voice as a deep, moving instrument, accenting the authenticity, the integrity, the credibility of their products. The words ad makers' use to define the qualities of this voice resemble those uncovered by Griffin—words like *rich, dark, sultry,* and *profound.* Missouri's tourist board chose Louis Armstrong's "Up the Lazy River" for an ad because his voice was "warm, rich, engaging." Together, this made for earthiness. When Coca-Cola chose Jaguar Wright and the Roots for their 2002 commercials, the brand manager said, "these commercials have an organic yet modern feel to them . . . realness is exactly why Coca-Cola, Jaguar Wright, and The Roots make perfect sense together."[43] To claim "realness" or "organic" as goals of an ad-making process that takes as its premise the manipulation of images might seem far-fetched. But ad makers prize these qualities in black music and black singers' voices. For the summer of 2002, African American adman Jimmy Smith cocreated a Nike commercial from the 1970s funk music of Bootsie Collins. The emotion derived from the 1970s idiom was "the freedom to express yourself however you wanted."[44] The emotion was that of a new-found personal freedom.

Ad makers seeking to project authenticity or realness from black musical backgrounds lead us back to the crafting of the Viagra commercial. Through some sleuthing, we have discovered that the ad's creators—all white—pursued a cultural ideal of what the black blues voice should sound like. In the recording sessions, they intervened to produce what they deemed to be a black sound. This comes through from an interview with Irving Louis Lattin—"the best Chicago bluesman in New York"—who rerecorded the Muddy Waters blues song for Viagra. He shadowed the Viagra ad text. As Barthes said, Lattin was necessary to the text, and his performance was fertile with cultural ideology. When Lattin auditioned for the ad, he performed "the actual track that they had put together for the commercial." They liked what he sang, with one major exception. Lattin recalls, "they called me back a week later, because they felt I had enunciated too well." He goes on, "I thought it was pretty funny. Here was a bunch of white guys saying, 'You are not quite blues enough. You said the words too properly.' So I went back and kind of like bit the words a little bit. They wanted me to, like, bend a word here and there."[45] They were recreating the black voice, ruralizing it, putting it in what they regarded as a down-home mode. Here, we witness a cultural feedback into black culture, forcing the black voice to mobilize and resonate in a particular way. The injunction: sing in that black bluesy way. It might be apocryphal, but it has been said that Frederick Douglass, in his early public speaking days, was urged by abolitionists presiding over antislavery rallies to speak more in the plantation style.

Shadowing the Ad Texts: Significance and Future

In a recent *Boondocks* cartoon, the main character Huey Freeman, the scornful intellectual, tells his friend Caesar he wants to go to the movies.

There is a problem, though. He is sick of the roles given blacks in movies. He disparages the old stereotypical characters (e.g., "asexual black sidekick") as well as the new hip ones ("black men dressed as women"). Finally, they decide on a film. But Caesar dismays Huey when he discovers "there's black people on the soundtrack." The cartoon's creator, Aaron McGruder, is saying that not only are black roles in Hollywood films clichéd, but appearing on the soundtrack is a stereotypical dead-end as well. Despite McGruder's disapproval, the agents of black musicians and songsters press to get their clients into commercials. Other musicians are doing so, too. "Selling out" is increasingly moot because of the rewards of ad insertions—contract money, exposure, and increased record sales. As a 1999 *TV Guide* joked, "Remember how shocking it used to be when you would hear an old Beatles or Motown melody turned up years later in a car commercial? We live in far more mercenary times. Today's rock groups don't just sell out—they presell out."[46] This derision followed Lenny Kravitz's instant selling of a song, "Fly Away," from his just-issued album.

In the future, will black music and singers sell everything on television? Obviously not. On the other hand, black music backgrounds will likely increase, especially as black-controlled ad agencies become more competitive. This means that television will rely on black music and black musical performances—such as the recent jazz combo on a Chili's restaurant ad or the performance of Gloria Gaynor's disco hit "I Will Survive" for Mervyn's department stores—to push its wares. Both of these ads present black performers in their own bodies, and maybe this begins a lowering of this prohibition. Regardless, there will be a continued subtle racialization of product depiction. Beyond this, other risks loom ahead.

Worry is necessary over what should be called the radical pairing of black music with products. Mention has already been made of the Senokot–James Brown nadir. Another horror was perpetuated not by an ad, but pairing of Stevie Wonder's "Happy Birthday," dedicated to Martin Luther King, Jr., with a photo tribute to Strom Thurmond (December 5, 2002) on *CNN Headline News.* This happened just hours before the infamous Trent Lott homage to Thurmond. This pairing tells us how wrong things can go. Reducing black music and black singers to mere shadows rather than seeing them as representatives of a monumental tradition within world culture can be ruinous, for art and business. Artists especially need to think about the use of their music.

There is another risk. Will black backgrounds on ad soundtracks (and movie soundtracks) eventually further limit the appearance of black musicians and singers as fleshed-out characters, appearing in their own bodies, on television and in movies? Queen Latifah was nominated for an Academy Award in 2003 for her appearance in *Chicago* as a singer, but will there be others? Connected to this problem is the risk posed by technology. Black computer characters are being created rapidly for media markets. Jason Kidd, the NBA basketball star, has a double as a "playable character" for a basketball video game. Jada Pinkett-Smith has been re-created for a game taken from "The Matrix" series.[47] Virtual performers, like BET's Sinita, an animated character introducing a cartoon show, are already upon us. How far are we from a computer-generated black singer, bearing a famous name or no famous name, using shadow soundtracks similar to those from commercials?

In looking at television commercials and their relationship to black cultural material—music produced by blacks—we have tracked a traffic that lives below the standard cultural radar screen. We have excavated a virtually subliminal black cultural material. This is a black cultural traffic based on an old premise, that of having a black performance while limiting the physical access of blacks to the main performance venue—in this new form, television. We have seen that while this relationship has produced some high moments in popular culture, it has problematic properties. It will continue to raise the question of whether the bargain created by advertising businesses for black musicians and black music is an arrangement that enhances their stature and their art. For the art of black music and black singers, television commercial creators, music brokers, and their artist collaborators should be careful. They should ponder Aretha Franklin's most famous demand for "R-E-S-P-E-C-T."[48]

NOTES

1. Melanie Wells, "Curls, Attitude Pushing Pepsi First-Grader Stars in New Campaign," *USA Today,* June 7, 1999, 8B.

2. www.Pepsico.com/news/pepsicola/1999/19990309p.shtml. A number of citations for this essay come from the Internet, where television commercial projects and ideas are often posted.

3. Roland Barthes, *The Pleasure of the Text,* trans. Richard Miller (New York: Hill and Wang, 1975), 32.

4. Martha Moore, "Ads Borrow a Slice of Black Culture," *USA Today,* July 25, 1994, 3B; Barnet D. Wolf, "Selling Out, Advertisers Use Familiar Tunes to Peddle Everything," *Columbus Dispatch,* September 29, 2002, lE.

5. Rawle Titus, "Black Music Gets Its Own Home with BBC," *Cityzine,* March 21,

2002, 1. "You cannot get away from black music, whether you are watching adverts on television, whether you are listening to pop charts, you are always coming across black music," said Ray Paul, a producer at the new BBC station 1xtra.

6. "Aretha to Sing for Pepsi," *Detroit News,* March 16, 1999, E3.

7. Leon Wynter, *American Skin: Pop Culture, Big Business, and the End of White America* (New York: Crown, 2002).

8. Wynter, *American Skin,* 175. See pp. 137 and 151 for other references to the commercial.

9. "Black Oldies Find New Life in TV Commercials," *Jet,* September 13, 1999, 60.

10. BBDO is Batten, Barton, Durstline, and Osborn.

11. Ted Sann's profile is represented on "21st Annual Kelly Award Judges" at www.kellyawards.org/judges/Bios.

12. www.vh1.com; and John Pareles, "There Are Divas, and There Are Divas," *New York Times,* April 16, 1998, E1.

13. For Pepsi's view of the ad, see Pepsi-Cola Press Release Archives, 1999, "Pepsi to Launch New 'The Joy of Cola' Ad Campaign on Academy Awards," www.pepsico.com/news/pepsicola, 1999.

14. Charles Barkley, *I May Be Wrong, but I Doubt It,* ed. Michael Wilbon (New York: Random House, 2002), 169.

15. Stephen Battaglio, "NAACP Plans Boycott Aimed at Networks," *Milwaukee Journal Sentinel,* September 14, 1999, 8; and "NAACP to Take New Actions to Increase Television Diversity," *NAACP News:Media Advisory,* May 24, 2001, www.naacp.org/news/releases/Tvdiv52401.html.

16. Barnet D. Wolf, "Selling Out: Advertisers Use Familiar Tunes to Peddle Everything from Arthritis Drugs to Chewing Gum," *Columbus Dispatch,* September 29, 2002, 2E.

17. www.lavender.fortunecityjudidench/584/calraisins.html; www.home.teleport.com/~v3d/.

18. For an analysis of the Ray Charles ad, see Wynter, *American Skin,* 126–27.

19. Sherrie Day, "Pepsi Says Its Pop Music Stars Can Reach Minorities and the Mainstream at the Same Time," *New York Times,* August 27, 2002, C2.

20. Stuart Elliott, "The Real Golden Oldies Are Popular Again," *New York Times,* October 17, 1991, D24.

21. Patricia Williams Lauro, "The Media Business: Advertising: Forget Jingles. Viewers Prefer Familiar Tunes in Commercials," *New York Times,* November 8, 1999, C1; Nick Lewis, "Flock of Ads: Commercials Are Giving Cash a New Lease on Life to Stars of the Past," *Calgary Herald,* January 27, 2002, C1.

22. Rick Lyon, "Music Viewpoint: Restart Me Up," *Advertising Age's Creativity,* May 1, 1996, 20–22.

23. Lyon, "Music Viewpoint," 21.

24. Kim Flotz, "The Media Business: Madison Avenue Turns an Ear to Rap Music," *New York Times,* July 6, 1990, 5.

25. Flotz, "The Media Business," 5.

26. Ibid.

27. Ibid.

28. Marc Spiegler, "Marketing Street Culture: Bringing Hip-Hop to the Mainstream," *American Demographics,* November 1996, 2–9.

29. Flotz, "The Media Business."

30. Stefano Hatfield, "A Number One? It's All in the Jeans," *The London Times*, February 13, 1998, 22. Also Robert Hilburn and Jerry Crowe, "National Exposure for a Song," *Los Angeles Times*, March 17, 1998, F1; and "Apple's Aesthetic Core," *Paper*, May 2002, 70–74.

31. "All over the Blues," *Fort Smith News*, October 19, 2002; Alfred Hickling, "Master of the Nine-and-a-Bit Bar Blues," *Guardian*, August 10, 2002, pp. 1–2.

32. Greg Johnson, "Company Town: Ads Boost Songs as Firms Get in Tune with Viewers," *Los Angeles Times*, October 3, 2001, pt. 3, pp. 6–7.

33. Jonathan Takiff, "More and More Pop Artists Offering Their Tunes to Madison Avenue," *Philadelphia Daily News*, March 24, 2001, Entertainment News, 5–7.

34. Sandy Hunter, "Pop Goes the Spot," *Boards* (Brunico Communications), October 1, 2001, 53.

35. Lyon, "Restart Me Up," 22.

36. Lyon, "Restart Me Up," 22.

37. "Television Commercials Resurrect '70s Music to Brand Products," *Tampa Tribune*, August 2, 1999, 14.

38. Delia Cabe, "A Tale of Black Women's Singing," *Radcliffe Quarterly*, fall 2001, 5.

39. "General Motors, Pontiac Debuts 'Fuel for the Soul' Advertising Campaign," *M2 Presswire*, September 16, 2002.

40. Quoted in Valerie Gladstone, "Advertisers Play a New Tune: Jazz," *New York Times*, December 6, 1998, 34.

41. Ann Douglas, *Terrible Honesty: Mongrel Manhattan in the 1920s* (New York: Farrar, Straus and Giroux, 1995), 15, 74–75, 104–5, 179–216.

42. Donna DeMarco, "TV Ads Go Pop: Advertisers Marry Modern Music with Their Products," *Washington Times*, May 12, 2002, A01.

43. "MCA/MotiveSinging Sensation: Jaguar Wright and Grammy Award Winning Artists," *PR Newswire*, February 11, 2002.

44. Chris Vognar, "Replay That Funky Music: Seventies Black Culture Is Cool Again," *Record*, July 2, 2001, F1.

45. Adam Gussow, "Journeyman's Road," *Blues Access*, spring 2001, 3.

46. *TV Guide*, October 14, 1999, 5.

47. Michel Marriott, "A Thin Line between Film and Joystick," *New York Times*, February 20, 2003, E1, 2. Julius Wiedemann, *Digital Beauties: 3-D Computer Generated Digital Models, Virtual Idols, and Characters* (New York: Taschen, 2003).

48. Norman Solomon, "In the Media Mix, What Happens to Music?" *Media Beat*, December 28, 2001, www.fair.org/media-beat/011228.html.

PART TWO

Stop Signs and Signposts

Stabilities and Instabilities in Black Performance and
Black Popular Culture

W. T. LHAMON, JR.

Optic Black
Naturalizing the Refusal to Fit

While he's working at the Liberty Paint Company, Ralph Ellison's naive youth in *Invisible Man* must learn the secret of whitewash. Because ten drops of black dope go into every tin of "Optic White . . . the Right White," the black foreman in charge of this mix proudly tells the youth, "we the machine inside the machine."[1] He knows blackness mixes ineradicably in the purported whitenings of official life, and Ellison's point, put simply in another register, is that blackness is the stealth ingredient in America's bourgeois public sphere. I will argue here that both Ellison's now widely known secret and its metacommentary are also true inversely. An optic blackness, to which whites have contributed all along, has grown up to prove the right white wrong.

My account cues on Ellisonian phrases that Harryette Mullen reads to good effect in her important article "Optic White: Blackness and the Production of Whiteness."[2] But my claims neither argue with her position nor follow in its path, for what I have to say on these issues runs awry from Mullen's emphases on racial passing and the marginalization of blacks by the creation of an optic white ideology. Optic blackness certainly is about performing a blackness, but it is not about passing. On the contrary, it always features its mixing of modes. It is about compounding affinities, not seamless cover. Nor do I think optic blackness marginalizes blacks or whites. Instead, it struggles to lever into view a particular blackness that disaffected peoples of every ethnicity in the United States evoke to signal their dissatisfied relation to American and Atlantic history. Optic blackness is a contrapuntal cultural style that opposes whiteness, is available to participants who include, but certainly are not limited to, blacks, and embodies a persistent countermemory of historical opposition.[3] Optic blackness was the earliest style of the first transnational popular culture that grew up around the blackface figure of Jim Crow.[4] Because its countermemory and gestural repertoire continually evolve, ever drawing, since its constellation in the 1830s, on its past, optic blackness is now transtemporal—that is, it keeps a running tab on its past that is legible in its successive signs.[5] Because optic black continues to attract downwardly mobile and alienated members of the middle class to its plebeian mode, it remains and sustains an important cross-class formation.

As surely as tiny measured amounts of black pigment are necessary to show off the "right white," American and Atlantic cultures have regularly constituted a particular blackness with white infusions. These white traces make the blackness more starkly apparent and perhaps more culturally abrasive to those who disdain, fear, and oppose it. Let me begin unraveling what's at stake in these inversions with six propositions:

1. Optic blackness is a function of cultural optics that do not render experiential reality for blacks or any ethnic group but give, instead, a convenient, pliable mediation of the real—a fiction that seems sufficiently real for cultural symbolism.
2. Thus optic black is less about "race" than about the positional binary of its own pretense and momentum.
3. Optic blackness persists across historical epochs, artistic periods, and political ideologies.
4. Optic blackness is not contained in any form, genre, or medium, be it high or low; it weaves through them all.
5. The contending forces of optic black and optic white center their dispute in American culture and defend their dominion everywhere Atlantic slavery was.
6. Optic black reconstitutes a "*plebeian* public sphere," which Jürgen Habermas notes "was suppressed in the historical process" that formed the bourgeois public sphere and incited historians to focus on its more familiar domain.[6]

Performers who underwrite these propositions drive the machine inside the machine of American vernacular art. They open spaces in public where an alternative to optic whiteness can do its oppositional work. That work is chiefly the display of a widespread refusal to fit.

The recurrent usefulness of optic blackness as a plebeian—and I will claim *lumpen*—alternative sphere is what I am after here, as well as its oppositional relation to the optic white public sphere. In optic whiteness, a seamless passing is necessary for survival. The black foreman at the Liberty Paint Company is proud that the paint he mixes makes a "chunka coal" seem white clean through. In the optic black alternative, the opposite is true: the compounding of multiple identities together is clear, and provisional rehearsal is their point. From T. D. Rice impersonating Jim Crow to Damon Wayans or Anna Deveare Smith or Eminem performing contemporary versions of optic black, members of their knowing publics always realize that the act is a put-on, and that being in the know is diagnostic of their cohort. In optic black, this mixing of identities is requisite for each successive reappearance of the mode. Optic white has a direct connection to identity politics. On the other hand, because its practitioners know its effects are not real but that they are instead tentative and imaginary, optic black's relation to identity is provisional and oblique.

Despite efforts by both white and black cultural beadles to stamp it out, optic blackness has an extensive genealogy. Its recurrence happens for real historical reasons embedded in Atlantic cultures that are ongoing and not likely to fade anytime soon. It is as naive to ignore optic blackness while analyzing American culture as it was for Ellison's youth not to reckon his invisibility. We cannot map the cultures that follow the peculiar institution of Atlantic slavery without understanding how optic blackness affects our mediations. In Atlantic history, blackness and whiteness developed an interactive relationship contesting each other during their assembly and display. This cultural history determines that we see the one fully only in the presence of the other. The fundamental corollary is that both optic white and optic black necessarily convey the very activating pasts they share. Optic white may prefer to escape or efface, to repress or deny this past; optic black calls attention to that history. Blackness produces optic whiteness; whiteness produces optic blackness; each bears the aura of the other in every move it makes.[7]

Although optic blackness has prominently marked its territory and media presence, it is certainly not the only available blackness. People can and do choose to stir up other sorts of blackness that aim to delete white addition or presence, just as many white writers (Hawthorne, James) have wanted to ignore black presence.[8] What bell hooks calls White Person Fatigue Syndrome has pushed some performers off into realms of their own definition.[9] When, in their plays and films, August Wilson, Julie Dash, and Charles Burnett deal in minstrel conundrums, exaggerated masking, or dis 'n' dat dialect, they do so chiefly to scourge them. Thus their professed blackness circulates in a black economy and attention. Julie Dash's film *Daughters of the Dust* (1991), for example, has moved in black circles just the way Henry James's novels have traveled a mostly white circuit since the 1870s. But, in both cases, audiences miss the full range of components that make up those artists' contemporaneous life. And this disengagement from the common run of experience—arguably from optic black contending with optic white—is what impedes Dash's and James's popularity.

Optic blackness is one among several black cultural modes, but its manifest recurrence, and the reasons for this persistence, engage me. Of all the available modes and images in their common registries, why should Atlantic peoples of many sorts and backgrounds continue to dredge and recycle those elements that represent the most disdained idioms of black culture and their most hardened partisans? My fundamental answer is that a much deeper history of mutuality undergirds passionate sections of Atlantic societies than most analysts remember. The stubborn codes of optic blackness derive from the way European industrial force pressed both whites and blacks into mutual labor on sailing ships and plantations, then sentenced them to canal digging and menial service at the end of the eighteenth century.[10]

That's why optic black is less black at bottom than lumpen. Its own adherents have identified themselves as black—whether they were or not—in order to understand their own scorned condition, and show its effectual condition to others. That black code became a convenient marker for their whole cohort.[11] Much has been written about the distinctive political and social ramifications of industrial labor, of course. But what is culturally distinctive about this Atlantic modernity stems from the unprecedented overlapping that occurred when the poor, pressed, and captured of Europe and Africa were moved together through the Americas to do mudsill work. This developing compound culture was what set Atlantic modernity on a diagnostic course that artists and analysts are still trying to figure out.

Thus the optic black strand of cultural imagery has been importantly enduring. More than others, the optic black mode enacts and replays the imbrication of Atlantic peoples, the problems they share, and their distinctive pain. Optic blackness has legs that run and run because many, if not all, of us dope up optic blackness—sometimes together, usually by turns—to engage our unevenly experienced, unevenly elected, but mutually disfranchised and peculiar history together.

What does the common obsession to sustain optic blackness serve? The process most obviously maintains the momentum of its own tradition, which is not trivial. Because optic blackness is where the culture works through the agony of its overlays, it is one mode that realistically undermines racism, even as it also inscribes the memories of Atlantic racism's history. Beginning in stereotypes, optic blackness acknowledges and works through stereotypic effects, usually turning them inside out, as in figures 1 and 2. When optic blackness does not sap the stigmata that it engages, then it fails. Or its makers fail *it*. That's the risk of the strategy. When it works, optic blackness serves the needs of many segments in the culture, producers and end-users of all colors, to show their disfranchisement, and thus their discomfort, at assimilative fit.

These first two figures show images by recent black artists Kara Walker and Michael Ray Charles that illustrate basic practices of the radically destabilizing stereotypes to which optic blackness gravitates. Walker and Charles register sedimented attitudes of disgust and humor written serially on bodies. The bodies in their art compose palimpsests that compound a life cycle of changing feeling. Both show their particular histories intensely impinging on the present and keep a running tab of that account. Both show how stereotypes can be made to reveal the painful history. That is why Spike Lee included several images by Michael Ray Charles, besides the title image, in his film *Bamboozled* (2000).

The Puritan errand to the wilderness—which Perry Miller named and Kara Walker nailed in her 1999 image, *Out of Africa*—has been an historically important North American concept, if not a widely shared experience. Walker produced this composite black-on-white cutout for the September 19, 1999, edition of the *New York Times Magazine* as part of a series they called "New Eyes: Scenes from the Millennium." The Puritan male is one of the many tokens that those groups controlling their eras have projected as standing for the whole. Alone, however, no Puritan directly evokes the triangulation of modes that the slave trade bequeathed. Thus Walker surrounds him with shadowy forms from the optic black imaginary. As in all her work, she gives a composite picture that explicitly refers to a shifting mélange of images cut out from a cultural history in which the peoples of the Atlantic have existed together, hardly happily, but doubtless interactively. Walker's images are always connected, extruding from and penetrating each other: warping, haunting, demonstrably still buggering our present.

Yankee peddlers and Erie canallers, Western keelboatmen and yeoman

FIG. 1. *Out of Africa* by Kara Walker. (Courtesy Brent Sikkema NYC.)

FIG. 2. *Scratch Yo Dirt* by Michael Ray Charles.

farm families, cowboys and Indians, thinker-tinkers and entrepreneurs: all these mark further significant identity types for disparate American publics. All variously have kindled imaginations, even of groups they did not immediately represent. But none encodes in its parts anything close to the complex history compressed in optic blackness. These other types lack the intensity of affect, the range of meaning, and the close identification that optic blackness commands. These other types have had their moments, their publics, and their persistence. But optic blackness surpasses their eras and conjoins apparently separate publics over time. It stretches from the power relations of the Middle Passage through the Jazz Age and the Harlem Renaissance to dump us among current headlines about racism in home-mortgaging for African Americans and the severity of the American penal system for black men. Only optic black performance shorthands the sullied depth of this shared past along with our difficult present. Optic blackness always codes both the uneven power and the mutuality of what it means to have passed through the Atlantic trade in peoples. Thus optic blackness, as in Kara Walker's imagery, holds together the painful intergroup relations that determine everyone in the Atlantic who ponders race, or who hopes for an inclusive society, whether or not their forebears were involved in the slave trade.

There was nothing optically black before black performers came into and defined Atlantic public spaces, making them Atlantic rather than Anglo, European, or African spaces. But there has been no stopping this creolization since. Optic blackness began in the earliest white fascination with black performance in the Americas, as in *The Old Plantation* (fig. 3). This beautiful watercolor of blacks dancing on what is probably a South Carolina lowlands plantation at the close of the eighteenth century is the earliest American graphic that figures blacks centrally and positively. The give-and-take here has its mutual aspect: The dancers know the covert white painter is watching their gathering at the edge of the plantation; they know the painter is making their private rite a public space.

Even as they figure themselves out for themselves, they prepare a version of blackness for white consumption. Within his European-derived perspective, the presumed white watercolorist sympathetically records a scene the dancers allow him to see. The charisma of these danced gestures effects a revolutionary change in Atlantic perspective here, for together the dancers and their painter invert the conventional grounds. They bring forward the cultural gestures of blackness while rendering the Big House small and distant. The painting highlights the mystery of the immediate

FIG. 3. *The Old Plantation.* (Courtesy Abby Aldrich Rockefeller Folk Art Museum, Colonial Williamsburg Foundation, Williamsburg, Virginia.)

movements. How *do* the women's clothes relate to the man's wand? What *are* these instruments tilted for viewers to see their features? While keenly observing these details, the painting belittles the plantation's enterprise, including the three boats plying the river between the black and white ways of being.[12]

Within two decades, but a good bit farther north, another vernacular drawing foregrounds white attention to black dance (fig. 4). This folk drawing, that I analyzed in *Raising Cain,* is *Dancing for Eels—1820—Catharine Market.* Whereas white attention was implied in *The Old Plantation, Dancing for Eels* makes white fascination its explicit content: the outsider artist sketches other white outsiders studying black moves. Along with the dancer's black support group, who likely also competed for eels and admiration, we see Bowery B'hoys leaning in, agog. After the 1820s, as whites draw out these moves to flag their own attitudes, their fascination melds with the gestures they crave. Precisely so: their involvement is the white dope in optic blackness.

FIG. 4. *Dancing for Eels—1820—Catharine Market.*

T. D. Rice—sometimes called Daddy Rice for his generative status in blackface performance—gave optic blackness its formal momentum when he blacked up as Jim Crow in an image dating from about 1830 (fig. 5). Here the white observer goes past fascinated leaning into the frame. He lives out his urge to join with blackness. He darkens his skin and inhabits gestures that the culture had already stereotyped as black. There is no evidence that Rice used grotesque makeup. Thick lips and shiny black caking became de rigueur during postbellum minstrelsy only after his death. There is plenty of evidence that Rice's impersonations created a craze for blackface singing and dancing. A large paradox awaits those who know Jim Crow only as the vicious segregation laws that the South rolled into place after the North betrayed Reconstruction. The early, 1830s Jim Crow was an extremely popular blackface character who could outsmart, outtalk, and outrage all the white devils, mad scientists, and dandy squires then peopling the Atlantic stage. My research in diaries and advertised theater prices from New York to Natchez shows that blacks as well as whites were

Fig. 5. *Jim Crow* by Edward William Clay. (Courtesy of the Harvard Theatre Collection, Houghton Library.)

eager to see how Jim Crow cavorted.[13] Rice as Jim Crow yoked previously disparate traditions into a stubborn form that attracted workers of all hues, as well as the disaffected *calicots* and clerks at the menial reaches of the urban middle class. This transracial, cross-class, and Anglo-American alliance could oppose the stolid conventions regnant in popular traditions before Jim Crow gave momentum to optic blackness.[14] Popular culture that is truly Atlantic-wide not only dates from this intervention, but also remains largely in the mold that Rice's early blackness fixed.

Like Kara Walker's imagery today, Rice's antebellum plays delighted in skewering Puritan pretensions. In *Bone Squash Diavolo* (1835) Rice played a charismatic black chimney sweep named Bone Squash who outwits and dumps back into hell a Yankee devil. In one of his last plays, *Yankee Notes for English Circulation* (1842), the Rice character, always in blackface, substitutes himself for a statue of George Washington in a hotel garden at Saratoga Springs. Arguing that "Gineral Washington must gib way to Gineral Necessity," he climbs onto the column that had supported Washington, and judges from that perch the capers of the visiting English and Yankee fools parading below him. This turning of the tableaus, so to speak, from the father of America's optic white public sphere to the daddy of her blackface public sphere—or optic blackness—is a kernel episode for the making and maintaining of black visual culture in the Atlantic.[15] It is precisely the move that followers in this vein, like Michael Ray Charles, also make.

Relevant here is a line of thinking Michael Ray Charles raised in the summer of 1998 when we discussed the relationship between his paintings and Kara Walker's collage. He correctly insisted their art was very different. What they share, however, is their mutual engagement with optic blackness. Charles and Walker both wade through stereotypes in order to upend them. They see and show how stereotypes judge their own formulators. The self-consciousness in Charles's and Walker's art points out the twisted field on which optic black plays.

Is this inversion of stereotypes doing what Ellison's famous term said it would—namely, changing the joke and slipping the yoke?[16] Yes and no. Yes, these inversions invoke and change the way racists continue to employ the old jokes in America. But the biggest joke is that this strategy actually detonates again the very tactics and imagery present in Jim Crow from the very beginning. In other words, what we see in transgressive postmodern, millennial art reinflects practices already rampant in popular culture of the 1830s. When T. D. Rice played his one-act version of *Bone*

Squash Diavolo in 1836 London, for instance, the curtain rose on a chorus of white actors in blackface singing these lyrics:

> We de Niggers dat do de White Washing oh
> We de Niggers dat do de White Washing oh
> On de scaffold we stand
> Wid de brush in our hand
> And de jenus shines out wid de slashing oh[17]

Before Victoria came to power in England, and during Andrew Jackson's parade of demotic energy in the United States, therefore, the Atlantic had popular spectacles that displayed white workers in blackface identifying with racial victimization and declaring their penetration of optic whiteness. Their lyrics slipped yokes more than a century before Ellison provided a proverbial term for it and gave us Lucius Brockway crowing about his own creation of the "right white" paint in *Invisible Man.* The whiteness of Rice's white washers peeked out from beneath their palimpsested black masks. They were not passing for black, but compounding themselves with a fictitious imagery that it was important to be able to achieve on both sides of the north Atlantic. Already this theater registered overlays and shared connections. Already in the 1830s audiences in both England and the United States saw and applauded the wink of blackness in whitewash, whiteness in blackness. All this persists through the wry remarks of black stand-up comedy, as well as the cutups of Kara Walker and the bitter paintings of Michael Ray Charles. They are all different, but they lie down together in optic blackness.

Each rejoining of black gesturation added energy to the mode over time, winding up the cumulative momentum that I call optic blackness. Constance Rourke called it "Long Tail'd Blue," after the song often associated with T. D. Rice.[18] But optic blackness has survived straight-up blackface and Uncle Sam's long coat. It is a mode that underlies and links blackface with subsequent theater in the Harlem Renaissance (Charles Gilpin and Paul Robeson in *The Emperor Jones* [1920]; Langston Hughes and Zora Neale Hurston's *Mule Bone* [1931]), with painting, fiction (from William Gilmore Simms's *The Lazy Crow* [1845] in the Young American movement to Darius James's shocking *Negrophobia* [1992] in postmodernism), as well as every form of American vernacular music. For 120 years, beginning when Rice started jumping Jim Crow in the 1830s and lasting until the 1950s, when the NAACP culminated a campaign against blackface performance that middle-class blacks had begun in the 1920s, the recrudescent mask has traced an enduring need to face the distinctive overlays of the Atlantic. Whether it was covering a white or black performer, the burnt cork both pointed to and hid the layers of complex history that the image coded. This obsession with the particular history that provokes these class, racial, and transnational maskings is what regenerates their specific codes even after the cork becomes taboo. Blackface is the most obvious signifier of optic blackness, which existed before actors blacked up (to make clear their connection to the mode) and survived its apparent policing by organized campaigns. The attempts to stamp out blackface had the unintended result of widening its spectrum, ranging from rock 'n' roll, to hip-hop, and such radioactive comics as Richard Pryor, Eddie Murphy, and Chris Rock.

The only possible cure of the root problem—as opposed to touching up the symptoms—would be the erasure of history. Since changing history is not possible, the recurrently ineffective approach to the problem by those with the power to enforce political correctness has been to outlaw blackface performance, as if scrubbing germs. But blackface is not a germ. It is a series of fetishized motifs that spawn anew in each generation to rehearse the history of status, race, and class in societies anguished by their relations to slavery.

I turn now to the spawning. When Karen Gorney admires John Travolta's dance steps in *Saturday Night Fever* (1977), she asks, did he "invent" them? He replies, "Yih, yih! No, see, I saw them on TV, and *then* I made 'em up." His remarks exemplify the ambiguity in vernacular theory about the resurgence of charismatic black dance. This vexing of dance inventions negotiates both a forgetting that the moves originated in optic blackness *and* their jagged remembrance. Popular cultures typically enact connections without articulating them consciously; indeed, it is important to their working that they do so. Thus Travolta's answer smartly illustrates the way succeeding generations always affirm their culture as astoundingly new while they incorporate the past.

Vernacular culture *is* ever new. But its core gestures in the United States also stem back, in a train of emulations, to the eighteenth century's opening of the Atlantic to stoke English sugar refineries and cotton mills. The conveyances of this informal culture are ever-changing: TV, in this case; sailing ships; woodcuts, watercolors, and lithographs; films; vinyl records, CDs, and then music videos and MP3 files, among many others. Each conduit has had its own momentum, and all have had their separate agenda. Running through them all is the genius they share with weeds: vernacularity travels the way burrs bum rides on the cuffs of those who would stamp them out. Both the burr and the stamping are requisite for the regeneration. The burr can lie in wait and travel by itself, but it will not activate without the hostile dominating culture's panic. Optic blackness exists in oppositional polarity with active disdain.

After it spawns, where should we seek optic black? Since developing its usable past by about 1830, as Constance Rourke demonstrated, American vernacular culture has continually sapped its class, ethnic, and genre borders, treating them like sieves. In addition to the content and vigor it carries, this transference brings news that crosses the grain of current models of cultural studies that usually argue that class and race formation has striven for exclusivity or, alternatively, for a melting pot in which dominant whiteness boils off black capacity for self-representation. These totalizing models hide the fact of contrapuntal cultures that survive, even thrive, in the littoral overlays of modern multiculturality.

The consensual analytic conventions currently in place are apt for a history of state power with its win-or-lose calculus, its unions, legislation, and power blocs standing to be counted in assemblies and polling booths. The consensual analysis is not fit, however, for cultural histories whose effects are as ambiguously mixed as their publics are fugitive and shifting. These publics are "running and dodging the forces of history," like Ellison's zootsuiters, "instead of making a dominating stand."[19] A cultural history determined to demonstrate exclusion and white dominance simply cannot account for such oddly mingled works as *Saturday Night Fever* (1977) nor the fiction of Thomas Pynchon's *Gravity's Rainbow* (1973), with its Schwarzkommandos and celebration of Red Malcolm and Charlie Parker's demisemiquavers. But it is not just recent works that are contrapuntally mingled. Exclusivity will explain neither George Lippard's 1844 novel *The Quaker City*, whose central grotesque figure, Devil Bug, is white in the novel but scripted black for the suppressed play, nor Toni Morrison's undervalued *Tar Baby* (1982), which contains a key passage that links all these works.[20] Morrison describes a "great class of undocumented men":

[T]hey were not counted. They were an international legion of day laborers and musclemen, gamblers, sidewalk merchants, migrants, unlicensed crewmen on ships with volatile cargo, part-time mercenaries, full-time gigolos, or curbside musicians. . . . Some were Huck Finns; some Nigger Jims. Others were Calibans, Staggerlees and John Henrys.

Anarchic, wandering, they read about their hometowns in the pages of out-of-town newspapers.[21]

Our current maps of dominance do not count these lumpen personifications of optic blackness as the appropriate context for the miscegenated painting of Robert Colescott, the music of Miles Davis, or the films of Melvin Van Peebles. All these performers have received attention, for sure, but primarily in single-form analyses rather than as exemplars of cultural littorals. Peebles's *Sweet Sweetback's Baadasssss Song* (1971) provides a creed for optic blackness when it dedicates itself "to all the brothers and sisters who have had enough of the Man" and ends with Sweetback running, always running, through the wasteland of urban infrastructure, refusing domination and making crucial alliances with disaffected whites. All these, performers of varying backgrounds and media, register the abiding power of optic black recalcitrance within the overriding fact of continuing racism. We need to understand and model the way vernacular and curated cultures mingle insistently to counter the overt, obvious, and one-dimensional claims of exclusivity. We need maps of a contrapuntal power that does not show up in legislation and is undeterred by governance.

To model this flowing hybridity we cannot rely only on allusion and acknowledged influence. Anyone observing culture hemorrhage through the skeins of genres, class protocols, and purported race can see that the heaviest transfers have been subtextual more than intertextual. To see how culture moves, therefore, we ought not thumb through biographies to find out when author X read novel Y in year Z. Pursuing solitary agency is not the only way to go. We hit deeper pay dirt by tracing cultural transmission beneath and before texts. That's where lore cycles truck charismatic gestures, phrasing, and other atomic facts. That's where fundamental cultural elements gravitate anonymously wherever people find them alluring or, conversely, repugnant. Attraction and repulsion alternate in the same current because lore cycles exist as the medium in which people contest enduring problems. Largely independent of curated texts, citizens rehearse in vernacular rites the problems they may not resolve in politics, exorcise in religion, or express in love.

These everyday, anonymous drills are the field that texts organize. We should understand texts as secondary harvests: they gather ripened practices, stack them as sheaves, and house them distinctively for subsequent digestion when fresh goods are scarce. The complex allusions in texts to other texts are rudimentary compensation for the unfathomable density of gesturation by which all peoples daily play out their saturated family resemblances and identity choices. Sometimes, these preserved goods, these texts to which curators give priority, bump into each other. They then produce the overt links that professionals call influence or cultural transmission. Thus T. S. Eliot's account in "Tradition and the Individual Talent." Thus Henry Louis Gates, Jr.'s account of signifyin(g) as the genesis of African American fiction. Thus Toni Morrison's figuring of black and white interdependence in *Playing in the Dark*.[22] What all these studies of cultural motion privilege is texts—even Gates's "Signifyin'" deals primarily with verbal patterns consolidated in changing but recognizable toasts. What they all ignore is vernacular gesturation—the phrasings, melodies, and motions that precede and constitute even vernacular texts ("Stagger Lee," "The Arkansas Traveler," hex signs, "The Titanic"). Around these rehearsed motions, all the texts gather.

Just as importantly, all the knotted-up texts will unwind back into the flow of these motions. All traveling goods fray back into the lore cycle, where they require neither museums nor anthologies nor the attention of particular performers to sustain them. Rather, the lore cycle transmits them in a slurry of subconscious atomic moves, those smallest distinguishable marks of identity that people play out.

Most important is why peoples act out this spawn in specific configurations—why they develop stubborn forms. This persistence is what links the black trickster figure Jim Crow to Stagger Lee and Sweet Sweetback, Topsy to Little Richard and Kara Walker, William Henry Lane (aka Juba) to Mick Jagger and M. C. Hammer, Dan Emmett to Al Jolson and Danny Hoch. All these figures share mutual antagonisms to the disdaining context that carries them, breaks them down, and runs them through the wastelands—but also passes their codes down the generations, spreading their trademark dis-ease from one cultural organ to another.

How did Harriet Beecher Stowe conjure the minstrel stereotypes in *Uncle Tom's Cabin*? Contemporary mores rigidly forbade women of her station—daughter and partner of preacher men—from attending blackface performances in the 1840s; nothing in her mature character challenged that taboo. Yet Stowe undeniably re-created minstrelsy in Aunt Chloe, Adolph, Sam, Andy, young Harry, and Topsy—though not in Uncle Tom. Alone from this list, Uncle Tom did not come from the panoply of stereotypes played out on the minstrel stage in the late 1840s. In every particular, the character of Uncle Tom counters the push of blackface performance. His steadfast piety and hallmark predictability are the precise opposite of the characteristic frame-breaking and surprising insouciance incarnate in both Topsy and in her blackface mentors of the 1830s and 1840s. Stowe's minor black characters exemplify the active circulation of lore via social osmosis. Stowe did not seek out her stereotypes. They somehow slipped through to her.

Stowe showed Topsy's continual resistance to fit without ever watching Gullah peoples dance "Knock Jim Crow," T. D. Rice sing "Jump Jim Crow," or William Henry Lane parody them all. Already this resistance to fit was becoming naturalized, traveling from blackface performance to other forms without any apparent connection between the forms' purveyors: it was flying under the radar.

Without ever viewing its major moments, Stowe ably reproduced blackface performance in prose fiction. After much more exposure, three Australian white men, the Bee Gees, even more closely copied three African American women in the soundtrack to *Saturday Night Fever*. The white actress Caroline Fox Howard created Topsy for the most famous stage version of *Uncle Tom's Cabin*, and George Christy, of the Christy Minstrels, played Topsy in drag on the minstrel stage. Just so, black performers from Ma Rainey and Ida Cox to Josephine Baker inaugurated their public figures playing this unsituatable character. All these attenuators performed within the intertextual aegis of Stowe's model. But they dipped their buckets in the much deeper subtextual slurry to draw up a widely seeping convention of "blackness." They were all able to relay blackface figures because the construction of such figures had been cross-racial and parallel from the outset, and because blackface gesturation continued below and beyond the canning of *Uncle Tom's Cabin* into a text. The gestures of blackface performance were always out there in daily practice, coursing independent of print. As my next examples show, when books swallow these charged marks of identity, they cannot help taking on board important dynamics.

Although Nathaniel Hawthorne's *The House of the Seven Gables* does not spring to mind in tandem with black vernacular performance, it nevertheless bears comparison to *Uncle Tom's Cabin*, and not only because it appeared the same year as that novel's initial serialization, 1851. Stowe sought and centered black performance; Hawthorne apparently trivialized and debased it. Both novels, in their contrasting ways, thereby revealed the already-ripened concept of cultural blackness and its pressure on reading publics and the authors who helped form them.[23] Even though Hawthorne seemed offhand, even dismissive, in rendering an extremely stereotyped blackness in *The House of the Seven Gables,* his treatment and its affects perhaps register just as much about the production of race as *Uncle Tom's Cabin.*

Various blacknesses deeply attracted Stowe, who showed several conflicting strands of behavior ranging from George Harris's violent self-defense through Topsy's insouciance, little Harry's Jim Crow dance and Adolph's fey mimicry to Uncle Tom's steadfastness, and many more. Blacks embody the major crisis in America for Stowe; around their behavior every conceivable issue—from feminist ethics and patriarchal religion to the underlying unity of economies North and South—turns, right through to the vexations of cultural transmission and historical recall. For instance, how *did* Topsy become herself? Is she a case of someone who "jes grew," as Topsy famously claimed? How Stowe came to create Topsy is important because she translates into mass culture the female version of optic blackness; Topsy remains proverbial for a special form of uncanny and inadvertent resistance.

The same moment when one powerful novel foregrounds cultural blackness as an emerging force, another esteemed novel tamps it into a mite whose mightiness it has taken a century and a half to appreciate. While Stowe displays many strands of blackness, Hawthorne admits just one, essentialized and apparently without affect. Blackness appears two ways in this novel. First, as slaves in the manse, like pathetic Scipio in Holgrave's story within the frame narrative. Second, blackness comes to us tokening a sweetened, palatable commodity—a commercially baked gingersnap. The slaves are nonbeings for Hawthorne; he seems to care little for them in Stowe's sense. However, the fate of their cultural tokens fascinates both the author and certain of his characters.

Hawthorne compresses and then deploys optic blackness as a delayed depth charge that can burst after characters and readers digest it. He freights this token with as much symbolism as any other in the novel. In scenes of rich tonality, remembered to varying extents more than ten times during the tale, Hawthorne dramatizes the moment of aristocratic collapse when the novel's now impoverished heiress must open a penny shop in her parlor to trade with the public. The very first item she sells is a gingerbread cookie stamped out as Jim Crow. The young purchaser immediately eats Jim Crow headfirst, soon returning for more with

crumbs and discoloration of the cannibal-feast . . . exceedingly visible about his mouth! . . . The little schoolboy, aided by the impish figure of

> the negro dancer, had wrought an irreparable ruin. The structure of ancient aristocracy had been demolished by him, even as if his childish gripe had torn down the seven-gabled mansion![24]

Hawthorne shrinks blackness to a gingersnap and disdains the youth who engages it. What does this mean? Neither this "cannibal" boy nor his breakfast compelled Hawthorne the way Topsy fascinated Stowe. How the urchin came to his particular hunger, what his outcome will be, what "the impish figure of the negro dancer" means to him—all these are trivial givens to Hawthorne, compared to the theme of Hepzibah's collapse from "lady" to "forlorn old maid." And that is doubtless why, until very recently, there has been almost no critical commentary on the role of blackness in *The House of the Seven Gables*. But readers today may take a different approach. Now that we have begun to fill out the history of Jim Crow, the blackness and the youth culture that Hawthorne seemed to belittle grows consequential to us—and we are in better position to ponder the cultural work of his compression.

By 1851, when Hawthorne's *House* appeared, Jim Crow had been the rage of young theatergoers on both sides of the Atlantic for fifteen years, significantly impacting both sides of the color line. Jim Crow's songs and drama, their popular vitality, formal experimentation, and surging dramatic subversions all loomed to compete with just the sort of romance/independence/imagination that Hawthorne professed. Hawthorne's appropriation of Jim Crow was probably as much a proleptic strike against the perceived vulgarity of white attraction to blackness—and its capacity to shape a public—as it was a blow against blacks, per se.

In consolidating optic black into cookies for working lads to consume, however, Hawthorne nevertheless confesses its kinetic power to wreak "irreparable ruin" in the "ancient aristocracy" that was his own obsessive topic. Attraction to that dance potentially tears down the house. The cost of Hawthorne's magic light manner, necessary for the swallowing of the bolus, locked the process away so that cultural commentary would not usefully rehearse its meaning until attention returned to antebellum performance history (as much as to American Renaissance masterworks), to such literary opponents of the New England patriarchy as George Lippard's Philadelphia sensation novels and Martin Delany's Black Nationalist fiction, to the cultural ethnography of blackface, and to the self-fashioning—or recocking—of a working-class mentality in the Jacksonian era.[25]

If we recall the watercolor *The Old Plantation* (fig. 3), in the presence of *The House of the Seven Gables,* we see that Hawthorne restores the binary proportions that the South Carolina watercolorist had overturned half a century before. Hawthorne's channeling of history's flow through a looming symbolic edifice, his display of black performance shrunk to enlarge the meaning of the manse and its life, his cooking of black performance for a youth culture to cannibalize—all these are, quite strikingly, social aspects that the radical perspective of the painting had inverted but that the momentum of daily life in the dominating culture had restored during the antebellum interval. Hawthorne's performance of the ironies in *The House of the Seven Gables* is certainly consciously within, and possibly against, that momentum of his era. The more impish, trivial, and otherwise stereotypical black *fetishes* become, he may be arguing, the more easily mass culture consumes them.[26] If we consider that their sliding signification and certain internal detonations will be more dangerous later, once they are inside the host, we might well argue that these gingersnaps are really Trojan crows, snuck into the belly of the dominating society. Binary inversions keep on happening. Thus where they take place really matters. To those who are within and addressing the New England patriarchy, there is a critical difference between an inversion that occurs on the margins of a South Carolina plantation (as in *The Old Plantation*) and those occurring in the cent shops and gut of the dominating culture (as in *The House of the Seven Gables*). Perhaps it is no accident that Ned Higgins, who cannot resist eating Jim Crow gingerbread, shares initials with Nathaniel Hawthorne, who had been noting and contemplating "Gingerbread figures, in the shape of Jim Crow and other popularities" since he first wrote about them in his journal on the Fourth of July, 1838.[27]

The fetish of "the dancing negro" thus acquires another association in its concatenated history. Its apparent slighting abets its compaction, familiarization, and linkage with national ritual. Now it is inside the gables, inside all the penny shops, swallowed by average consumers, a token of mechanical reproduction exciting insatiable hunger for its introjection. The irony that packs its presence, like boots that would stamp out weeds, chocks it further into domains it had not previously affected. Its presence there shows the keepers of those zones that they fail to maintain their exclusivity. Swallowing these unseatable images of mass culture guarantees that what Harry Elam (after Homi Bhabha) has described as their "productive ambivalence" will subvert the dominating culture from within.[28] *Saturday Night Fever, Uncle Tom's Cabin,* and even *The House of the Seven*

Gables are all spectacles of lumpen provenance that reckon implications for optic black culture proliferating inexorably within the fascinated, fearful, and containing host.

I want to mention yet one more strong text of canonical literature to which optic blackness spread and profoundly determined. In Herman Melville's tale "Benito Cereno," optic blackness is the machine inside the machine of Babo's performance.[29] The story's driving secret is manifest during the brilliant centerpiece of the story, when the servant shaves and slices the titular master. This scene is memorable to everyone who has read it. Seeing Babo prepare to shave Cereno moves Amasa Delano to his most piquantly racist preconceptions. These manipulable positions are exactly what Babo intends to hide behind. "Napkin on arm," Babo performs an optic blackness that he knows will mask his revolutionary intentions. Babo's performance causes Amasa Delano to compare him, and all his apparently servile kind, "to Newfoundland dogs." All who have read the story will know how the scene constructs its stereotypical dimensions and will know how far astray they lead both Amasa Delano and those readers whose agency he represents. Realizing that this scene is not in the famous source tale—chapter 18 in the historical Captain Amasa Delano's 1817 *Narrative of Voyages and Travels*—readers have believed that Melville invented this shaving scene for his riddling narrative.

Melville did not invent it. The scene was standard on the late 1840s minstrel stage in New York City. Dan Emmett wrote it as a sketch called "The Barber Shop in an Uproar," and Melville alluded to it when his narrator asks, "what could be the object of enacting this play of the barber before" Delano?[30] Is Melville's re-creation of this blackface chestnut an example of a great artist transcending his banal sources? Certainly the writing in Emmett's skit nowhere approaches the cunning, measured surprise in Melville's masterpiece. But Emmett's sketch does trap the initial and apparently logical agent of the majority audience, the European-descended customer in the black barbershop, and maul him. The play forces the audience to switch allegiance from the white man being shaved to the blackened barber, causing in compact form the identity transfer that Melville's story would elaborate. The doubleness and anger in Emmett's skit anticipates the revolutionary feelings that Melville exploits. Emmett's blackface barber whets his razor on the floorboards, mutilates the face of the racist visitor, then wipes all the sudsy, bloody gore all over his victim's shirt. In short, he tricks and terrorizes the European dupe who had been insulting him. Emmett's story delivers immediately; Melville's ontological puzzle embeds Babo's frustration in paralysis and deferred repayment. Yes, Melville's story is more ironic and its narrative more sophisticated. But Emmett's skit was effective lumpen theater, and both play in the same sphere of optic blackness. Both depend upon operative lore cycles to convey coded visuality they can manipulate for their own ends. Both set turning the same cultural inversions. It has taken more than a century for many readers to see that Melville's sympathies extended to, or were even with, Babo; audiences who attended blackface theater in the late 1840s and early 1850s, when Melville would have seen Emmett's play, recognized the sympathy for the optically black figure as soon as the play was under way, and they certainly were cheering for *him* rather than the bloodied German farmer.

Optic blackness has an important contested authenticity. Optic blackness is not authentically or experientially black—as various as that must be—but authentically corrupt, like Atlantic life and history. As Paul Gilroy argues, all the copyrights on this blackness are expired. Kid Rock and Eminem have as much right to it as Kara Walker or Toni Morrison. Its continually reanimated existence registers a specifically American co-involvement in the struggle to redefine what blackness is: every contending group claims always to know the truth; every group leaves its thumbprints on the construct. The compulsion to perform optic blackness further compounds with time, as more and more people punch and kick the assemblage, wanting it to speak in their preferred diction—just the way Brer Rabbit caught himself in the tar baby. That's why everyone keeps returning to the same totemic context, literally trying to figure out its sufficiency. That's why black *and* white artists keep returning to the contrapuntal excess of blackface performance. The artists I would point to here range from the minstrel Billy Kersands in post-Reconstruction traveling shows to the comedians Williams and Walker from the turn of the nineteenth to the twentieth century, and on more recently to Donald Byrd's late-1990s choreography of *The Minstrel Show*. But I would also include such white singers as Moran and Mack (who began to record comedy and songs in the spring of 1927 for Columbia as The Two Black Crows, and were perhaps more popular among black audiences than white); also Emmett Miller (his recordings through the 1920s have been collected on *The Minstrel Man from Georgia* [Columbia CK 66999]) and Kid Rock, along with performance artist Danny Hoch (both late 1990s)—even when, as in the cases of Kid Rock, Eminem, and Danny Hoch, the burnt cork is implied. To participate in this contrapuntal blackness is why Frank Chanfrau blacked up a white dancer as Porgy Joe to act in and advertise his 1848 play *New York As It Is,* the most popular drama before *Uncle Tom's Cabin* in New York City. That's why DuBose Heyward (*Porgy* [novel 1925, play 1927]) and George Gershwin (*Porgy and Bess* [opera 1935]), and Miles Davis and Gil Evans (*Porgy and Bess* [LP 1959]) have returned to the same fetishized motif. All have sought to represent the most recurrent strain of American vernacular culture, a particular blackness. It is past time to recognize its distinctiveness and assess its mixed behest.

Whether or not their cohort was present in the United States prior to Emancipation and Reconstruction, all Atlantic constituents engage optic blackness. Indeed, after the NAACP effectively made blackface impossible to perform publicly in the 1950s, other means of playing out its arguments had to emerge—like black stand-up comedy, rock 'n' roll, and, now, hip-hop. Stamp out *Amos 'n' Andy* in the United States and *The Black and White Minstrels* in the United Kingdom, and what do you get? Richard Pryor, Chris Rock, Public Enemy, N.W.A., *In Living Color,* and the Clash singing "White riot, we want a riot of our own." One way or another, the beat of an Atlantic culture goes on. The beat need not always be aggressive; sometimes it sugars its defiance, as in Taj Mahal's wistful grunts anchoring Michelle Shocked's high wiry melody on "Jump Jim Crow / Zip-A-Dee Doo-Dah": "Hip Zip Coon," she sings, "you sure look slick. . . . How *do* you do that walkin' trick?" Her chorus, with its surely intentional ambiguity, could be the chorus for optic blackness:

If I knew your secret, I would make it mine.
If I knew your secret, I would make it mine.[31]

Each successive ethnicity claiming its place on these shores, and every mass mode of communication (theater, fiction, radio, film, LP, TV, video) blacks up, acts black, and thus negotiates its arrival. These rites of passage constitute a fundament of optic blackness. But let's be clear about the results. Do these negotiations, as Michael Rogin argued in *Blackface, White Noise* (1996), *replace* ethnicity with whiteness?[32] Or do they *compound* Atlantic identity?

I believe doping up optic blackness is additive. In its performance, people may discover their mutuality. One is not less Jewish for blacking up in *The Jazz Singer* (1927) or less Puerto Rican for singing, as Big Punisher does on the *Whiteboys* (1999) soundtrack, that he is a "thug for life." Rather, by turns, T. D. Rice, Dan Emmett, William Henry Lane (aka Juba), Billy Kersands, Bert Williams, Al Jolson, Ida Cox and Josephine Baker, Mezz Mezzrow, Little Richard, Elvis Presley, Mick Jagger, Richard Pryor and Eddie Murphy, Sandra Bernhard (in *Without You I'm Nothing,* 1990), Wesley Brown (in *Darktown Strutters,* 1994), Danny Hoch, Kid Rock, and Big Punisher meld their ethnicities to an abstract body of symbolic pain that optic blackness has conveyed all these years.

What they perform amounts to a naturalization ceremony. Think of these catalogs as immigrants reciting aloud a Declaration of Independence that affirms no optic white aspect of the United States and undermines its superiority. To claim blackface creates whiteness is vastly to simplify and essentialize its practitioners. The optic black impersonators I have been listing play for riskier stakes than constituting whiteness. To misread them as creating whiteness can only occur if the reader is a day-tripper who does not know the complex history of the form, and who mistakes its crudest signifiers for the whole. So long as they experience exclusion and disdain, these performers will bristle back with optic black. They await a time when their way of living within the maw of the dominant culture will force it, as the invisible youth's grandfather told him in Ellison's novel, to "vomit or bust wide open."[33] This waiting is not an overtly revolutionary stance. Rather, it calculates its odds on the steeply tilted playing fields of the Atlantic economy and its globalizing successor—and acts accordingly. The tactics of optic blackness dissatisfy those who yearn for frontal resistance and less-complicated identities.

I conclude with Big Punisher's hip-hop gloss on these themes. Big Pun died of heart failure early in 2000 at age twenty-eight—that same break point at which such other optic black performers as Janis Joplin, Jimi Hendrix, Brian Jones, and Jim Morrison also succumbed to excess. Born Chris Rios, of Puerto Rican parentage, Big Pun rose from Bronx street culture with his single "Still Not a Player" in 1998 to become the first solo Latin emcee with a platinum single. Embodying the consumer wing of popular culture (when his heart failed, he weighed nearly seven hundred pounds), Pun had a delivery that was speedy, smooth, and entirely in the groove of optic blackness. On the soundtrack to his limited-release film *Whiteboys,* in 1999, performance artist and playwright Danny Hoch gave the lead position to Big Punisher's anthem "Who Is a Thug." This song verifies that the ideals of optic black are still cruising every domain of popular culture. Even though structural and officially valorized slavery is now a distant memory in the western Atlantic, performers of all hues assume optic black positionality as much as if they were still working out how to represent themselves at the far edges of plantation life at the end of the eighteenth century. Those values continue to model what passes for counterauthenticity in multiethnic culture.

Big Pun does his chorus as a dialogue with a woman who answers to "6430." She tests him: who delegitimizes the dominant culture? Are you sure? He replies:

> . . . word bond, I bring my brothers wit' me,
> Definitely, and start off my own thug committee.

Thugness here stands as the oppositional party, those who seek not assimilation but its opposite, those who stand tough against legitimacy. And here we are, back again, with T. D. Rice and Sweet Sweetback, with Harriet Beecher Stowe and John Travolta: seeing others move and then making them up. "Word bond," says Big Pun, "I . . . definitely . . . start off my own thug committee." Then the chorus, always the chorus:

> 6430: Who's a thug? Are you sure?
> Pun: Big Pun, baby, I'm a thug for life,
>   I'm a thug for life, I'm a thug for life.
> 6430: Who's a thug? Are you sure?
> Pun: Aiyyo, my word is bond, long as I'm
>   alive, I'ma put it on.
>   Coulda gone legit shit, thug nigga 'til
>   I'm gone.

Repeat Forever

Within months, Big Pun would be gone. But others, like Eminem, have taken his place, and will continue to do so until it no longer makes sense. As one performer, writer, painter, or joker falls under the pressure, another steps in "to do the Calinda against the Dude," as Ishmael Reed wrote in *Mumbo Jumbo* (1988).[34] The determination to avoid legitimacy, the adoption of thugness (here standing in for optic blackness and flagging one's own disdained status), the brotherhood of bravado, the hard-to-copy delivery (like Little Richard, a generation earlier, singing so fast that

Pat Boone could never force his lips around the syllables): these are as much the passport to what's real in America—and all the places that hearken to "America"—as those values have been for almost two centuries.

No end in sight for optic black. All sorts of people—doubtless the largest, most active cohort participating in the cultural life of Atlantic modernity—use optic black to display their starkest refusals to fit even as their involvement in the mode displays their paradoxical naturalization in the most resurgent cultural pattern of the long modern era. It waxes, it wanes, but it lasts.

NOTES

1. Ralph Ellison, *Invisible Man* (1952; reprint, New York: Random House, 1982), 165.

2. Harryette Mullen, "Optic White: Blackness and the Production of Whiteness," *Diacritics*, summer–fall 1994, 71–89.

3. Lauren Berlant reformulates Michel Foucault's concept of "countermemory" as "the residual material [that] is not identical with the official meanings of the political public sphere [and is] in contradistinction to the official material that so often becomes the 'truth' of a historical period and political formulation." *The Anatomy of National Fantasy: Hawthorne, Utopia, and Everyday Life* (Chicago: University of Chicago Press, 1991), 6.

4. I expand this point later in this essay and try to nail it in my two books on the topic.

5. I thank Lisa Clark, the jacket designer, for illustrating this point efficiently on the cover of *Raising Cain*. There one sees M. C. Hammer performing on TV in 1990 the same dance step John Diamond (a white dancer in blackface) performed at the Bowery Theatre in 1843: W. T. Lhamon, Jr., *Raising Cain: Blackface Performance from Jim Crow to Hip Hop* (Cambridge: Harvard University Press, 1998); also pp. 61 and 224.

6. Jürgen Habermas, *The Structural Transformation of the Public Sphere: An Inquiry into a Category of Bourgeois Society*, trans. Thomas Burger with the assistance of Frederick Lawrence (1962; reprint, Cambridge: MIT Press, 1991), xviii.

7. The many works on the historical production of race and class in the Atlantic include Paul Gilroy, *The Black Atlantic: Modernity and Double Consciousness* (Cambridge: Harvard University Press, 1993) and *Against Race: Imagining Political Culture beyond the Color Line* (Cambridge: Harvard University Press, 2000); Noel Ignatiev, *How the Irish Became White* (New York: Routledge, 1995); Winthrop Jordan, *White over Black: American Attitudes toward the Negro, 1550–1812* (Chapel Hill: University of North Carolina Press, published for the Institute of Early American History and Culture at Williamsburg, Virginia, 1968); Peter Linebaugh and Marcus Rediker, *The Many Headed Hydra* (Boston: Beacon, 2000); David R. Roediger, *The Wages of Whiteness: Race and the Making of the American Working Class* (London: Verso, 1991); Sterling Stuckey, *Slave Culture: Nationalist Theory and the Foundations of Black America* (New

York: Oxford University Press, 1987); and Vron Ware, *Beyond the Pale: White Women, Racism, and History* (London: Verso, 1992).

8. I deal provisionally with Hawthorne's difficulties later in this essay. Ralph Ellison memorably addressed similar issues in his too-seldom-read essay "Society, Morality, and the Novel," originally included in Granville Hicks's collection *The Living Novel* (1957) and reprinted recently in *The Collected Essays of Ralph Ellison,* ed. John F. Callahan (New York: Modern Library, 1995), 694–725.

9. bell hooks, "Representing Whiteness in the Black Imagination," in *Cultural Studies,* ed. Cary Nelson, Lawrence Grossberg, and Paula A. Treichler (New York: Routledge, 1992), 346.

10. Peter Way, *Common Labour: Workers and the Digging of North American Canals, 1780–1860* (Cambridge: Cambridge University Press, 1993); also Lhamon, *Raising Cain.*

11. The work of Catherine Cole on current African blackface and Manthia Diawara on James Brown's reception and effectiveness in Africa confirms this claim even for the southeastern Atlantic: the west African coast. See Catherine M. Cole, "Reading Blackface in West Africa: Wonders Taken for Signs," *Critical Inquiry* 23, no. 1 (1996): 183–215; and Manthia Diawara, *In Search of Africa* (Cambridge: Harvard University Press, 1998).

12. *The Old Plantation* hangs in the Abby Aldrich Rockefeller Collection of Folk Art in Williamsburg. As part of a longer study, I am preparing a full reading of this painting. It is often referenced as documenting banjo history, clothing, dance, or ritual, all of them important, but its composition also requires reading beyond these separating significations.

13. On April 12, 1836, in Natchez, a free black man, a barber, and lifelong diarist named William Johnson, went with his best friend Robert McCary to T. D. Rice's benefit performance. They sat in the segregated gallery, but Johnson vowed not to return until rowdy conditions at the theater improved. See William Johnson, *William Johnson's Natchez: The Ante-Bellum Diary of a Free Negro,* ed. William Ransom Hogan and Edwin Adams Davis (Baton Rouge: Louisiana State University Press, 1951), 114. From Boston to Charleston and around to New Orleans, all the theaters regularly advertised Negro seats for Rice's plays. His audience included blacks.

14. For more on Rice, Jim Crow, and the publics they yoked together, see chapter 4 in *Raising Cain* and W. T. Lhamon, Jr., *Jump Jim Crow: Plays, Lyrics, and Street Prose of the First Atlantic Popular Culture* (Cambridge: Harvard University Press, 2003).

15. These plays are published in Lhamon, *Jump Jim Crow.*

16. Ralph Ellison, "Change the Joke and Slip the Yoke," in *The Collected Essays of Ralph Ellison,* ed. John F. Callahan (1958; reprint, New York: Modern Library, 1995), 100–112.

17. Text of T. D. Rice, *Bone Squash: A Burletta,* British Library Add MS 42953 ff. 312–19.

18. Constance Rourke, *American Humor: A Study of the American Character,* ed. W. T. Lhamon, Jr. (Tallahassee: Florida State University Press, 1985), 77–104.

19. Ellison, *Invisible Man,* 333.

20. The playbill for the stage version of *The Quaker City,* never produced, is at the Historical Society of Pennsylvania.

21. Toni Morrison, *Tar Baby* (New York: Plume, 1982), 166.

22. T. S. Eliot, "Tradition and the Individual Talent" (1919) in *Selected Essays* (New York: Harcourt, Brace and World, 1960), 3–11; Henry Louis Gates, Jr., *The Signifying Monkey: A Theory of African American Literary Criticism* (New York: Oxford University Press, 1988); and Toni Morrison, *Playing in the Dark: Whiteness and Literary Imagination* (Cambridge: Harvard University Press, 1992).

23. Nearly everything written about *Uncle Tom's Cabin* has been about its representation and misrepresentation of race and gender. But almost nothing published on *The House of the Seven Gables* has focused on Hawthorne's concern with racial production. An excellent start has been made by David Anthony, "Class, Culture, and the Trouble with White Skin in Hawthorne's *The House of the Seven Gables*," *Yale Journal of Criticism* 12, no. 2 (1999): 249–68. Less centered on race but wrestling significantly with the instability of all categories of representation in the novel is Cathy N. Davidson, "Photographs of the Dead: Sherman, Daguerre, Hawthorne," *South Atlantic Quarterly* 89, no. 4 (1990): 667–701. See also Susan Mizruchi, *The Power of Historical Knowledge: Narrating the Past in Hawthorne, James, and Dreiser* (Princeton: Princeton University Press, 1988); and Robert K. Martin, "Haunted by Jim Crow: Gothic Fictions by Hawthorne and Faulkner," in *American Gothic: New Interventions in a National Narrative*, ed. Robert K. Martin and Eric Savoy (Iowa City: University of Iowa Press, 1998), 129–42.

24. Nathaniel Hawthorne, *The House of the Seven Gables*, ed. Millicent Bell (New York: Library of America, 1983), 395–96.

25. My influences here include Dale Cockrell, *Demons of Disorder: Early Blackface Minstrels and Their World* (Cambridge: Cambridge University Press, 1997); Harry Elam, Jr., "The Black Performer and the Performance of Blackness: *The Escape; or, A Leap to Freedom* by William Wells Brown and *No Place To Be Somebody* by Charles Gordone," in *African American Performance and Theater History: A Critical Reader*, ed. Harry Elam, Jr., and David Krasner (New York: Oxford University Press, 2001), 288–305; Eric Lott, *Love and Theft: Blackface Minstrelsy and the American Working Class* (New York: Oxford University Press, 1993); David R. Roediger, *The Wages of Whiteness: Race and the Making of the American Working Class* (London: Verso, 1991); Joseph Roach, *Cities of the Dead: Circum-Atlantic Performance* (New York: Columbia University Press, 1996); Shelley Streeby, "Haunted Houses: George Lippard, Nathaniel Hawthorne, and Middle-Class America," *Criticism* 38, no. 3 (1996): 443–72; Shane White, *Somewhat More Independent: The End of Slavery in New York City, 1770–1810* (Athens: University of Georgia Press, 1991) and *Stories of Freedom in Black New York* (Cambridge: Harvard University Press, 2002); Edward L. Widmer, *Young America: The Flowering of Democracy in New York City* (New York: Oxford University Press, 1999); and Sean Wilentz, *Chants Democratic: New York City and the Rise of the American Working Class, 1788–1850* (New York: Oxford University Press, 1984).

26. I use *fetish* here as earlier in this essay in the sense that William Pietz has taught: "novel productions resulting from the abrupt encounter of radically heterogeneous worlds." See William Pietz, "The Problem of the Fetish, I," *Res* 9 (spring 1985): 6.

27. Nathaniel Hawthorne, *The American Notebooks*, ed. Claude M. Simpson (Columbus: Ohio State University Press, 1972), 172.

28. Elam, "Black Performer," 288–89.

29. In considering Melville's ironic production of race, I have been most

influenced by Philip Fisher, *Hard Facts: Setting and Form in the American Novel* (New York: Oxford University Press, 1987); C. L. R. James, *Mariners, Renegades, and Castaways: The Story of Herman Melville and the World We Live In* (1953; reprint, Detroit: Bewick/ED, 1978); Carolyn L. Karcher, *Shadow over the Promised Land: Slavery, Race, and Violence in Melville's America* (Baton Rouge: Louisiana State University Press, 1980); Michael Paul Rogin, *Subversive Genealogy: The Politics and Art of Herman Melville* (New York: Alfred A. Knopf, 1983); and Sterling Stuckey's chapter, cowritten with Joshua Leslie, "The Death of Benito Cereno: A Reading of Herman Melville on Slavery," in Stuckey's *Going Through the Storm: The Influence of African American Art in History* (New York: Oxford, 1994), 153–70.

30. I have transcribed this short play from the holograph manuscript in the Dan Emmett papers at the Ohio State Archives. Along with my headnote, brief analysis, confirming playbills, and evidentiary photographs of blackface actors performing the shaving scene, it will be published in Jay Fliegelman's edition of "Benito Cereno," forthcoming from St. Martin's Press.

The vernacular brilliance of other Emmett scenes of optic blackness are presently available in Hans Nathan, *Dan Emmett and the Rise of Early Negro Minstrelsy* (Norman: University of Oklahoma Press, 1962). See particularly "Bressed Am Dem Dat 'Spects Nuttin,' Kaze Dey Aint a Gwine to Git Nuttin'!" (410–12). A wonderful analysis of this stump speech is in William F. Stowe and David Grimsted, "White-Black Humor," *Journal of Ethnic Studies* 3 (1975): 78–96.

31. *Arkansas Traveler* (1992), Mercury 314–512101–2. Her liner notes include this remark: "My early intention was to present this record with a cover photo of myself wearing blackface. Aside from providing controversy for hatemongers or offending the delicate sensibilities of the politically correct, my sincere intention was that it would provide a genuine focus on the real 'roots' of many of the tunes included: blackface minstrelsy. It's my contention that a blackface tradition is alive and well hidden behind a modern mask. I believe that 'blacking up' should be done correctly: as an exploration for the source of that hollow ring we mistakenly believe was immaculately conceived in Las Vegas." She did not include that photograph. The tour that accompanied the release was not a minstrel show, either.

32. Michael Rogin, *Blackface, White Noise: Jewish Immigrants in the Hollywood Melting Pot* (Berkeley and Los Angeles: University of California Press, 1996).

33. Ellison, *Invisible Man*, 13–14.

34. Ishmael Reed, *Mumbo Jumbo* (1972; New York: Atheneum, 1988), 134.

KOBENA MERCER

Diaspora Aesthetics and Visual Culture

Contemporary artists offer intriguing insight into the often surprising ways in which blackness travels. Referencing works from African American and black British contexts, this contribution examines call-and-response dialogue in visual culture and asks why critics have so far failed to recognize the creative energies of such cut-and-mix aesthetics. By way of an overview of unresolved issues in African American art historiography, I suggest that one obstacle to the recognition of such dialogic interaction lies in the implicit notion of a hierarchy of bodily senses that assumes an inherent dichotomy between the aural and the visual.

Michele Wallace insightfully identified such dilemmas in her landmark essay "Modernism, Post-modernism, and the Problem of the Visual in Afro-American Culture," although unprecedented shifts associated with contemporary globalization require a thorough rethinking of the Ellisonian metaphors of "invisibility" and "visibility."[1] While these terms have been profoundly influential in critical understandings of the politics of "race" and representation, there are limitations to dichotomous evaluations in which black cultural criticism often counterposes the innovative qualities of black music against what are seen to be the imitative qualities of black visual arts. Taking account of why this distinction arose, I argue that an interactive approach to diaspora aesthetics rejects the necessity of such either/or positions. Showing how the Fanonian iconography of the mask does indeed respond to "the problem of the visual" initiated by the supremacist gaze, I suggest that the need to question the politics of visibility opens up a wider horizon for understanding diaspora culture's complex histories and future possibilities.

Web, Text, and Flow

In installation works featuring manufactured fabrics as ready-made materials for neoconceptual interrogations of culture and identity, the artist Yinka Shonibare unravels a fascinating story of cross-cultural exchange. In *Double Dutch* (1994), the dressmaking fabric known in West Africa as the Dutch wax-print, or fancy-print, takes the place of blank canvas that is stretched over fifty individual frames arranged in a grid on the gallery walls. In the piece entitled *How Does a Girl Like You Get to Be A Girl Like You?* (1995), Shonibare creates a finely tailored replica of a Victorian bustle remade in the ornately patterned "West African" fabric. In *Alien Obsessives: Mum, Dad, and the Kids* (1998), a sculptural family of science-fiction puppets has been remade with wax-print fabrics, provoking a visual pun on perceptions of cultural "otherness" by substituting stereotypical space aliens in place of human "aliens" such as migrants and travelers.

Throughout his body of work, Shonibare's practice serves to unstitch a complex history of global interaction woven into the very threads of the fabric chosen as his source material. Although wax-print fabric is widely perceived in the West as quintessentially "African" due to its elaborate patterning and bold color combinations, it actually originated in Indonesian and Javanese batik fabric-making traditions typically employing wax-resistant color dyes, layered in organic patterns, and featuring exquisite "cracking." Late-nineteenth-century Dutch colonialists copied these indigenous crafts, converting the process into industrial manufacture whereby factories in the Netherlands would export mass-produced "copies" back into the Asian Pacific periphery. British competitors in the textile trade soon emulated the Dutch initiative. Similarly, indigenous West African batik methods were imitated and "translated" by designers in factories in Manchester and other Midlands cities, producing fabrics specifically intended for export to western and central African markets. Indeed, the circuit of supply and demand between center and periphery was so finely tuned that, as it continued into the postindependence era, photographic portraits of political leaders would often appear on fabrics commissioned to celebrate such occasions.

Shonibare's art brings to light the twist to the tale occurring when the wax-print cloth is "retranslated" into diasporic cultural spaces. When African American fashions in the sixties employed the fabric in head-wraps, dashikis, and joromi, it became a potent emblem of Pan-African identification. Worn with pride, the fabric enunciated the wearer's affilia-

FIG. 1. *Double Dutch*. Photo by Yinka Shonibare. (© Museum of Contemporary Art, Chicago.)

tions with an "imagined community" that connected black people globally by way of an instantly recognizable badge of belonging. In the early seventies, Europeans also appropriated the fabric during the brief rage for "ethnic chic," which recycled modernist primitivism by fastening onto the wax-print as an exotic icon of otherness. The irony in this is that both strands of translation were equally dependent upon a prior history of circulation and exchange that effectively decontextualized the material from its origins.

Shonibare's art reveals that the cultural "meaning" of the fabric is not intrinsic to its ethnic origins. Rather, it constantly acquires layer upon layer of altered meanings as it travels through diverse sites and locations in which users and consumers encode their own local tastes and preferences into the intentions and interpretations of their semiotic choices.

Shonibare's project resonates with concepts of "traveling culture" put forward by James Clifford[2] in that his art draws attention to the material entanglement of cultural identities, which is unthinkable for essentialist or separatist ideologies that require monologic notions of "pure" origins and symbolic unanimity. However, insofar as art's aesthetic autonomy cannot be reduced to an illustration of theory, it is helpful to have a sense of Yinka's self-description in which cultural mixing and hybrid interaction

FIG. 2. *How Does a Girl Like You Get to Be a Girl Like You?* Photo by Yinka Shonibare. (© Museum of Contemporary Art, Chicago.)

are taken for granted as the background to his artistic choices and procedures. Illuminating the concerns that animate his neoconceptual methods of inquiry, he has said:

> Is there such a thing as pure origin? For those of the postcolonial generation this is a difficult question. I'm bilingual. Because I was brought up in Lagos and London—and kept going back and forth—it is extremely difficult for me to have one view of culture. It's impossible. How do I position myself in relation to that multi-faceted experience of culture?[3]

Comfortable with the multiculture made available by his "back and forth" background, and thus questioning monolithic conceptions of blackness, Shonibare goes on to suggest that the acceptance of hybridity is not the conclusion but merely a starting point for his open-ended investigations:

> My own sense of culture evolved out of what I watched on television, the music I listened to, the people I knew and what I read and the obvious impact of a postcolonial history. . . . I listened to the music of Fela Kuti, James Brown, Sugar Hill Gang and King Sunny Ade. I read Shake-

speare, Charles Dickens, Wole Soyinka and Chinua Achebe at school. I am a post-colonial hybrid. The idea of some kind of fixed identity of belonging to an authentic culture is quite foreign to my experience.[4]

What is striking about Shonibare's outlook as a "post-colonial hybrid" is the extent to which it is generationally shared. The Nigerian-born and New York–based artist Ike Ude has voiced a similar perspective on his artistic aims:

> I have found that, irrespective of ideological rhetoric, any strict adherence to a single cultural approach is flawed and practically impossible. Looking beyond colonial impediments, I see the circumstances of my artistic practice as inextricably informed by the multiplicity of conflicting cultural influences I have inherited and delineated to serve myself. . . . I am nobody's artist but my own.[5]

The main thread I want to pull out here is not that postcolonial hybridity is a uniform or universal experience for everyone in a given diaspora, but that the two-way process of cultural traffic is now increasingly understood not as special or exceptional but as an ordinary and normal aspect of everyday life. To better understand distinctive diasporic experiences (that are nonetheless deeply interconnected by the practice of culture) not as territory, property, or ownership, but as a living fabric of web, text, and flow, we can pinpoint three key issues arising out of the interactive, rather than essentialist, model of cultural identity.

First, we can say that blackness travels through routes that were initially opened by trade, commerce, and market-based exchange. Each of these economic and political forces entails the exploitative inequalities determined by capitalism, but also encounter resistances, subversions, and stoppages in their path. Unlike the Marxist world-system model, which tends to assume that structural asymmetries in the control of production inevitably determine social and cultural inequalities, the concept of "traveling cultures" allows us to grasp the contradictions that capitalist globalization produces as an unintended consequence of its intrinsic need to find new markets. Paul Gilroy's brief analysis of soul and funk LP covers is an excellent example of how profit-driven motives in the music industry were constantly accompanied by countervailing discourses created by the message in the music—if not the visual images through which it was marketed.[6]

FIG. 3. *Alien Obsessives: Mum, Dad, and the Kids.* Photo by Yinka Shoni-bare. (© Museum of Contemporary Art, Chicago.)

Second, insofar as Africa, Europe, and the Americas have been histori-cally entangled in a global system more or less since 1492, then the "big story" of twentieth-century modernity is the story of black innovation and white imitation—a story that runs as a countercurrent to modernist pop-ular culture. I employed the phrase "black innovation/white imitation" in an essay on diasporic hairstyles so as to pinpoint a paradox.[7] On the one hand, excluded from access to conventional channels of democratic expression, African Americans encoded political aspirations for self-determination in cultural forms such as music, dance, vernacular speech, and even in the medium of hair. On the other hand, however, such stylis-tic innovation was also highly attractive to white Americans—and indeed to nonblack people globally—who then copied and imitated such styles and, in the process, drained them of exclusively "black" content and detached them from their initial meanings as covert or encoded signifiers of resistance.

Since we have seen a similar dynamic in the cultural history of the wax-print fabric, I would want to complicate the axis of black innovation/white imitation on two accounts. It is crucial to bear in mind, however, that this axis subverts the one-sided supremacist view of mimicry as applying to blackness alone. In light of the critique of Marxist reductionism, the commonplace notion of "commodification" as a unilateral, top-down process of co-option is called into question. Rather than see the appropriation of stylized blackness as an inevitably exploitative practice perpetrated by nonblacks, we might want to bear in mind that one of the first African American millionaires was Madame C. J. Walker, whose hair pomade and preparations drew enormous profits from mainly black, female, and working-class customers. In Britain, the hair-care products of Caribbean-born entrepreneurs Dyke and Dryden have also made millions. In other words, the "traveling culture" model encourages us to resist conflating cultural and economic processes. Departing from deterministic approaches, we can further identify contradictions that arise within and between spaces of the black diaspora itself.

In the realm of style and fashion, an interesting example of such contradiction arose with the African American passion for kente cloth in the eighties. When kente was adopted to make unequivocally Afrocentric statements of pride in one's heritage, we saw on the surface a reworking of the sixties repertoire that was extended from traditional garments, such as flowing robes or waistcoats, into everyday apparel such as sweat-tops and even baseball caps. Besides the irony that the fabric used was often printed material imported from Korea rather than traditionally hand-woven kente from Ghana's Ashanti region, it might also be argued that, despite the intended Afrocentric message of authenticity, the translation of kente into what Manthia Diawara calls Afro-kitsch may have been unintentionally disrespectful—the fabric, in its original context, is usually reserved for ceremonial occasions such as births, marriages, and funerals.[8] With wit and humor, the African American artist Daniel Tisdale opened space for consideration of such questions in the ironic museological display of sixties fashions in his neoconceptual installation *The Black Museum* (1990).

Third and finally, the key question for thinking about the future possibilities of the diaspora's cultural politics is to ask: what breaks the flow? What codes cover over and conceal the processes of cultural mixing that have generated the inventive energies of Afro-diaspora modernisms? What are the boundaries that cut off the flow—not just with the dualism of whiteness and blackness, but within and between the distinctive experiences that differentiate and enrich the internal diversity of Afro-diaspora identities?

To the extent that diaspora-based webs of cultural connectedness might offer alternatives to market-driven pressure to penetrate cultural barriers in the name of the performance principle of pure profit, I want to ask whether the historical demand for visibility that has been so vital to the counterpractice of expressive performativity in the aesthetic codes of black culture has now reached a turning point. I asked, "What breaks the flow?" I want to work through the question by looking specifically at "the problem of the visual" in the received narrative of modernism.

Modernism Was Always Multicultural

Romare Bearden's collage *Three Folk Musicians* (1967) has a call-and-response relationship to Pablo Picasso's painting *Masked Musicians* (1921). Taking the blues tradition as subject matter, Bearden returned to the composition of his earlier gouache, *Folk Musicians* (1941–42). Having worked through social realism and abstract expressionism in the forties and fifties, Bearden arrived at the photomontage projections that became his medium of choice in the sixties. As Ralph Ellison observed, the visual methodology of collage was highly suited to Bearden's outlook on African American life.[9] The cut-and-mix approach involved in collage resonates with the improvisational aspects of the vernacular, which selectively appropriates what is given or found in one's environment and transforms it into raw material for one's distinct stylistic signature. Just as bebop musicians transformed melodies from familiar standards as the basis for solo-in-the-circle antiphony, vernacular speech "signified" on Standard English by using tropes such as inversion or irony that carried traces of the syntax and tonality of African oral languages.[10]

In the sense that the cut-and-mix collage aesthetic of *Three Folk Musicians* exemplifies a condition of "double consciousness," it can be said to bring about a quality of dialogic doubleness that enriches our understanding of how deeply African and European cultures interacted and intertwined under modernity. Bearden openly acknowledged his postcubist interest in the flatness of the picture plane against the realist illusion of verisimilitude. While his almost mathematical inquiry into geometric rhythm and formal spacing is indebted to Matisse and Mondrian, whose *Broadway Boogie Woogie* (1942) was inspired by stride piano, Bearden also brings into the mix his own intimate knowledge of the syncopated rhythms and angular intervals associated with the compositions of Thelonious Monk, for example.

FIG. 4. *Three Folk Musicians*. Photo by Romare Bearden. (© Romare Bearden Foundation/ Licensed by VAGA, New York.)

Bearden, therefore, does not passively celebrate black culture. Rather, he actively "translates" back and forth between European modernism and the African American vernacular. In fact, this is how he arrived at collage as a pictorial method that refused the either/or dichotomies of an art world that often counterposed the terms *Negro* and *artist* as if they were inherently antithetical. Bearden's unique position as a midcentury African American modernist allows us to examine why this dialogic doubleness has thus far gone mostly unrecognized in twentieth-century art criticism. Briefly touching on moments from the Harlem Renaissance in the twenties and the Black Arts movement in the sixties, I want to pinpoint two key reasons why this has occurred.

Broadly speaking, the first reason concerns the dominance of the formalist master-narrative that tends to regard the history of modern art as a linear, goal-driven sequence in which the mastery of pure form triumphs over the chaos of random matter. This is my own simplification, admittedly; nevertheless, it conveys the ideological thrust of a grand narrative that began with critics Roger Fry and Clive Bell, was transferred to Alfred Barr, chief curator of New York's Museum of Modern Art, and continued with critic Clement Greenberg until it was radically called into question, during the sixties, by conceptual artists who extended Marcel Duchamp's interrogative practice of institutional critique.

My point is that, insofar as this dominant version of the modern art narrative was widely influential, what results is the bicycle-race model of art history: who got there first, who was fastest, and what prize did they win? When the story is told as a sequence of heroically transgressive acts, in which the mantle is passed from Manet and Cezanne to Picasso and Mondrian and then to post-1945 American modernists such as Jackson Pollock and Barnett Newman, what we find is that minority artists always tend to be excluded. I would argue that such exclusion from the canon is not so much accidental as obligatory, for the core modernist values of originality, transgression, and a unified oeuvre are based on an either/or logic. Just as the very existence of "high" culture entails the rejection and exclusion of "low" culture as its Other (in the sense that the fine arts necessarily exclude folk crafts, for example), each of high modernism's core aesthetic principles excluded various minor traditions in order to provide a foil to its own identity. What is interesting is how this exclusionary logic of "othering" dovetails with ideologies of ethnocentrism and supremacism.

When the beholder assumes the unquestioned values of high modernism, the dialogic interplay between Bearden and Picasso is canceled out. Because *Masked Musicians* was made first, it attains pride of place and thus makes *Three Folk Musicians* secondary or derivative. Because Bearden restlessly experimented with diverse methodologies, moving through realism and abstraction to collage, whereas Picasso's stylistic shifts are held to be problem-solving progressions within a unified oeuvre, the former is seen as less accomplished than the latter, who thus wins accolades for his individuality. Finally, Picasso's transgressions were pitched against earlier masterpieces in European painting, such that the shock of his *Demoiselles D'Avingnon* (1907) lay not so much in the influence of African sculptures but in the work's intertextual reference to Eugene Delacroix's *Women of Tangier* (1824), which was both acknowledged and undermined in a quasi-Oedipal drama of filiation and independence. For diaspora artists like Romare Bearden, however, the question of belonging to a tradition had been in doubt from the very beginning.

Because white supremacism posited that Africans were entirely stripped of an original culture by the Middle Passage, African American artists were obliged to refute such racist assumptions. Art historian Albert Boime reveals that such nineteenth-century artists as Robert Scott Duncanson, Edward Mitchell Bannister, Mary Edmonia Lewis, and Henry Ossawa Tanner were each obliged to demonstrate the Negro's capacity for artistic "competence."[11] That each of these artists did so, enjoying successful careers that won them national and international recognition, serves only to highlight the disparity, at that time, between European American artists (who all emulated a European aesthetic) and African American artists, who faced a double imperative. Not only did African American artists have to prove competence to gain admittance to an art world profession, but their achievements in searching for an artistic voice and style of their own were overshadowed by the need to refute widely held misrepresentations of the "Negro" as a whole.

Add to this cultural scenario the intensified ideological investment in ethnic stereotyping after Reconstruction, and we can see how visual artists of the 1895–1925 New Negro movement were overburdened by contradictory expectations and demands. Implicitly expected to "represent the race," each generation of artists has had to negotiate this dual dilemma.

When W. E. B. DuBois set forth his wide-ranging "uplift" agenda in "Criteria of Negro Art" in 1926, he wanted artists to "represent the race" by demonstrating the capacities and potential of black people. At the same time, he wanted artists to refute vulgar and degrading stereotypes. When Alain Locke edited *The New Negro* anthology in 1925, emphasizing the cultural rather than political dimension of African American creativity, he too urged such artists as Aaron Douglas, Sargent Johnson, and Lois Mailou Jones to form a "racially representative idiom of group expression."[12] Less preoccupied with the need to refute stereotypes, but sharing DuBois's concern that white America recognize the talents and achievements of black artists, Locke saw the nineteenth-century generation as broadly imitative of outmoded European academic conventions. He wanted the Harlem Renaissance generation to learn from the modernist examples of Picasso and Modigliani, all the more so to reactivate the "ancestral heritage" of precontact African cultures as a source of originality and distinction for African American visual art.

Like many others, Locke felt that the distinctively expressive features of African American cultural identity were manifested mainly in speech, in music, and in dance. Although such broad brushstrokes inevitably simplify the complexity of cultural history, my point is that the second reason why the interactive energies of African American modernisms have not been fully recognized stems from the ideological pressures that led successive generations of intellectuals to assume a hierarchy of the arts. By placing literature and music at the top, the survivals and traces of African influences throughout the diaspora highlighted the distinctiveness of African American identity. By virtue of being culturally distinctive, the "Negro" was entitled to social recognition as an equal contributor to modern American civilization. Seeking to refute the supremacist idea that black culture was merely imitative, the emphasis on aesthetic distinctiveness in the literary and performing arts led cultural critics to an implicit hierarchy in which the aural culture of the voice would be championed over and above the visual culture of the eye.

Once we grasp that this move was being driven by the deeper demand for the social recognition of African American identity, we come to understand how aesthetics and politics were further conflated in subsequent moves that posited an entirely separate black aesthetic in the sixties. When Black Arts Movement (BAM) advocates such as Larry Neal and Amiri Baraka sought to fuse aesthetics and politics into the all-encompassing demand that black art be made "by, for, and about" black people, the result was a hierarchy in which music, theater, and performance poetry, being closer to the vernacular rhythms of the streets and the long-standing wisdom of folk belief, would be championed as more "authentically black" than potentially elitist and more esoteric fine arts like painting or sculpture.[13]

Curiously, the didactic and prescriptive rhetoric of the BAM agenda echoed the idealistic "uplift" espoused by DuBois and Locke: artists in both eras were supposed to "represent the race" and refute stereotypes. Although the political atmosphere of the sixties could not be more different from that of the twenties, the common outcome was that visual artists were subjected to conflicting expectations. During the thirties, the philanthropic agenda of the Harmon Foundation wanted black artists to win white approval by adopting conservative styles that would demonstrate their competence; but affluent white patrons, such as Charlotte Osgood Mason and Carl Van Vechten, whom Zora Neale Hurston dubbed "Negrotarians," wanted black artists to fulfill primitivist desires for absolute otherness.

During the sixties, when black artists had embraced abstract expressionism (painter Norman Lewis, for example, had represented the United States at the 1956 Venice Bienale; MoMA purchased mid-1950s works by sculptor Richard Hunt), they now found that, because their work was nonrepresentational, they were not "black enough." Conversely, artists such as Wandsworth Jarrell, Ben Jones, and Jeff Donaldson, who participated in the Chicago-based artist's collective Africobra in the late 1960s, sought to produce a participatory aesthetic that was accessible to popular audiences and which represented populist aspirations. Despite innovative works, however, such artists were rarely valued by mainstream art institutions, and are rarely remembered in BAM narratives. What we find from the twenties through the sixties is that when artworks are made secondary either to the artist's cultural identity or to the art world's institutional obligations to reflect society, then art is rarely appreciated for what it actually is—a painting, a mural, a sculpture, a collage—but is constantly interpreted for what it is held to represent about African American culture in general, or American society in the abstract.

One consequence of this overdetermined reading of artworks as necessarily "representing the race" or "reflecting society" is that art historians fail to observe the "back and forth" dialectic set in motion when artworks talk to one another. Faith Ringghold's painting *Flag Is Bleeding* (1967) articulated a searing indictment of America's inability to fulfill its democratic ideal. Yet such dissent depended on the signifying difference she inscribed in relation to a work such as Jasper Johns's *Flag* (1954), which, despite its questioning of depiction (was it a representation of a flag or a flag abstracted into a painting?), avoided the underlying question of national identity. When David Hammons's *African American Flag* (1993) replies to Jasper Johns—it is an actual flag made of fabric, not a representation or a depiction—Hammons performs further critical "signifyin" by substituting Marcus Garvey's red, black, and green colors in place of the red, white, and blue.

Art historians cannot "see" such critical conversations in visual culture because the interactive dimension is occluded by absolutist ideologies that assume a fixed or essential "difference" between European and African cultures. To examine the legacies of such hegemonic divisions, we need to locate the problems in African American art historiography in a deeper historical perspective. By defining "the problem of the visual" as a product of the cultural history of Western modernity as a whole, we may retain the value of Ellison's insights into the dilemma of invisibility while registering the conceptual limitations of the demand for visibility. This in turn opens wider perspectives on the complexity of the diaspora's cultural history and highlights dilemmas regarding future possibilities in an era of global media culture.

Unmasking Metaphors of Visibility and Invisibility

Observing the institutional history of African American exclusion from both the metropolitan art world and the mainstream narrative of modernism, Michele Wallace rightly argued that:

> the problem remains the unilateral unwillingness of Euro-American culture to admit and acknowledge its debt, or even its relationship, to African and Afro-American culture. In fact, this problem—which lies at the heart of the problem of the visual in Afro-American culture—has such a long and convoluted history that its enunciation has become one of the telling features of Afro-American Modernism. One of the early practitioners of Afro-American literary Modernism, Ralph Ellison, even gave it a name: invisibility.[14]

While this insight is crucial to understanding the obstacles African American visual artists faced in the struggle for recognition, it is, however, only part of the story. For, as I have tried to indicate in this rapid round-trip from the twenties through the sixties, the expectations and demands voiced by African American critics also heightened the pressure on artists to be representative, placing them at odds with the idea of individual freedom of expression.

In this light, "the problem of the visual" was reinforced when the artwork was overshadowed by an emphasis on identity and exclusion driven by the demand for social recognition. The implicit hierarchy of the senses, which regarded the aural cultures of black music as original and distinctive at the same time that black visual arts were perceived as imitative or derivative, also diminished the aesthetic specificity of African American modernisms.

As Wallace observed, once we go back to Ralph Ellison's text, there is a key distinction between music and visuality, characterized by the dichotomy between positive and negative scenes of instruction. As a site of cross-cultural interaction that created the soundtrack to twentieth-century modernity, from ragtime, blues, and jazz to rock and hip-hop, music bears witness to the deep interinvolvement of African Americans and European Americans in creating uniquely modernist forms. In the aural domain of music, African American aesthetics are widely recognized and appreciated as universal values that, in terms of the recognition of cultural identity, created a space of autonomy in which black musicians have innovated and experimented freely.

So why, on the other hand, would the visual be the scene of negative instruction? Why is it that African American visual artists are often perceived through the lens of particularity as dependent or even imitative in contrast to the freedom of expression that European American artists have enjoyed? The answer, in part, lies in the crucial role of vision and visuality in establishing the very ideology of "race" as a matter of visible difference.

While numerous societies may be characterized by structures of racialism, ethnocentrism, and ethnic chauvinism, what distinguished the worldview that sought to rationalize racial slavery with Enlightenment sciences such as biology, anatomy, and genetics was the reliance of its optical and chromatic distinctions on the epistemological privilege of vision. Western modernity is, in a fundamental sense, inaugurated by the privilege of the visual. The Copernican revolution in the natural sciences ushered in empiricism and placed the eye at the center of the observable world. In painting, the rediscovery of linear perspective regarded the world as immediately accessible to rational knowledge through the transparent "window" to which visual representations aspired. While art's increasing prestige and autonomy reflected a vision-centered world, the profound paradox of Western modernity is that its power and wealth depended on the existence of others whose very humanity was denied by the color-coded optical and chromatic metaphors of a classical racism that made them invisible.

When Ellison wrote *Invisible Man,* his insights into the psychic and social worlds of African American identity resonated with those put forward by Frantz Fanon in *Black Skin, White Masks.* Published in 1952, both texts address what happens to human identity when the dialectic of mutual recognition is socially denied. For Ellison, when African humanity went unrecognized in American society, it created a condition of "invisibility" in which the all-too-visible difference of blackness was perceived within the supremacist imagination as the embodiment of its antithesis— whiteness needed the Other in order to know what it is not. For Fanon, the colonizer's fantasy of omnipotence meant that the colonized was also denied equal recognition. Fanon saw the colonizer, like the master in Hegel's master/slave dialectic, unable to acknowledge his dependence on the Other. In Fanon's view, the colonized, by turning from the object of his labor to the unfulfilled demand for recognition, became—unlike Hegel's slave—locked into a double bind in which he wore the mask of compliance that performed alterity.[15]

When Wallace underscores the unwillingness of the European American art world to acknowledge its indebted or interdependent relation to the African artifacts that inspired Picasso's cubist revolution, she reveals the enduring legacy of a worldview anchored by the privilege of vision. Whereas whiteness arrogates universality on account of an unmarked or anonymous existence that equates with a subject position of mastery, blackness is fixed into the field of vision as an object for the gaze. To the extent that the subject/object dichotomy has been historically aligned with the visible polarity of whiteness and blackness, one may speculate that black visual artists were denied freedom of expression because their difference fixed them on the side of the object that they were expected to depict or represent. In contrast to the subjective freedom enjoyed by musicians, visual artists were seen as representatives, expected to refute stereotypes, and to depict black cultural identity. Such imperatives arose from the overarching ideology of the visual that had equated whiteness with the control of the gaze and thus assigned blackness, qua other, to the side of the object.

I want to conclude with two points in this regard concerning the past and the future, respectively. Both entail rethinking the value and limitations of the modernist critique of "invisibility" that was predicated on political demands for cultural visibility as an emancipatory goal.

First, just as art historians have been unable to "see" the interactive "back and forth" that characterizes the dialogic forms of Afro-diaspora modernisms, art criticism has failed to grasp the iconography of the mask in diaspora aesthetics. The image of the African mask recurs, from the Harlem Renaissance through Bearden to Basquiat, as a constant and distinctive visual trope of the diasporic imagination. It signifies something profoundly important to the condition of double consciousness, for it is crucial to note that a mask always has two faces.

Where the outward face of black masking performs survival strategies that comply with social roles scripted by the stereotype, it does so in order to tame and appease the predatory force of the master gaze. The paranoid and narcissistic fantasies Fanon diagnosed under colonialism were active under supremacism, as both involved an anxious investment in the visual culture of the gaze. Looking relations were highly regulated under Jim Crow segregation, such that it was customary that blacks would avoid eye contact when addressing whites, and it was forbidden for black men to look at white women. Far from being securely centered in the world, the Other-directed dynamics of paranoid projection betrayed the psychic insecurities of whiteness, which could only be equated with mastery by virtue of the social violence at its disposal. Relatedly, narcissism conceals dependence on the other such that, when blacks were related to as objects of pity or fear, the black subject who often appeared to play along with such ascribed identity did so in order to ward off and abate the potential for violence. From minstrels and mammies to mau-mauing and woofing, the outward face of the mask performed otherness so as to ensure survival of black subjectivity and to create room for maneuver within the social asymmetry of power. But what was taking place on the other side of the mask?

To the extent that the inner face of the mask concerns its protective function, I would suggest that masking is a cultural form of central importance to the psychic life of the black diaspora because it seeks to hide and protect an inward relationship to Africa. What it protects is a contemplative or meditative space that allows spiritual and emotional reflection on the time and place left behind by the trauma and rupture that inaugurated diaspora.

When poet Countee Cullen asked, "What is Africa to me?" his question was not so much a problem in search of a solution but a riddle voicing his awareness of a potentially unanswerable enigma. To the extent that the catastrophic separation from one's origin or homeland engenders any diaspora's physical or metaphysical narratives of return, the visual iconography of the mask may be placed alongside broader cultural patterns of masking, such as the survivals and retentions of West and central African religious elements beneath the expressive forms of Afro-Christianity. Just as New World syncretic religions, such as candomblé in Brazil, vodun in Haiti, or Santeria in Cuba, masked and protected the worship of Yoruba deities behind the outward face of Catholic saints, the wide-ranging scholarship on the aesthetics of African diaspora spirituality calls for closer attention to the reworking of such mixed or hybrid cultural forms in the more secular domains of modernist music or art.[16]

Once we consider the enigmatic relationship to "home" that is preserved on the inward face of the mask, we may understand its deeply layered meanings as performing a protective function for diaspora subjectivity. Not only does the mask seek to protect the inner world from the social violence of supremacist ideology, it aims to conserve, through secrecy if necessary, a psychic or emotional space for open-ended contemplation wherein the enigmatic relationship to the unknown or unnamed ancestor may be nurtured as a source of growth and renewal. These speculative lines of inquiry open a fresh angle on the interpretation of masking in the visual cultures of the black diaspora. Clearly, it cannot be reduced to a mimetic or dependent relationship to dominant forms of European American visuality where masquerade tends to be associated not so much with the release of the soul into spirituality but with concealing the self from social identification.

Leaping from past to present, I want to suggest that a broader understanding of the importance to diaspora aesthetics of double-faced masking—Janus-like and ambivalent in its acceptance of contradiction as integral to the flow of human existence—helps us to grasp the highly contradictory condition of black "visibility" in contemporary culture. I would like to extrapolate here from the insights of media sociologist Herman Gray, whose observations on the rapid changes in black popular culture associated with media-driven globalization over the past decade cast the modernist demand for visibility in a critical light.

Taking account of the commercial success of hip-hop in the music industry, of black-themed cinema in Hollywood, and of the plethora of African American images on U.S. network television, Gray notes, "Given the level of saturation of the media with representations of blackness, the mediascape can no longer be characterized using terms such as invisibility. Rather, we might well describe ours as a moment of hyperblackness."[17] Far from implying a simple shift out of "invisibility" into hypervisibility, Gray encourages us to take stock of the massive economic, political, and social changes that have made the clear-cut boundaries addressed by Fanon or Ellison much more ambiguous in both the postcolonial context and in what could be called the post-civil-rights predicament in the African American context. Whereas the earlier modernist demand for public visibility implied a struggle for the full recognition of equal rights of entitlement to the claims of citizenship, it may be said that the structural shifts brought about by postmodernism have decoupled the underlying equations between visibility and empowerment. What led to this contradictory about-turn?

Even though media images of blackness are now more globally visible than ever before, we witness the deepening of racial inequalities in U.S. society as evidence of the structural decoupling of culture and politics. The signifying difference of the black vernacular now feeds into the global marketing of postmodern capitalism, from Nike and Coca-Cola to Benetton and Tommy Hilfiger; such heightened visibility appears to merely mask a growing sense of disenchantment and disillusionment with politics per se.

Gangsta rap's almost grotesque exaggerations of stereotypical alterity are highly indicative as cultural symptoms of this ambivalent shift. While images of unlimited wealth and luxury seem to parody capitalism's normative definitions of the good life, the excessive irony can barely conceal the rage that results from a pervasive sense of disappointment with the very idea of political engagement. As a generational emblem of this outlook, one might recall N.W.A.'s first music video when the group burst through a paper banner emblazoned with the words "I have a dream."

Under such changed social conditions it may be said that the visible signifiers of blackness have become detached from their referents in social reality. "Hyperblackness" in this sense concerns the proliferation of black representations that primarily refer to other representations. This process is characterized by an escalating reflexivity generating excessive parody and irony, as well as diminishing emphasis on the referential dimension in which blackness was once held to stand for, or represent, clear-cut ethical and political commitments. Whereas Gray's observations align "hyperblackness" with the broader dilemma of the hyperreal under postmodernism—in which media simulacra of reality appear more real than reality itself—I would regard the "hyper" as a form of hyperbole in which performative and rhetorical excess and exaggeration mask the decoupling of black culture and politics. "Too black, too strong" was a slogan often heard in the early nineties; like the strident voices heard in gangsta rap or the defiant imagery associated with black cinema after Spike Lee, the hyperbolic tone seems to suggest uncompromising resistance. But does the very loudness of such hyperbole not merely mask and mute an increasing sense of a loss of direction within the black body politic? To the extent that the post-civil-rights era entails sharpened polarities *within* black society—between an expanded middle class struggling to coexist with a growing underclass, for example—the antagonistic and exclusionary boundaries once anchored by the chromatic distinctions of race are no longer so clearcut. It may be said that it is precisely this postmodern condition of radical uncertainty that is evaded by performative hyperbole.

During late modernism, cultural forms encoded political desires that were blocked from official channels of representation. The increasing disenchantment with the belief that politics can deliver significant social change has led to a compromise formation of cultural substitutionism whereby the increasing quantity of media images are held to have satisfied the demand for public visibility. What was at stake in the very meaning of visibility as a desirable and emancipatory goal of collective empowerment has been profoundly altered under contemporary conditions of hyperblackness; the ethics of commitment has given way to the seductions of consumption. As a provocation to further inquiry I want to suggest that hyperblackness amounts to a form of global branding in which the signifying difference of vernacular culture produces an instantly recognizable cultural identity. Given this, hyperblackness would not be able to survive in the marketplace were it not for the presence of white consumers. Perhaps hyperblackness has merely updated the masquerade of performing alterity. When so-called "Generation Xers" are happy to embrace such hyperbolic expressions of blackness—in gangsta rap, club culture, or designer-label clothing—we find that, rather than a more open-ended or honest acknowledgement of the interdependence in which our cultural identities unfold, we are beholden to the most recent twist in a long-standing story: the interaction of African and European elements in American culture is thoroughly mediated and shot through with intransitive fantasies of otherness. If fantasy prevents the recognition of another's subjectivity and ethical autonomy, perhaps the interrogative space of the arts— whether literary, musical, or visual—allows room for a questioning outlook otherwise off-limits in a globally saturated media culture. In light of the wide-ranging journey into the diaspora's cultural history undertaken here, the search for alternatives to, and exit points from, contemporary dilemmas requires a deeper understanding of the complexity of the spaces through which blackness has traveled so far.

NOTES

1. Michele Wallace, "Modernism, Post-modernism, and the Problem of the Visual in Afro-American Culture," in *Out There: Marginalization and Contemporary Culture,* ed. Russell Ferguson, Martha Gever, Trin T. Minh-ha, and Cornel West (New York: New Museum of Contemporary Art; Cambridge: MIT Press, 1990).

2. James Clifford, "Traveling Cultures," in *Cultural Studies,* ed. Lawrence Grossberg, Cary Nelson, and Paula Trichler (New York: Routledge, 1992). See also James Clifford, *Routes: Travel and Translation in the Late Twentieth Century* (Cambridge: Harvard University Press, 1997).

3. Yinka Shonibare, cited in Kobena Mercer, "Art That Is Ethnic in Inverted Commas," *frieze* 25 (November–December 1995): 40.

4. Yinka Shonibare, "Fabric and the Irony of Authenticity," in *Mixed Belongings and Unspecified Destinations: INIVA Annotations 1,* ed. Nikos Paperstergiadis (London: Institute of International Visual Arts, 1996), 40.

5. Ike Ude, "Artist's Statement," in *In/Sight: African Photographers, 1940 to the Present,* ed. Clare Bell, Okwui Enwezor, Olu Oguibe, and Octavio Zaya (New York: Guggenheim Museum, distributed by H. N. Abrams, 1996), 296.

6. Paul Gilroy, "Wearing Your Art on Your Sleeve: Notes towards a Diaspora

History of Black Ephemera," in *Small Acts: Thoughts on the Politics of Black Cultures* (London: Serpents Tail, 1993).

7. See the chapter entitled "Black Hair/Style Politics" in Kobena Mercer, *Welcome to the Jungle: New Positions in Black Cultural Studies* (New York: Routledge, 1994).

8. Manthia Diawara, "Afro-Kitsch," in *Black Popular Culture,* ed. Michele Wallace (Seattle: Bay Press/Dia Center for the Arts, 1992).

9. Ralph Ellison, "The Art of Romare Bearden," in *Going to the Territory* (New York: Random House, 1986).

10. Henry Louis Gates, Jr., *The Signifying Monkey: A Theory of Afro American Literary Criticism* (New York: Oxford University Press, 1988).

11. Albert Boime, *The Art of Exclusion: Representing Blacks in the Nineteenth Century* (London: Thames and Hudson, 1990).

12. W. E. B. DuBois, "Criteria of Negro Art," in *Selections from "The Crisis"* (New York: Kraus-Thompson, 1983), 444–50; Alain Locke, "The Legacy of the Ancestral Arts," in *The New Negro: An Interpretation* (New York: Atheneum, 1983), 266–67.

13. Larry Neale, "The Black Arts Movement," and Amiri Baraka, "The Changing Same (R&B and New Black Music)," in *The Black Aesthetic,* ed. Addison Gayle (New York: Doubleday, 1971).

14. Wallace, "Modernism," 43.

15. Ralph Ellison, *Invisible Man* (New York: Random House, 1952); Frantz Fanon, *Black Skin, White Masks,* trans. Charles Lam Markmann (New York: Grove Press, 1967).

16. Robert Farris Thompson, *Flash of the Spirit: African and Afro-American Art and Philosophy* (New York: Vintage, 1983); Theophus Smith, *Conjuring Culture: Biblical Formations of Afro-America* (New York: Oxford University Press, 1994).

17. Herman Gray, *Watching Race: Television and the Struggle for Blackness* (Minneapolis: University of Minnesota, 1995), 230.

TIM'M T. WEST

Keepin' It Real
Disidentification and Its Discontents

You and me, what does that mean?
Always, what does that mean?
Forever, what does that mean?
It means we'll manage, I'll master your language,
and in the meantime, I'll create my own.
    —Tricky, *Pre-millennium Tension*

[I]n the diverse invitations to suspend artistic experimentation, there is an identical call for order, a desire for unity, for
identity, for security, or popularity (in the sense of "finding a
public"). Artists and writers must be brought back into the
bosom of the community, or at least, if the latter is considered
to be ill, they must be assigned the task of healing it.
    —Jean-François Lyotard, *The Postmodern Condition*

Disidentification's Discontents

The Bay Area rap group Deep Dickollective[1] (of which I am a founding
member) came together with buckets on which to bang, a piano, freestyle
rhymes, and the daunting task of consoling a friend's post-HIV crisis. I
was that friend in crisis. Dis/ease with hip-hop is not so figurative these
days. It is the performance I enact each time I step on the stage and check
the mic; it is the vantage point through which I theorize my movements in
hip-hop culture as a black gay-identified man.

    The burgeoning hip-hop subculture called "homo hop" is the inevitable
outgrowth of a tension between hip-hop's greatest taboo and the figurative
dis/ease experienced by its "homiesexual" disciples. Homo hop has an origin narrative of its own: romantic and revolutionary, just like the origin

narrative of hip-hop, the global and cultural movement out of which it was born. Some will come to say that the momentous year was 1999. D/DC was founded on beats, rhymes, and the dis/ease of a gay black man moved to self-treatment: making hip-hop music with his "niggaz." As black queer men we came together having accepted the idea that there are few "safe" spaces in which to live, and therefore, claiming all space as salvageable for whichever ways it supports our breathing. During that first freestyle and spoken word session "check the breath" became a mantra not only marking our testimony to life beyond dis/ease, but also a declaration that hip-hop would be our most viable pulpit for broadcasting resurrection.

The notion of revival connotes the spiritual proselytizing inherent in black gospel tradition, but at the turn of the twenty-first century, it was accompanied by break-beats and a beat-box. This time the "faggots" are not the silent choir members, deacons, or ushers assuming a compulsory silence after a pastor's rebuke of Sodom. This time we would be the ones "mic checking." In hip-hop the person who "mic checks" tests the viability of the medium for communication. Nothing is voiced until the microphone is checked. Some will come to say that gay hip-hop terrorists began seizing control over microphones in this new millennium. Others will praise us for doing so. What is certain is D/DC's focus on empowerment and agency—not obsession with marginalization or complaints without action—has ultimately spawned an empowered and visible community that has been referenced everywhere from the *New York Times* to *Newsweek*.

For members of my rap group, D/DC, there was no way around the hip-hop culture that had been so central to our rites of passage into black manhood in America. The insults in hip-hop music, uncomfortable and badgering to our gay identities as they have been, either become the tropes that make us cringe at every other refrain, or the thing we merely manage or tolerate—finding neither identification nor counteridentification with hip-hop culture. This tension, this in-betweenness mediating identification (e.g., assimilation) and counteridentification (e.g., defiance), is what José Muñoz calls *disidentification*. The disidentifying subject necessarily mediates an unhappy attachment to something often inextricable to his or her very sense of self. The queer's relationship to hip-hop reflects increasing grounds for divorce, even when there is love enough to justify "till death do us part." Like the ironic failure of some of our most liberal states to honor same-sex marriage in 2004, the inextricable bond between the "homiesexual" and his or her hip-hop muse reflects a desire for some-

Fig. 1. Deep Dickollective. *Left to right:* Jeree Brown (JB RapItUp), Tim'm T. West (25Percenter), and Juba Kalamka (Pointfivefag). (Photo: Ayanna M. U'Dongo/Phireye Media.)

thing foreclosed and perhaps more treasured as a result. It is the ironic double bind of saying this marriage isn't working, because one so desperately wants it to work. It is queer rappers defending hip-hop to gay activists who fail to see its complexity as art offering an array of social messages, many of them homophobic, but many not.

In the introduction to his book *Disidentifications: Queers of Color and the Performance of Politics,*[2] Muñoz takes off from Michael Pêcheux's theorization of the "good subject/bad subject" dichotomy in order to explain that disidentification is neither the enjoyment of nor the betrayal by majoritarian ideology. In Muñoz's summarization of Pêcheux's view, it is not as simple as the "good" subject identifying with the dominant ideology and the "bad subject" counteridentifying with it. There exists for Muñoz a third modality for mediating this tension.

Disidentification is the third mode of dealing with dominant ideology, one that neither opts to assimilate within such a structure nor strictly oppose it; rather, disidentification is a strategy that works on and against dominant ideology.[3]

An opportunity for gays in hip-hop culture opposed to the dichotomous "hate hip-hop, or love it and hate yourself," this third modality of disidentification is the gay rapper's partial assimilation of hip-hop ideology while she or he simultaneously works to *deconstruct* it. The gay subject in hip-hop does not seek to *destroy* hip-hop, as she or he relies upon it as part of his or her fundamental self-definition (e.g., B-boy, emcee, deejay, etc.). Disidentification is hip-hop music as it flows in the very veins of New York City gay rapper Cashun,[4] who has enough dignity as a gay man to challenge the homophobia of a fundamental aspect of the culture in which he evolved, and yet who is one of its responsible and loyal disciples. Muñoz says of this strategy:

> Identifying with an object, person, lifestyle, history, political ideology, religious orientation, and so on, means also simultaneously and partially counteridentifying, as well as only partially identifying . . . [Disidentification] resists an unproductive turn toward good dog/bad dog criticism and instead leads to an identification that is both mediated and immediate, a disidentification that enables politics.[5]

Black gay folk who live at the intersection of various hegemonies often find this practice of disidentification more seductive and enabling than majority subjects. Even in black (and presumed heterosexual) or gay (and majority white) contexts, black queer subjects find that having a more tentative identification with larger groups is a more enabling and liberatory strategy for survival than those people who have everything to gain by identifying with more dominant ideologies.

Black queer rappers like Hanifah Walidah[6] hold the double-edged sword that has potential to both wound and defend them. Their disidentificatory relationship with hip-hop—the practice of "making do" with a cultural medium that has been so central to their formation as black folk in America—is about the decision to manage dis/ease rather than live as invisible men and women and deny themselves the medium that most clearly brings them into view.

In 1999, faced with the news about a drop in my T cells and the anticipated harmful side-effects of life-saving toxins, I could have either chosen to die or struggle to live inside dis/ease. It is the analogous relationship between my dis/eased body and disidentification with hip-hop that I wish to explore in this essay. "Keepin' it Real," being true to oneself, is the colloquial point of reference for an analysis of how black queer bodies assimilate and deconstruct the choice medium for their creative expression. For D/DC, "checking the breath" signifies an allegiance to the metonymic microphone that will give voice to our experiences as both black men and queer men. "Checking the breath" also denotes that if we are to "keep it real" then we must "check" hip-hop culture for its hypocritical marginalization and degradation of its queer sons and daughters.

Between Rocks and Hard Places: The Search for Community

I utilize the two epigraphs in this essay to illustrate the tension between the stability one desires in a shifting and turbulent culture and the simultaneous enjoyment one finds in ambivalence—in a noncommittal allegiance to the idea of stability. Without delving deeply into how this mediation or tension is a marker of our postmodernity, I think that both Tricky and Jean-François Lyotard offer statements that explicate the dis/ease, the disidentification, and tension I will explore throughout this essay. Tricky questions essential conceptual frameworks (e.g., Always, Forever, You and Me), only to conclude that mediating the dependence on such terms, and their very interrogation, requires a new language. Gay rappers disidentifying with the heteronormative conditions of the hip-hop nation must often employ the very premises intended to badger them.

Deep Dickollective recontextualizes the popular "conscious" rapper Common's infamous gay-diss "In a circle of faggots, your name is mentioned" (from the album *Like Water for Chocolate*) such that it reappears as a badge of honor for "homiesexual" rappers. Recontextualized, the fag becomes not the butt of the joke, but rather the praiseworthy topic of conversation among his peers, his fellow "faggots." Interestingly, in Common's album following his fag disses, the fag morphs into his best friend, who in 2003 is receiving the sympathy and understanding of a man who has outgrown his homophobia. In hip-hop, tension often is the impetus for change. Perhaps not so surprisingly, many hip-hop headz relish Common's older material, preferring the homophobic battle-rhyming B-boy to the self-aware ex-homophobe renouncing his ignorance.

"Premillennium tension" is, as Tricky might argue, expressed in other plays on hip-hop lingo as well. It is moving beyond the intention of language to uncover new meanings. In one issue of the popular magazine *Hip Hop Connection*, London-based deejay Mister Maker, founder of the international hip-hop site gayhiphop.com, relays an instance in which assimilating the terms of his objectification becomes the tool for both self-affirmation and a counter-diss to his homo hop haterz:

> I know some rappers who are "out" and it's for this reason they don't get anywhere with regards to recording and club spots. There is a deep-seated prejudice in our society that gay artists have to deal with. It's funny because I've played clubs and totally rocked the spot, and I wonder to myself would some of these people still be happy knowing that they are listening to a gay Hip Hop deejay? However, I have a good battle routine for people who know I'm gay and think faggot samples are funny. I use Cage's verse "Can you guess who the faggot deejay is?" Most people think I'm fooling until I scratch in the Simon Harris cut "It's me."[7]

While Tricky contemplates personal resistance to the discursive ideologies given, Lyotard discusses disidentification on the macrolevel, a significant topic since most of this essay will ponder the hip-hop *nation*. Although the homiesexual plays with language and experiments with the terms made available to him by the larger culture, he still seeks some sense of unity or community. Even the enjoyment in disidentificatory practices by gay rappers is met with the drive for something analogous to the unification inherent to nation building. There is no enjoyment in the misery of hip-hop's gay bashing by homiesexuals without spaces in which to share the feelings. In the case of homo hop, yes misery loves company . . . but is working to strategize a come-back.

This come-back, however, assimilates the character of its enemy in an ironic way. Gay hip-hop artists, in vast and increasing numbers in 2004, now debate with each other about who is *best* "keepin' it real" or "representin'" as a gay rap artist. It should be a surprise to no one that there are queers even at the margins of the gay hip-hop movement. How does the building of a new hip-hop nation—one challenging the sexism and homophobia that has become so synonymous with mainstream rap music—avoid the same hegemonic policing that has kept gays marginalized for so long? Where the desire for free creative expression (an essential element of hip-hop's origins) and the boundaries created to keep the mic and breath "in check" collide, there is no easy answer; there are uncomfortable contradictions, and "making do" is often the best one can do with the tools given.

Is It Really Real, Though? A Nation without Borders

Does it make sense to refer to a hip-hop nation? The task of nation building is clearer when the focal point is the nation-state—an entity defined by geographical, ethnic, cultural, or linguistic borders. But shift retrospectively to the year 1999 and the term *nation* (as challenging a term as it is to define) and bear witness to a generation of young people who are self-proclaimed members of the hip-hop nation. These are B-boys who break dance, graffiti artists who "tag" with urgency before their disappearance into the night, and deejays who reassert the musical past into our present through their mixing and scratching. Hip-hop's origin in New York City among black and Latino youth was Ralph Ellison's invisible man wailing for recognition over a four-by-four dub beat. These men were setting the record *straight* that they are not invisible men. If invisibility marks an emasculated space where men are powerless, then visibility marks a declarative Yes to the question: are we not men? However, given the burden of invisibility, the struggle to voice black manhood, there is no tolerance for the black sissy.

Youth in hip-hop culture today are much more diverse in their ethnic backgrounds and sex, but still negotiate their identities in a culture where the act of verifying one's "realness" compels an especially heteronormative gendered performance. The demands today as hip-hop culture diversifies is that black youth "represent" and "keep it real." These are slogans indexing the increasing anxiety around authenticity as white boys and women and everybody else struggles for a taste of the American pie that is our hip-hop culture. But is the real ever really "real"? The slogan "keep it real" itself articulates angst around the authenticity and stability of the real. The real must be perpetually managed and kept in check by those who want to secure hip-hop's connection to "straight" black and Latino men who started hip-hop. But the straightness of the men in early hip-hop is questionable—though those vested with the authority to control hip-hop's image would prefer that none of us believe this. One's approximation to "realness" (figuratively speaking) has less to do with which men get to call the shots than whether some individuals are given a gun. When the ability or failure to "keep it real" determines one's access or exile from the hip-hop nation, expect the kind of angst it has experienced going into the twenty-first century. Also expect that so much of the angst in the hip-hop nation around "realness" and authenticity would be regulated through gender performances.

The relationship between regulated gender performances and concepts of the hip-hop nation are mediated through popular slogans. Among them is the demand that hip-hop patriots "keep it real." As black youth in the United States emerge in the new millennium, how might scholars who study youth culture and performance account for the increasing proliferation and value accorded to the slogan "keepin' it real"? Paradoxically, "keepin' it real" is one's authentication of allegiance to a norm that seems to struggle against itself; realness is never proven once and for all, but must be compulsively reconfirmed. Angst around authenticity exists because, ironically, the illusion of permanence must be stabilized over and again. Similar to the ways in which African-ness has often operated as an authenticating sign of blackness, "realness" becomes a crucial marker among black youth who embrace a hip-hop aesthetic. A discursive trope among youth in hip-hop culture, "keepin' it real" not only signifies a set of codes (performative and discursive) that authenticate one's identification with urban black culture, but also indicates that both the black nation and the hip-hop nation have similar processes through which its people are produced.

In *Race, Nation, Class: Ambiguous Identities* Étienne Balibar says:

> The fundamental problem is therefore to produce the people. More exactly, it is to make the people produce itself continually as a national community. Or again, it is to produce the effect of unity by virtue of which people will appear, in everyone's eyes, as a people, that is, as the basis and origin of political power.[8]

This "problem" explains the performative unity that the hip-hop nation must perpetually reenact to ensure its stability. Through performative and discursive codes, youth in America and around the globe are interpellated as citizens of the nation through their appropriation of hip-hop lingo, styles of dress, cultural, and political sensibilities.

Some of the most significant discourses on the subject of blackness now occur through hip-hop music and culture. Given its origins and its prominence in the black cultural landscape, it is clear that hip-hop provides an imperative lens through which to examine blackness at the turn of the twenty-first century. Considering the rigid policing of gender that occurs in most instances of nation building, what connections might scholars draw between the cultural production of "straightness" and the stability of the hip-hop nation? Specifically, how have the regulative practices of a heteronormative hip-hop nation affected its queer constituency?

As hip-hop culture has been compelled to shift in order to give expression to women and nonblacks, it is interesting that the homosexual becomes a figure indicating the proverbial death of hip-hop. The rallying call for "real" hip-hop patriots to "stand up"9 for hip-hop articulates an angst in hip-hop culture around authenticity. This rally attempts to resuscitate its origins as the politicized cry of urban underclass youth. The vast appropriations and evolutions in hip-hop over the past three decades are, necessarily, responses to the insular hopes to keep hip-hop music black people's music, to "keep it real." Because the music indexes a culture of protest—the metonymic battle cry of urban black young men—nonblacks, women, and queers are often viewed as trespassers diluting hip-hop's realness. In the opinion of many black nationalist hip-hoppers, feminism and queers can be blamed for the dilution of hip-hop's "real" elemental foundation. There are various dynamic examples of this slippage.

In 1999, Busta Rhymes dressed his hypermasculinity in skirts, silk pajamas, and Pippi Longstocking braided dreadlocks. Lauryn Hill rapped with a voice "harder" than many of her male counterparts. Missy "Misdemeanor" Elliott chanted a celebratory refrain "I'm a bitch" as if it were a black womyn's mantra. MeShell Ndegeocello crooned a blues song in a low and sexy timbre that aroused even straight-identified women. In 1999, RuPaul was not a real woman but looking as good as many, and Erykah Badu had a secret pre-Afrocentric past hidden underneath her headwrap. Responding to these eccentric expressions, hip-hop's Afrocentric nationalists were nostalgically starving for a time when girls were girls, boys were boys, and black folk could keep the lid on the gumbo that is our hip-hop nation.

Today there exists this tension between those who enjoy the shifting, erratic openness hip-hop is experiencing and those who like their gumbo traditional—without all the extra pizzazz and especially the sugar. The hip-hop nation senses its crisis, and the burden of proof for the hip-hop nation's security is encapsulated in the nation's mantra: "keepin' it real." Terrified that hip-hop will become a virtual beat into which anyone could break-dance, hip-hop's national guard becomes more watchful of its borders. Guarding one's territory is the duty and honor of every good soldier. Hip-hop's soldiers are those given voice over the airwaves, and hip-hop halls to continue the ministry. And if homiesexuals at the site "phatfamily.org" are noting what these ministers are saying, it's clear that there's no place for "faggots" when emcees break bread at the hip-hop table:

Though I can freak, fly, flow, fuck up a faggot
Don't understand their ways, I ain't down with gays.
    —Brand Nubian, from *Punks Jump Up To Get Beat Down*

She took her panties down and the bitch had a dick
I had to put the gat to his legs, all the way up his skirt
Cuz this is one faggot that I had to hurt.
    —Eazy-E, from *Nobody Move*

Man to man, I don't know how they did it
From what I know the parts don't fit (Aw shit!).
    —Public Enemy, from *Meet the G That Killed Me*[10]

Hip Hop Connection writer Nick Ellis notes this disdain for gays in hip-hop when he writes, "As a genre, Hip Hop has profited on being homophobic."[11] The soldiers keepin' it real have spoken, the battle lines have been clearly drawn, and the new millennium marks the last stand for hip-hop in the minds of those for whom homo hop is antithetical to the very fabric of hip-hop culture.

Perhaps the better question is not who is keepin' it real, but who gets to define realness. What discourses, which aesthetics come to predominate in attempts to reclaim an enduring "real" blackness? Indeed, the very interrogations around realness indicate that aspirations to exhibit "real" blackness are nothing more than the perpetual iterations of an impossible stability. That youth must *keep* it real underscores the instability of postmodern hip-hop aesthetics. "Realness" is always threatened by the inevitability of time and change, and therefore hip-hop enthusiasts must perpetually safeguard the limits of tolerance. Each moment there is some new attempt to authenticate a new standard of "real" black heteronorma- tivity, to expose fakes: endless numbers of persons who do not portray "the real" in the right way. The problem is that the right way usually translates into the "straight and narrow" way; and with the *turn* of the century, the anxiety in the hip-hop nation about authenticity is understandable.

Premillennium Tension in the Hip-Hop Nation

Is anything "real" in hip-hop anymore? Perhaps nothing has ever been real. A postmodern hip-hop aesthetics is Jameson's notion of nostalgia without memory that manifests when a deejay samples an oldie outside of his or her experiential frame of reference. It is the ironic subversive poten- tiality of anticapitalist lyrics proliferating across MTV or going triple plat- inum; it is the suspicion of a gay rapper, more "hardcore" than all others, his same-sex desire guised under a performative cloak of hypermasculin- ity. Going into the new millennium, it is not uncommon to see a white boy with dreadlocks or a black woman with an Afrocentric headwrap and blue contact lenses to match. Lauryn Hill's video for "That Thing" juxtaposes a sixties and premillennium bohemian black aesthetic; the song itself is a blending of doo-wop and a deejay scratch. Musically, a postmodern hip- hop aesthetics might be thought of as the diasporic fusion of soul genres that have fashioned the hip-hop-influenced "trip-hop" music or "jungle" music.

Premillennium tension is Tricky—the Afro-Brit godfather of trip-hop venting a southern blues guitar sample with techo-industrial clamor at his New Jersey studio. It is black "girls in the hood" referring to his "Vent" as "white-boy music." The implication is that Tricky is not "keepin' it real." The conflation of his music with whiteness serves to blackball him as a race traitor—one who is not in the service of promoting the agenda of the hip- hop nation. The cultural gatekeepers are not necessarily hip-hop artists who are anxious about infiltration, but any enthusiast who is interested in transferring racial, sexual, or gender anxiety onto the hip-hop landscape. It is easier to point a finger at hip-hop for its unique brand of intolerance for gays. Much more difficult is tackling the overarching homophobic cul- ture grounding the seeds in which fear and intolerance grow. In this new millennium there seems to be a final call to resuscitate the hip-hop nation's agenda. Which is what? one might ask. And therein lies the problem. There has never been an agenda—just bodies with power and patriarchy and a big stick: hip-hop police who will protect and serve their nation.

I have suggested that the anxiety around realness in hip-hop is clearly related to the angst around black authenticity. The instability around black authenticity being so dynamic in the current environment, youth have an almost infinite range of ways they can express their blackness. There is the juxtaposition of a feminist Afro-matriarch aesthetic of Lauryn Hill or Erykah Badu to the high-fashion Jezebel seductress image of a Lil' Kim or Foxy Brown. There is the bohemian nationalistic strain of Blackstar or The Roots that can be juxtaposed to the gangsta thug aesthetic of the late Tupac Shakur or a flashy producer/entrepreneur like Puff Daddy. But even these juxtapositions—ones that appear to assign a politicized consciousness around race and gender to natural hairstyles and conscious lyricism, while critiquing the latter for glamorizing the excesses of capitalism—represent a communal angst around authenticity in the hip-hop nation. It is an anxiety that leads to the rigid policing of identity. On BET, MTV, and every urban radio station the most visible and vocal rap representatives articulate this apprehension to the masses in their rebuke against "punks" and "sissies." That these kinds of slurs against gays inundate the airwaves without public censure is evidence enough that "keepin' it real" is keeping the facts *straight*. Hip-hop history relies on the reiteration of a particular origin narrative in which "gay niggaz" like Deep Dickollective do not exist.

In the new millennium, as the range of African diasporic personalities explode the more stubborn boundaries of a seventies Black Arts movement or an eighties new black aesthetics, there is a deep sense of loss for that which can never be recovered—a melancholia for authentic blackness that stubbornly recommends nostalgia as a cure. Black youth today are dreadlocking Afrocentrists, high-fashion mafia mimics, self-proclaimed "bitches" and "niggas," "homiesexuals," and everything in between. "Keepin' it real" represents the clash between anti-identity multiculturalists who check "other" or "all" on ethnicity questionnaires and wannabe Black Panthers born twenty years too late. I sometimes find myself between these dichotomies struggling for the breath to voice both my marginality and investment in hip-hop culture. It is this disidentificatory space that is indicative of what I've called premillennium tension. The current generation of hip-hop enthusiasts is the first to shatter hip-hop's narcissistic delusion with its presumed straight reflection.

Public Enemy front man Chuck D. refers regularly to the "hip-hop nation" of which he is an integral member; and in the year 2000 a museum curated the exhibition "Hip Hop Nation" at San Francisco's Yerba Buena Center for the Arts. A scholar of cultural theory who is thoroughly interested in the policing of "national" boundaries, I wish to draw a few parallels between how gender is managed in more finite nation-states and the more loosely constituted "community" of people unified by their relationship to hip-hop music and culture. The point here is hardly to give verity to the notion that hip-hop enthusiasts have a nationality, but rather to emphasize that the same heteronormative and sexist practices at work in the hip-hop nation are active as well in most nation-states. The regulatory policing of gender continues to delimit which bodies in the nation are "real" citizens of the nation and exiles those not "keepin' it real."

About the historical relationship between the nation and its female subjects, Anne McClintock, in her provocative text *Imperial Leather: Race, Gender, and Sexuality in the Colonial Contest,* writes:

> All nations depend on powerful constructions of gender. Despite many nationalists' ideological investment in the idea of popular unity, nations have historically amounted to the sanctioned institutionalization of gender difference. No nation in the world gives women and men the same access to rights and resources of the nation-state.[12]

If we examine the marginalization of female bodies in early hip-hop alongside the courageous entry of the women who dared to rap, deejay, and break-dance, we might notice a relationship between the visibility of women in the nation and their foreshadowing of sexually diverse members also seeking recognition, representation, and a share in the power to define the nation, even when this share in power is not equal.

Imagined Communities, Real Communities

Hip-hop artist Lauryn Hill popularized a sentiment that "Everything is Everything" and that "what is meant to be will be." One response to such deterministic ambivalence has been a vehement nostalgia for a time when there was more simplicity and certainty about what was constitutive of black identity. While the unity and stability of either blackness or hip-hop realness are largely imagined and illusory, there is a commitment by those concerned with the health of the nation to keep its national citizens in check. The politics of policing are therefore enacted and reinforced not just by national authorities but by citizens as well.[13] The irony of such cultural policing in the hip-hop is that its "people" have never been as unified as the nostalgic imagination sometimes projects. Such is the case with most nation-states as well. There is the reactionary unification when a "threat" is posed to the nation. In the case of hip-hop, many have mobilized on the basis of their fear of infiltration by white boys or women or faggots who do not belong there. Often, clarity around the constitution of the nation or community, imagined as their unity can sometimes be, is strengthened by the threat posed by perceived outsiders. Interestingly, people sometimes find it easier to say what they are not, than to clearly state what they are.

In *Imagined Communities,* Benedict Anderson suggests that the nation is imagined "because the members of even the smallest nation will never know most of their fellow-members, meet them, or even hear of them, yet in the minds of each lives the image of their communion."[14] This illusory communion or unity is a concept often seized upon by scholars who are in the practice of deconstructing and destabilizing hegemonies. Still, the flip side of such interrogations is often the lazy dismissal of the very "real" effect that gender policing has on women and queer people in the "nation." In fact, nation building is often predicated on the notion that its citizens reproduce the ideas of heteronormativity and patriarchy crucial to its development.

White rapper Necro, in a *Hip Hop Connection* article in which he appears with machete in hand, sunglasses, and a scarf over his mouth, protests: "Who the fuck wants to hear a fag rap? It's bad enough these straight rappers sound like they're gay; do we really need real gay motherfuckers on the mic. That shit is wack."[15] The queer who challenges Necro's patriarchy might be considered a national threat and therefore rendered insubordinate or might be altogether ignored. Perceived to be an internal enemy to the national project, gay rappers are relegated to the underground and margins. White rappers like Necro might be hip-hop's most fervent antigay ministers, as his "diss" of gay rap not only fulfills the representation of hip-hop as straight boy music, but also placates the "real *Negro*" who would otherwise challenge white-boy "realness."

I have suggested that while the nation might be "imagined" or "illusory," its effects are very real. People are exiled, ostracized, marginalized, and put to death because of *difference,* even (or perhaps, especially) in the imagined communities. Quite often invisibility, displacement, and expulsion are the impetus for emerging nationalisms, neonationalisms, counternationalisms. These are imagined communities born out of struggle and resistance to nationalist hegemony. They are self-proclaimed "homiesexuals" and "rap faggots" who in name, and in their celebratory reappropriation of hateful slurs, both redefine and shift the predominant culture and create their own illusory repository for free expression.[16] Taking a second look at the work of José Muñoz, we see how marginal space can become a generative and lucrative space for the creation of communities provoked by their struggle for representation. In "Performing Disidentifications," Muñoz writes that "performance permits the spectator, often a queer who has been locked out of the halls of representation or rendered a static caricature there, to imagine a world where queer lives, politics, and possibilities are representable in their complexity."[17]

Queer rap artists are engaged in the simultaneous process of expanding the boundaries of hip-hop imagination and fashioning a community of their own. Expulsion from the hip-hop nation becomes a mixed blessing, the space of marginality a lucrative opportunity for not only inventive political praxis, but new communities unified by their love for hip-hop culture and their refusal to be denied identification with the music. But is it counterproductive or hypocritical to critique the policing of gender inside of communities and simultaneously celebrate the formation (and sustained energy) of a women's or queer hip-hop community? I hope to illuminate, through narratives about the hip-hop nation and its discontents, this elemental paradox.

Hip-hop scholar Tricia Rose depicts hip-hop as a space where youth are able to vent their marginality in an American culture where race and class oppression is elemental to the nation's development and prosperity. But if hip-hop is summarized as a cultural resistance to white American hegemony, then policing is how its enthusiasts attempt to insulate its "realness." Yet while the counterhegemonic cry of black urban youth is celebrated, there is very little interrogation of hip-hop's own oppressive hegemony. In her groundbreaking text, *Black Noise: Rap Music and Black Culture in Contemporary America*, Rose states:

> Rap's stories continue to articulate the shifting terms of black marginality in contemporary American culture. Even as they struggle with the tension between fame and rap's gravitational pull toward local urban narratives, for the most part, rappers continue to craft stories that rep-

resent the creative fantasies, perspectives, and experiences of racial marginality in America.[18]

But those bodies at the margins of the margins have their own battle cry. There is a way in which forms of nationalism born out of oppression fail to recognize their own capacity to oppress. I have said that the "opening up" of national boundaries is often perceived as a threat to national stability. In hip-hop, the multidimensionality of identity must be reducible to blackness and blackness alone (read: male and heterosexual), and other agendas are seen as threats to the utopian illusion of unanimity and sovereignty.

How do communities and nations—which by the account of scholars like Benedict Anderson are illusory and highly contingent states of unity— sustain themselves if not through a rigid policing of gendered bodies? Such a question hints of the "inescapable hegemony" that I have struggled with when theorizing gender and nationalism. Is it just a matter of choosing a kinder, gentler hegemony? Can one who claims to be counterhegemonic ever embrace an imagined community and not also embrace the related policing that is essential for its self-definition? Is counterhegemonic discourse itself illusory?

Even as the foundation of many forms of nationalisms is necessarily unstable, what remains consistent between communities and nations is the ongoing tension between those vested with the power to speak and those who not only challenge the people in power but who do so by adapting the very popular discourses that communicate national consciousness. Clearly the patriarchs maintain the luxury and power not only to remain seduced by the illusion of their hegemony, but also to affect people and policy through their illusion. However, those on the margins are by no means immobilized by the powers that be. If anything, they imagine their own communities and the potentialities for the representation of their "real."

Forced Entries, Ironic Identifications

In *Imagined Communities,* Benedict Anderson seizes upon the simultaneity of citizens reading the morning paper as a metonym for an imagined sense of national unity that might otherwise be referred to as a nation. Though the imagination and popular media are conduits for the imagined sense of community to which Anderson refers, he does not undermine the very real political, social, and economic effects of even the most vivid imaginations. Empires rise and fall invested in the illusion of not only a shared constituency, but also a shared set of complementary beliefs. Consider that in 1999 the premillennium tension I have referenced describes the bubbling over of an unchecked and uncensored proliferation of identities once thought external to the hip-hop empire. As the water is on the verge of boiling over, enter Eminem.

Imagine that around the United States the hip-hop anthem is the repetitious "My name is . . ." song that became not only the introduction of Eminem (Slim Shady) but a space where hip-hop realness was being exploited by a white body—and accepted as such. Eminem, unlike many of his white predecessors in hip-hop, was a talented and skilled emcee who hailed Detroit as his authenticating "hood." His rise from poor white inner-city kid to stardom has much to do with the empathetic sensibility of an urban underclass able to overlook race as long as the white subject is keeping his real "real." To boot, Eminem is led by an entourage of successful black rappers and producers who confirm that he is the "real" Slim Shady (e.g., Dr. Dre, formally of Niggas With Attitude). His expanded affiliation with 50 Cent and D12 are ongoing testaments to his associative authentication. The extension of "realness" to nonblacks reflects the very openness that excited me about hip-hop as a teenager in the 1980s. Seeing the Beastie Boys and 3rd Base, I felt that there was some possibility that hip-hop would open up enough to accept my sexual difference. I had failed to consider that where either straightness or blackness stands trial before the hip-hop jury, straightness is the enduring quality that will never be compromised.

Russell Potter in his essay "L'Objet X: Performing Race" points to what Michael Eric Dyson calls the "anxiety of authenticity." This anxiety is heightened when the subjects entering hip-hop "realness" are not black. Problematizing the parodic appropriations of "blackness" by artists like Eminem, Potter says:

> This [appropriation of blackness] reflects a sort of perverse romanticization of the racialized "Other," even as (and perhaps in part because) that Other is daily demonized via the media spectacle of the young, drug-dealing, gat-packing black male.[19]

This demonized black male who we witness on television screens on glamorized shows like *Cops* and (ironically) HBO's Hollywood prison show *OZ* is never a homosexual. In fact, he hates homosexuals. Like the explosive dialogue about down-low behavior among black men who have sex with men but identify as straight, the self-hating homosexual proves that a man is not necessarily what he does. The rupture between behavior and self-identification overstates the abjectification of same-sex relationships, particularly among men of color in homosocial hip-hop contexts.

It is not so ironic that the "My name is . . ." song that stormed the airwaves also boasts the cruelty and degradation of a "fag" teacher. Is this brand of fag-dissin fundamental to "real" hip-hop? Perhaps Slim Shady is just an inner-city kid venting his marginality, right? Keepin' it real in the hip-hop nation is authenticated through not only one's sexual prowess and masculinity, but often through the degradation of women and especially "fags." While many women have been able to penetrate and influence hip-hop, the worst insult in hip-hop banter is to call an emcee or rapper a "fag"; and even women sharing their responsibility of keeping the hip-hop nation "real" exhaust this insult. In one of the few challenges to heterosexism in *Black Noise,* Tricia Rose notes:

> In a number of raps by women, men who are being insulted are referred to as "fruity" or "punks," hinting at their possible homosexuality as a way to emasculate them. This sort of homophobia affirms oppressive standards of heterosexual masculinity and problematizes a simplistic reading of female rappers' sexual narratives.[20]

That the gender police in the hip-hop nation are not just its patriarchs but women who have also internalized heteronormative standards of behavior speaks volumes about the demands for reproduction and family inherent in black nationalism. In *Race, Nation, and Class,* Étienne Balibar elucidates the comfortable relationship between sexism and nationalism:

> That is why nationalism also has a secret affinity with sexism: not so much as a manifestation of the same authoritarian tradition but in so far as the inequality of sexual roles in conjugal love and child-rearing constitutes the anchoring point for the juridical, economic, educational and medical mediation of the state.[21]

The present-day conflation of queerness with whiteness denies the voice of black queer subjects who stand at the intersection of racial and sexual marginalization. In the eyes of those popularly believed to be hip-hop's conscious sons and daughters, homosexuality is a white man's problem. There is the conjoined anxiety about racial authenticity and sexual normalcy that predominates many disses of "homiesexuals." Present-day proponents of Pan-Africanism, black nationalism, and Afrocentricity believe that blackness has become so many things that blacks lack the sense of unity or solidarity needed to ground social and political mobilizations against oppression. Hip-hop shares this angst. Concerned, and perhaps rightly so, that an "everything is everything" sentiment is a privilege afforded only to a people who have not had their forms of artistic expression appropriated and exploited by the white capitalist patriarchal machine, there are some who argue that "realness" travels better light. That is, in this procession of a loosely defined blackness into the twenty-first century, what baggage gets left behind, what is indispensable, what can we afford to leave behind?

Jamarhl Crawford, a hip-hop critic greatly influenced by the politics of black nationalism, argues that gay infiltration into hip-hop is the final straw for enthusiasts who want to protect the nation. In his controversial essay "Will You Stand Up for Hip Hop or Bend Over?" he states:

> Wait a minute! [Homosexuals] crossed the line now! . . . until recently, Hip Hop had been safe, at least from all outward displays of frilliness . . . I overstand that every special interest group is clamoring to get a piece of Hip Hop pie (now that it's popular) but can we draw a line somewhere in Hip Hop . . . Can Hip Hop handle a sexual revolution, especially a homosexual one?[22]

Crawford strategically deploys the language of combat—referring to the lines drawn, revolution, and safety as his rallying call for comrades to "stand up" for hip-hop. Crawford, a black male, in his attempt to safeguard hip-hop from queer infiltrators resuscitates Black nationalist rhetoric that exiles blacks who do not reproduce (both figuratively and sexually) the patriarchal order. He says in an email (dated May 17, 2001) to Juba Kalamka, a member of the Deep Dickollective: "My problems with homosexuality begin at the fact that I believe it is dangerous for Black People in large groups to choose not to reproduce. Also it is not our heritage or culture, yet another habit shown to us by our good buddy the white man."[23] Crawford's original article is not just a pink alert publicizing his opinion on gays in hip-hop, but he boldly hints at a violent curative for homosexual infiltration:

I think the leap from backpackers to fudgepackers might be extreme. Gay Hip Hop sounds as crazy as gay reggae and the urban environments of Jamaica and America have bred Rudeboys and Homeboys who are very protective of their manhood. The boom bap ain't too far from the boom bye bye and for that reason, I believe that Hip Hop and reggae will be the toughest battlegrounds for homosexual integrationists.

The threat of violence indexed by the controversial Buju Banton song "Boom Bye Bye" in which Banton advocates and encourages the homocide of Jamaican "batty boys," or homosexuals, is Crawford's way of defending the hip-hop turf. The cancellation of dance hall emcee Beenie Man's concerts in 2004 might be proof that more than just queers are protesting homophobia in hip-hop.

Juba Kalamka (pointfivefag) and other members of Deep Dickollective mobilized not just to stand up against gatekeepers like Crawford, but to challenge the general illusion of heteronormativity in hip-hop culture. The construction of the collective, Kalamka notes, is an attempt to escape the hard-and-fast hegemony that ostracizes gay and bisexual men from hip-hop culture:

> We specifically called ourselves a collective because of what it implies in the greater cultural sense of a space for people to enter and exit based on their interests and needs rather than a "band" with a hard and fast membership.[24]

But the self-reflexive awareness of how hard-and-fast boundaries can duplicate the hegemonic and oppressive structures that alienate is not a solution to the problem of hegemony. Not everyone can be a member of Deep Dickollective. We are a decidedly African American queer male hip-hop collective whose lyricism is steeped in challenges to Black nationalist hip-hop rhetoric. The reasons why we have drawn the lines as we have with respect to the desired participation of either straight allies or non-blacks has everything to do with our own allegiances to the idea that hip-hop is fundamentally black music. To boot, as black queer men many people consider "straight acting" and who are very Afrocentric in our aesthetic, our challenges to the hip-hop nation are taken more seriously than they would be if an effeminate white guy were part of our performance. Such membership would feed into the very conflation of queerness with whiteness that we want to challenge. Deep Dickollective is, otherwise, as open as we can be within these boundaries. We perform regularly with a straight white deejay whom we affectionately refer to as "Double Token" and have welcomed a black female-to male transgendered person to our collective. This does not exempt D/DC from particular conformities to the hip-hop nation. That there have not yet been effeminate gay black men in our collective is something I ponder regularly. We continue to interrogate and scrutinize the ways in which we duplicate the hegemonic ousting of other black queer men. It is this kind of self-critical examination that I propose will save hip-hop, not because its agents (including D/DC) won't occasionally act irresponsibly, but because we the artists, and especially our fans and enthusiasts, will demand that we be not only more responsible, but inclusive as well.

I have attempted to elucidate the burden and blessing of disidentificatory practice in hip-hop, especially among its queer constituency. It is this same double-edged sword that transgender rapper Katey Red assumes when she "passes" as a codified black jezebel figure similar to Trina. It's what happens when homo thug rapper Young Harith declares, "I don't fuck around with simple ass people, the niggas I deal with be bustin like Rhymes, Jump in the Ranger just to load up the clip and the 9, and roll up to a spot where some haters talk shit."[25] Clearly the politics of disidentification generates a counter-Lordean[26] politic of having to rely on the master's tools in order to dismantle his house. This is the double bind that is the gay rapper's disidentification with hip-hop.

Interviewed by the *Dallas Voice*, a gay paper interested in covering my August 2002 performance at a local record shop, I was asked to explain why I had invested so much energy in critiquing, writing about, and yet producing hip-hop music, the perception being that hip-hop hates homosexuals. Without seeing any direct connection to my theoretical work around the politics of disidentification, I made a statement that I later discovered echoes Lyotard's trajectory toward healing the communities in which we live. This path of identification, counteridentification, and the willing acceptance of a politics of disidentification presupposes the call for hip-hop's sons and daughters to heal the nation's suffering with dis/ease about homosexuality. Seizing upon my understanding of hip-hop's origins, I stated:

Hip Hop was a form of black creative expression that was used to supplement the voice people weren't given in the inner city to convey their lives and experiences. . . . I'm following in the same Hip Hop tradition of giving voice to issues and experiences that aren't being heard. So when people say there shouldn't be gay people in Hip-Hop, I think that's contradicting Hip Hop's very origins.[27]

As the boundaries of hip-hop continue to shift, from the inside and out, we might consider a sharper awareness of how boundaries preserve "the real." "Keepin' it real" might indicate one who is true to a multidimensionality of identity; one that is sensitive to gender, class, sexuality and other dimensions of identity. The challenge, or perhaps hope, for loyalists to the hip-hop nation is that it will continue to expand and shift—able to respect its origins in inner-city black culture, but malleable enough to voice unanticipated identities that emerge on its landscape.

NOTES

1. http://sugartruck.tripod.com.

2. José Esteban Muñoz, *Disidentifications: Queers of Color and the Performance of Politics* (Minneapolis: University of Minnesota Press, 1999).

3. Muñoz, *Disidentifications*, 1.

4. http://www.thegayrapper.com.

5. Muñoz, *Disidentifications*, 8.

6. http://www.trustlife.net.

7. Nick Ellis, "Homo Hop," *Hip Hop Connection: The World's Original Rap Monthly*, September 2001, 40.

8. Étienne Balibar, in *Race, Nation, Class: Ambiguous Identities*, by Étienne Balibar and Immanuel Wallerstein (New York: Verso, 1994), 93–94.

9. Jamarhl Crawford's essay "Will You Stand Up for Hip Hop or Bend Over" will be thoroughly engaged later in this essay.

10. The "Diss List" is a list managed by members of Phat Family, a gay hip-hop Listserv. Members of this site regularly contribute additions to the growing list of homophobic lyrics. These were among three of many examples I use to illustrate the normalization of verbal bashing of gays in hip-hop music. That the lyrics come from among the more popular and famous songs by respective artists seems to clarify who the hip-hop police are.

11. Ellis, "Homo Hop," 41.

12. Anne McClintock, *Imperial Leather: Race, Gender, and Sexuality in the Colonial Contest* (New York: Routledge, 1995), 353.

13. In their introduction to *Between Woman and Nation: Nationalisms, Transnational Feminisms, and the State*, ed. Caren Kaplan, Norma Alarcón, and Minoo Moallem (Durham, N.C.: Duke University Press, 1999), the editors note that "we have the never ending experience of nation making, through which the vulnerability of certain citizens, some of whom are often in question, can be mapped. Often these sub-

jects stand on the edge of contradictory boundaries—equality and liberty, property and individual self-possession, and citizenship itself—the modern nation-state cannot resolve. In this sense of the process of nation making, we can agree with Benedict Anderson's notion of the 'imagined community' as an unstable fiction whose desire must be continually posed and questioned" (6).

14. Benedict Anderson, *Imagined Communities*, 2nd ed. (London: Verso, 1991), 6.

15. Ellis, "Homo Hop," 41.

16. Given the impress hip-hop has had on culture internationally, the interventions lyrically and politically of five queer Negroes is bound to have ripple effects. Black queer rap group Deep Dickollective represents a "coming out" in hip-hop about what some of us have known for a long time: that any black cultural renaissance needs fags. There is no cipher without the sissy—whether they appear as the abject reference of the insecure closet fagrapper or whether the fervor with which they approach lyricism, beat making, graffiti art, or breakin' has inspirations that have been cloaked in compulsory silence. (http://www.deepdickollective.com/ddc.html)

17. Muñoz, *Disidentifications*, 1.

18. Tricia Rose, *Black Noise: Rap Music and Black Culture in Contemporary America* (Hanover, N.H.: Wesleyan University Press, 1994), 3.

19. Russell A. Potter, "L'Objet X: Performing Race in a Postmodern World," *Literature and Psychology* 41 (1995): 18.

20. Rose, *Black Noise*, 151.

21. Balibar, *Race, Nation, Class*, 102.

22. Jamarhl Crawford, "Will You Stand Up for Hip Hop or Bend Over?" *Elemental Magazine*, November 2000, http://www.elementalmag.com.

23. Jamarhl Crawford, email to Juba Kalamka, May 17, 2001.

24. Juba Kalamka, email to Jamarhl Crawford, May 19, 2001.

25. http://www.pradahblack.blakout.net/?about=1.

26. Audre Lorde has a popular adage, "You cannot dismantle the master's house with the master's tools." It is possible that the disidentificatory performances that Muñoz refers to suggest something different—that it is indeed possible to use the master's tools to construct a different kind of house, or perhaps a shelter different from a house.

27. Mekado Murphy, "Rapper's Delight, Queer Emcee Tim'm Leads the Homo Hop Revolution," *Dallas Voice*, August 2, 2002, 41.

CAROLINE A. STREETER

Faking the Funk?
Mariah Carey, Alicia Keys, and (Hybrid) Black Celebrity

In this essay I read the careers of performers Mariah Carey and Alicia Keys as barometric indicators of how "blackness" is rendered intelligible in an American popular cultural landscape that is fragmented, yet less segregated than in the past, and replete with "white" Americans who idolize "black" American celebrities. The term *blackness* is used here in the sense in which Herman Gray has defined it, "as a way to examine various positions and claims on it both from within the African American community and from outside of it."[1] I look at the representation of Carey and Keys in black media—magazines such as *Vibe* and television broadcasts such as the NAACP Image Awards—as well as how they are depicted in the mainstream media. The notion of racial authenticity to which the title of this essay implicitly refers is germane to an American cultural environment in which individuals are racially classified and commodities are marketed with an eye toward racialized groups. The notion of "race" itself is complicated by the tendency in American culture to regard whiteness as a deracialized norm—rendering those who are not white as racially marked "others." American jurisprudence has tended to identify those of mixed racial descent not as white but as either wholly a part of, or as a subset of, the racialized group to which they are also related.[2] There is a doubleness inherent in the notion of the racial hybrid that both troubles the ways in which distinctions are made between groups and has the potential to undermine the stable sense of identity within a group. While the hybrid is a sign of difference, he/she is also a reminder that the races are not successfully segregated and there are not always clear physical distinctions between them. Whereas the hybrid may move with relative ease across boundaries and up hierarchies, he/she is also marginalized for being frag-

mented and multiple. Thus the hybrid occupies a complex node of privilege and stigma in the American racial imaginary.

The anxiety that arises over racial mixing is matched by the sexual
desire that provokes "miscegenation" in the first place. Hazel Carby has
theorized the mulatto character in literature as "a vehicle for an exploration of the relationship between the races and, at the same time, an
expression of the relationship between the races."[3] I am arguing here that
contemporary images of people of mixed descent still function in this symbolic fashion—a fact complicated by the ways in which their representations have been appropriated by discourses of multiracialism and multiculturalism. Biracial women such as Carey and Keys are not only the
embodied result of sex between the races but also function as a symbolic
fetish object from more than one point of view: for white males intrigued
by the idea of sex with a woman who is racially taboo but not so different
from a white woman, for black males intrigued by the idea of sex with a
woman who approximates the physical aesthetic of whiteness that is the
feminine beauty ideal. Carey and Keys are figures that help to illuminate
how the marketing of hybrid bodies as popular cultural icons becomes
synonymous with the commodification of miscegenation—a conceptual
negotiation of racial difference through sexual desire. The idea of race
mixing implies both miscegenation and heterosexuality, and thereby oper-
ationalizes the inherent conflict between the taboo against interracial sex
and the imperative of normative heterosexuality. In the U.S. cultural
framework, then, the racially mixed female body becomes symbolic of
both illicit sex and the incitement to an apparently transgressive heterosexuality that is quickly recuperated and normalized through processes of
desire, spectacle, and commodification. The careers of Carey and Keys
have also benefited from what seems to be an emerging role for multiracial
celebrities in the post-civil-rights era as enablers of the consumption of
black popular culture without sacrificing the appeal of what Homi Bhabha
might call a "not quite white" female body.[4]

The pejorative roots of terms like *hybrid* and *mulatto* remain implicit
despite the increasing frequency with which the term *hybridity* figures in
postcolonial theory[5] and *mulatto* can be appropriated by people of mixed
descent as a badge of identification.[6] Carey and Keys are part of a generation of post-civil-rights "rainbow babies"—young adults born in the 1970s
and 1980s—whose parents could legally marry and whose mixed racial
identity, however problematic it might be on a personal level, has inexorably become part of America's social and cultural landscape (especially

in urban areas, and states such as Hawaii and California). By the same token, popular cultural representations of women like Carey and Keys frequently emphasize a hypersexual image, a stereotype that derives from conflating mixed-race people with the taboo interracial sexuality that brought them into being.[7] Moreover, in the case of women of mixed black and white descent, the mulatta-as-whore image (prevalent in slavery days on more than one continent) is an enduring archetype.[8]

There are significant parallels between Mariah Carey and Alicia Keys, both in terms of their personal lives and their career ascents. Both are biracial with African American fathers, and were raised by single European American mothers, Carey in New Jersey and Keys in New York. Both became world famous and won Best New Artist Grammy Awards on the strength of their debut albums—Carey in 1990 and Keys in 2001. One key difference that characterizes media representations of the two performers is that whereas biracial identity has remained a consistent theme and has functioned as a site of stigma for Carey, for Keys being biracial has been significantly more normalized. How much this difference can be attributed to the ten-year span between the performers' emergence, how much to the ways in which they have been marketed, and how much to the women's own personal style are questions I engage here. I begin by exploring the very public excoriation of Carey that accelerated following the terrorist attacks on the United States of September 11, 2001, before moving on to a more explicit comparison of how representations of Carey and Keys engage in popular cultural discourses of "blackness."

"Is Mariah Carey exhausted, or just tired?" So began the African American music magazine Vibe's "20 Questions" in the November 2001 issue, a monthly list of sardonic non sequiturs dishing the latest celebrity gossip. The dig referencing Carey's high-profile collapse and hospitalization at the end of summer 2001 also described a low point in her illustrious career.[9] The first feature film starring Carey, Glitter, a rags-to-riches tale of a biracial singer who becomes fabulously successful in 1980s New York, performed abysmally at the box office, and the soundtrack similarly failed to wow critics or fans.[10] Carey's vulnerability seemed evident in her performance at the first benefit concert for victims of the terrorist attacks, recorded on soundstages without audiences and broadcast less than two weeks after September 11 (on the same night that Glitter premiered). During her ballad Carey's voice sounded weak and underrehearsed; at one point she actually turned to her backup singers to provide the powerfully sustained notes that she is famous for.

All celebrities participate in regrettable projects at some point. In the weeks following September 11, however, the failure of *Glitter* became a running joke—and Mariah Carey a safe target for a media that was jittery about content. A *Saturday Night Live* parody of a news broadcast featured the item that the Bush administration was looking for Osama bin Laden in remote, unpopulated places—so they searched every theater playing *Glitter*.[11] Days later, in his capacity as host during another televised benefit concert, the actor Billy Crystal deadpanned, "Regardless of our differences, we can all come together as Christians, Jews, Muslims, Buddhists—and agree that Mariah Carey should never make another movie."

Why did the failure of *Glitter* provoke so much gleeful scorn, and why did it play a prominent role in popular culture's postmortem period of recovery following September 11? As I watched the nation becoming "unified" in a spectacularly censorious fashion, I began to think about what has to be displaced to provide coherence to a statement like "United We Stand." In Danzy Senna's 1998 novel *Caucasia,* in which circumstances force a post-civil-rights era biracial teenager to pass as a white girl, her African American father, obsessed with the fate of his daughters, writes a seven-hundred-page historical thesis on the fate of the mulatto. For him, the metaphor for the mulatto in a racist society is "Canaries in the Coal Mine." In other words, the health and well-being of the children of interracial unions directly reflect the virulence of racism: in a climate poisoned by it, they die. Does the fact that Mariah Carey became such an easy target reflect our culture's generalized love/hate relationship with celebrities? Or is a hybrid body, symbolic of racial ambiguity and ethnic multiplicity, the type of body U.S. culture needed to disavow at a time when "the enemy" assumed no fixed body? In the multiple identity crisis that followed September 11, the incitement to rally around Carey's failed body (of work) points to a heightened hostility toward subject positions "marked by a border condition, a position at the rim . . . neither fully inside nor fully outside."[12]

The virtually universal derision of Carey in the media coincided with the emergence of Alicia Keys, who gave an electrifying performance in one of her first nationally televised appearances at the same benefit concert featuring a below-par Carey. Overall, Alicia Keys's career has been characterized by a marketing strategy that fixes her more firmly in the realm of black celebrity despite her ambiguous look and biracial heritage. Her music is classified in a "black" category as part of the late 1990s and early millennial "neo-soul" R & B movement typified by solo artists such as Erykah Badu, Angie Stone, India Arie, and D'Angelo, whereas Carey has for the majority of her career been marketed in the "pop" category that is coded "white."

At the beginning of her career, a combination of factors rendered Mariah Carey's racial identity opaque and, as such, inconsistently interpreted by the media. As Lisa Jones has observed, Carey's launch benefited from the kind of marketing resources usually lavished on promising white artists. Promotional materials that made no mention of Carey's racial heritage seemed to exploit her physical ambiguity. For some, the absence of explicit racial classification combined with aggressive marketing made her whiteness a given. Thus in July 1990 the *Los Angeles Times* called her a "white soulster . . . poised to give the British singer Lisa Stansfield a run for her money."[13] Eight months later in a review of Carey's first music video, the *Los Angeles Times* had not changed its reporting of Carey's racial classification, although a reviewer complained that the video gave no clues as to "how Carey, who is white, acquired such strong black-gospel roots and why she comes across so vividly as a product of the black culture."[14] In that same month, March 1991, *Ebony* magazine published a feature on Carey entitled "Not Another White Girl Trying to Sing Black."[15] In that interview Carey expressed that she was a biracially identified woman with mixed musical influences. The *Ebony* piece was subsequently hailed as Carey's "coming out" as a black woman and indicative of a belated effort to stop capitalizing on the racial ambiguity that her record label seemed to coyly promote.

At an early stage of Carey's career in 1990, before her racial heritage had been made public, she appeared on two late-night talk shows, *Arsenio Hall* and *The Tonight Show with Jay Leno*.[16] There is a significant contrast in the content of the two programs because the African American television host Arsenio Hall was not permitted to interview the emerging star (although she performed twice on his show within three months). Is it possible that Carey's record label, Sony/Columbia, feared that Hall would "out" Mariah by exposing her black heritage? Jay Leno, it seems safe to say, was utterly clueless. Leno appeared smitten by Carey in a manner that exceeded the usual flirtatious banter that characterizes conversation between male hosts and female guests. Well-known musicians and producers Jimmy Jam and Terry Lewis have deconstructed Leno's demeanor in a documentary about Carey's career. The film cuts back and forth between Leno's remarks and commentary by Jam and Lewis:

JL: "You look like my wife when I met her."

JJ & TL: "Jay was trying to get a date or something."

JL: "That's why I was staring at you."

JJ & TL: "Jay was like, flabbergasted—he was like stumbling over words and stuff."

JL: "You have the same . . . twenty years distant . . . I mean you're very pretty."

JJ & TL: "I thought Jay was gonna lose it."

JL: "I don't mean to embarrass you."

That Leno would comment, "You look like my wife," indicates that he was unaware of Carey's black heritage. Making such a statement would connote at the least an uneasy statement about his wife's heritage, if not an outright insult. Adrian Piper observes:

> No reflective and well-intentioned white person who is consciously concerned to end racism wants to admit instinctively recoiling at the thought of being identified as black herself. But if you want to see such a white person do this, just peer at the person's facial features and tell her, in a complementary tone of voice, that she looks as though she might have some black ancestry, and watch her reaction. It's not a test I or any black person finds particularly pleasant to apply . . . and having once done so inadvertently, I will never do it again.[17]

Rather, that Mariah Carey might look like Jay Leno's wife indicates the extent to which Carey's racial appearance exceeds a black/white paradigm. Her "look" at that point in her career—dark curly hair and deep-colored cosmetics—could be interpreted as stylistic markers for Latina, Jewish, and (specifically in relation to Leno and Tommy Mottola, Sony Records executive and Carey's future husband), Italian ethnicity. (These same features would, subsequent to the *Ebony* article, be read as "black" and evidence of America's one-drop rule.) As an Italian-American, Leno is part of an ethnic group that has become "white" yet is subject to enduring racial myths, including the idea that Italy's proximity to Africa has permanently "tainted" that genetic pool.[18] His televised interview with Carey took place in Southern California at a point in 1990 when awareness of multiracial identity was becoming increasingly common. Thus, the discourses of miscegenation and intergenerational desire that surface in the interview compete with other discourses about the unstable status of "whiteness" and monoracial classifications in general.

Fig. 1. Mariah Carey on VIBE cover, November 1998. (Courtesy VIBE Magazine.)

The collapse of such complex dynamics of ethnicity into the black/white paradigm, however, facilitated the myth that Carey's critics and fans were allowed to believe that she was white, however briefly. Thus, the specter of racial passing has become a fixed aspect of her image, and her ethnic identity and racial allegiances continue to be foregrounded in all of the media reaction to her. Mariah Carey can pretend to be white before audiences to whom she looks white enough, but the one-drop rule always already renders any claim to whiteness—even an implicit, silent one—inauthentic. Although there was no consensus among black journalists and music fans about Carey's ethnic heritage when her first album was released, some maintained that contrary to what was being reported in the mainstream press she wasn't "just" white. Rather than being publicly outed, however, Carey and her record label were able to orchestrate the terms of the revelation about her heritage, which the black press then led the way in reporting.[19] The pleasure of gossiping about celebrities who "pass" is a recurrent theme in ethnic communities, a phenomenon that may become conflated with an imperative for complicity that has deep historical resonance for African Americans. As anachronistic as racial passing might seem, in late 2001 the television talk show hosted by Ananda Lewis featured the dilemma experienced by black people whose relatives have passed as white.[20] As Lisa Jones has observed, the 1990s tendency for celebrities to emphasize multiracial identity is less likely to engender resentment among contemporary black audiences who understand market forces: if multiculturalism is in, claiming mixed identity may not be about rejecting one's blackness, but about getting paid.[21]

The deliberate marketing of Carey's racial ambiguity illuminates the complex stakes at play in a popular music world in which the ability to "cross over," with regard to both musical genres and racial boundaries, is extremely lucrative. It seems fair to say that in their packaging of her, Carey's record label capitalized on the multiracial/multicultural vogue that has swept visual culture since the 1980s.[22] Yet the shifts in how Carey has been marketed (from "assumed white" and "ambiguous" to "black") draw as well upon the increased social and cultural intelligibility of mixed-race identity that makes Carey's particular difference a possibility and her blackness not necessarily a given.

Although Carey's collaborations with black songwriters, musicians, and producers dates from the beginning of her career and she has consistently worked in black musical idioms such as gospel and rhythm and blues, it was only when she began collaborating with rappers and hip-hop artists (on the 1997 album *Butterfly*) that her involvement in a black-identified musical idiom was not only newsworthy but also met with reactions that ranged from skepticism to outright hostility. In July 2000 an Internet site reported that the single from *Rainbow* (an album released in 1999) was a chart flop. The site warned, "Her forays into hip hop and r&b, and her work with 'urban producers' may be alienating top 40 listeners." It is also significant that Carey's management does not appear to have solicited her participation in black entertainment venues until after the shift in her musical collaborations. Her separation from Tommy Mottola after a five-year marriage seems to have accelerated her emergence as a black female celebrity. Since their divorce in 1998, she has made appearances at the NAACP Image Awards, pursued high-profile collaborations with African American superstars like Whitney Houston, and been linked romantically with a number of prominent black men (including the baseball star Derek Jeter, another biracial celebrity). In addition, Carey's image on magazine covers and in music videos became significantly more sexual, with copy that repeatedly alluded to her desirability.

As Adrian Piper implies, there is an odd double standard regarding racial passing, in that "passing for black" is assumed to constitute an oxymoron because of the one-drop rule.[23] Yet, Carey's phenotypic ambiguity and cultural hybridity mark her difference in ways that make her claims to black identity subject to controversy as well. Interestingly, the most persistent contestations of Carey's perceived claims to black identity through her alliance with hip-hop have been articulated by the Jewish-American actress Sandra Bernhard, a performer known for her ironic explorations of racial mimicry and masquerade. In her performances Bernhard routinely parodies her own ambiguous position with regard to ethnicity, sexuality, and conventional standards of female beauty. She is also very attuned to the American obsession with celebrities. The conflation of Carey's mixed racial heritage and her sexuality was thematized in Bernhard's one-woman show, *I'm Still Here . . . Damn It!* Published excerpts of Bernhard's comments include: "Now (Mariah's) trying to backtrack on our asses, gettin' real niggerish up there at the Royalton Hotel suite, with Puff Daddy and all the greasy chain-wearing Black men. '*Oooh*, Daddy . . . I got a little bit of Black in me, too. I didn't tell you that?'"[24] When I saw this performance onstage in San Francisco in 1999, I distinctly recall this part of the monologue referencing Carey's desire for "big black dick." In such a discourse Carey assumes a position analogous to titillating advertisements that feature black men and white women, the latter eroticized as the light-skinned vessel for a "big black dick."[25] As the most taboo yet familiar visual representation of miscegenation, such images of interracial couples are burned into the American racial imaginary and have been a focal point during virtually every political, social, or cultural debate about race relations in the United States for well over three centuries. After interracial marriage became legal throughout the United States in 1967, demographers were quick to observe the significant preponderance of black men marrying white women that characterized black-white intermarriage.[26] Black nationalist rhetoric of the 1970s excoriated intermarriage in general, and black feminists wrote scathing critiques of black men's sexual desire for white women.[27] Despite the fact that statistics demonstrate that in the United States black-white intermarriage occurs at a much lower rate than intermarriage between other racial groups (already a small percentage of marriages overall), anecdotal observations about prominent black men who marry white women—both in history and in contemporary times—continue to inform the exaggerated emphasis on this social phenomenon.[28] Thus highly sexualized representations of interracial couples featuring black men and white women reflect less upon actual behavior and more upon the nature of fear and desire about miscegenation and its ramifications for the status of "whiteness."[29]

Bernhard's humor simultaneously frames Carey as a white-looking woman and a mulatta subject, exploiting her racial ambiguity to fuel stereotypical images of white women and black men in interracial relationships as well as insatiable mulatta sexuality. In a May 1999 interview with *Mirabella* magazine, Carey herself offered commentary on Bernhard's monologue:

> Sandra Bernhard used words that every African-American I know—and definitely I, personally, find inappropriate. If my skin were two shades darker, she wouldn't have done it . . . [C]alling me a "phony white bitch" and saying I was "acting niggerish" is acceptable because she figures, "Who's gonna stick up for her?" . . . And yeah I'm a freaking mutt, I'm a triracial freak, but she implied I was a white person trying to be black. And it's offensive to me, because I've been a victim of racism on both sides.[30]

Carey is astutely aware of the ways that her "white-looking" features can be read as defusing Bernhard's racial slurs. And her question, "Who's gonna stick up for her?" goes to the heart of her liminal position. The vitriol that fuels Bernhard's mockery of Carey is reminiscent of Piper's experience of the hostility directed toward her by white people who are inexplicably furious when they discover that, despite "visual evidence" to the contrary, Piper is African American:

Once exposed as a fraud of this kind, you can never regain your legiti-macy. For the violated criterion of legitimacy implicitly presumes an absolute incompatibility between the person you appeared to be and the person you are now revealed to be, and no fraud has the authority to convince her accusers that they merely imagine an incompatibility where there is none in fact. The devaluation of status consequent on such exposure is, then, absolute, and the suspicion of fraudulence spreads to all areas of interaction.[31]

Carey's statement about being a victim of racism on both sides alludes, I think, less to the idea that she has suffered from "black racism" than to the conundrum that Piper has likewise deconstructed regarding the hostility that white-looking blacks can experience from other blacks who withhold acceptance of a person judged "not black enough." Such experiences have given Piper insight

> into the way whites feel when they are made the circumstantial target of blacks' justified and deep-seated anger . . . because the anger is justified, one instinctively feels guilty. But because the target is circumstantial and sometimes arbitrary, one's sense of fairness is violated. One feels both unjustly accused or harassed, and also remorseful and ashamed at having been the sort of person who could have provoked the accusa-tion.[32]

Carey's question, "Who's gonna stick up for her?" particularly evokes the dilemma of light-skin privilege for women, who, when they become "rep-resentative" of black women, are implicated in the racist standards of beauty that make them icons. Carey's remarks seem to indicate her aware-ness of the dearth of empathy that attends being an oppressive symbol to the women whom Alice Walker has called "black black women."[33]

And yet, the new "mulatto" celebrities that have emerged in the 1990s like Mariah Carey and Tiger Woods embody precisely the kind of racial multiplicity that belies the power of the dominant racial binary. In Carey's case, Latina ethnicity emerges repeatedly to challenge the tendency to place her on one side of the black/white opposition.[34] She has been fea-tured on the cover of *Latina* magazine and is included in a volume in the series *Famous People of Hispanic Heritage*. In another era Carey might have attempted to deploy Latina identity to escape the stigma of blackness much as Philippa Schuyler, the biracial concert pianist, created the "Iberian" alter ego Felipa Monterro for a brief period in the early 1960s.[35] In the contemporary United States, however, hip-hop culture includes numerous Latino groups, stylistic and linguistic elements, as well as celebrity icons such as Jennifer Lopez, who is representative of both hip-hop culture and the "Latino explosion" of the late 1990s. Carey has had a high profile in Spanish language media, particularly when she was romantically involved with the Latin pop superstar Luis Miguel.[36]

Although the way that Mariah Carey is styled and photographed can signify as black, white, or Latina, it is nevertheless striking that over the years a whitened aesthetic increasingly characterizes images of her. We could almost say that the "blacker" she gets, the "whiter" she looks, a factor that in her case derives significantly from the way that her hair is styled: "bone straight," as African American stylists say, and platinum blonde. In August 2001 the tabloid magazine *Star* ran a feature of "before" and "after" photographs of celebrities, contrasting their looks early in their careers with contemporary shots. The early photograph of Carey depicted her with the dark curly hair that she had in the television appearances that I discussed earlier. Of this look the *Star* wrote, "Mariah Carey had a voice like a songbird and hair like a bird's nest when her first album *Mariah Carey* debuted in 1990. The 20-year old scored four hits off the album—but it wasn't until she went from shaggy to sleek sex bomb that she truly conquered the world."[37]

This kind of deracializing process—hair that becomes straighter and blonder, bodies photographed so that skin appears lighter, the use of pastel rather than deep-toned cosmetics—seems to be an unfortunate byproduct of fame for many female celebrities (including those of European descent unproblematically classified as "white"). We see evidence of radical transition in a dramatically short period of time in figures like Jennifer Lopez, who went from a raven-haired "Butter Pecan Rican" in *Vibe* magazine in 1997 to a blonde-streaked "Diva Loca" in a *Vibe* issue of 1999. The rapper Lil' Kim provides a more extreme example of the same phenomenon, moving from a fleshy, dark-haired, and chocolate-skinned vixen to a platinum-blonde, gym-toned, surgically enhanced, and mahogany-hued creation in just one short year. Although it is important to note that artifice is part of the transgression of the hip-hop aesthetic, it is also striking that so many female celebrities undergo this process of lightening and Anglicization, recalling the ultrawhite aesthetic developed for Hollywood film actresses of the 1950s that Richard Dyer has astutely analyzed.[38] While it can be argued that such transitions are a matter of style and spectacle, it is crucial to ask how much they depend upon bodies that more easily conform to normative notions of female beauty that incorporate an aesthetic hierarchy that devalues "racial" features.

It is clear that Mariah Carey and Alicia Keys—young, slender, light-skinned, and conventionally attractive—are examples of hybrid bodies that have the potential to move across boundaries and, as such, are ideal subjects for the type of molding that female celebrities undergo. But whereas Carey mutated, if you will, from an ambiguously raced figure to a "black diva," Alicia Keys's career has been managed so that she will not be required to make such a transition. In the marketing of both her music and style, black signifiers are deployed consistently and strategically. Significantly, early in her career Keys appeared on the cover of several magazines aimed at black women, including *Essence* (March 2002) and *Today's Black Woman* (October 2001), in the cornrows that have become her trademark.[39] Although Kobena Mercer justifiably cautions us against equating racial authenticity with hairstyles, representations of Keys support Mercer's contention that hair is "the most tangible sign of racial difference."[40] As Mercer implies, what is at issue on the topic of hair is the way that the substantial range of textures and colors that occurs "naturally" intersects with questions of political and social value.[41] The two images that accompany this essay, which are covers from the African American music magazine *Vibe*, deploy hair among other signifiers. In November 1998 Carey was depicted with wavy, blonde-streaked tresses and dressed in a silver lamé bikini with a caption that declares: "Mariah breaks it down! Miss Carey busts loose on Whitney, Derek Jeter, love and lust and mixed-race melodrama." Keys was photographed for the September 2002 cover with a halo-like Afro framing her cornrows and wearing jeans emblazoned with a black power salute. Keys's skin appears more brown-skinned than in earlier magazine covers and her hair looks black rather than brown. She has been rendered significantly darker than in the aforementioned covers of *Essence* (March 2002) and *Today's Black Woman* (October 2001).[42]

Keys's style points toward an aesthetic popularized by neosoul female artists like Lauryn Hill, Erykah Badu, Angie Stone, Jill Scott, and India Arie. These women self-consciously embody "positive" representations of blackness that both derive from black cultural nationalist discourses and constitute a more contemporary feminist challenge to the gendered aesthetic that dictates that the body become progressively thinner and lighter-skinned and the hair straighter with fame. That racialized political and

FIG. 2. Alicia Keys on VIBE cover, September 2002. (Courtesy VIBE Magazine.)

social meanings tend to be inscribed on the bodies of female celebrities is linked both to the generalized Western cultural tendency to conflate appearance with femininity (as in John Berger's assertion that "men act, women appear")[43] as well as to the more distinctly African American struggle over the politics of appearance. As Patricia Williams has written,

Black women's hair anxiety has a lot of history, even a legal history. Legal theorist Paulette Caldwell has written about how black women have actually had to sue for the right to wear their hair naturally—i.e., unstraightened, kinky, liberated from chemical "enhancement"—without being fired from their employment. (My favorite case in that litany involved a woman who sued to be able to wear her hair in "cornrows," cornrowing being nothing less than an ancient African style of braiding hair. Not only was she required to conform to her employer's demands, she was then chided for "imitating Bo Derek.")[44]

Notwithstanding Williams's astute comments, it bears consideration that some black women do not have to manipulate their hair in order to conform to normalized standards. In fact, the "Afro" hairstyle of the 1960s and 1970s eluded many African Americans who simply didn't possess a kinky enough hair texture.[45] Thus, the question of racial authenticity that stereotypically plagues mixed-race people is not at all limited to "hybrids." Vibe's representations of Carey and Keys reflect the decreasingly marginalized status of mixed race in African American popular culture over the past decade. Vibe's 1998 cover of Carey, with the reference to "mixed race melodrama," was published when there was significantly more public interest in mixed-race identity: at a time when the question of whether a "multiracial" category would appear in the census of 2000 was widely debated. Although a multiracial category was not instituted in the census, Americans were able for the first time to check more than one racial category (under the assumption that the information would be tabulated and used to generate data). In the weeks prior to the distribution of the census of 2000, however, Americans of African descent reported in majority numbers that they were likely to check only the "black" category, regardless of whether they were of mixed descent.[46] Neither Vibe's September 2002 cover of Keys nor the article about her makes an issue of her biracial heritage—both her white mother and her black identity are unproblematic givens. The normalization of biracial subjects over the ten-year period that has elapsed between the emergence of Carey and Keys as stars may account for the media declining to "take the bait," as it were, constituted by Keys's heritage.

At the same time, Alicia Keys benefits from flattering comparisons to artists like Mariah Carey because of the way in which musical styles are rendered as binary and racialized opposites. While pop is a style that, through its virtue as a mainstream form, becomes classified as "white"—

which comes with undeniable privileges—it is also represented as a paradigmatic model of illegitimacy when compared to black urban music forms that are equated with authenticity. As P. David Marshall has written, pop is associated with commercialism and superficiality, and pop artists and their audiences, especially when they are female, are stereotyped as being controlled, manipulated, and duped.[47] Such distinctions are meaningful for media and contemporary audiences well versed in the notion that "blackness" constitutes the currency, the vernacular, and the standard not only for "realness" but also for what constitutes the artistic cutting edge. And yet, that type of binary is ultimately not sustainable, as such an interpretation of blackness is limited to consumers with specific cultural interests and values, and is contingent upon historic and material circumstances.

Moreover, proximity to what is considered authentic does not always rub off. Although Carey has collaborated with hip-hop artists of impeccable pedigree such as the producer-performer Missy Elliott and female rapper Da Brat, she is characterized as alienating her core audience of "pop" fans while failing to convince the targeted audience—assumed black—that she is "real." In contrast, Keys's collaboration with the rapper Eve on the summer 2002 hit "Gangsta Love" enacts the singer's seemingly effortless boundary-crossing between R & B and rap. As I have argued, such ease is attributable to the privileged hybrid body. But it is also, I think, linked to the fact that Keys traverses a genre boundary rather than a racial one. The aesthetics of the video for "Gangsta Love," directed by Little X, are arresting in that some scenes are shot so that Keys, who is significantly lighter-skinned than Eve, looks as if her skin is the same color as the rapper's. The darkening of Keys in both *Vibe* magazine's cover and the "Gangsta Love" video functions as a fascinating aesthetic counterpoint to phenomena such as *Time* magazine's infamous darkened cover photo of O. J. Simpson in their issue of June 27, 1994, reframing the familiar association of darkness with stigma.

When Alicia Keys was recognized at both the mainstream Grammy Awards and the "subcultural" NAACP Image Awards of 2002, what struck me most was the extent to which both ceremonies emphasized multiculturalism in their programs. At the Grammies, Keys sang a medley of her hits in a Spanish-styled production number, performing the tango with a noted flamenco dancer (who has also toured with Madonna). The album of the year was awarded to a roots revival band from Appalachia, and the

African American group Destiny's Child sang in Spanish with the Latino pop sensation Alejandro Sanz.[48]

At the NAACP Image Awards, Keys made a presentation accompanied by two other young singers, the African American Tyrese and the Canadian Nelly Furtado.[49] During the teleprompter-fueled banter that precedes an award, Keys introduced herself as "a biracial New Yorker," followed by Furtado, who introduced herself as "first-generation Portuguese." After each of these declarations the brown-skinned Tyrese acknowledged, "Me, too," prompting laughter from the audience. On one hand, the inclusion of racial and ethnic hybrids like Keys and Furtado at such an event is very familiar, since white communities have traditionally, whether through means de facto or de jure, excluded hybrids from their midst. Simultaneously, such a public claiming of positions that do not fit neatly into the racial classification system is a product of the post-civil-rights era's remapping of identity. The deployment of the multicultural in-joke—Tyrese's "me, too"—seems to gesture at the types of boundaries that prevent the acknowledgment of multiplicity—in the American context, one of the most potent of those boundaries being "the color line."

It is tempting to place Mariah Carey on the "tragic mulatto" side and Alicia Keys on the "well-adjusted and black-identified mulatto" side of a racial identity binary, just as they seem to be placed on racially defined sides of a musical binary. The realm of black celebrity and the ways that it intersects with the spectrum of ethnic identity and hierarchies of value, however, demand a more complex assessment of their meaning as icons. In the brilliant comic strip *The Boondocks,* in which creator Aaron McGruder regularly pillories politically conservative African Americans such as Condoleezza Rice, Mariah Carey appeared in March 2002 as a nominee for "Most Embarrassing Black Person of the Year" (for her performance in *Glitter,* of course). Yet in the strip's last frame McGruder's biracial character Jazmine protests "Hey! I liked *Glitter!*" McGruder's double gesture—toward a political critique of Carey's artistic choices as well as the empathetic representation of a young girl's desire to claim a "positive" role model—perfectly captures the mode of analysis demanded by the hybrid figure in contemporary culture.

As this article goes to press, representations of Mariah Carey and Alicia Keys are poised at a new intersection of the cultural traffic mapped in this anthology. Their positions as indicators of intelligible "blackness" have continued to reflect racial dualism even as ruptures continually undermine such binaries. Media about Carey reflects the ways that the discourse of the mulatto continually haunts the figure of mixed-race. In April 2005 she appeared on the cover of *Essence* magazine with the caption: "America's Most Misunderstood Black Woman: the story only we can tell." The photograph of Carey pictures her as an ethereal blonde beauty with rosy cheeks and pale pink lips. The African American friend who alerted me to the magazine told me that when she saw the image from a distance her first thought was, "Who is that white woman on *Essence*?" The article begins by declaring that Carey bears no resemblance to Sarah Jane, the tragic mulatto of the film *Imitation of Life* (dir. Douglas Sirk, 1959). This rhetorical move works to associate Carey with the tragic mulatto even as it denies her resemblance to that figure. It is also striking that the article cites the remake of the film in which a white actress played the tragic mulatto Sarah Jane, rather than the 1934 original directed by John Stahl, in which African American Fredi Washington depicted Peola (the name for the character in Fannie Hurst's 1933 novel). The article delineates Carey's struggle to be accepted as racially authentic. Da Brat insists, "Hip-hop is in (Mariah's) bones, in her soul. That child is black. That girl is ghetto."[50] In a *Vibe* interview of 2003, Carey demonstrated characteristic insight into how her reputation as a musical lightweight—an artist known primarily for a pretty face and a beautiful voice—likewise begs the question of her authenticity. "If you're not strumming a guitar or playing the piano like Alicia Keys, people assume you're not involved."[51]

As for Keys, the conversation is very different as she continues to solidify her status as an artist whose idiom is unambiguously black. In 2005 Keys won four Grammy Awards for her second album *The Diary of Alicia Keys,* including best R&B performance by a duo or group and best female vocal performance.[52] The video for her award-winning duet with Usher for the song "My Boo" featured a fascinating transition in Keys's style as she morphed from a "raw unabashedly street persona"[53] to a video vixen, complete with flowing straight hair and satin slip. That Keys now appears more frequently with straightened hair on magazines that are not targeted at African American audiences (for example, on the covers of *Lucky* magazine in February 2005 and *Seventeen* magazine in April 2005) indicates that it is now "safe" for her to straighten her hair and to expand her market. The fact that Keys's braids were her Afro-centric signature for so long makes it likely that her straight hair will be interpreted as a style choice rather than symbolic acquiescence to "white" standards of beauty. Interestingly, the question of Keys's authenticity has arisen with regard to Black

English. Anecdotal evidence indicates that she slips in and out of dialect, prompting the observation that "(W)hile some question the sincerity of her ghetto vernacular, she insists it is all her."[54] Interestingly, the label "ghetto" is referenced in media about Carey and Keys, emphasizing the extent to which this term has been rehabilitated. Thus the imperative for multi-millionaire music stars to stay "real" by remaining linked to the black urban underclass is likewise for Carey and Keys the standard for their continued relevance to contemporary consumers.

At the Cannes Film Festival of 2004, Alicia Keys announced that she would be playing the biracial concert pianist Philippa Schuyler in a biographical film produced by Halle Berry. Such a role would represent the collaboration of two celebrity biracial women in a project about another biracial woman who was a significant celebrity in the 1930s and 1940s. The ways in which blackness and mixed-race continually cross paths shall no doubt remain one of the prominent aspects of black cultural traffic. At such intersections the mixed-race woman remains a critical node of negotiation and transformation.

NOTES

1. Herman Gray, *Watching Race: Television and the Struggle for "Blackness"* (Minneapolis: University of Minnesota Press, 1995), 13.

2. G. Reginald Daniel, "Passers and Pluralists: Subverting the Racial Divide," in *Racially Mixed People in America* (Newbury Park, CA: Sage, 1992); F. James Davis, *Who Is Black? One Nation's Definition* (University Park: Pennsylvania State University Press, 1991); Ian Haney López, *White by Law: The Legal Construction of Race* (New York: New York University Press, 1996).

3. Hazel V. Carby, *Reconstructing Womanhood: The Emergence of the Afro-American Woman Novelist* (New York: Oxford University Press, 1987), 89.

4. Homi K. Bhabha, "Foreword: Remembering Fanon: Self, Psyche, and the Colonial Condition," in *Black Skin, White Masks,* by Frantz Fanon, trans. Charles Lam Markmann (London: Pluto, 1986). A recent example of this phenomenon is the actress Jessica Alba in the recently canceled television series *Dark Angel.* The show liberally deployed signs of black urban culture—graffiti and hip-hop music and fashion—and featured black actors in smaller roles (even a recurring black lesbian character!). The plot, however, revolved around a human-cyber mutant—played by the "exotic" and not-quite-white-looking Alba. The actor is of Mexican and European descent, with features that could be read as Asian and Latina.

5. Trinh T. Minh-ha, *Cinema Interval* (New York: Routledge, 1999).

6. Lise Funderberg, *Black, White, Other: Biracial Americans Talk about Race and Identity* (New York: William Morrow, 1994). "I am *two* things, you know? And then people say, 'Well, you're not. You're biracial.' But people don't make it into one thing.

It's not a legally noticed race. That's why I like the word *mulatto*. Because mulatto means only black and white" (48).

7. Cynthia Nakashima, "An Invisible Monster: The Creation and Denial of Mixed-Race People in America," in *Racially Mixed People in America* (Newbury Park, CA: Sage, 1992); Carla K. Bradshaw, "Beauty and the Beast: On Racial Ambiguity," in *Racially Mixed People in America* (Newbury Park, CA: Sage, 1992).

8. The fetish for light-skinned women—"quadroons" and "octoroons"—and the notion that they made ideal concubines was institutionalized in the nineteenth-century New Orleans practice of plaçage, in which wealthy (white) Creole men chose partners from among the mixed-race women of the free black community. See Monique Guillory, "Under One Roof: The Sins and Sanctity of the New Orleans Quadroon Balls," in *Race Consciousness: African American Studies for the New Century* (New York: New York University Press, 1997). In his comparative study of race and slavery in Brazil and the United States, Carl Degler cited a familiar Brazilian folk saying: "White women are for marrying, Mulattas are for fornicating, Black women are for service." See Carl N. Degler, *Neither Black nor White: Slavery and Race Relations in Brazil and the United States* (New York: Macmillan, 1971).

9. Mariah Carey was the biggest-selling female recording artist of the 1990s, with more number one singles than any other woman artist in history and surpassed in number one hits on the charts only by the Beatles and Elvis Presley. Carey negotiated an early release from her contract with Columbia and brokered her own record deal with Virgin Records in 2001. Her new agreement paid her 23 million dollars for the *Glitter* album soundtrack before record executives heard a single note. In the weeks following the U.S. entry into the war with Afghanistan, Carey appeared to be recovering from the humiliation of her film flop, ignoring her scapegoat status by traveling to Bosnia and entertaining American troops, being photographed on the shoulders of American soldiers resplendent in cleavage-baring khaki fatigues. Subsequently, however, her record company paid Carey 28 million dollars to release the label from her contract following the disappointing sales of the *Glitter* album.

10. Parenthetically, the press reported that *Glitter* was no greater a financial debacle than contemporaneous films starring musical artists, including a project with members of the boy band N'Sync and two films featuring Snoop Dogg, *Bones* and *The Wash* (both 2001). The vitriol reserved for the commercial failure of Mariah Carey's film would seem to reflect not only the ambivalence directed toward her as a hybrid figure but also the considerable misogyny that not even a "diva" is immune from. See Nick Madigan, "Pop Stars Try to Parlay Fame into Big-Screen Success, but Few Quit Their Day Job," *New York Times*, March 6, 2002, B1.

11. Noel Holston, "Viewers Get a Dose of Comic Relief; Late-Night Shows Struggle to Find Humor after the Tragedy," *Newsday*, October 1, 2001, pt. 2, B02.

12. Victor Burgin, *In/Different Spaces: Place and Memory in Visual Culture* (Berkeley and Los Angeles: University of California Press, 1996), 257.

13. Connie Johnson, "Pop Beat/Soul: Kipper Jones' 'Ordinary Story' Is Anything But," *Los Angeles Times*, July 28, 1990, F (20) 5.

14. Dennis Hunt, "Pop Music; Mixed Media: Mariah Carey: The First Vision," *Los Angeles Times*, March 17, 1991, Calendar, 64.

15. Lynn Norent, "Mariah Carey: 'Not Another White Girl Trying to Sing Black,'" *Ebony*, March 1991, 54.

16. Carey's appearances on the talk shows were excerpted in the VH1 documentary *Mariah Carey's Greatest TV Moments.*

17. Adrian Piper, "Passing for White, Passing for Black," *Out of Order, Out of Sight:* vol. 1, *Selected Writings in Meta-Art, 1968–1992* (Cambridge: MIT Press, 1996), 292.

18. For example, the film *True Lies* (dir. James Cameron, 1994) contains an arresting scene in which one character taunts another that Sicilians are "niggers." Scholars have written about the identification that much "gangsta" rap music expresses with Italian-American iconography through citing images that derive from mobster vernacular. See John Gennari, "Passing for Italian," *Transition* 6, no. 4 (1996): 36–49.

19. The controlled way in which this information was released to the press was enacted more recently when the popular talk-show host Rosie O'Donnell revealed that she is a lesbian. Unlike the attention lavished on Carey's racial identity, however, Rosie's coming out was greeted with little fanfare. As *Vibe*'s "20 Questions" remarked, "We're glad Rosie O'Donnell came out of the closet, but didn't everyone already know she's gay?" (June 2002).

20. "Who Am I? Mixed Race and Passing," *The Ananda Lewis Show*, exec. prod. David Armour, KTVU-TV Fox (San Francisco), broadcast October 29, 2001. Provocatively, the show's synopsis defines "passing" as "being biracial, and passing as only one race." The original source for this information was the theanandalewisshow.com. The website is no longer online as the show was cancelled in 2002. The source for information about the show's cancellation is the website tvtome.com.

21. Lisa Jones, *Bulletproof Diva: Tales of Race, Sex, and Hair* (New York: Doubleday, 1994), 202.

22. The success of multiracial and multiethnic models on the runways and in advertising images does not, for the most part, extend to acting careers. Actors of mixed descent who appear racially ambiguous routinely express how hard it is to get cast. A recent example includes the now-successful Vin Diesel, *People*, August 19, 2002.

23. Piper, "Passing," 275.

24. "Now she's trying to backtrack on our asses, gettin' real niggerish up there at the Royalton Hotel suite, with Puff Daddy and all the greasy chain-wearing Black men. 'Oooh, Daddy . . . I got a little bit of Black in me, too. I didn't tell you that?" Joan Morgan, "Free at Last: Mariah Carey," *Essence*, April 2005, 118.

25. I refer here to an advertisement for Jordache jeans that I analyzed along with other ads that feature images of interracial couples and people of mixed racial descent. See Caroline A. Streeter, "Ambiguous Bodies, Ambivalent Desires: The Morphing Mulatta Body in U.S. Culture, 1965–1999," Ph.D. diss., University of California, Berkeley, 2000.

26. Paul R. Spickard, *Mixed Blood: Intermarriage and Ethnic Identity in Twentieth-Century America* (Madison: University of Wisconsin Press, 1989).

27. Michele Wallace, *Black Macho and the Myth of the Superwoman* (New York: Verso, 1990. Reprint, New York: The Dial Press, 1978).

28. Gloria Wade-Gayles recorded the disbelief among her black female students at Spelman College upon learning that Frederick Douglass's second wife was a white woman. See *Rooted against the Wind: Personal Essays* (Boston: Beacon Press, 1996). Among the number of prominent black men married to white women, popular stereotypes have singled out successful black athletes among the worst "offenders." As African American cultural theorists have observed, the drama of the O. J. Simpson

trial revolved around the enduring fascination and dread about miscegenation, black masculinity, and white femininity. See *Birth of a Nation'hood: Gaze, Script and Spectacle in the O.J. Simpson Case,* edited by Toni Morrison and Claudia Brodsky Lacour (New York: Pantheon, 1997).

29. It is apparent not only from advertising images but also from any cursory look at contemporary pornographic imagery, that an obsession with the black phallus and its potential to "contaminate" the white gene pool through sexual intercourse with white females, a fear that was so often the pretext for the repression of black social and political power in the past, continues to inform popular fantasies about race relations.

30. James Patrick Herman, "There's Something about Mariah," *Mirabella,* May 1999, 128.

31. Piper, "Passing," 276.

32. Piper, "Passing," 277.

33. Alice Walker, "If the Present Looks Like the Past, What Does the Future Look Like," in *In Search of Our Mother's Gardens* (New York: Harcourt Brace Jovanovich, 1983), 291.

34. The classification of "Latino" (depending upon the geographic area, "Hispanic," "Mexican American," or "Chicano" might be the term of choice) is, of course, a multiracial and multiethnic signifier. At the same time, however, many Latin American countries deploy binaries similar to the black/white binary of the United States. In Mexico, for example, although the national identity is "mestizo," a recognition of the European and indigenous heritage of the country, people with Indian features are routinely discriminated against and subject to degrading stereotypes. The myth of noble Indian origins is celebrated while actual Indians are at the bottom of the social, economic, and political hierarchies. See Richard Rodriguez, "Mixed Blood," *Harper's,* November, 1991. In Brazil, which enjoys a reputation as a multiracial paradise, people with "more" African blood or more visible African features are also at the bottom of a complex racial taxonomy. See Degler, *Neither Black nor White.*

35. Kathryn Talalay, *Composition in Black and White: The Life of Philippa Schuyler* (New York: Oxford University Press, 1995).

36. Interestingly, I've been told that during the relationship between Miguel and Carey, Latino talk shows and tabloids labeled her as a tramp that brought him down. There are fascinating implications here regarding discourses of purity and contamination that are projected onto Carey, both as a woman of black heritage and as an American. Such a characterization brings to mind Jennifer Brody's research on the ways that the identity of the gentleman in Victorian England was elaborated as distinct from the image of the American as feminized and racially impure. Jennifer DeVere Brody, *Impossible Purities: Blackness, Femininity, and Victorian Culture* (Durham: Duke University Press, 1998).

37. "When Today's Stars Were Almost Famous," *Star,* August 14, 2001, 30.

38. Richard Dyer, "White," *Screen* 29, no. 4 (1988): 44–64.

39. Although Mariah Carey has appeared on the cover of numerous magazines aimed at (white) women, including *Mirabella* (May 1999), *Glamour* (November 1999), *Jane* (April 1999), and *Elle* (July 2001), until April 2, 2005, when *Essence* featured Carey, she had not, to my knowledge, been featured on the cover of any black women's magazines.

40. Kobena Mercer, "Black Hair/Style Politics," *Welcome to the Jungle: New Positions in Black Cultural Studies* (New York: Routledge, 1994), 101.

41. Mercer, "Black Hair/Style Politics," 105.

42. Although Carey's hair can be kinkier than in the *Vibe* cover image, even in what the tabloid *Star* called her "bird's nest" stage, it would hardly qualify as "nappy." By contrast, Keys's hair texture had been something of a mystery since it has either been styled in cornrows or hidden by scarves she has worn. Although people might assume that styles such as braids or locks require a certain hair texture, in fact any type hair can assume any style with the right products and stylist. Thus, there was no reason to assume that Keys's hair was particularly kinky until images such as *Vibe*'s cover exposed her naps.

43. John Berger, *Ways of Seeing* (London: Penguin, 1972).

44. See Patricia J. Williams, "American Kabuki," in Morrison and Lacour, *Birth of a Nation'hood*, 283–84.

45. Kathe Sandler, *A Question of Color* (Film Two Productions: San Francisco: California Newsreel, 1992). Danzy Senna, *Caucasia* (New York: Riverhead Books, 1998).

46. Diana Jean Schemo, "Despite Options on Census, Many to Check 'Black' Only," *New York Times*, February 12, 2000, A1.

47. P. David Marshall, *Celebrity and Power: Fame in Contemporary Culture* (Minneapolis: University of Minnesota Press, 1997).

48. The path for this type of cultural fusion was surely blazed when Aretha Franklin sang an aria at a Grammy ceremony some years ago, replacing an ailing Luciano Pavarotti.

49. Furtado, with features that can be read as "white" and a Latino-sounding surname, has like Keys solidified her association with black popular culture through the idiom of hip-hop music.

50. Joan Morgan, "Free at Last," *Essence* (April, 2005), 119. The same issue of *Essence* features two articles by African American women that also articulate stuggles linked to the persistence of racial essentialism and notions of racial authenticity. "Will I ever be black enough?" expresses how a woman with two black parents who nevertheless looks "mixed-race" experiences hostility and rejection from African Americans (Kenya Jones, 124). "This child is mine," conveys the frustration of a woman who is often not recognized as the biological mother of her biracial daughter (Lisa Teasley, 106).

51. Lola Ogunnaike, "Through the Fire," *Vibe* (March 2003), 118.

52. In an example of successful cross-promotion, Keys's book *Tears for Water: Songbook of Poems & Lyrics* (New York: G. P. Putnam's Sons, 2004) was published to coincide with the release of her album. Half of the book consists of lyrics for songs from her two albums *Songs in A Minor* (2001) and *The Diary of Alicia Keys* (2004). The book was listed as number one in Hardcover fiction on the *Essence* best-seller list in March and April 2005. ("The *Essence* Best Sellers list is based on reports of retail sales. Respondents are African-American bookstores." *Essence*, April 2005, 104.)

53. Mimi Valdéz, "Blaze of Glory," *Vibe* (March 2004), 126.

54. Ibid.

Interlude

Black Artists on Issues of Culture and Performance

All interviews with these artists were conducted by Elena Becks and Kim Fowler of the Committee on Black Performing Arts at Stanford University. The artists were interviewed individually.

On Black Cultural Genesis

Christian McBride: I really have to say that all of the styles, that whatever hip styles that have been part of America for the last one hundred years—all of that has emanated from the black community. Anything that's hip, in my opinion, looking out through the years, has come out of the black community.

Will Power: I kind of feel like African American culture, especially like aspects of music and style and dress and language and communications and that kind of stuff, African Americans have always been innovators around the world, as far as influencing other cultures. You look at jazz, rock and roll, funk, and not just the music but the whole social cultural stuff that came out of that. When I go a lot of places, there's a couple of things I see. Sometimes I see, well, obviously there's an influence which is cool, but sometimes I see people kind of like perpetrating.

Christian McBride: Even though it may have emanated and originated in the black community, the influence it has on other cultures in America, it's going to somehow bleed into other cultures. I think that's okay as long as we are secure enough that we know where it came from. As long as we know where it came from, there really shouldn't be an issue.

On Cultural Appropriation

Euzhan Palcy: I have no problem having nonblack people adopting elements of my culture as long as they acknowledge the fact that they did. I truly wouldn't have any problem, if a white filmmaker, male or female, would come and say to me, "Oh, you know what, I discovered that great story. I wrote a beautiful story about a family that I met in Africa and these people are so wonderful." And the person is very sincere and wants to tell the story, because he's a human being before being white. I have no problem with that. As long as they have respect for it and they don't portray black people like they have been portrayed for centuries. I feel like you have to allow people to do that, but as long as they do it with respect. I am very proud of my cultural heritage and, yes, I like when people embrace it because it's bigger than them. I like to give them a chance to educate themselves.

Chike Nwoffiah: If we are talking about appropriations, just by the mere definition of a word, this is not good, whether it's black or white. Nobody should appropriate, so to speak. If you're talking about people adapting or adopting our art forms into theirs, I think we should welcome it. . . . But we should also be vigilant. And be able to call it wherever we see or hear that black work has been mislabeled, so that the credits do go to where they belong. If this is ours and there are traces of ours in yours, you should be able to say, yes, I've created new work, but it is a combination that I got from this and that and that.

Will Power: I think when a music if it's in true form or art, it belongs to everybody. I think it's for everybody. I think it's for anyone that gets touched and inspired by it. The problem comes when people co-opt it and then call it their own and then don't give respect to the ones that developed it. I really don't know how to deal with that in a society that's dominated, in America at least, by white folks. That's a real interesting kind of thing. I know someone like, you know, Bonnie Raitt, when she does blues and stuff, but she's very clear about where it came from. She gets a lot of respect, whether it's raising money for old . . . I mean that's cool. She's doing her own thing, she loves blues music, which is African American music. As opposed to someone like Elvis or like in hip-hop, back in the day when Vanilla Ice came out. It was like, "I'm the best rapper on the planet." I think it just depends.

Christian McBride: You see someone like an Eminem, so to speak, you say, "Oh yeah, that's cute, but we all know where he got that from." You take someone like Elvis, and I know in certain parts of this country I would probably be shot for saying this, but Elvis to me is like far from "the King." Elvis was good. He was the best, he was the luckiest copycat. Had there not been Little Richard or Louie Jordan or somebody like that, Elvis would never have existed. . . . Elvis was RCA's guinea pig.

Will Power: But then there's some other groups and other people, like there's this one group we met in Canada called Orishas which is a Cuban hip-hop group. The way they took it was like they had American influences as far as beats, but then they had their own culture in there, their own music, their own spirituality, their own language. So that's kind of a way how you might get influenced by something, but make it your own. I see both of those dynamics coming out of African American cultures throughout the world. Some people kind of take it, but they incorporate their own stuff and make it their own. Some people kind of, like, it's just straight perpetrating. Like they've got a lot of hip-hop groups in Canada and Europe who are quote-unquote hard hard-core hip-hop groups. They just look like a joke to me. But that just might be a bias of being from America too.

Michael Franti: I look at it from an overall perspective. When you look at Eastern cultures, there was no such thing as intellectual property. Some guy would sit down with his guitar or his drum or whatever instruments they had, and he would write a song. He would sing that song, and if people enjoyed it, it was his gift. Coming through the creative spirit first, the creator's gift to the whole community of a song that now we have in our midst that we could sing whenever we wanted. Anybody could sing it. Anybody could add their little parts to it or change it in any way they felt like it. That song could grow over time.

Euzhan Palcy: I'd kill for the rights to be inspired by other people's cultures if it was taken away from me . . . So it is good to allow other people to improve their life, their spirit and soul, their creativity, by diving into your culture as long as they do not forget to pay a tribute to it. Like Picasso. Negro art (l'Art Negre) enriched tremendously Picasso's work . . . Take Giacometti, as well . . . look at the shape of his sculptures. I mean what inspired them? L'Art Negre. I welcome that as long as they say it as it is, they recognize in the face of the world the importance of Negro

Art in their work and what Negro art taught them, brought to them, and how it contributed to make them who they are. Anyway it would have been very difficult for Picasso to really deny it. When you take both volumes of "Primitivism and Modern Art," they really show the African piece and then how it has been copied. That's what has been happening to us for centuries. People have been stealing Negro Art (in its entire diversity) and referring to it as "primitivism." The minute they copy it, and put their famous name on it, it becomes all of a sudden a piece of art and it costs millions.

On Black Artistic Control

Robert Moses: I want to control how my work is seen. I want to control where it's seen. I want to—I want control—whatever that means. Whatever you can think of when you say "control." Whether you think it's a negative thing or a positive thing. I'll be a benevolent dictator. And I want control.

Euzhan Palcy: That's what I'm talking about. We have been robbed for years and years and centuries. So we must be very careful. Now, what can we do? The key is money. How can you fight and protect what belongs to you, when you do not have the economic freedom, when nobody gives it to you? Why when a white fellow comes and does [the same thing]—here comes the money. Why can't black folks get money to do their projects? We know we are in a world that doesn't like the black thing. So I'd say let's be more supportive of ourselves. Let's develop a real solidarity among ourselves. Let's acknowledge our value, praise our artists, and be strong supporters of them.

Michael Franti: At the moment, the Internet is helping a lot of us artists who are underground to get our stuff out there and have it be traded around. People hear a song or two that they enjoy and then they'll go out and buy the whole album. But when people can just click a button and it just streams into their [computer] in seconds, it's going to really change the music industry as a whole. What that means is that we as artists really have to define clearly what it is that we do and what our motives and intentions are for doing this, then try to create a new economic model for making a living and doing music. I think what I like about what's happening now is that it's a time when music can go back to the artist. I got out of a major label contract and I started my own label. Through the Internet I'm able to sell records directly to people at a rate that's cheaper than they can get in the stores, but is earning me a royalty rate that's much, much higher than I would get if I was on a major label. I don't have to sell nearly the amount of records that I would if I were on a major label in order to break even or turn a profit. That changes things in that it puts [the music] back into the hands of the artists. For somebody like me, I can develop a fan base of fifty to a hundred thousand people around the world, and if I can sell records to them, I can earn a great living and support myself and my band. Whereas if I'm on a major label, I have to sell like a million or two million.

Keith Antar Mason: I think for me as an artist, I'm more interested in our sacred space than cyberspace. As I speak, I'm having someone create a web page for the Hittites right now. But notice I'm not creating it. I understand there's an impetus among African Americans at this time to move on to the next thing because we get commodified so quickly. Things get bought up and sold so quickly. Michael Jordan went from being the number one basketball player to *Space Jam.* Things in America are accommodated and then co-opted and then finally, brothers and sisters say: "You sold out." It's a process to that process. I'm very much concerned about it, but I don't want us to be hesitant about us seeing the new vision while trying to preserve the traditions that we come from. I very much respect the traditions that we come from.

Euzhan Palcy: I'm a black filmmaker no doubt, but when I bring a project to a studio executive I never say: "I'm bringing you a black film or a black story," because you limit yourself. So they give you this limited money to do it to. For example, we are dealing with a story and that story costs 10 million to be done. The same story with only white folks in it will get the $10 million. Just change the color and you put black, and they cut the budget in half. They give you $5 million, half of the amount just because it's black. So let's not ourselves accept those limitation. We got to find a way to appeal to Hollywood and make them understand that we are human beings just like the other folks, and that we pay to see their movies just like the others! We've got to appeal to the wealthy black folks; [they need] to put part of their money into production to support their artists.

On Commercialism and Artistic Responsibility

Christian McBride: As far as the commercialism of jazz, it's probably at an all-time low. Jazz record sales count for 1 percent of all of the recording industry's music. You think about all the records that these country music artists sell, like Faith Hill and Garth Brooks and these hip-hop artists and these pop artists, the Britney Spears and the Christina Aguileras, and I'm surprised that New Age music—what they call the Yannis and the John Teshes—I'm surprised at how many records those guys sell. But jazz only counts for 1 percent. If jazz is going to survive and if jazz is going to get to that next level, we need support. The young kids are really going to have to know what's going on. When they get to their thirties and forties, they have some idea of what's going on with jazz. It's not only with jazz, it's with theater. It's a whole bunch of little aspects of black culture that they really have no idea about.

Chike Nwoffiah: It speaks to the responsibility of the artist. The artist, especially given where we come from, the artist has all through time played a series of roles. The artist has been the historian. The artist has been the social commentator. The artist has been the vigilante. The artist has been the revolutionary. The artist [has been all these], and on and on and on, all through time. I think it is important because art, especially our type of art, performance art . . . [has] this awesome power, that those of us artists oftentimes forget or are not conscious of. What I'm saying is, if people are drawn to my dance and drumming, I should be able to consciously give them more than that, whether it is directly or indirectly. I can invite you then to come and see my dance performance. That has been with us even through the African American experience in America, or the experience of Africans in America through time, where through our songs and through our dances, we told the story of the struggles of our people. We sent coded messages out to the communities. Today, I think we still have to keep that responsibility, where if people are interested in what we do, albeit just curious, we should be able to use that to teach them a few things about who we are.

Keith Antar Mason: I think the artist gives us a place to be the shaman to heal ourselves and to figure out a way to envision the future for ourselves.

Rhodessa Jones: I'm interested in shamanism in theater. How can I take you to another place with my work? Any kind of theater that does that interests me. Tiny Tim says, "I don't care what you feel about me. Just feel something."

Keith Antar Mason: If you allow me to do the political thing, it was Mexico City 1968. John Smith and Tommy Carlos doing the black power sign. That erased all of my childhood nightmares of lynchings, when they held up the black power sign. I remember that they showed an Aztec pyramid, an American flag waving in the background, and these two brothers up on the platform with the power sign. I wanted to write that down. I wanted to somehow write that down in a poem. I wanted to create a poem. How do you re-create that visual image so it has the same impact? For me I can actually say, that was the [moment of] conception for me wanting to be a poet.

On Popular Culture

Christian McBride: There's no soul in anything that's popular right now. There's absolutely no soul or any depth in anything that's popular. I don't think it can really keep going on like that. Pretty soon people's souls are going to die and they're going to think, "Wait a minute, I need something else."

Will Power: A lot of kids like around my way probably think that jazz or blues is for white folks. 'Cause if they walk by the San Francisco Blues Festival, it's all white people. There's a couple of black acts, but mostly white acts and all white people are there. But it's kind of like it's hard because blues, I'm not saying that blues is old fashioned or something like that, but it was created at a certain time when a certain thing was going on. By the time you see the one dance or mainstream stuff, black people done created something else. We think, why we want to do that? It's old. We're on to something else. But it creates a challenge because the generations need to know the true history. It's kind of like a challenging thing, because we continue to innovate and then . . . A lot of the jazz artists now, there are some black jazz artists, but a lot of them are white. Definitely the audience is white. A lot of black people say, "Yeah, jazz is cool," but a lot of young people [say], "I need something to speak to me right now."

Christian McBride: Even though jazz is not necessarily a part of American popular culture any more, it's still very much at the root of American culture. Even though it's not really as popular as it once was, you can't do without it. It's always going to be there. I find that a lot of people still . . . you know, people love jazz, but we're all kind of trying to figure out a way that it can become . . . you know, I don't know if jazz should necessarily become the music of American popular culture, because I think that's one of the beauties of jazz is the fact that it's not so popular. That way we can always kind of experiment and try new things and develop. You know how the American press is nowadays. If Branford Marsalis and Wynton Marsalis or Joshua Redman or someone like myself was on the cover of *People* magazine and *Access Hollywood* every week, then the music probably wouldn't have as much impact as it does.

Michael Franti: One thing I find is that, among black American artists in particular, and especially in hip-hop, there's been this movement of really defining what is hip-hop, what is real, what is the authentic thing. I think in some ways it's a positive thing because it helps us to really progress and further push some of the ideals of our community. Like the beat has to be strong and it has to be funky and the lyrical flow has to be creative and has to follow some certain standards and codes. Just like you have scales for blues or scales for jazz, it's the same for hip-hop. It's just that we don't have names for them. In another way, I find that it hampers people from being creative. They start saying like, well, is this real or is this authentic or is this. . . . What ends up becoming real and authentic is what's selling millions of units rather than what is true and coming from the heart. The economics of hip-hop, especially, is something that I feel like is trying to stifle creativity because people say, well, what's selling and let me do something that sounds like that—rather than, I woke up this morning and I felt like sunshine, so I'm going to make this beat sound like sunshine. . . . Because a lot of people who have been drawn to hip-hop are coming from neighborhoods where we grew up poor, one of the main goals of being involved in hip-hop is to get paid. It is a critique, but [what determines] where music goes is what is making money for people. That's why music shifted from being about Public Enemy and KRS-1 and really consciousness-raising music to being about gangsta stuff.

Will Power: You know Robert Johnson? The blues singer? That's like gangsta rap! It ain't no different. He had this one line, you know, "I want you to squeeze my hand till the juice run out, mama." He's like, "I'm gonna beat my woman 'til I'm satisfied, me and the devil walking side by side." That blues stuff was gangsta music. It was like young cats. . . . And the other thing is—but see that's what I'm saying—people forget. Now, people think the blues is, "Hey, hey. The blues is all right." They go to blues concerts and they eat their hot dogs and they've got these old blues catches. Not to diss them, you know, they're jamming along with them. People forget that blues was made by some young, angry, bad-assed motherfuckers, excuse my French, down in the delta that was running from the Ku Klux Klan, had razorblades in one hand, gun in another, whiskey, you know what I mean, women. That's where blues was made. Black people trying to survive. Young cats. Robert Johnson was like twenty, twenty-one years old. But we forget.

On Black History and Consciousness

Euzhan Palcy: When you talk to the new generation of black Americans, they don't know anything about their black history if you try to teach them about it, you know, because we Caribbeans, we Africans, we are very proud of that heritage. I try to talk to them about it. They look at you with big eyes and empty eyes. This is history, this is the past. Who cares about that? The only thing they want to hear is they are American, period. They don't want to hear that. Talk to them about how many cars they can have, how many women they can have, you know, that's what they want. That's so sad. But it's the whole system.

Michael Franti: When hip-hop was really talking about black conscious-ness, it had black buyers and black listeners. Although there were white people who enjoyed dancing to the music, I don't know how much they really got into the politics of it. When it got gangsta, with bitches and whores, it became a thing where a lot of white kids in the suburbs wanted to just see what was on the other side of the tracks. They were able to get that vicarious experience through listening to hip-hop.

Will Power: I feel like those are some of the challenges of how to keep the historical stuff true and give respect where it's due. African Americans are a mixture of difficult cultures. Even though I feel like for the most part we're African, we're from African roots, but we also have white in us and we also have indigenous in us. If you look at a dance like the cakewalk, they weren't doing no cakewalk in Africa. That was the African people reacting to a European thing.

On Africa

Chike Nwoffiah: Africa is still misunderstood outside its borders. It is my opinion that historical distortions and blurred interpretations have led to very, very blurred perceptions of Africa and its people. In trying to create a theater company, what we intentionally decided to do was we would create a theater company that would present Africa and its people in a sharing way. To us, it wasn't going to be about showing off what we know, but more of sharing who we are and what we say and how we define ourselves. We wanted to stay true to the art of the African. Now, that takes me to the next level of who now, not what now, is African? Is it African in the sense that it comes from this place that is defined as Africa, the continent? Is it African because it comes from those that were born in that place or those that their ancestors came from that place?

Christian McBride: What jazz is basically is a combination of African rhythms and European harmonies, which came to America. Then, the black people of America took it and made it into something completely their own. So it turned out to be something that wasn't really, even though the roots were African, it turned out to be something completely different from anything you would hear in Africa or Europe. But the roots of it were from Africa.

Chike Nwoffiah: If you go to the African continent—in fact, let's take for instance today what is called the highlife music of western Nigeria. Now, we have, if you look at highlife music and the different variations of high-life music, you have juju music, Afro-jazz, and all that. It's interesting because the Africans in America have used the native vernacular of music from these African cultures, woven them with the American tapestry coupled with their own, and called it distinctively African American. What happens generations later is that this new art form has now gone back to the continent. So now you have all this [mixture of] other new art forms that are not indigenous to Africa. So it's amazing. A lot of the African American influence on the African music shouldn't be underestimated. It just is there. It's incredibly there.

PART THREE

International Congestion
Globalization, Dispersions, and Black Cultural Travel

TYLER STOVALL

Black Community, Black Spectacle
Performance and Race in Transatlantic Perspective

We wear the mask that grins and lies,
It hides our cheeks and shades our eyes,
This debt we pay to human guile;
With torn and bleeding hearts we smile,
And mouth with myriad subtleties . . .
Let them only see us, while
We wear the mask.
    —Paul Lawrence Dunbar, "Lyrics of Lovely Life."

This quotation from Paul Laurence Dunbar suggests that African American life in general is often a performance given before an alien, hostile, and uncomprehending audience. One reading of it implies that blacks in white society have been forced to disguise their real feelings and nature, instead acting out a series of stereotypes to please their oppressors. But the final stanza, "We wear the mask," prompts one to ask where the mask ends and the "real" face begins. Rather than emphasizing authenticity, or viewing blackness as an unchanging essence, this perspective suggests that racial identity is itself constituted through performance, shifting in myriad ways along with the relations between blacks and the wider society they inhabit and help shape. Blacks thus create not only themselves, but also their white interlocutors, through the conscious and unconscious acts that constitute performative strategies.[1]

In a recent essay, bell hooks distinguished between two types of black performance: performance as complicity in racial oppression for the sake of survival, and performance as ritual play. The first involves a display of blackness as a consumer product for a larger, nonblack audience, whereas in the second case black performance functions as a liberatory practice that emphasizes the creation and articulation of languages of identity.[2] These two aspects of black performance cannot be separated, but are constantly interacting and changing over time. To adapt Dunbar's metaphor, there is no hard-and-fast distinction between the face of affirmative performance and the stylized mask worn for outsiders; each shapes the other. Consequently, following hooks, any approach to black performance must be grounded in a broader, antiessentialist perspective, one that privileges continual interplay between performances in different contexts over notions of authentic black culture.[3]

I wish to adapt hooks's insights on the two faces of black performance by underscoring the role of expressive culture in the creation of community solidarities and traditions. In this perspective, one can develop a kind of insider/outsider motif, opposing performance for others to performance as a ritualistic act that binds a group of people together. This practice subverts the traditional pattern of black/white relations in Western societies, making the outsiders insiders and vice versa. In exploring the nature of black community from both nationalist and diasporic approaches, the role of performance in creating and politicizing them must be acknowledged.[4]

This essay will discuss black performance in Paris during the era of the Harlem Renaissance. It will consider black performance from the standpoint of both community solidarity and voyeuristic spectacle, exploring the differences and intersections of both. Paris during the Jazz Age has long been famed for its exciting avant-garde culture in a variety of fields ranging from literature to drama to music.[5] Although many have commented upon the spectacular career of Josephine Baker, making her a symbol of "the crazy years," the central role of other African American performers in the creative spirit of interwar Paris has often been overlooked. At the same time, the contribution of Paris to the history of black performance has generally not received due consideration. I will argue here that Jazz Age Paris represented an extreme example of both black community and black spectacle, therefore casting an interesting and instructive light on the interrelationship of the two. Yet Paris was not an exceptional island; rather, it shared a key role with New York, Chicago, and other centers of black modernity in the early twentieth century. This transatlantic example of black performance will hopefully demonstrate the manifold uses of black culture and the many ways in which it exemplified the anxieties of the interwar years.[6]

Black Modernity, Black Performance

Throughout the history of the African diaspora, performance has been both an expression of black consciousness and the product of the interactions between blacks and the dominant white culture.[7] On the one hand it has been rooted in and shaped by African traditions. On the other, blacks have adapted these traditions to the radically different conditions they encountered in the New World, from the era of slavery to the present day.[8] Many scholars have shown how manifestations of African American performative culture, from jazz to the call-and-response tradition of the black church, reveal African antecedents.[9] Black American culture, and American culture in general, cannot be understood without attention to the contributions of the ancestral black continent. At the same time, the necessity of surviving in a hostile white world has shaped black performance in numerous ways as blacks adapted to their surroundings. The different creole languages of the Caribbean reflect a complex series of linguistic negotiations between white masters and black slaves, as the former tried to use language to control their slaves and the latter saw it as a means of resistance.[10] Capoeira, the ritualized martial art invented by the slaves of northern Brazil, represented a response to slavemasters' bans on fighting that still permitted black men to demonstrate power and agency.[11] Similarly, the intricate *tignons,* or headscarves, of women of color in antebellum New Orleans represented an assertion of black female beauty and equality in the face of laws restricting elegant coiffures to whites.[12]

Given these and many other examples, it is not surprising that some theorists have come to regard performance as a key element of the relationship between the dominant and the subaltern. In his celebrated essay "Of Mimicry and Man," literary critic Homi Bhabha has addressed the ways in which the imitation of their masters by colonial subordinate groups serves symbolically to renegotiate the relationship between the two.[13] Scholars of whiteness like David Roediger, Eric Lott, and Michael Rogin have studied blackface minstrelsy as a performative style that both challenged and reinforced distinctions between black and white in American culture.[14] More recently, philosopher Judith Butler has used the concept of performativity to show how instances of hate speech constitute discourses of discrimination and power.[15] Such scholarship underscores the importance of performance to African American history and culture, and its power to mark and subvert racial distinctions.

Performance has become especially significant to black cultures of modernity. I would in fact argue that one distinguishing characteristic of blackness in the age of modernism is the heightened importance of the performer as a representative of black culture in general. In the history of the African diaspora since the end of slavery, black actors, dancers, and musicians have taken center stage as symbols of what it means to be black (and, by extension, what it means to be white).[16] This is due not just to changes in black history, but also to the nature of modernity in general during the early twentieth century. One important aspect of the rise of modernist culture has been a shift in the relative importance of production and consumption as cultural tropes. In both Europe and America, the dawn of the new century witnessed the rise of a middle-class society more distanced from the work of industrial development and capital accumulation than its nineteenth-century forebear. The result was a culture in which styles of consumption, be they in fashion, housing, food, or other areas, took pride of place over labor in the definition of social identities.[17]

Few blacks shared in such affluence, of course, but the rise of consumer culture had its impact upon blackness as well. The end of black slavery in America meant that the issue of labor and production was no longer so central to what it meant to be black.[18] At the same time, the African American migration from rural South to urban North in the late nineteenth and early twentieth centuries created a new type of black presence, constituting an urban symbol of blackness as an alternative to the plantation. Ghettos in northern cities constituted a segregated, autonomous urban space, separated from white areas by social practice but also available to white city dwellers as zones of transgression, both of pleasure and of danger. Urban modernity thus reinforced the status of blackness as a consumer product, one central to the definition of avant-garde white racial identity.[19]

These were the kinds of trends that produced the Harlem Renaissance, the cultural flowering of black urban modernity that owed so much to interracial interactions.[20] Although the Harlem Renaissance is usually identified with writers like Langston Hughes, Zora Neale Hurston, and Jessie Fauset, musical performance certainly also had a deep impact upon it. Recent scholarship has, in fact, questioned traditional views of this period as primarily a literary movement, emphasizing in addition the centrality of music to intellectual life.[21] From the emphasis placed by the Talented Tenth upon the contribution of spirituals to classical music to the profusion of black musical theater, even on Broadway, the new black culture sang and danced as well as wrote its redefinitions of African American life. Jazz became a key symbol of black musical creativity during the Harlem Renaissance, and much of the generational tension between black intellectuals centered around reactions to this new form of music, and to black popular culture in general. As Langston Hughes wrote in 1926:

> Let the blare of Negro jazz bands and the bellowing voice of Bessie Smith singing Blues penetrate the closed ears of the colored near-intellectuals until they listen and perhaps understand. . . . We younger Negro artists who create now intend to express our dark-skinned selves without fear or shame. If white people are pleased we are glad. If they are not, it doesn't matter . . . If colored people are pleased we are glad. If they are not, their displeasure doesn't matter either.[22]

As this quotation makes clear, jazz became a prime symbol of black identity as well as blackness as a consumer product in America during the early twentieth century. When many outsiders thought of Harlem and other African American urban neighborhoods, they summoned up images not of literature, churches, and spirituals, but of hot jazz bands, rent parties, and fancy nightclubs. Yet jazz was overwhelmingly produced and consumed by and for black people, and certainly cannot be reduced to "black culture for sale." For a variety of reasons, the creative tension between community and spectacle was even more pronounced in the expatriate black life of interwar Paris. As an analysis of the Parisian experience will reveal, this tension was key to perceptions of blackness by both blacks and whites in the modern era.

White Spectatorship

The important role played by whites in the history of the Harlem Renaissance is well known. White patrons of the arts like Charlotte Osgood Mason and Fannie Hurst exercised a supportive and at times controlling influence on several important writers and artists, bringing to bear their own ideas about what black art should be upon those who created it. White intellectuals like Heywood Broun, Fania Marinoff, and, most notoriously, Carl Van Vechten were fascinated by Harlem's nightlife and culture, claiming to find in them answers to the troublesome questions posed by the modern age.[23] Beyond such noteworthy individuals, Harlem attracted a large population of white tourists, especially during the late

1920s, who came to the neighborhood in search of thrills not readily available at home. These outsiders were drawn above all by plush, often segregated nightclubs like Connie's Inn and the Cotton Club, entertainment spaces that featured lively jazz bands and other performances. At a more profound level, they offered whites a sanitized, carefully controlled glimpse of black life, one that enticed with a daring sense of racial transgression, yet left underlying hierarchies undisturbed.[24] Yet whites also ventured to humbler nightclubs like Ed Small's or the Clam House, and even made their way to rent parties where one could hear "real jazz." George Gershwin, for example, frequently attended and played piano at such modest but exciting venues.[25]

The white vogue for Harlem had a number of reasons. Jazz was the primary attraction, and certainly appealed to many on its musical merits alone. However, one could hear jazz without going to Harlem, and the Jazz Age represented more than music. Prohibition contributed to the popularity of black nightlife in the 1920s and 1930s. The banning of alcohol gave all nightclubs a more illicit air, so that going to hear black music in a black neighborhood seemed less of a stretch than it might have before the war.[26] More generally, the interest in jazz and black culture represented a rejection of the dominant conservative mood in America in the twenties that Prohibition symbolized. Finally, the presence of a large black "city within a city" was a relatively new phenomenon in the North. New York's prewar black population had been not only smaller but more decentralized, scattered throughout Manhattan. Growth and ghettoization thus constituted Harlem as an alternate cultural space, a new world, exotic and unknown.[27] The result was an unprecedented increase in white Americans' public fascination with black life, leading to a sharp rise in white spectatorship.

The intensification of white interest in black culture was, if anything, even more pronounced on the other side of the ocean, leading to the re-creation of a famous Parisian neighborhood, Montmartre, as a sort of transatlantic Harlem. The fascination with blackness in interwar Paris arose from changes in both French and American life. Starting with the first major exhibition of African sculpture in 1905, many avant-garde Parisian intellectuals had transmuted their own disenchantment with positivist European civilization into a romanticization of the black aesthetic. World War I accentuated this interest by demonstrating the destructive depths to which the Western world could descend and by providing French women and men a glimpse of real-life alternatives in the form of African, Afro-Caribbean, and African American soldiers.[28] By the end of the war, writer Guillaume Apollinaire was able to write that prewar negrophilia had turned into negromania.[29] The war also brought a new prominence to American mass culture in France, symbolized by the triumph of Hollywood movies in Parisian theaters.[30] At the same time, not only American culture but also Americans themselves came to France in unprecedented numbers during the 1920s. American prosperity, the desire to visit wartime gravesites and battlefields, favorable exchange rates, and the lack of prohibition in France all contributed to an explosion of American mass tourism to that country.[31] The double consciousness of African American life, representing both Africa and America, thus exercised a dual fascination upon the French avant-garde.

Montmartre had a long history as a center of popular entertainment. During the early nineteenth century, before its annexation by the city of Paris, the area was home to numerous wine shops where one could drink more cheaply because of the absence of city taxes. The end of the century saw the golden area of music halls like the Moulin Rouge and Le Chat Noir, immortalized by impressionist painters. By the 1920s, artists and intellectuals had largely deserted Montmartre, and the neighborhood reverted to its former emphasis on nightlife.[32] In particular, although not exclusively, the area's music clubs specialized in African American jazz and performance. A group of small nightclubs just south of the Place Pigalle, places like Zelli's, Bricktop's, Chez Florence, and L'Abbaye claimed to offer the latest in hot sounds, direct from America. A diverse crowd of socialites, aristocrats, American expatriates, and Parisians, all intent upon seeming as modern as possible, made black American jazz a hit in Montmartre. Night after night throughout the 1920s and early 1930s, this archipelago of black performance became the place to let loose and "shake that thing" until the morning light.[33]

In this respect, Montmartre did indeed resemble Harlem. Many of its musicians, most notably Bricktop, had come there directly from New York, and people constantly circulated between the two neighorhoods.[34] Yet Montmartre was Harlem with a difference. Unlike New York's black ghetto, Montmartre, although home to a diverse population of immigrants, was overwhelmingly white and French. As a result, the audiences at its jazz clubs were also mostly white. One could find in Montmartre the equivalent of the Cotton Club (in fact, a bar named the Cotton Club opened there in 1929), but it offered no real parallels to Harlem's rent parties, or other spaces where mostly blacks gathered to hear black music. In Montmartre, much more than in Harlem, black performance equaled black spectacle, a show to a large extent put on for outsiders. Some whites in New York may have erroneously believed that most blacks in Harlem were jazz musicians. In Montmartre this was actually true; most African Americans there were in fact jazz musicians. Blackness, jazz, and performance were equated to such an extent that some of the few French musicians in Parisian jazz bands during the 1920s routinely performed in blackface.[35] In other words, the stage was for blacks, the audience was for whites. This distinction was all the more important in that much of the audience in Montmartre's jazz clubs consisted of American tourists, people for whom a night in Montmartre represented at once a daring foray into the underworld and a taste of home. Interwar Montmartre thus represented an extreme version of black performance as spectacle, a show that catered to primitivist preconceptions of black culture and music for the benefit of white viewers. As Claude McKay put it, "The Montmartre of the cabarets and music halls never excited me. It is so obviously a place where the very formal French allow foreigners who can pay to cut up informally. It has no character of its own."[36]

The African American Community in Paris

However, there was another side to black life in Montmartre. Although largely white, the neighborhood was home to a small but well-defined and interconnected African American community with its own institutions and practices. Moreover, black performance, although largely aimed at white audiences, at the same time brought African Americans together in a strange, foreign city. Black jazz clubs, several of which were owned and operated by black Americans, fulfilled a dual purpose in interwar Montmartre: not only did they offer exciting new music and exoticist fantasies to white audiences, they also served the black community in Paris as a kind of "home turf," a space where they could go and feel at ease. In 1925, for example, the poet Gwendolyn Bennett described a night on the town in tones that illustrated this sense of identity and belonging:

> Then at 4:15 AM to dear old "Bricktop's" . . . extremely crowded this night with our folk. "Brick" singing as well as ever her hits— "Insufficient Sweetie" and "I'm in Love Again" . . . Lottie Gee there on her first night in town and sings for "Brick" her hit from "Shuffle Along"—"I'm Just Wild About Harry." Her voice is not what it might

have been and she had too much champaign [*sic*] but still there was
something very personal and dear about her singing it and we colored
folks just applauded like mad.[37]

Everything about this passage reflects a view of the jazz club as community institution, from the fond, familiar terms in which Bennett refers to
Bricktop, to the intense personal and collective identification with Lottie
Gee's song. This was all the more notable in that Bennett was probably not
a regular at Bricktop's (as a student on scholarship she couldn't afford it),
but nonetheless saw it as *her* place. The description of Lottie Gee exemplifies the idea of black performance as a ritual that binds a community
together, with familiar songs that provoke an enthusiastic response. This is
all the more significant in that there were doubtless many whites at Bricktop's that night, but Bennett doesn't mention them. The only thing that
counts for her is the applause offered by "we colored folk."

Most African Americans in Paris between the wars were jazz musicians,
people for whom France represented, at least initially, another gig. Unlike
the white American writers of the Lost Generation who came to learn from
the French, these individuals were in Paris because their hosts wanted what
they had to offer, and in many cases were willing to pay handsome salaries
for it. Many of them stayed in France throughout the 1920s and 1930s, setting down roots in the French capital and only leaving when a new war
threatened their survival. Both their numbers and their enviable positions
thus made musicians the leaders of the black expatriate community in
Paris. In contrast, the writers, artists, students, and other black Americans
who did not play jazz for a living had less money and stayed more briefly,
often for a summer or a year on fellowship. The prominence of jazz musicians in Paris, at a time when many elite African Americans still considered
jazz lowdown and undignified, created an interesting inversion of class
status hard to imagine in Harlem or most other black neighborhoods in
the United States. The example of Langston Hughes, middle class and college educated, working as a busboy in a Montmartre jazz club provides a
case in point. In Renaissance Harlem, literature seized the high ground as
representing the new black culture; in Montmartre, black music reigned
supreme.[38]

The community of African Americans in interwar Paris was small,
never more than one or two thousand, and tightly knit. Although its
members came from many different parts of the United States, not just
New York, they seem to have developed a variety of communal networks

and associations. Not all of them lived in Montmartre, yet that neighborhood quickly became the place for black expatriates in Paris to find each other and some semblance of the culture they had left behind. As Joel Augustus Rogers, the Paris correspondent for several African American newspapers, put it:

> The Boulevard de Clichy is the 42nd and Broadway of Paris. Most of the night life of Paris centers around it, and most of the colored folks from the States, too. If you hear that some friend from the States is in Paris, just circulate around this boulevard from the Moulin rouge down Rue Pigalle as far as the Flea Pit, and it's a hundred to one shot you'll encounter him or her, at least twice during the night.
>
> Most of the colored folk live in this neighborhood. There is a surprising number of them, and it is increasing every year.[39]

Within Montmartre, cafes, cheap hotels, a few American restaurants, and above all jazz clubs served as places for black Americans to congregate. The African Americans of interwar Paris did not constitute the kind of black community familiar to people in the United States; there were few children or families and few individuals who had been there for longer than a few years at any given point. One notable contrast to the central role played by churches in the black life of the United States was the almost total absence of any black church or other religious structure. In effect, the nightclubs of Montmartre constituted an alternative to the black church at home: a place where one could go to get a taste of African American life and, to a certain extent, see blacks in positions of power and authority. Consequently musicians, not preachers, became the leaders of the black expatriate community in Jazz Age Paris. When, for example, the American army sent black Gold Star mothers (those who had lost sons in the war) to France on a segregated ship, it was the African American musicians of Montmartre who organized to meet the ship in Le Havre as a protest against this discriminatory treatment. More so than in Harlem, perhaps because they had so little competition, Paris' black nightclubs brought the black community together.[40]

No one symbolizes black performance in 1920s Paris more than Josephine Baker, and this essay will explore her presence there in more depth subsequently. From her triumphant debut in the *Revue nègre* as a living representation of torrid primitivism, to her later success as a star of the Paris music hall, Baker was the epitome of black performance as a spectacle for enthusiastic white audiences. Yet Baker also had her ties to black Montmartre. Not only did she carry on a close, if conflicted, relationship with Bricktop, the godmother of the neighborhood, but also frequently worked with local musicians. At the end of 1926 she opened her own nightclub, Chez Josephine, in the heart of Montmartre's entertainment district. Like other jazz clubs in the area, Chez Josephine welcomed both the African American community and white café society. While her successful career soon took her far beyond black Montmartre, for a time even the great Josephine balanced the contrasting imperatives of performance in black and white.

Montmartre in the Jazz Age was therefore not just a pleasure ground created for tourists, but a small yet vibrant African American community. In Paris, the difference between black performance as spectacle versus community ritual stood out in a more extreme fashion than in the ghettos of America. Yet this difference was not rigid or immutable. In the rest of this essay, I will outline the ways in which these two aspects of black performance interacted with and reinforced each other, producing a black culture of modernity.

Complicity and Resistance

The role of jazz in the histories of blacks and performance in both Montmartre and Harlem leads one to consider the relationship of popular African American music to the political agenda of the Harlem Renaissance. Traditionally, many of those who studied the period have considered jazz peripheral to the literary and political struggle for black uplift after World War I. While an important aspect of black culture at the time, jazz and black performance are portrayed primarily as entertainment, somehow separate from the fight against Jim Crow. Contemporary literary figures often went further, condemning jazz—and indeed all popular culture—as debased and politically unimportant. Writers in both the *Crisis* and the *Messenger* editorialized against jazz, seeing in it the culture of the least respectable, most degenerate segments of the black community. At bottom, much of this hostility arose out of the suspicion that the vogue for jazz owed more to white primitivist fantasies than to the music's artistic integrity, that it was yet another way of expressing convictions about black inferiority.[41] More recently, scholars like Ted Vincent have challenged this view, emphasizing jazz's revolutionary aestheticism and the importance of intellectuals, such as Langston Hughes and Cyril Briggs, who championed it. Yet the central issue remains posed: how can black performance function simultaneously as spectacle and as community ritual?[42]

This was certainly an important problem for the African American performers of Jazz Age Paris. Bricktop, for example, has been criticized for fawning over a series of white aristocrats—most notably the Prince of Wales—who viewed their visits to her nightclub more as exotic slumming than as a rejection of racial distinctions. Some musicians who worked at her fabled nightclubs have accused Bricktop of forcing them to "tone down" their music, playing bland sounds to cater to an audience that viewed jazz as a distraction, not a serious art form.[43] Not surprisingly, Josephine Baker's performative style has attracted even more censure. Her debut in the *Revue nègre* rested upon some of the oldest stereotypes of black womanhood, and the banana skirt for which she became famous closely resembled derogatory images of Africans found in French advertising and popular culture. After all, her celebrated *danse sauvage* was in fact invented by a French choreographer, Jacques Charles, based upon his own ideas of what constituted black culture.[44] In her theatrical performances, Baker portrayed a succession of innocent waifs in the French empire, usually in love with dashing young military officers.[45] Such romanticized justifications of colonialism in general, and the sexual exploitation of women of color in particular, illustrate the aesthetic and political dangers that can attend black performance in certain historical contexts.

Yet attention to historical context must also consider the various ways in which Bricktop, Josephine Baker, and other African Americans in Jazz Age Paris also resisted the pressures of performance as spectacle, striving to perform their art on their own terms.[46] Jazz musicians' early morning jam sessions—after the clubs had closed and the tourists had gone home—constituted a symbolic reclaiming of performative space for and by those who had created it. Such sessions gave them the chance to play the music they loved for themselves, replicating the group experimentation that is the heart of jazz. For all the resemblance between Bricktop's and Harlem nightspots like the Cotton Club, Parisian clubs differed from their New York cousins in one key respect: in Paris, blacks were always welcome, as patrons as well as performers, and interacted with whites as equals.[47] However much Bricktop may have adored the titled nobility, she reserved her warmest welcomes for African American celebrities like Paul Robeson and Jack Johnson. Years before her public challenges to racial segregation in America, even Josephine Baker at times sought to transform the stereotypical frame in which the French placed her. Her signature song, "J'ai deux amours," originally came from an operetta in which Baker portrayed a Vietnamese girl torn between her love for her homeland and for a handsome young Frenchman. Baker gradually changed the meaning of this song to represent her position between America and Paris, shaping it into a subtle critique of the homeland whose racism had forfeited its right to her love.

For Josephine Baker and many other African Americans in Paris, exile in and of itself was an act of performative resistance. Unlike the self-conscious expatriates of the 1950s, most had initially come to France for money and opportunity, not politics. Yet, once in France, many came to value the unprecedented experience of comparatively kind and egalitarian treatment at the hands of the French, seeing in it a hard-to-imagine alternative to life in the United States. Life in Paris enabled them to perform in conditions that in several ways represented an improvement on those available at home. Moreover, the creation of an expatriate black community was itself a kind of dress rehearsal for the freedom many hoped would one day be available on the other side of the Atlantic. In considering the relationship of black performance to the liberationist agenda of the Harlem Renaissance, the dynamics of complicity and resistance offered by Jazz Age Paris exemplify the complex character of black culture in the age of modernity.[48]

Princess Tam Tam

Few texts illustrate the intricate interweavings of community and spectacular performance in the Jazz Age better than Baker's 1935 film *Princess Tam Tam*. A colonial and primitivist fantasy, the film relates the story of Aouina, a young Tunisian child of nature who is "discovered" by a bored French writer in search of tropical inspiration. Pygmalion-like, he attempts to teach her civilized values and brings her to Paris, disguising her as "Princess Tam Tam" (Princess Tom-Tom) from a far-off, exotic land. The beautiful dark-skinned "princess" soon takes Parisian high society by storm (much as Baker did herself), yet ultimately learns that "East is East and West is West," that she belongs not in the West but back home in Tunisia. Her civilized ways are only a thin veneer that she soon sloughs off as she returns to a life of carefree savagery in the desert.[49]

Two contrasting scenes from *Princess Tam Tam* highlight the differ-

FIG. 1. *Princess Tam Tam*, Kino Video. (Courtesy Kino International.)

ences between black performance for one's own community and performance for outsiders—and, to a certain extent, they call into question that very distinction. The first occurs in Paris when Baker, tired of society parties, decides she wants to go out and have fun the way ordinary people do. She and a servant joyfully explore an amusement park and a variety of popular entertainments before ending up in a working-class bar. This establishment, which resembles nothing so much as a seedy sailor's dive in a tropical port rather than a Parisian café,[50] features blacks and whites dressed in shabby clothes, as well as an orchestra of black men singing softly about the beauties of African skies.[51] The clientele is mostly masculine, with the notable exception of one white actress in blackface. Although the atmosphere differs in many ways from the elegance of Montmartre nightclubs, like them this bar offers a sense of black community, of a place where blacks come to meet and be with each other. Here subaltern identities based upon class and upon race mutually reinforce each other, so that a proletarian bar becomes the natural setting for a black subculture.[52] Of course, the entire scene (like the subsequent one I will discuss) is an excuse to display Baker's acting and dancing talents. She starts singing with the band and then dances with a white sailor, displaying an easy joy at being among her people and living for the moment. This is performance that emphasizes a comfortable sense of belonging and community, the ease of being with one's own in a strange land.

The next scene features a very different presentation of Josephine Baker. She attends a lavish party given by a maharaja (also a white actor in blackface) visiting Paris. The party showcases one elaborate dance routine after another, very much resembling the geometrical choreography of Busby Berkeley. A Frenchwoman, who had seen Baker at the sailor's bar while slumming with some society friends, gets her drunk and entices her to go out onto the dance floor. Baker of course needs little encouragement. She tears off her shoes and her high-fashion gown, hurls herself into the middle of the dancers and moves frenetically to the beat.[53] This is pure performance as spectacle. Baker is the only black person in the scene; the only black musician one sees is an African tom-tom drummer who is presented not as a real person but as an abstract symbol of the African beat. Whereas the music in the sailor's bar is gentle and winsome, at the maharaja's party the sounds are pulsing, exciting, dramatic. As the figure of the African drummer makes clear, here the beat is everything. This inversion of traditional associations between low social status and rough music reinforces the contrast between community and a performance for outsiders. The scene ends with Baker receiving wild applause from the other guests, much to the bitter disappointment of the envious white women who had set up her performance. Her reversion to savagery on the dance floor becomes, like her real-life success in the *Revue nègre*, a triumph of the primitivist aesthetic.

These two performances by Josephine Baker differ markedly, highlighting the contrast between community ritual and spectacular display. At the same time, however, the two scenes have much in common, and these various levels of kinship raise the issue of the slippage between solidarity and spectacle. Most obviously, both scenes are part of a film directed and produced by whites and intended for a white audience. The sailor's bar is no more an authentic black space than the *danse sauvage* was an authentic African dance; rather, it is a fantasized representation of such a space. Moreover, both scenes contain, and are in fact linked by, white spectators. Like the princess herself, the whites who visit the sailor's bar are searching for an authentic black experience, although for different reasons. The music and the dancing prove attractive, as does the prospect of entering a strange new world usually closed to whites. It is not just black performance, but black performance in its social and cultural context, that is so alluring.

In short, the phenomenon of white slumming in *Princess Tam Tam* shows how the distinction between black performance for outsiders and for one's own can be undermined when the black community itself is the spectacle. The attraction of black nightclubs was not just the performers, but also the audiences; whites as well as blacks enjoyed and sought out what Gwendolyn Bennett described as being among "our folk." In America, whites who tired of the staged black culture featured in establishments like the Cotton Club would seek out more modest nightclubs and rent parties. Not only could one supposedly find "real" jazz there, but also one could observe authentic black life, not just black performance. Such black spaces also served as refuges for whites involved in asocial behavior, such as extramarital or homosexual social relations, since one need not worry about being seen there by others from "respectable" society.[54] More generally, in a society where relations between whites and blacks had been highly regimented and structured, avant-garde whites found themselves tempted to pierce the protective veils around black life and enjoy the privilege of seeing African Americans the way they saw themselves.

Ultimately, such attempts at transgression bring us back to an initial theme of this essay: In many ways, all aspects of African American life can be seen as performance, because they can never be completely divorced from their context of a minority subculture in a larger white world. Therefore, rather than looking for distinctions between the community-based or spectacular aspects of black performance, it is perhaps more useful to consider the many ways in which they intersect. In Jazz Age Paris, the small size of the African American population and the dual role played by its jazz clubs, both as centers of community and as exotic stagings of black culture, present this intersection in dramatic fashion. Such intersections lie at the heart of black modernity, and their Parisian version merits consideration in any exploration of the cultural history of race and performance in the twentieth century.

NOTES

The epigraph comes from Paul Laurence Dunbar, "Lyrics of Lovely Life," in *The Collected Poetry of Paul Laurence Dunbar,* ed. Joanne M. Braxton (Charlottesville: University Press of Virginia, 1993). See also Paul Gilroy's analysis of this poem in "'. . . to be real': The Dissident Forms of Black Expressive Culture," in *Let's Get It On: The Politics of Black Performance,* ed. Catherine Ugwu (Seattle: Bay Press, 1995).

1. The literature on performance studies provides important theoretical insights into the constitution of social identities. See Peggy Phelan and Jill Lane, eds., *The Ends of Performance* (New York: New York University Press, 1998); Richard Schechner and Willa Appel, eds., *By Means of Performance: Intercultural Studies of Theatre and Ritual* (Cambridge: Cambridge University Press, 1990); Andrew Parker and Eve Kosofsky Sedgwick, *Performativity and Performance* (New York: Routledge, 1995).

2. bell hooks, "Performance Practice as a Site of Opposition," in Ugwu, *Let's Get It On.*

3. On questions of racial identity and essentialism, see Henry Louis Gates, Jr., *"Race," Writing, and Difference* (Chicago: University of Chicago Press, 1986); Houston A. Baker, Jr., Manthia Diawara, and Ruth H. Lindeborg, eds., *Black British Cultural Studies: A Reader* (Chicago: University of Chicago Press, 1996); Paul Gilroy, *The Black Atlantic: Modernity and Double Consciousness* (Cambridge: Harvard University Press, 1993); Kobena Mercer, "Diaspora Culture and the Dialogic Imagination," in *Blackframes: Critical Perspectives on Black Independent Cinema,* ed. Mbye Cham and Claire Andrade-Watkins (Cambridge: MIT Press, 1988); Anna Stubblefield, "Racial Identity and Non-essentialism about Race," *Social Theory and Practice* 21, no. 3 (1995): 341–69.

4. On theories of black community, see Stuart Hall, "Cultural Identity and Diaspora," in *Identity: Community, Culture, Difference,* ed. Jonathan Rutherford (London: Lawrence and Wishart, 1990); Tyler Stovall, "Harlem-sur-Seine: Building an African American Diasporic Community in Paris," *Stanford Humanities Review* 5, no. 2 (1997): 202–18.

5. On the interwar Parisian avant-garde, see George Melly, *Paris and the Surrealists* (New York: Thames and Hudson, 1991); Paul Rabinow, *French Modern: Norms and Forms of the Social Environment* (Cambridge: MIT Press, 1989); Douglas Johnson and

Madeleine Johnson, *The Age of Illusion: Art and Politics in France, 1918–1940* (London: Thames and Hudson, 1987).

6. On interwar black Paris, see Michel Fabre, *From Harlem to Paris: Black Writers in France* (Urbana: University of Illinois Press, 1991); Tyler Stovall, *Paris Noir: African Americans in the City of Light* (Boston: Houghton Mifflin, 1996); Jody Blake, *Le Tumulte Noir: Modernist Art and Popular Entertainment in Jazz-Age Paris, 1900–1930* (University Park: Pennsylvania State University Press, 1999); Phyllis Rose, *Jazz Cleopatra: Josephine Baker in Her Time* (New York: Doubleday, 1989).

7. Henry Louis Gates, Jr., *The Signifying Monkey: A Theory of Afro-American Literary Criticism* (New York: Oxford University Press, 1988); Sandra L. Richards, "Writing the Absent Potential: Drama, Performance, and the Canon of African American Literature," in Parker and Sedgwick, *Performativity and Performance.*

8. For an interesting review of the debate between Afrocentrists and diasporic theorists on the relationship between African and African American culture, see Tunde Adeleke, "Black Americans, Africa, and History: A Reassessment of the Pan-African and Identity Paradigms," *Western Journal of Black Studies* 22, no. 3 (1998): 182–94.

9. Gale Jackson, "The Way We Do: A Preliminary Investigation of the African Roots of African American Performance," *Black American Literature Forum* 25, no. 1 (1991): 11–22; Joanne K. Henning, "Black Theatre and Performance: A Pan-African Bibliography," *Ariel* 23, no. 1 (1992): 160–62; Gerald L. Davis, *I Got the Word in Me and I Can Sing It, You Know: A Study of the Performed African-American Sermon* (Philadelphia: University of Pennsylvania Press, 1985).

10. Chris Bongie, *Islands and Exiles: The Creole Identities of Post/Colonial Literature* (Stanford: Stanford University Press, 1998).

11. John Lowell Lewis, *Ring of Liberation: A Deceptive Discourse in Brazilian Capoeira* (Chicago: University of Chicago Press, 1997).

12. Kimberly S. Hangar, *Bounded Lives, Bounded Places: Free Black Society in Colonial New Orleans, 1769–1803* (Durham, N.C.: Duke University Press, 1997), 137; Carolyn Cosse Bell, *Revolution, Romanticism, and the Afro-Creole Protest Tradition in Louisiana, 1718–1868* (Baton Rouge: Louisiana State University Press, 1997). On Creole performance, see also Helen A. Regis, "Second Lives, Minstrelsy, and the Contested Landscapes of New Orleans Afro-Creole Festivals," *Cultural Anthropology* 14, no. 4 (1999): 472–504; Pamela Franco, "'Dressing up and Looking Good': Afro-Creole Female Maskers in Trinidad Carnival," *African Arts* 31, no. 2 (1998): 62–67.

13. Homi Bhabha, "Of Mimicry and Man: The Ambivalence of Colonial Discourse," *October* 28 (spring 1984): 121–33.

14. David Roediger, *The Wages of Whiteness: Race and the Making of the American Working Class* (London: Verso, 1991) and *Towards the Abolition of Whiteness: Essays on Race, Politics, and Working-Class History* (London: Verso, 1994); Theodore Allen, *The Invention of the White Race,* vol. 1, *Racial Oppression and Social Control* (London: Verso, 1994); Michael Rogin, *Blackface, White Noise: Jewish Immigrants in the Hollywood Melting Pot* (Berkeley and Los Angeles: University of California Press, 1996); Eric Lott, *Love and Theft: Blackface Minstrelsy and the American Working Class* (New York: Oxford University Press, 1993); Matthew Frye Jacobson, *Whiteness of a Different Color: European Immigrants and the Alchemy of Race* (Cambridge: Harvard University Press, 1998).

15. Judith Butler, "Burning Acts: Injurious Speech," in Parker and Sedgwick, *Performativity and Performance.*

16. Angela M. S. Nelson, ed., *"This Is How We Flow": Rhythm in Black Cultures* (Columbia: University of South Carolina Press, 1999); David Toop, *The Rap Attack: African Jive to New York Hip Hop* (London: Pluto Press, 1984); Amiri Baraka, *Blues People* (New York: William Morrow, 1963).

17. On consumer culture and modernism, see T. J. Jackson Lears, *No Place of Grace: Antimodernism and the Transformation of American Culture, 1880–1920* (New York: Pantheon, 1981); Neil McKendrick, John Brewer, and J. H. Plumb, *The Birth of a Consumer Society: The Commercialization of Eighteenth Century England* (Bloomington: Indiana University Press, 1982); Rosalind Williams, *Dream Worlds: Mass Consumption in Late Nineteenth Century France* (Berkeley and Los Angeles: University of California Press, 1982); Lizabeth Cohen, *Making a New Deal: Industrial Workers in Chicago, 1919–1939* (Cambridge: Cambridge University Press, 1990); Victoria de Grazia and Ellen Furlough, *The Sex of Thing: Gender and Consumption in Historical Perspective* (Berkeley and Los Angeles: University of California Press, 1996).

18. This certainly does not imply that black labor lost its economic importance in the post-Emancipation era. Rather, I suggest that its symbolic significance changed.

19. See, for example, Allan Spear, *Black Chicago: The Making of a Negro Ghetto, 1890–1920* (Chicago: University of Chicago Press, 1967); Kenneth Kusmer, *A Ghetto Takes Shape: Black Cleveland, 1870–1930* (Urbana: University of Illinois Press, 1978); Theodore Kornweibel, Jr., ed., *In Search of the Promised Land: Essays in Black Urban History* (Port Washington, N.Y.: Kennikat Press, 1981).

20. On the Harlem Renaissance, see Nathan I. Huggins, *Harlem Renaissance* (New York: Oxford University Press, 1973); Houston A. Baker, Jr., *Modernism and the Harlem Renaissance* (Chicago: University of Chicago Press, 1987); Alain Locke, ed., *The New Negro* (New York: Atheneum, 1992); Jervis Anderson, *This Was Harlem: A Cultural Portrait, 1900–1950* (New York: Farrar, Straus and Giroux, 1982); David Levering Lewis, *When Harlem Was in Vogue* (New York: Vintage, 1979); Cheryl Wall, *Women of the Harlem Renaissance* (Bloomington: University of Indiana Press, 1995).

21. Samuel A. Floyd, Jr., ed., *Black Music in the Harlem Renaissance: A Collection of Essays* (New York: Greenwood Press, 1990); Ted Vincent, *Keep Cool: The Black Activists Who Built the Jazz Age* (London: Pluto Press, 1995); Jon Michael Spencer, *The New Negroes and Their Music: The Success of the Harlem Renaissance* (Knoxville: University of Tennessee Press, 1997).

22. Langston Hughes, "The Negro Artist and the Racial Mountain," *The Nation,* June 28, 1926, cited in Lewis, *Harlem in Vogue,* 191.

23. Leon Coleman, *Carl Van Vechten and the Harlem Renaissance: A Critical Assessment* (New York: Garland, 1998); George Hutchinson, *The Harlem Renaissance in Black and White* (Cambridge: Harvard University Press, 1995); Jeffrey C. Stewart, "Black Modernism and White Patronage: African American Art during the Harlem Renaissance," *International Review of African American Art* 11, no. 3 (1994): 43–55.

24. Note that the segregated nightclubs in fact reinforced these hierarchies, bringing a sense of plantation life to the North.

25. Ann Douglas, *Terrible Honesty: Mongrel Manhattan in the 1920s* (New York: Farrar, Straus and Giroux, 1995); George Chauncey, *Gay New York: Gender, Culture, and the Makings of the Gay Male World* (New York: Basic Books, 1994).

26. Malcolm Cowley, *Exile's Return: A Literary Odyssey of the 1920s* (New York: Norton, 1934). On the history of Prohibition, see Herbert Asbury, *The Great Illusion: An Informal History of Prohibition* (Garden City, N.Y.: Doubleday, 1950); Thomas Coffey, *The Long Thirst: Prohibition in America, 1920–1933* (New York: Norton, 1975); Edward Behr, *Prohibition: Thirteen Years That Changed America* (New York: Arcade, 1996).

27. Gilbert Osofsky, *Harlem: The Making of a Ghetto: Negro New York, 1890–1930* (New York: Harper and Row, 1966).

28. Marc Michel, *L'Appel à l'Afrique: Contributions et reactions à l'effort de guerre en A.O.F.* (Paris: Publications de la Sorbonne, 1982); Arthur E. Barbeau and Florette Henri, *The Unknown Soldiers: Black American Troops in World War I* (Philadelphia: Temple University Press, 1974).

29. Gérard G. Le Coat, "*Art Nègre* and *Esprit Moderne* in France (1907–1911)," in *Double Impact: France and Africa in the Age of Imperialism*, ed. G. Wesley Johnson (Westport, Conn.: Greenwood Press, 1985); William Rubin, *"Primitivism" in Twentieth Century Art: Affinity of the Tribal and the Modern* (New York: Museum of Modern Art, 1984); James Clifford, "Negrophilia," in *The New History of French Literature*, ed. Denis Hollier (Cambridge: Harvard University Press, 1989). A fine example of interwar "Negrophilia" is Paul Morand, *Magie Noire* (Paris: Ferenczi, 1936).

30. Richard Abel, *French Cinema: The First Wave, 1915–1929* (Princeton: Princeton University Press, 1984), 9–11; Charles Rearick, *The French in Love and War: Popular Culture in the Era of the World Wars* (New Haven: Yale University Press, 1997), 20–21.

31. Harvey Levenstein, *Seductive Journey: American Tourists in France from Jefferson to the Jazz Age* (Chicago: University of Chicago Press, 1998).

32. Louis Chevalier, *Montmartre du plaisir et du crime* (Paris: Éditions Robert Laffont, 1980).

33. Stovall, *Paris Noir;* Bricktop with James Haskins, *Bricktop* (New York: Atheneum, 1983); Chris Goddard, *Jazz Away from Home* (New York: Paddington Press, 1979); Ralph Nevill, *Days and Nights in Montmartre and the Latin Quarter* (New York: George H. Doran, 1927).

34. Tyler Stovall, "Music and Modernity, Tourism and Transgression: Harlem and Montmartre in the Jazz Age," *Intellectual History Newsletter* 22 (2000): 36–48.

35. Goddard, *Jazz Away from Home*, 278.

36. Claude McKay, *A Long Way from Home* (New York: L. Furman, 1937), 230; Wayne F. Cooper, *Claude McKay* (Baton Rouge: Louisiana State University Press, 1987).

37. Gwendolyn Bennett, diary entry of August 8, 1925, cited in Stovall, *Paris Noir*, 62.

38. Langston Hughes, *The Big Sea* (New York: Hill and Wang, 1979), 144–88.

39. Joel Augustus Rogers, "The Paris Pepper Pot," *Pittsburg Courier*, July 27, 1929.

40. P. J. Carisella and James W. Ryan, *The Black Swallow of Death* (Boston: Marlborough House, 1972).

41. Cary Wintz, ed., *The Critics and the Harlem Renaissance* (New York: Garland, 1996); Tony Martin, *Literary Garveyism: Garvey, Black Arts, and the Harlem Renaissance* (Dover Mass.: Majority Press, 1983).

42. Ted Vincent, *Keep Cool*, 106–73; Angela Davis, *Blues Legacies and Black Feminism: Gertrude "Ma" Rainey, Bessie Smith, and Billie Holiday* (New York: Pantheon,

1998). This is true most notably of debates about black television situation comedies, which both appeal to a wide African American audience and at the same time frequently replicate traditional stereotypes. See Herman Gray, *Watching Race: Television and the Struggle for "Blackness"* (Minneapolis: University of Minnesota Press, 1995).

43. Goddard, *Jazz Away from Home*, 219.

44. Rose, *Jazz Cleopatra*, 5–6.

45. Angela C. Pao, *The Orient of the Boulevards: Exoticism, Empire, and Nineteenth Century French Theatre* (Philadelphia: University of Pennsylvania Press, 1998); Pierre Sorlin, "The Fanciful Empire: French Feature Films and the Colonies in the 1930s," *French Cultural Studies* 2, no. 5 (1991): 135–51.

46. In considering the broader issue of cultural resistance to racial oppression, see Robin D. G. Kelley, *Race Rebels: Culture, Politics, and the Black Working Class* (New York: Free Press, 1994). Also important theoretically is the work of James Scott. See *Weapons of the Weak: Everyday Forms of Peasant Resistance* (New Haven: Yale University Press, 1985) and *Domination and the Arts of Resistance: Hidden Transcripts* (New Haven: Yale University Press, 1990).

47. James Haskins, *The Cotton Club* (New York: Random House, 1977).

48. A classic statement of the liberating nature of Parisian exile for African Americans is Richard Wright, "À Paris, Les G.I. Noirs Ont Appris À Connaître Et À Aimer La Liberté," *Samedi Soir,* May 25, 1946.

49. See the analysis of this film by T. Denean Sharpley-Whiting in *Black Venus: Sexualized Savages, Primal Fears, and Primitive Narratives in French* (Durham, N.C.: Duke University Press, 1999), 111–18.

50. In effect, it seems to resemble nothing more closely than the Marseilles of Claude McKay. See also the film version of the novel *Big Fella* (1937), starring Paul Robeson.

51. This fictional creation of a sailor's bar in a city far from the ocean is fascinating. It alludes both to the romanticization of colonial port cities, and to the fantasy of Montmartre as a port created by certain nineteenth-century Parisian intellectuals.

52. There is now a rich historical literature on the interplay of race and class in modern Europe. See, for example, René Galissot, "Nationalisme français et racisme: À l'encontre d'idées reçues," *Politique Aujourd'hui* 4 (1984); Étienne Balibar and Immanuel Wallerstein, *Race nation classe: Les identités ambiguës* (Paris: La Découverte, 1988); Ann Stoler, *Race and the Education of Desire* (Durham, N.C.: Duke University Press, 1995); Richard Lebow, *White Britain and Black Ireland* (Philadelphia: Institute for the Study of Human Issues, 1976).

53. For another example, this one from French popular literature, of a civilized black woman reverting to her native barbarism, see Morand, *Magie Noire,* the story of Pamela Freedman.

54. For example, in the novel *The Bridges of Madison County,* the adulterous white lovers go to a black juke joint, secure in the knowledge that they won't meet anyone they know there. James Robert Waller, *The Bridges of Madison County* (New York: Warner Books, 1992).

The 1960s in Bamako
Malick Sidibé and James Brown

I was looking at a book of Malick Sidibé's photographs, put together by André Magnin, with my friend Diafode, who has been living in France since 1979. As we flipped through the black-and-white photos of our teenage years in Bamako, Diafode's attention was suddenly drawn to a photo of a group of boys entitled *Friends, 1969.* "Les Beatles!" he exclaimed, and added, putting his index finger on the photo, "voilà les Beatles." I looked closely at it, and before I could even say a word, Diafode started identifying them one by one: there was John Lennon, Ringo Starr, and all the other members of the Beatles of Medina-Coura, one of the hip neighborhoods of Bamako in those days.

Diafode and I spent that evening in my Paris apartment, looking at the Beatles of Medina-Coura and reminiscing about our youth in Bamako. Sure enough, I now could see Nuhun, aka John Lennon. He's wearing a "Col Mao" jacket with six buttons, just like the one John Lennon wore on the cover of one of the Beatles' albums. Nuhun now lives in Canada. And there's Cissé, with his arm on Nuhun's shoulder. He's wearing a tight-fitting shirt, with a scarf à la Elvis Presley, a large belt, and bell-bottom pants. We used to call him "Paris" because he was so elegant and smooth. When he lived in Bamako-Coura, a neighborhood on the southern tip of the commercial center, and did not have a motorcycle to come to Medina-Coura on the north side, he would walk for forty-five minutes to cross the busy commercial center—under the hot sun at two o'clock—to join the group at Nuhun's house listening to music, playing cards, and drinking tea.

The elegance of Paris's style was also marked by a pack of "Craven A" cigarettes, which he placed in his shirt pocket while holding one unlit cigarette between his lips. He walked slowly through the busy crowd of the market and across the railway, without losing his rhythm and without sweating a drop. When he arrived at Nuhun's place, his shoes were always shiny and his face was as fresh as ever. He would always say, "Salut, les copains" before taking a napkin out of his pocket, wiping off a chair, and sitting down. We used to say that one day, Paris would surely leave Bamako for Europe. With his Craven A cigarettes and tailored shirts, he looked like the actors from the Italian photo-novellas. Cissé, aka Paris, now lives in Canada too.

Other guys in the photo reminded Diafode and me of more Bamako stories. There is Addy, who went to Switzerland to study hotel manage-ment and returned to Bamako in 1970 with the first copy of Crosby, Stills, Nash, and Young's *Four-Way Street*. We had organized "Woodstock in Bamako" with Addy's record collection. Since then, Addy has worked for hotels in Abidjan and Bamako before opening his own business in Bamako. Niare, who's sitting on the floor and holding the album by Sly and the Family Stone that contains "I Wanna Take You Higher," now works for the Malian government as an accountant. In the back, Amara, aka "Harley-Davidson," is wearing a flowered shirt. In those days, every-body had to have a flowered shirt to feel part of the youth culture—not only in Bamako, but also in Paris, London, and Amsterdam. Harley is now an abstract painter and conceptual artist in Bamako. He was always a dreamer; in those days, he was convinced that he would seize history one day and become the center of it.

Malick Sidibé's photographs enable us to revisit the youth culture of the 1960s and our teenage years in Bamako. They show exactly how the young people in Bamako had embraced rock and roll as a liberation movement, adopted the consumer habits of an international youth culture, and devel-oped a rebellious attitude toward all forms of established authority. The black-and-white photographs reflect how far the youth in Bamako had gone in their imitation of the worldview and dress style of popular music stars, and how Malick Sidibé's photographic art was in conversation with the design of popular magazines, album covers, and movie posters of the time. To say that Bamako's youth was on the same page as the youth in London and Paris in the sixties and seventies is also to acknowledge Mal-ick Sidibé's role in shaping and expanding that culture. To the youth in Bamako, Malick Sidibé was the James Brown of photography: the godfa-ther whose clichés described the total energy of the time. Today, we go back to the music and films of the sixties and seventies in order to give meaning to the culture. We can also go back to Malick Sidibé's photographs to gain access to the style, vibrancy, and ethos of those times in Africa.

So implicated are Malick Sidibé's photographs in the culture of the sixties that when we look at them, our youth comes back to life. They are the gateway to everything that was fashionable then, everything that constituted our modernism. They are documents through which we can see the passage of time in Bamako as marked by dress style (from B-boys to hippies), music appreciation (from Latin beat to James Brown), movies (from westerns to *Easy Rider*), hairstyle (from Patrice Lumumba and Marlon Brando to the Afro), and dance moves (from the twist to the camel walk).

In Sidibé's photographs, one can see the turbulence of youth and the generational conflict that characterized the sixties. The desires of youth are inscribed in most of the photos as a determined break with tradition and as a transformation of the meaning of the decolonization movements of the sixties into a rock-and-roll revolution. It is clear from Sidibé's photographs that what the youth in Bamako wanted most in those days was James Brown and the freedom and existential subjectivity that linked independence to the universal youth movement of the sixties. The photographs show that, in attempting to be like James Brown, Jimi Hendrix, the Beatles, and the Rolling Stones, they were also revealing their impatience with the political teachings of the nationalist state and the spirit of decolonization.

As Diafode and I looked at these photographs now, more than a quarter of a century later, I felt a strange familiarity, a simultaneous desire and repulsion. I looked intently at every photograph in the book, each more than once, looking for myself, but at the same time dreading the possibility of finding myself there. These photographs are speaking to me now, not only as important aesthetic documents of sixties culture, but also as documents that both problematize the narrow meaning of nationalism extant at that time, and open the door for a pan-African and diasporic aesthetics through rock and roll.

I am proposing here to go beyond the nostalgic function that the photographs served for my friend Diafode and me that night in Paris. This is not to underrate nostalgia as a significant element in photography and the other arts. On the contrary, photo albums and home videos of weddings and naming celebrations play an important role in the lives of African immigrants in Paris and elsewhere. They protect them from the effects of segregation in the host country by providing entertainment and pleasure.

FIG. 1. *Friends 1969* by Malick Sidibé. (Courtesy of the C.A.A.C.—The Pigozzi Collection, Geneva. © Malick Sidibé.)

They also constitute a link between the immigrants and their original homes, and thus foster a sense of community culture.

But to understand the conditions of emergence and evolution of Sidibé's formal style in these photographs, it is important to place him in the social and historical context of the sixties in Bamako. Malick Sidibé was one of the first studio photographers in Bamako to take a lighter and cheaper 35mm camera outside, to house parties and picnics, in order to take pictures of young people. As he followed the youth, who themselves were following a universal youth movement, he discovered his style in what I will call rhythmic or motion photography. But how did we arrive at the finished product that we have in this book today; how did the bodily dispositions and the structure of feeling of the subjects in Sidibé's photography change from those in the work of his predecessor Seydou Keita?

It is important to understand that at the time they were taking people's pictures in Bamako, neither Malick Sidibé nor Seydou Keita considered himself an artist. It is also important to understand that the types of photos each took and the perfection they both achieved in their work were a condition of the demand that existed at their respective times. Photographers in Bamako were no different than the barbers or tailors; they all beautified their clients or provided them with styles for the visual pleasure of people in Bamako. Their success depended on word of mouth, which contributed, as Pierre Bourdieu would put it, to increasing their symbolic capitals. They only became artists by first pleasing their customers, by providing them with the best hairstyles, dresses, and photographs.

Seydou Keita's photography was both enhanced and limited by the economic, social, and cultural conditions prevailing in Bamako between 1945 and 1964, when he had to close his studio and become a civil servant for the socialist government in Mali. The people he photographed in his studio were from the middle class. They were from traditional Bamako families: businessmen and their wives, landlords, and civil servants (schoolteachers, soldiers, and clerks for the colonial administration). As a photographer, Seydou Keita's role was to make his subjects look like they belonged to the bourgeoisie, to make them feel modern and Bamakois. The women were very beautiful, with their hair braided and decorated with gold wings, and their long dresses with embroidery at the neck. The men wore European suits or traditional boubous, and they exhibited their watches, radios, or cars. Seydou Keita produced artifice through studio mise-en-scène and makeup to ensure that every one of his subjects looked like an ideal Bamakois, a bourgeois civil servant invested with the authority of the colonial administration.

When independence arrived in 1960 and the colonial administration had to cede its place to the new government of Mali, people's relation to photography, as to many other things in Bamako, began to change. Civil servants were no longer content with their intermediary roles between whites and Africans; they were now competing with the traditional leaders for control of the country. In Seydou Keita's studio, they no longer wanted to mimic the colonial administrator; they wanted to be seen occupying the colonial master's chair at the office, his house, and his places of leisure. As these patterns of life changed in Bamako, new structures of feeling emerged and studio photography became devalorized as something conservative and artificial. Soon the studio's customers would be largely composed of people who needed passport and identification photos as well as visitors from rural areas. Seydou Keita's reaction to the changes was also conservative: not only did he have problems with the new socialist government, but he also found women in pants, miniskirts, and Afro hairdos to be neither beautiful nor religiously acceptable in a predominantly Muslim country.

Thus, the change in power from a colonial system to an independent state brought about a profound transformation in people's sense of aesthetics in photography. Young people especially began to look upon studio photography as old-fashioned or as something reserved for people who were pretending to be Bamakois. To be photographed in the studio was associated with being a fake and a powerless pretender. In other words, studio photography was seen as unreal; realism had become the criterion for defining the new aesthetics of Bamakois photography. By insisting on realism, people were demanding a new photography that portrayed them as actors in situations, a photography that was neither a studio reenactment nor an imitation of something previously done. The new Bamakois wanted to be filmed while he or she took the center of the action that was unfolding. Photographers therefore had to come out of the studio and follow the action wherever it was taking place.

These limitations of studio photography, a genre fostered by colonialism, led to Malick Sidibé's emergence as the photographer of the young generation. While maintaining his studio largely for passport photos and camera repair, Sidibé took his camera to where the youth were and photographed there. I will therefore define the youth's sense of a new realism in photography less as an absence of artifice, mise-en-scène, and mimicry, and more as something tied to the location and historical action of the subjects in the photos. In other words, each photo tells a story located in space and time that serves to empower the subject. The emphasis on action was meant to bring photography as close to live action as possible.

There is, however, another problem, related to a change in power relations in Bamako, that needs to be addressed when discussing Sidibé's photography. It would seem that his photos of young Bamakois are in contradiction not only with colonial-era studio photography, but also with the patterns of life that one would expect in a decolonized state. According to the famous theses on culture developed by Aimé Césaire and Frantz Fanon, it is not only impossible to create a national culture under colonialism, but it is also equally evident that artifacts like these photos are signs of neocolonialism and Western imperialism. Writing about African independence in the 1960s, Césaire stated that whereas the colonial era was characterized by the "reification" of Africans, the transition to independence would give rise to a revival of creative energies, and a recovery of authentic ways of being that had been forbidden by the colonizer. Independence would awaken in the individual the African personality that had for so long been suppressed. For Césaire, "after the 'moment' of precolonial Africa, a moment of 'immediate truth,' and the colonial 'moment,' a moment of the shattered African consciousness, independence inaugurates a third dialectical 'moment,' which must correspond with a reconciliation of the mind with its own consciousness and the reconquest of a plenitude."[1]

For theoretical purposes, it is important to retain Césaire's use of the terms "moment," "immediate truth," "own consciousness," and "plenitude." All of them refer to independence as an authentic state of being, a state of genuine creative and natural harmony between the precolonial past and the present. In contrast, the colonial and neocolonial state was characterized by the assimilation, alienation, and depersonalization of the African. Authors like Césaire expected the continent to create a new man with an African style in politics and culture. Lumumba, Sékou Touré, and Kwame Nkrumah were the prototypes of the postindependence ideal image, and they were all fiercely nationalist, authentic, and anti-imperialist. That the images of the youth in Sidibé's photographs did not seem to reflect the Africa that these leaders were attempting to shape has been interpreted as an indication of how alienated the youth were, as a sign that the youth were not in continuity with the political history of the nation. The photos could be said therefore to reveal the presence of neocolonialism among the youth.

Indeed, in Mali, the socialist government created a militia in the mid-sixties to monitor the behavior of the people, in conformity with the teachings of socialism. This militia was aimed not only at the abolishing of traditional chiefs and other tribal customs, but also at correcting the youth's habitus. In Bamako, curfews were set and youth caught wearing miniskirts, tight skirts, bell-bottom pants, and Afro hairdos were sent to reeducation camps. Their heads were shaved and they were forced to wear traditional clothes. The situation did not get any better for the youth after the military takeover in 1968. Even though the former regime was castigated for taking people's freedom away, for being worse than the colonizer in its destruction of African traditions, and for being against free enterprise, the soldiers who replaced the militia continued to patrol the streets of Bamako in search of rebellious and alienated youth. It was clear, therefore, that to both the independence leaders and the military regime in Bamako, the youth in Sidibé's photographs were not obeying the teachings of independence, nationalism, and tradition. They were mimicking the culture of the colonizer, which shut the door to authentic self-actualization.

Looking at Sidibé's photographs today, it is possible to see what was not visible then on account of the rhetorical teachings of revolution. It is indeed clear to me that the youth's refiguration of the independence movement, their appropriation of the political history of decolonization, and their representation of their freedom were all misrecognized by their elders. According to Bourdieu, one can obey the past without representing it.[2] In assessing the youth's continuity with and transformation of the political history of independence in Bamako, it is therefore critical to look at the degree to which the youth had internalized and incarnated the lessons of the revolution. The youth had quickly internalized African culture, collapsed the walls of binary opposition between colonizer and colonized, and made connections beyond national frontiers with the diaspora and international youth movements. That the theory of decolonization could not recognize this at the time as anything but mimicry and assimilation is an indication of its failure to grasp the full complexity of the energies unleashed by independence.

First of all, the youth saw in the departure of the colonizer from Bamako an opportunity to seize the city for themselves, to become the modernizing agents of their hometown, and to occupy its leisure spaces. Independence also enabled them to exhibit African cultures that until then had been forbidden by the colonizer. Thus, they could go back and forth in history without interruption, and without the permission of the new government or the traditional religious and tribal leaders. The youth in Bamako felt free to pick and choose as a prerogative of their new freedom. Their dress style, their point of view, and their corporal deportment constituted a new habitus in Bamako that was misrecognized by their parents. What I call here change of habitus, following Pierre Bourdieu, can also be understood through Raymond Williams's notion of change in patterns of life. For Williams as well, the training of youth in social character and cultural patterns may result in youth's developing its own structures of feeling, which will appear to come out of nowhere: "The new generation responds in its own ways to the unique world it is inheriting, taking up many continuities that can be traced, and reproducing many aspects of the organization, which can be separately described, yet feeling its whole life in certain ways differently, and its shaping its creative response into a new structure of feeling."[3]

Clearly, what Bourdieu and Williams are saying is that one cannot predict the outcome of a revolution, nor the new habitus that will develop out of power relations, nor from where the youth will draw the resources for their creative and epistemological ideas. As the civil rights leaders in America have learned from the generation that succeeded them, it is much easier to liberate people than to tell them how to live their freedom. Unlike revolution, freedom cannot be taught; otherwise, it is a freedom that is no longer free, a freedom under siege. The youth in Bamako did not want to be restricted in their freedom, and therefore used it to express the themes and aesthetics of Pan-Africanism, the black diaspora, and rock and roll, some of which were in continuity with the independence movement, and some in contradiction with it.

If one follows Bourdieu's statement that habitus plus capital equals action, the challenge in Sidibé's photographs becomes how to describe the components of the youth's actions, the extent to which they represent an accumulation of social and cultural capitals in relation with diaspora aesthetics and bodily dispositions that Bourdieu terms, appropriately, habitus.

The youth in Bamako, as in most modern African capitals in the sixties, began building their social networks in high schools and soccer clubs. High schools were important centers of intellectual and cultural life in Bamako because, in the absence of a university at that time, they constituted the sites where the future elite of the nation gathered. Most young people in those days met at high school or at soccer games organized between schools, before forming their own clubs or grins, to use the common Bamako term of reference. By the time high school youth had formed their own grins, they had already self-selected among the masses of students, cemented their friendships, and developed attitudes and styles specific to them. They would have already chosen a name by which they were known—the Rockers, the Temptations, the Rolling Stones, the Soul Brothers, the Beatles—and they spread their reputation throughout Bamako.

The name was not the only important thing about a club; it was also crucial to have a permanent location associated with it (e.g., the Beatles of Medina-Coura), a sort of meeting place or headquarters for the group, with a turntable and a good collection of records, magazines, and detective novels that club members exchanged among themselves. Most grins also had a shortwave radio that received BBC Radio, the Voice of America, and Radio France International. The Beatles of Medina-Coura regularly had the local newspaper *L'Essor,* and occasionally one could find French papers like *Le Monde* and magazines like *Paris-Match* and *Salut les copains,* from which they removed the posters of the Beatles of Liverpool, Jimi Hendrix, and James Brown to put on the wall. Finally, every grin had green tea, which the members drank while listening to music and debating several topics of the world at the same time. Every club built its reputation and symbolic capital by accumulating these important resources at the headquarters, and by organizing parties and picnics to which rival members of other groups were invited. It has been estimated that by the time Malick Sidibé was at the height of his career, there were more than 250 clubs in Bamako.[4]

Besides debating over favorite rock stars, political discussions constituted an important characteristic of grins in 1960s Bamako. Indeed, the way the youth talked about the music, movies, or detective stories was always related to their own condition in Mali. They always made a comparison between themselves and the people they saw on album covers, magazines, and movie posters, as well as fictional characters in movies and novels. They debated the rock stars' stances against the war in Vietnam, racial discrimination in America, the peace movements associated with Martin Luther King, Jr., and Mahatma Gandhi, and Muhammad Ali as the world's heavyweight boxing champion. Discussion of African politics was generally concerned with the heroes of independence Sékou Touré, Lumumba, and Nkrumah, who defied France, Belgium, and England, respectively. The youth elevated these freedom fighters to the rank of icons like Mao Zedong, John F. Kennedy, André Malraux, Marilyn Monroe, James Dean, Malcolm X, Angela Davis, Che Guevara, and Fidel Castro.

The grins were important centers of social criticism about what was lacking and what was needed in Bamako. People talked heatedly about the government, the restriction of people's freedom, and the incapacity of African nations to unite. Some argued that neocolonialism was the reason that the leaders could not get together, and that France and the CIA still had their hands in our affairs. People at the grin also saw themselves as rebels in Bamako against traditional societies, which wanted to interject more religion into their lives and control the way they dressed and behaved. The youth thought of themselves as open-minded and tolerant toward each other, regardless of ethnic and caste origins. They therefore did not want to go back to the separation of people by tribe that was encouraged during the colonial era. They defined themselves first of all as Bamakois, Malian, and Pan-African, as opposed to Bambara or Fulani. Not only did the youth in Bamako organize their own Woodstock to listen to music in a public sphere and protest against apartheid in South Africa, Ian Smith's regime in Rhodesia, and the imprisonment of George Jackson and Hurricane Carter in the United States, but they also continued to resist the military dictatorship in Mali until its overthrow by a mass movement in 1992.

When I look at Sidibé's photographs today, I see as political action the way in which the youth of Bamako transformed the themes of independence and adapted them for themselves, to the point of not being recognized by their elders. Because Bamako's youth could not content themselves with the mechanistic application of the political theory of independence, nor return to certain African traditions that would have imposed limits on their freedom, they turned to Pan-Africanism and the African diaspora as powerful sources for the expression of their freedom.

The Impact of James Brown

Looking back at the period between the midsixties and the early seventies in Bamako, it is clear that the single most important factor, after independence, that introduced change into youth's habitus was their exposure to diaspora aesthetics through rock and roll and the black power movement. And in this respect, it is also clear from the visual evidence in Sidibé's photographs that James Brown was the most important reference that combined the ethos of black pride with the energy of rock and roll. As independence changed power relations in Bamako, the reception of diaspora aesthetics through popular culture opened a floodgate of youthful energy and creativity. The youth could see themselves more easily in James Brown or in a glossy photograph of a defiant Muhammad Ali than in any other motif of independence at that time.

This enthusiastic embrace of popular culture from the United States may seem odd in a newly independent socialist country like Mali. In Mali, as in other African countries, the United States had at that time been identified as the symbol of imperialism and capitalist exploitation. It is therefore crucial to explain what James Brown and other diaspora aestheticians from North America were able to provide to Bamako's youth that could escape the critical eye of anticapitalism and anti-imperialism, but that was lacking in the other independence-era social formations.

The identification with James Brown was total and uninterrupted; from the way he appeared in album cover photographs as if caught in the middle of a trance to the way his music and dance provoked the youth to action, James Brown was captivating. The dress styles that his influence popularized among Bamakois included tight turtleneck shirts with buttons or a zipper, which the local tailors made from looking at the pictures on the album covers. The same tailors in Bamako also made the "James Brown" style of shorter, above-the-ankle bell-bottom pants; which were thought to enhance one's ability to dance the jerk or the mashed potato.

In 1967, Malick Sidibé photographed two young women holding between them a James Brown album, *Live at the Apollo,* released that same year. I remember that white suits similar to the one James Brown is wearing on that album cover were all the rage at dance parties in Bamako. It is also a measure of the popularity of *Live at the Apollo* that it appears more often than any music album in Malick Sidibé's photography. There were also some songs on it, such as "Cold Sweat," "There Was a Time," "I Feel Good," and "It's a Man's World," without which no dance party in Bamako could rise to greatness. These James Brown hits, along with "Papa's Got a Brand-New Bag" and "I've Got a Feeling," remained at the top of the charts in Bamako for more than a decade.

One of the girls in the photo is wearing a sleeveless blouse and skin-tight pants, while the other has on a checkered minidress reminiscent of the Supremes. They are both laughing and looking into the camera, each with one knee bent forward and the other leg spread back as if to mark a dance step. The girl on the left, wearing the minidress, is holding the record album in the center, between herself and her friend. The other girl is pressing her body against the album as if she were dancing with it. *Live at the Apollo* thus becomes an important part of the composition of this photo. Inasmuch as James Brown is clearly identifiable here by his picture and by his name written in big letters on the album, one can say that he has become the third person in the photograph. By putting him in the center against their hearts, the two young girls transform him from a lifeless photo on an album cover to an omnipresence in front of Malick Sidibé's camera. It is as if, in the photo, they were dancing with the "real" James Brown.

It is also important to understand that the presence of the album in the photo helps redefine the young women. By seeing themselves in James Brown, identifying with *Live at the Apollo,* and becoming one with their idol through dance, they change themselves. The person looking at the picture also begins to see the two girls differently. For him, they assume a new identity that is secular and cosmopolitan. They are no longer stuck in the Malian identities defined by the tribe or by Islam. For example, in Mali, young women were not allowed to be seen by their parents dressed the way they were in this photo. Such conduct would have been deemed indecent by Islam. When young women went to the grin or to a dance party, they smuggled their pants and miniskirts out the window beforehand, and then walked out the door dressed in traditional clothes. They only changed into their modern outfits once they were far from home and unrecognizable.

Clearly, therefore, diaspora aesthetics were opposed to the habitus, imposed by tradition, home, and Islam, which sought to control the young girls' bodies. In this sense, identification with James Brown was an indication of where the youth in Bamako wanted to be at the time of independence, as well as nationalist leaders' blindness to these desires. As the two young women take on a new identity, influenced by James Brown and diaspora aesthetics, that had begun to emerge at the same time in Zambia, Liberia, Harlem, Senegal, Ghana, and elsewhere, the origin of this photo becomes indeterminate. The presence of James Brown in this photo helps therefore to explain the new habitus of postindependence, why young people dressed the way they did, and how they freed their bodies from the limitations imposed by older power relations.

I call this a diaspora aesthetic, as opposed to a Malian or even an African aesthetic, because it was defined beyond the national boundary and it united black youth through a common habitus of black pride, civil rights, and self-determination. The civil rights movement in America and the worldwide movement of decolonization were resources for this new aesthetic, and James Brown was the dominant symbol for the youth. James Brown, as a figure mediated through civil rights and worldwide decolonization, had become for this youth the link between the new freedom and an African identity that had been repressed by slavery, Islam, and colonialism. By that I mean that a storehouse of African cultural and spiritual practices, forced into silence and rendered invisible by colonialism and Islam, emerged when the youth entered into contact with James Brown's music.

It is no secret that both colonialism and Islam fought hard to rid Africans of their gods, rituals, and cultures. Colonialism imposed itself in a binary manner, collecting African statues and masks in order to burn them or send them to museums in Europe, replacing them with the Bible. For both Islam and Christianity, polytheism was the root of evil, and they therefore sought to fill Africans' needs for several gods with one God. In the process, they banned the priests who represented different gods, and left the rituals and dances unattended by an intermediary between the people and their creator. This destruction of the spiritual and technical base of African cultures is eloquently described in masterpiece after masterpiece of the creative writing of the African diaspora. In Chinua Achebe's *Arrow of God,* the African priest loses his place in the harvest ritual to the Christian missionary. In Yambo Ouologuem's *Bound to Violence,* the anthropologist assists in the destruction of an African kingdom by collecting the masks and the oral traditions. In Maryse Condé's *Segu,* Elhadji Oumar's army of jihad destroys the Bambara Empire, burns the fetishes, baptizes the king, and puts a Muslim priest in charge of Segu.

By the time of independence in the 1960s, therefore, what we call "African" had been changed through and through by Islam and Christianity. Most importantly, the connections with the pre-Atlantic-slavery African had been destroyed or forgotten. The rituals seen today, performed for tourists or at the celebrations of the anniversary of independence, are fixed in time and devoid of any spiritual and technical meaning. They can no longer cure an epidemic, nor teach people the meaning of a puzzle. The presence of Islam and Christianity also means that people adopt a different way of praying that excludes dance, as well as a different disposition of the body that involves submission to God rather than an imitation of God through dance. It is therefore safe to say that Africans, who were famous in the literature of primitivism for their sense of rhythm, were without rhythm at the time of independence.

James Brown's music reconnected Bamako's youth to a pre-Atlantic-slavery energy that enabled them to master the language of independence and modernity and to express the return of Africanism to Africa through black aesthetics. The term *Africanism* has been used in a varied manner by diaspora authors and theorists, including Amiri Baraka (LeRoi Jones) in *Blues People,* Robert Farris Thompson in *Flash of the Spirit,* V. Y. Mudimbe in *The Invention of Africa,* and Toni Morrison in *Playing in the Dark.* My use of *Africanism* here is closer to the way Baraka and Thompson have adopted the term, and to Houston Baker's concept of the "vernacular" in *Blues, Ideology, and Afro-American Literature*—all of which indicate the survival, transformation, and influence of pre-Atlantic-slavery African cultures on modernist cultures. By subverting Christianity and Islam as the spiritual guardians of modernity, Africanism endows itself with distinctive resources that Clyde Taylor calls "pagan modernism."

To understand the impact of James Brown's music on the youth in

Bamako (and what is here called pagan modernism), it is important, first, to make a detour to one of the pre-Atlantic-slavery cultures that seems to have survived in James Brown's own performance. I refer here to the Dogon of Mali. According to Marcel Griaule, in his classic book *Dieu d'eau,* Dogon cosmology revolved around men and women's desire to be perfect like the Nommo.[5] The Nommo were twin offspring of Amma, the Almighty God. Unlike their older brother, the incestuous jackal, who was ill-conceived through a union between Amma and the Earth, the Nommo were perfect in everything they did. They each had male and female organs, and would therefore reproduce without the other's help. That is why the Dogon refer to the Nommo both as singular and plural; every Nommo is identical to the other, but also depends on the other like the left hand depends on the right. It is through their function in identity and binarism that the Dogon believe the Nommo to be part god and part human, part fluid and part solid, part water and part snake.

The symbol of Nommo, variable and unlimited in Dogon cosmology and iconography, is also the vehicle for language. For the Dogon, the Nommo revealed the secret of language to men in three stages, each corresponding to a specific work and form of prayer. The first language, which is also the most abstract, came with the transformation of baobab barks into fibers with which to clothe the nakedness of the earth. Even today, the Dogon dress their masks and statues with these multicolored fibers that contain the most ancient language of Nommo, which is understood by very few people. The second language was revealed through the technique of weaving, and it was clearer, less sacred, and available to more people. Finally, the third language came with the invention of drums. It was a modern and democratic language understood by all. For the Dogon, mastery of these languages brought men closer to the purity and perfection of Nommo and placed them in control of their environment.

Through imitation of the Nommo's language, men could therefore partake of a divine essence and, like the eight ancestors of the Dogon, become Nommo themselves. If Nommo were in the drums that they had made to teach men language, then men, by beating drums, were speaking the language of Nommo, and they themselves were Nommo at that moment. As Ogotemmeli, Griaule's interlocutor in the book, puts it, men were "learning the new speech, complete and clear, of modern times."[6]

When we return to James Brown in the sixties and consider his impact on the youth of postindependence Africa, we realize his Nommo-like quality: the desire to elevate men and women to perfection. James Brown is a

Nommo (known as "shaman" elsewhere in the world): part god and part human, who teaches the world, through his music and dance, the complete and clear language of modern times, and who makes Bamako's youth coincide with the Dogon desire for perfection. Just like the Nommo was one with the drum, the beating of which taught men the language of modernity, James Brown was one with his band, though his was never complete without his red cape and his invitation to the masses to become part of his groove. People often say that James Brown, the hardest-working man in show business, does not say much in his songs, that he is notorious for limiting himself to a few words like, "I feel all right," "You've got it, let's go," "Baby, baby, baby." In fact, James Brown, like the Nommo, uses his voice and vital power to imitate the language of his instruments, the trumpet and drums, to make his audiences understand better the appropriate discourse of our modern condition. James Brown's mimicry of the sound of his instruments—letting them speak through him as if he were one with them—communicated more clearly with his audiences the meaning of sixties social movements than any other language at the time. By subordinating human language to the language of the drums, or the language of Nommo, James Brown was partaking in the universalization of diaspora aesthetics, the freedom movements, and the discourse of black pride.

The reception of *Live at the Apollo* in Bamako was due in part to the fact that it contained a complete and clear language of modernity with which the youth could identify. James Brown's didactic concern with history and the names of dance steps and American cities was an important factor of identification with the album for the youth who knew that their independence was tied to the civil rights gains of people in the diaspora. If we take, for example, a James Brown song, "I Feel All Right," it is easy to account for its popularity in Bamako. James Brown begins the tune in a ritualistic manner by addressing everybody in the building. Like the high priest in a ritual about to begin, James Brown, calling himself the "groove maker" (as if a rainmaker, the priest of a harvest ritual or funeral), makes sure everyone is ready for the amount of soul, or vital energy, that he is about to unleash. He even summons the spirit of the Apollo Theater in these terms: "Building, are you ready? 'Cause we're gonna tear you down. I hope that the building can stand all the soul. You've got a lot of it coming." Then James Brown, at once the son of Nommo and Nommo himself, proceeds to explain the dance steps he is about to teach the world. He performs the dance a few times, asking the audience to repeat after him. Repetition is the key word here for diaspora aesthetics: it marks the rhythm and accent of this new language. By imitating James Brown, one becomes James Brown, just as the imitation of Nommo's acts brings men closer to him.

Interestingly, as in all rituals, there is the risk of impurity, of something not working properly, and therefore threatening the success of the performance. During the song, we hear James Brown struggling with a man who was not properly following the directions he was giving: "My man always got to get his own extra thing in there," says an amused Brown. But, luckily for the people at the Apollo that evening, the groove prevailed and the ritual was a success, as James Brown screams: "You got it? Yeah, you got it! Now, let's go!" It is at such moments that James Brown reminds us most of Nommo, who could empower men and women and put them in control of their environment.

In Griaule's book, Ogotemmeli states that the first dance ever was a divination dance: "The son of God spoke through dance. His footsteps left marks on the dusty dance floor, which contained the meaning of his words."[7] Ogotemmeli goes on to say that the masked society that performs the dance rituals symbolizes the whole system of the world. When the dancers break onto the scene, they signify the direction in which the world is marching, and predict the future of the world. Similarly, one can say that, in *Live at the Apollo,* James Brown, son of Nommo and Nommo himself, was speaking with his feet and tracing, on the floor of the auditorium, the divination language that contained the future directions of the world. The youth in Bamako as well were interpellated by this movement, the language of which was absent from the other political movements of the time in Mali. They found the political and spiritual articulation of independence through James Brown's music, and thereby could become Nommo themselves; that is to say, connect with the African culture before Atlantic slavery.

Ogotemmeli, the Dogon philosopher, likes to state that, for human beings, articulation is the most important thing. That is why the Nommo provided men and women with joints, so that they can bend down and fold their arms and legs in order to work. According to Dogon cosmology, the Nommo had placed one pebble at every joint at the waist, the knee, the ankle, the wrist, the elbow, the neck joint, and so on, to symbolize a Dogon ancestor that facilitated the articulation of the joint. The movement of every joint is therefore tied to the presence of Nommo, who blesses and instructs it. The concept of articulation is also important for the system of language that permeates all Dogon activities. Language, for the Dogon, is opposed to silence and nakedness, while being at the same time the essence of action, prayer, and emancipation. Language prolongs action through prayer, and articulation provides every language system with its accent, rhythm, semantic content, and form. Ogotemmeli states that for each one of the eight Dogon ancestors, there is a language that is different from the others, and which is spoken by people in his village. The way a specific language is articulated by a people can also be read through the way they dance and communicate with God. In a word, articulation determines for the Dogon the rhythm of the world by relating, through a system of alliance, left and right, up and down, odd and even, male and female. It is thus easy to see how important the system of articulation was for both communication and aesthetics among the Dogon people. It was that which united opposites and created meaning out of seeming disorder, enabling men and women to enlist the help of their God and prolong their action on earth.

For me, two components of diaspora aesthetics—repetition and articulation, in other words, the incessant presence of Nommo and the joining of opposites in time and space—were missing in Bamako before the time of independence. It obviously had been suppressed by colonialism and Judeo-Christian and Islamic religions, which understood modernism as teleological, lacking in repetition and contradiction. To state this differently: before independence, the youth in Bamako were mostly Muslim boys and girls without rhythm, because they were detached from Nommo and other pre-Atlantic-slavery cultures.

So imagine James Brown in *Live at the Apollo* when, in a song called "There Was a Time," he invokes Nommo in these words: "But you can bet / you haven't seen nothing yet / until you see me do the James Brown!" To "do the James Brown" in this instance is to speak a different language with one's body, to improvise a new dance different from the ones mentioned before, like the jerk, the mashed potato, the camel walk, and the boogaloo. It is to dance with Nommo's feet, and to leave on the dance floor the verb of Nommo (i.e., the complete and clear new speech of modern times). Finally, it is to perform one's own dance of Nommo, without an intermediary, and to become one with Nommo and James Brown.

In Bamako, in those days, James Brown's music had an intoxicating power to make you stand up, forget your religion and your education, and perform a dance move beyond your ordinary capacities. As you move your legs and arms up and down in a scissors-step, or slide from one end of the dance floor to another, or imitate the blacksmith's dance with an ax, your steps are being visited by the original dancers of pre-Atlantic-slavery African peoples. The Nommo have given you back all your articulations so that you can predict the future through the divination dance of the ancestors.

For Ogotemmeli, to dance is to pay homage to the ancestors and to use the dance floor as a divination table that contains the secret of the new world system. Clearly, therefore, what James Brown was preparing the world for at the Apollo was the brand-new body language of the sixties, a new habitus that would take its resources from the civil rights movement, black pride, and independence. The catalog of dances that James Brown cites, from the camel walk to the mashed potato, is composed of dances that the Nommo taught men and women so they could clearly understand the language of civil rights, independence, and freedom.

In Bamako too, young men and women, upon hearing James Brown, performed dances that were imitations of the way Nommo swam in the river or the way the chameleon crawled and changed colors. The sun dance of the Great Dogon mask, the thunder dance of the Kanaga mask, and the undulating movement of the snake were included too. In this way, the Bamakois took charge of their new situation, showed how the system worked, and predicted the future. Just as the mashed potato or the camel walk were coded dances that told different stories of emancipation, the dances the youth performed in Bamako were also expressions of independence and connection with the diaspora. James Brown's music and other rock-and-roll sounds of the sixties were therefore prefiguring the secular language that the youth of Bamako was adapting as their new habitus and as expression of their independence. The sweat on the dance floor, reminiscent of James Brown's sweat at the Apollo, itself reminiscent of the sweat that runs down the body of Dogon dancers possessed by Nommo, is the symbol of the new and clear language pouring out of the body of the dancers. James Brown, with his red cape, heavy breathing, and sweat, is none other than Nommo.

Looking at the Malick Sidibé photograph of the two young girls holding *Live at the Apollo,* one revisits this new language and habitus of the sixties. Curiously enough, at the same time that Malick Sidibé was taking photographs of the youth in Bamako, Ali Farka Toure, a blues guitarist from the north of Mali, was also imitating the songs from the diaspora. First, people would gather at night in schoolyards and cultural centers to dance to his modernized music. Then, Radio Mali in Bamako began to play his music on the air. There is one particular song by Ali Farka Toure from those days, "Agoka," which takes several riffs from James Brown's "There Was a Time." It is therefore obvious that the youth used independence as an opportunity to latch onto diaspora aesthetics—that is, a pagan modernist style opposed to religious modernism and the "nationalist" and conversionist modernism of Fanon, Aimé Césaire, and Jean-Paul Sartre, thinkers who considered postindependence Africans only as part of the proletariat.

Copying the Copiers

In Malick Sidibé's photography, we see an encounter, between pre-Atlantic-slavery Africa, post-civil-rights American culture, and postindependence youth in Bamako, that produces a diaspora aesthetic. Thus, to say that Sidibé's photographs are "black photographs," as a photographer friend, Charles Martin, has stated to me, is to affirm his participation in shaping the new and universal look of the youth of African descent. Because Sidibé's photographs made Bamako youth so stylish, au courant, and universal, it was easy to identify with them. The youth in Bamako saw themselves in his photographs, and they wanted to be in them because the photographs made them look like the rock-and-roll idols and movie stars they wanted to be.

To say that the youth in Bamako saw themselves in Sidibé's photographs is to state that his style was modern, and that his photographs presented a Bamakois that was beyond tradition. By leaving the studio to follow young people outside, Sidibé was also discovering his style. At the conscious and unconscious levels, Sidibé's eye was being trained to recognize the youth's favorite movements and postures during dancing as well as their preferred hairdos and dress styles. By following Bamakois youth, he began to acquire their aesthetic taste, instead of imposing old-fashioned photographic models on them. This is why the youth in Bamako considered Sidibé's photography to be realistic: he recognized their style and used his camera to immortalize it. Sidibé saw the emergence of a rebellious youth in Bamako who wanted to demarcate themselves from the rest of the culture through their love of rock music, dancing, and dress style. By photographing them in the manner in which they wanted to be seen, Sidibé too was able to distinguish himself from other photographers in the city.

Sidibé, then, copied the youth who themselves were copying rock stars and movie stars. And if we consider that the youth in Bamako acquired their habitus by carefully watching images of James Brown, Jimi Hendrix, James Dean, Angela Davis, Aretha Franklin, and Mick Jagger in glossy magazines and movies and on album covers, it becomes possible to see these media outlets as important sources of Sidibé's style. It is therefore no exaggeration to state that Sidibé, who never attended a photography school, had learned from the best in the field. By following the youth of Bamako, who were wearing flowered shirts made by famous designers because they saw their idols wearing them in magazine photos, Sidibé was training his eye by emulating great photographers. And by following the copy of the copy, he was internalizing the history of photography without knowing it.

It is possible to see the influence on Sidibé's photography of great contemporary photographers from Richard Avedon to Andy Warhol, as well as that of black-and-white movie images. But what is important about Sidibé's art is its ability to transform the copy into an original and to turn the images of Bamako's youth into masterpieces of the sixties' look. Looking at Sidibé's photographs today, it becomes easier to see how productive they were in the sixties in shaping the youth's worldview and in uniting them into a social movement. In this sense, Sidibé is the James Brown of photography: he was not only the premiere photographer in Bamako, but his photographs also helped universalize the language of the sixties. Consider his single portraits of young men and women wearing bell-bottom pants and flowered shirts. It seems as if the individuals in the portraits define their identities through the outfits they are wearing. In claiming its position as a signifier of the sixties and seventies, bell-bottoms become, in these pictures, as much a feature of the portrait as the person wearing them. In a way, the person wearing the bell-bottoms is, like a model, celebrating the greatness of the pants to the onlooker.

There is one particular portrait of five friends, all of them wearing the same color of shirt and bell-bottom pants. They are standing facing the wall, with their backs to the camera. What dominates the visual field in this portrait are the bright black-and-white colored pants, which come all the way down to the floor and cover the young models' feet. The rhetoric of the image implies that the five friends are identical and equal in their bell-bottom pants. In fact, this Sidibé masterpiece of the representation of the sixties conveys a sense of redundancy, a mirrorlike excess that keeps multiplying the image until it produces a dizzying, psychedelic effect on the viewer.

This photograph is still remarkable for the youths' daring and eccentricity in wearing the same outfit to a party. The expressionist patterns of their shirts and the black-and-white designs of the pants work together to produce a kitsch presentation, which erases individual identities and replaces them with a group identity. In other words, the portrait creates the illusion that we are looking at a photograph of a painting of five young men in the same outfit, instead of a live photograph. By wearing bell-bottom pants and sacrificing their individual identities for that of the grin or the new social movement, the young men were indicating a break with tradition and a commitment to the new ideas symbolized by their eccentric outfits. Sidibé's photograph captures a moment of self-parodic humor and kitsch, but also a moment marked by the universalism of its language. In this photograph, we not only see the location of the sixties dress style in kitsch—the artifice associated with bell-bottoms, tight shirts, Afro-hair, and high heels—but also the labor that went into getting it right. Sidibé's photography defined bell-bottoms for Bamako's youth and told them that they had to wear them in order to be modern.

I have argued that Sidibé attained mastery of his craft by copying copies, by following Bamako's youth, who were themselves following the black diaspora and the rock-and-roll social movement. It is now important to point out the significance of movement in Sidibé's art. We have seen that the youth's desire to have Sidibé follow them at dances and beach parties was based on their belief that studio photos were not real enough. For them, the way they dressed and comported themselves at the grin and at parties was more original in terms of reproducing the energy and savoir faire of the 1960s worldwide than was the photography studio's mise-en-scène, which was stuck in the past. Sidibé had therefore to capture them in the details of their newly acquired habitus. They wanted to be photographed looking like Jimi Hendrix, dancing like James Brown, and posing like someone in the middle of an action.

The subjects of Sidibé's portraits look like they are posing in the middle of a ritual. Their action can sometimes even reveal the content of the ritual they are performing. It is easy enough to imagine who was photographed in the middle of dancing the twist, the jerk, or the boogaloo. It is even possible to hear certain songs while looking at Sidibé's photographs. In a way, one can say that the postures and the forms of the body's disposition in Sidibé's portraits contain signifiers specific to youth habitus in the sixties.

Space is most significant in Sidibé's shots, because the subjects are moving in different directions and the camera needs to account for the narrative of their movement in the shot. A depth of field is always required in order to reveal where the dancers are going and where they are coming from. It is therefore through the configurations of space that Sidibé captures rhythm in his photographs. We see the characters leaning backward and forward, pushing each other around, or moving in the same direction to mark the groove, as in a James Brown song. Sidibé's portraits are possessed by the space, which they fill not only with the traces of the great music of the sixties and the symbolic gestures of rock stars, but also with the spirit of great dancers, from Nommo to James Brown.

There is always a narrative occurring in Sidibé's group portraits. Instead of the subjects revealing themselves for the camera to photograph, they engage in different activities, as if some of them were unaware of the camera's presence. We see this already in shots with three or four people: they treat the camera more as a spectator to an unfolding story than as the reason they are posing. Looking at the images taken on the beach, for example, we can see the complexity of narrative in Sidibé's photography and how the subjects seem to invite the camera to participate in their unfolding. Sometimes, each subject in a Sidibé portrait acts as if he or she were the main character in the shot. Sidibé attempts to achieve this level of characterization by manipulating the narrative time in the shot through a behavior that differs from the others. In one of the photos at the beach, there are six persons who all seem to be engaged in different activities. Each individual is defined in space as if he were the focus of the shot and the others were there to enhance the mise-en-scène. At the same time, the facial expression of each one of the six people invokes a different emotion in the photo, whether contemplative, self-absorbed, playful, fatigued, or reacting to something off-field. At any rate, each of the characters in this shot seems to occupy a field of his own that is totally independent from the others.

I believe that this predilection for narrative indicates two things in Sidibé's art. First, the characters in Sidibé's photography pretend to ignore the camera, or not to act for it, or simply to be caught in medias res, because they are posing like their idols on record albums, movie posters, and magazines. They are waiting for the moment of the photo to be like James Brown and Nommo, and to become like gods of entertainment themselves. It is their belief that Sidibé's photos can transform them into stars, make them bigger than life, and that is why they act so dramatically in the photos. Each of Sidibé's portraits looks like an actor in a black-and-white movie who has been asked to carry the action to the next level.

By capturing movement (an action caught in time and space, which here I call narrative) in his portraits, Sidibé also enables each character to tell his own story. This act is political insofar as it allows the youth in Bamako to seize upon their own individuality, away from tradition and the high modernism of the independence leaders. By looking like the modern black image, deracinated from nation and tribe, the youth in Bamako were also showing their belonging to Pan-Africanism and the African diaspora. Therefore, to say that Sidibé's photographs reveal Bamako's youth as alienated is to address their politics, which were more aligned with the diaspora and the universal youth movement.

Finally, as I look at Sidibé's album with my friend Diafode, I think of the pervasive influence of hip-hop in Africa and the rest of the world. The young people participating in the movement today in Bamako are the ages of Diafode's and my children. Sidibé's photographs teach us to be more tolerant of today's youth, to understand that their action is not devoid of politics, and to see in them the triumph of the diaspora.

NOTES

1. Aimé Césaire, "La pensée politique de Sékou Touré," *Présence Africaine* 29 (December 1959–January 1960): 67.

2. Pierre Bourdieu, *Seminar at College de France: Edouard Manet* (Paris: 2000).

3. Raymond Williams, *Marxism and Literature* (Oxford: Oxford University Press, 1977).

4. See André Magnin, *Malick Sidibé* (Zurich: Scalo Press, 1998).

5. Marcel Griaule, *Dieu d'eau* (Paris: Fayard, 1966).

6. Griaule, *Dieu d'eau,* 74.

7. Griaule, *Dieu d'eau,* 198.

HALIFU OSUMARE

Global Hip-Hop and the African Diaspora

Global hip-hop youth culture is the most recent manifestation in the story of the exportation of black American cultural production that started with nineteenth-century minstrelsy, thrived during the 1950s crossover rock-and-roll era and continues today. What has changed is the speed at which black music and dance are marketed and the global reach that they now command. The result is that U.S. black American culture continues to be mired in social narratives of "blackness" that proliferate multidimensionally in the international arena, commingling with other countries' issues of social marginality. However, these narratives take on different meanings in Africa and its diaspora than in other areas of the world like Asia. Hip-hop aesthetics, steeped in polyrhythm, antiphony, an orality of social commentary, and a vital embodiment of all of the above, is repositioned by sub-Saharan black African, Afro-Caribbean, and Brazilian youths because of their connection to the transiting black aesthetic itself. African diasporic cultural connections, situated within particular issues of social marginality in each site by hip-hop youths, are the subject of this essay.

By investigating the international diffusion of a culture, one is essentially inquiring into an interactive, dialogic process that links discrete local sites and real people. Popular music scholar Tony Mitchell, using Roland Robertson's (1995) term *glocal* to capture the relationships between global and local, contends that "each is in many ways defined by the other and . . . they frequently intersect, rather than being polarized opposites."[1] At one end of the global-local paradigm is international political economy, with the contrived mechanisms of multinational corporations (Time-Warner, Microsoft, Viacom, BMG, EMI, etc.) as purveyors of pop culture, creating virtualized desires that we define as global postmodern culture. At the other end exist discrete loci of exchanges of information, aesthetics, pleasure, and perspectives on age-old issues of human hierarchies in various local manifestations. The global-local interchange is indeed complex and is continually metamorphosing. Hip-hop culture has become a binding youth subculture that has enabled young people in disparate local communities to share a sense of a common attachment. Yet the fact that the global hip-hop generation is being reared on MTV and music videos does not completely explain the intricacies of various international sites' identification with hip-hop and its adaptation to local issues and aesthetics. I turn now to a brief investigation of other locally based historical implications of this global youth phenomenon.

Connective Marginalities of the Hip-Hop Globe

While most adults over forty get their impressions of hip-hop from the hypersexed, spoon-fed, commercialized music videos of MTV, BET, and VH1, there exists a multifaceted and empowered hip-hop "underground" movement that generally tends to promote a more socially conscious rap music. This branch of hip-hop culture has evolved from the "political" and "conscious" rap era in the late 1980s and early 1990s. Groups and artists from that era like Public Enemy, Brand Nubian, Poor Righteous Teachers, Queen Latifah, and A Tribe Called Quest popularized probings connected to Afrocentricity and the Nation of Islam and were laced with streetwise allusions that spread social critiques of America globally.[2] For example, Queen Latifah's "Ladies First" 1991 video combined her talents with black British rapper Monie Love to render a searing indictment of both sexism and black social marginalization in general and South African apartheid specifically.[3] Today's emcees who do not receive regular rotation on the music video channels or commercial radio's Top 40, like The Roots, Dead Prez, The Coup, Bahamadiya, Talib Kweli, Common, and Mos Def, continue today's socially conscious and self-empowering thrust of hip-hop. Through expanding international tours, artists such as these motivate youths internationally to explore their own issues of marginalization through layered, nuanced metaphors and rhyming allusions, and sometimes through direct political projects.

Exactly how do the youth of other nations, who often speak languages other than English, decode and reinvent African American and Latino hip-hop culture emanating from the urban United States? The answer partly lies in what I call hip-hop's *connective marginalities*. These are resonances acknowledged by youth internationally with black expressive culture first generated from the Bronx, Compton and South Central in Los Angeles, and East Oakland and Marin City in northern California. Corresponding international sites where rap music, break dance, and graffiti art took on early strongholds were working-class French housing projects in the *banlieues* (outer suburbs) of French cities like Paris and Marseilles, housing projects in Poznan, Poland, poor areas of war-torn Bosnia and Croatia, and the Roppongi club district of Tokyo, where black servicemen congregate in nightclubs owned by the Japanese wives of African expatriates. In Africa and the diaspora, corresponding sites are found in South African shantytowns like Soweto, the favelas of Brazilian cities like Rio de Janeiro and São Paulo, and the poor Afro-Cuban district of Cojimar in Havana.

Yet class is only one of four major connective marginalities that tend to bind the hip-hop generation internationally. Connections or resonances can take the form of culture (Jamaica and Cuba), class (North African Arabs living in France), historical oppression (Native Hawai'i), or simply the discursive construction of "youth" as a peripheral social status (Japan). Joe Austin and Michael Nevin Williard, editors of *Generation of Youth* (1998), remind us that the term *youth* can become "a metaphor for perceived social change and its projected consequences; as such it is an enduring locus for displaced social anxieties."[4] Along these lines, black rap is an in-your-face rebellious youth style that *does* challenge the adult status quo wherever it expresses itself on the globe. The generational dynamic of hip-hop's international subculture remains, even as hip-hop "heads" themselves grow older.

However, rap and the entire expressive culture of hip-hop (deejaying, breaking, and aerosol art) resonate not only with the anxiety of youthful social rebellion, but extant global sociopolitical inequities as well. France's rap group NTM is a prime example of a growing Arab underclass in France. They have been dubbed the Public Enemy of France for their toughness and the rage in the content of their rap lyrics. Historical oppression can be viewed in Sudden Rush, Hawaii's most developed rap group. This Big Island–based group of emcees raps about Native Hawaiians' historic bonds of oppression with African Americans and Native Americans through strong pro-Hawaiian sovereignty messages. Sudden Rush posits the political hegemony of the *haole,* or foreign white, plutocracy in the Pacific that eventually led to the overthrow of the Hawaiian monarchy as a part of the last five hundred years of general displacement of people of color. Figure 1 shows a diagram detailing the ways these various sociohistorical realms overlap and inform the proliferation of global hip-hop. The generational connection of youth is the largest connection, but class, historical oppression, and culture link many hip-hop communities, complicating the global phenomenon.

Hip-hop culture, as an extension of African American and Latino popular culture, then, becomes a global signifier for several forms of marginalization. In each case "blackness," along with its perceived status, is implicated as a global sign. Together with the aesthetics of the music's low-register bass drum beats, whether digitized or played live, rapped messages of hip-hop have created a worldwide cultural phenomenon that we are only beginning to fathom.

Hip-Hop on the African Continent

In Africa and its diaspora, hip-hop is less of a sign to be appropriated and adapted for indigenous purposes than a sharing across a root aesthetic. From this viewpoint, hip-hop culture illuminates a connective marginality of culture in Africa and its diaspora. Both hip-hop culture itself and academia's growing embrace of hip-hop as a valid site of intellectual inquiry has acknowledged this cultural link. To open the UCLA "Power Moves" hip-hop conference on May 10, 1999, a Cuban music ensemble played sacred rhythms of the Yoruba *orisha* (deities) and secular rumba songs. After the powerful rhythms and songs had subsided, Richard Yarborough, acting director of UCLA's Center for African American Studies, explained in his welcoming address that "we started with the drums because that's where hip-hop comes from." Hip-hop culture's continuity with African diasporic practices is not only based in the orality of rap as a trajectory of the West African griot tradition or the toasting and boasting traditions of Jamaica, but the deeply affecting rhythm through which oral text is transmitted.

Today, rhythm is the component of Western popular music that universally defines the modern cool of pop culture. The pulse of the drum and the thump of the electric bass overlay one another to create the propelling drive in all contemporary pop music. In 2002 the studio equipment of choice includes the Akai MPC 2000 drum machine that loops body-pumping rhythms and the Korg Triton sampler that inserts repetitive phrases of, for example, P-Funk grooves of George Clinton or jazz riffs of Donald Byrd. Rhythm is the foundation of the emcee's oral phrasing and metaphoric allusions, creating a dense, polyrhythmic bricolage, just as

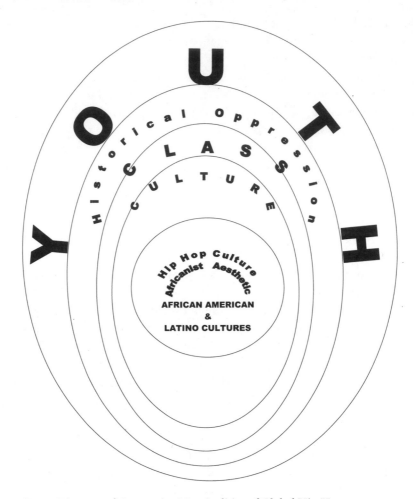

FIG. 1. Diagram of Connective Marginalities of Global Hip Hop.

ancient West Africa Ewe or Mande cross-rhythms do for festivals and ceremonies in their respective cultures today. In this sense, the discussion of the African diaspora's continued cultural links with Africa has little to do with Eric Hobsbawm's paradigm of "invented traditions," but rather has everything to do with modernity's generalized process of secularization of often sacred traditions.[5]

The continuing twenty-first-century secularization of African aesthetics in U.S. and Caribbean forms is the historical legacy now bequeathed to the African homeland from its diaspora. To be sure, Africa has recognized these New World resonances as evidenced by the mid-twentieth-century rumba orchestras of Kinshasa, the jazz bands of Accra, and the popular dance styles in Dakar's urban discos after the early-1970s Soul to Soul tour. The contemporary hip-hop movement has intensified this repatriation of black American music and dance, linking distant African sites such as Lagos, Dakar, Cape Town, Dar es Salaam, and Nairobi.

A current Pan-African hip-hop website, www.africanhiphop.com, serves as an explicit example of the multivocal concerns of Africa's pioneering hip-hop youth as they take their place in their continental, African diasporic, and global communities. The June 1998 theme for the website's home page was "Africa—Wake Up & Unify." Rap crews from six African countries were invited to contribute their rhymes on that theme, often in their indigenous languages, all posted as the "Hip Hop Show for the Month." African unity was not only served, but Africa's connection to the roots of hip-hop in African American culture was also declared. This latter point is implicit in any culture's participation in the global hip-hop youth phenomenon, but is not always directly acknowledged. "Africa—Wake Up & Unify" also included American rappers KRS-One and Busta Rhymes, as two of the culture's "elders" from the United States. The site read: "With artists from six African countries and one verse contributed by KRS-One, we come full circle." The site also provided a link that month to American "old school tracks" described as "the oldies of which date back to 1983!"[6] Africanhiphop.com demonstrates African youths' indebtedness to African American hip-hop culture.

The Internet has allowed African youths across nations and ethnic groups to connect through hip-hop culture. One can go online and read interviews with emcees such as PBS (Powerful Black Soul) and rapper Pee Froiss in Senegal, Prophets of Da City in South Africa, Pox Presha of Nairobi, and Sos-Bi of Tanzania. African female rappers are also represented, such as Nubian Sister and Godessa of South Africa. These emcees list their artistic lineage to specific African American rappers, internationally known African singers such as Yousou N'Dour or Miriam Makeba, and to Caribbean pop stars. Cultural and aesthetic resonances across Africa and the diaspora through hip-hop abound. Africanhiphop.com also formed a partnership with a South African site called Afribeat.com to sponsor a series of web-based rap shows known as Hip Hoperation (June 15–July 6, 2002). With the assistance of new technology, African youth are linking the continent through hip-hop in ways that their parents could never have imagined.

People-to-people hip-hop connections between Africa and its diaspora do not, however, negate international pop culture industry and technological hierarchies. Hip-hop culture takes its place within the larger context of Africa's neocolonialist umbilical cord, linking the continent to the Western-dominated media for news and popular taste. Malian film scholar Manthia Diawara observes that the global media "wired Africa to the West . . . to the extent that Africans are isolated from nation to nation, but united in looking toward Europe and America for the latest news, politics and culture."[7] Although the World Wide Web has ameliorated this dynamic to a degree by linking people to people—community to community—aspiring African emcees are definitely in competition with the hegemony of American music promoted by the global pop culture media. The African American rhythm and blues that influenced their parents and grandparents' generations dominate the airwaves. Rap music is only beginning to get mainstream radio airplay in Africa's urban centers, and, when it does, American stars like Jay-Z and P-Diddy are more likely featured than the country's own indigenous rappers. Cultural resonances across Africa and its diaspora through hip-hop subculture are manifest within continuing international hierarchies and the exigencies of global capital.

Hip-Hop in the Diaspora

African-based music and dance aesthetics, globally diffused by the transatlantic slave trade, are central to the forming of what Paul Gilroy calls the black Atlantic experience. They served as the foundation of what was eventually to be called popular, vernacular culture throughout the Americas. When deciphering the origins of contemporary hip-hop in the South Bronx, we discover that diasporic expressive practices were the bedrock of the inchoate youth subculture, rather than a monolithic African American one. Indeed, Robert Farris Thompson reminds us that contrary to the concept of a singular black culture in North America, the Bronx in the 1970s, as it does today, was truly representative of the black Atlantic:

> [H]ip hop history is the appreciation that these creative people can be divided into at least five distinct African-influenced cultures: First, English-speaking blacks from Barbados. . . . Afrika Bambaataa's mother and her two sisters were from Barbados, as was the family of that other

prominent Bronx DJ, Grandmaster Flash. Second, black Jamaicans, . . . among them figures most famously DJ Kool Herc. . . , originally from Kingston. . . . Third, thousands of blacks from Cuba. . . . It was only natural for Afro-Cuban conga drums to become one of the favored percussive springboards for early breakdance improvisation. . . . Fourth, there are thousands and thousands of *boricuas*—Puerto Ricans. . . . Fifth and finally, there are the North American blacks, whose music was jazz and soul and funk.[8]

In reality, hip-hop culture comes from an amalgam of African diasporic cultures that reflect U.S. urban life in New York. Concomitantly, the creolization process in the Caribbean and parts of South America was and is a reflection of this cross-cultural fertilization expressed in music and dance.

It is quite easy to construct hip-hop affiliations to English-speaking Jamaica, with its dance hall, sound system culture that specifically influenced hip-hop's beginnings as a deejay's culture. Jamaican-born DJ Kool Herc is credited with bringing his culture to Bronx parks and clubs in the early seventies, switching from dub and reggae music to funk and soul tracks that were more familiar to his black North American audience. Nearly twenty years later, in hip-hop's full-blown mass-market era, the same cultural sensibilities appeared in the collaboration between Bronx emcee KRS-One and Jamaican dub artist Shabba Ranks on their seminal track "The Jam" (Shabba Ranks, *As Raw as Ever,* Epic Records, 1991). The two artists made explicit the close association between hip-hop's rhythmic orality and Jamaican dub's cadenced rhymes.[9] Similar associations exist with Trinidad, steeped in the often scathing calypsonian social commentary tradition. Trinidad and Tobago's contemporary *rapso* movement, for example, facilely blends its oral tradition often with soca rhythms. Similar hip-hop connections exist within the non-English-speaking Caribbean and South America. Youths whose first language is Spanish, French, or Portuguese are making multilayered, metaphoric rhymed verse to a hip-hop beat-box pulse mixed with Latin-flavored rhythms. Below, I summarize scholars and journalists who are doing extensive research on hip-hop in Spanish-speaking Cuba and Portuguese-speaking Brazil.

Cuba's Ambivalent *Raperos*

In Cuba one of the few rap groups that has been able to traverse the tricky politics of Castro's cultural revolution is indicative of the dynamics of hip-hop culture in that country. Cuban rap group Orishas debuted on the international pop music scene in 2000. As journalist Rodrigo Salazar explains about two of the rappers in Orishas, Yotuel and Ruzzo, they "dared to wax poetic about conditions in present-day Cuba," first in Wu-Tang Clan-like beats, and then eventually in Cuban rumba rhythms with a smooth rap flow.[10] Their moniker, the term for Yoruba deities or *orishas* who are at the cosmological center of the Afro-Cuban Santeria religion, alludes to their privileging of indigenous Cuban culture through American rap. Yet they eventually found Cuba to be stifling for their artistic development. Although the Cuban immigration authority originally granted Orishas permission to leave the country on occasional tours, continuing tensions with the government about the length of time it took to receive exit visas and the resulting missed engagements abroad resulted in the group's move to Europe.

Eventual exile creates another kind of struggle for Cuban artists. This is a situational peculiarity of the would-be Cuban hip-hop emcee trying to join the international music circuit. Salazar captures the dilemma poignantly:

> Unlike their North American contemporaries, whose meager economic background created the "bling bling" culture, Orishas' struggle is exile. Every song is tinged with that sense of displacement. Songs like "A Lo Cubano" and "Madre," a letter to a mother worried about her son living abroad, capture this sense of melancholy.[11]

Orishas' melancholy because of their expatriate status echoes a theme that resonates throughout the African diaspora experience. The displacement of political exile is reminiscent of forced exile as a result of slavery and the longing for Mother Africa in various metaphoric dimensions running throughout the history of the Americas. "A Lo Cubano" (Cuban style) represents Orishas' recounting of "the best of what it means to be Cuban," an idealization to which they now must cling while forced to live outside of their beloved homeland for their artistic freedom.

The tension that exists between the Cuban government and some of its exiled citizens reached a crescendo during a U.S.-Cuban crisis in 2000, the Elian Gonzalez family custody battle in Miami. An April *San Francisco Chronicle* newspaper cartoon represented the essential strain between Castro's socialist revolution and the hegemony of American-generated world popular culture and commodification. Figure 2 shows little Elian return-

FIG. 2. Elian cartoon, *San Francisco Chronicle*, 2001. Cartoon by Walt Handelsman. Used by permission.

ing to Cuba in a Nike T-shirt and with protruding tongue, flippantly chanting "WHAAAAASUUUP." A dismayed, hands-akimbo Castro reacts defiantly, responding, "Send him back." Hip-hop exists within the global commodification of popular culture and the rampant materialism that attracts so many poor black and Latino youth in America's ghettos.

In the cartoon, expensive athletic wear promoted by many black sport and rap stars and Budweiser beer's multi-million-dollar campaign appropriating yet another black slang term, "What's up?" become global signifiers of American late capitalism and its entrenchment in pop culture in the postmodern era.

Many governments, weary of the effects of pervasive U.S. popular culture on its youth and ultimately its national lifestyle, have taken steps to reject or slow down the intrusion of American music and dance media. They know all too well that popular culture goes hand in hand with the fetishization of consumer goods and attendant superficiality. For example, both India and China tried successfully, until recently, to keep MTV out of their countries. Hip-hop scholar Tricia Rose explains,

Rap's ability to draw the attention of the nation, to attract crowds around the world in places where English is rarely spoken are fascinating elements of rap's social power. Unfortunately, some of this power is linked to U.S.-based cultural imperialism, in that rappers benefit from the disproportionate exposure of U.S. artists around the world facilitated by music industry marketing muscle.[12]

Popular music, promoted by major U.S. transnational music conglomerates, sets the world standard. The U.S. stars associated with R&B, reggae, salsa, and particularly rap, underpinned by the economic and distributionary clout of these companies, leave little room for success by indigenous artists throughout the world, unless they are promoted by one of the regional subsidiaries of these companies. Although the hip-hop underground, with its stalwart local adherents, attempts to counteract this global U.S. music domination, American musicians, and particularly rap emcees, dominate the global scene.

Despite the Cuban government's strident attempts to either stave off American hip-hop's commercial influence from the United States or to control it by bringing rap groups under the Ministry of Culture, Cuban hip-hop has largely developed as an underground movement. Smuggled CDs and tapes and roof-top rigged antennas that receive commercial Miami radio stations become the antidote to the two government-run radio stations that play only Latin music and speeches by Fidel Castro. Early Cuban hip-hop aficionados may very well have become influenced not only by black American rappers, but also by Cuban American rappers heard on Miami radio stations like DJ Laz (Lazaro Mendez) rapping in Spanish over merengue rhythms, long a musical staple throughout the Caribbean. In many ways the beginning scenario of Cuban hip-hop is reminiscent of the early Bronx days when poor youth would tap into Con Edison electrical poles to run their outdoor sound systems, as well as sell bootlegged hip-hop mixed tapes out of the trunks of cars as an underground economy. Poverty, whether under democracy or socialism, promotes creative contrivances by youth to find their pleasure in alternative popular culture forms and similar social counternarratives against attempted marginalization.

Cuba's government-controlled hip-hop movement consists of over 250 rap posses. These Cuban rappers or *raperos* often appear at Club Las Vegas in downtown Havana or in the funkier Club La Mona in the backyard of a cultural house in central Havana. According to journalist Annelise Wunderlich, who did fieldwork in Cuba, one of the main Cuban rap producers is Pablo Herrera, original producer of Orishas. According to Wunderlich, Herrera "managed and produced Amenaza, who took the top prize in one of Havana's four-year old Swing hip hop festival." Herrera also worked with female rap groups Instincto and Sexto Sentido who appeared in the festival.[13]

Herrera's conception of the underground Havana hip-hop scene is that it is congruent with Cuba's revolutionary ideals. Directly under the Ministry of Culture, Herrera espouses the direct party line when he positions Cuban hip-hop as "the empowerment of youth as a battle spear for a more conscious society. . . . [Hip-hop is a revolutionary force that] is serving the country, not being an antagonistic tool."[14] Yet given the flagrant consumerism of rap in the United States, Herrera's representation of rap as promoting the revolution's ideals is not without merit. After coming to New York and interfacing with the New York hip-hop community, he has realistic assessments of Cuban hip-hop vis-à-vis the commercial rap business:

> I don't want to see Cuba go down the drain with consumerism and our hip-hop community bought out by major labels, like it has in the U.S. I want Cuba to be an important world voice for hip-hop, in the same way that Cuba now represents for progressive leftists, those who want a righteous, socially conscious, warm life with real human development.[15]

Herrera makes critical points about the path that U.S. hip-hop has taken and its diluted progressive potential over time.

One Cuban rap group produced by Herrera, and therefore enjoying a degree of government sanction, is Anonimo Consejo, consisting of Afro-Cuban *raperos* Kokino and Yosmel. In an interview with Wunderlich, they discuss their revolutionary role models that include Latin Americans, black Americans, and Africans.

> Along with Che Guevara and Jose Martí, Yosmel and Kokino admire Malcolm X, Mumia Abu Jamal, Nelson Mandela and other black icons. They were among thousands of Cubans that went to hear Mumia's son speak at an anti-imperialist rally last year.[16]

World revolutionaries of all nationalities stand side by side in black Cuban emcees' social vision. Afro-Cuban hip-hop aficionados report an increasing awareness of their African identity, as well as a perception of racial difference in Cuba that links them to black American rappers. Wunderlich reports that after Yosmel and Kokino performed a rap about the police and racial profiling, they were arrested and thrown in jail. Like many international rappers, they allude to an allegiance founded in the aesthetics and culture of hip-hop that transcends nation states. The rap duo writes: "My country is my text, and my flag is the paper I write it on."[17]

Anonimo Consejo recognizes that skin color, despite the best efforts of the government, can still be a marker of class difference and perceived delinquency in Cuba. Yosmel poignantly reveals the difference between culture and perceived racial difference when he simply says, "When I feel African, I don't feel black."[18] Here "black" is associated with degradation and marginal social status that is part of the construction of race itself even in Cuba. On the other hand, Yosmel's feeling of being "African" confers an empowering preslavery cultural tradition to which the aesthetics of hip-hop is tied. Cuban hip-hopper's political consciousness, heightened by socialist Cuba, has always been attracted to the more politically conscious U.S. hip-hop underground that focuses on racism, the enslaving quality of capitalist materialism, and the promotion of black history and culture. This connection between Cuban hip-hop youth and the U.S. underground represents an important connective marginality within global hip-hop. Cuba's connective resonance, hence, is not only black aesthetics, but also based on the historical oppression of African descendants throughout the Americas. In postrevolution Cuba this translates as continued differential treatment of black Cubans, even as the current regime has sought to eliminate prerevolution racism.

Simultaneously, a generational resonance connects black hip-hoppers in Cuba and the United States. In a sociological study conducted on race in contemporary Cuba, Fuente and Glasco discerned a distinct difference between young and old vis-à-vis the place of blacks in the postrevolution era. The sociologists posit that Afro-Cubans in general feel that they are better off since the 1959 Cuban Revolution; however, "younger blacks do not equate the fall of the socialist regime with the end of racial inequality as much as older blacks do. For younger blacks it is possible to maintain racial equality even if the revolution falls."[19] The generational divide between black Cubans was further demonstrated by a majority of *younger* black Cubans who participated in a 1994 riot in a Havana plaza:

Those who rioted at Malecón were referred to as young blacks and mulattos, and our survey shows that, in fact, younger blacks share a more critical view of the revolution and its impact on racism than do older blacks. . . . What is at stake here is a generational rather than a racial issue.[20]

Young Afro-Cubans, with their political awareness piqued by the socialist revolution while simultaneously involving themselves in U.S. hip-hop's race-conscious underground, walk a thin line with Cuban authorities. As Wunderlich points out, Cuban hip-hoppers grew up on CDs like Public Enemy's 1989 *Fear of a Black Planet*. In PE's seminal track, "Fight the Power," lyrics like "Cause I'm black and I'm proud / I'm ready and amped? Most of my heroes don't appear on no stamps" help to promote a sense of their racial difference in an era of the island's history that was trying to minimize race while elevating Afro-Cuban culture. Wunderlich records Yosmel's sentiments about Public Enemy: "Their songs spoke to me in a new way. There was nothing in Cuba that sounded like it."[21]

With the New York–based Black August Hip Hop Collective and many community-based activist groups throughout the country, today's socially conscious wing of hip-hop culture continues in a more activist stance. The Black August Hip Hop Collective constructed a direct link to Cuba, while attempting to promote consciousness-building hip-hop movements globally. Key members of the collective are recognized rap artists such as Dead Prez and Black Star (emcees Mos Def and Talib Kweli), who have been touring to Cuba since 1998. On its website, the Black August Hip Hop Collective states that they strive

> to support the global development of hip hop culture by facilitating exchanges between international communities where hip hop is a vital part of youth culture, and by promoting awareness about the social and political issues that effect [*sic*] these youth communities. Our goal is to bring culture and politics together and to allow them to naturally evolve into a unique hip hop consciousness that informs our collective struggle for a more just, equitable and human world.[22]

The organization traces its inception back to "the 1970s in California prison system by men and women of the Black New Afrikan Liberation Movement." This politically activist branch of U.S. hip-hop culture, never promoted by the major pop culture media, strives to continue the political tradition of the community-building aspects of the Black Panther Party through the arts. The result is a two-city August hip-hop event: The Annual Black August Hip Hop Benefit in New York City, the proceeds of which go to establish a hip-hop library in Havana, and the Festival Nacional de Rap Cubano in Havana.

This contemporary hip-hop link between Cuba and the black revolutionary movement in the United States has a historical connection to a few black political activists of the late 1960s and early 1970s who fled the United States when accused of crimes against the state and received asylum in Cuba. Assata Shakur, Tupac Shakur's godmother, has been exiled in Cuba since 1986 when she escaped from prison while serving a life sentence imposed in 1973 after a highly disputed trial. Nehanda Abiodun is another political exile from this period and has been particularly close to the hip-hop community in Cuba, mentoring Cuban hip-hop youth to think critically. Wunderlich has noted that Abiodun has held "informal sessions about African American history, poetry, and world politics" with them.[23] As a result, rapper Yosmel perceives Afro-Cuban connective marginality in the rhymes of Black Star: "It was amazing to hear rappers from another country worried about the same issues I was."[24] Hence, meeting and rapping on the same show with some of the top underground U.S. artists through the Black August Collective validates the aspiring Cuban emcees' growing Pan-African consciousness.

Cuban emcees are still often caught between conflicting allegiances. Socialization within a revolutionary society that teaches one to challenge the world's status quo and, at the same time, de-emphasizes racial difference in a Caribbean region historically based on class and color, creates an ambivalence reflected in the work of young Afro-Cuban *raperos*. They struggle to express their generational concerns through hip-hop's less publicized counterhegemonic movement. But their challenge to their own country's continuing race and class problems can only have so much impact in a controlled society where freedom of political and artistic expression is not encouraged. However, Cuban hip-hoppers are not deterred; they continue to make associations with their black and Latino counterparts in the United States aesthetically, culturally, and politically through the music.

Brazilian Favelas' Connective Marginalities

Influenced by the U.S. hip-hop movement of the late 1970s, the emergence of hip-hop in Brazil dates back to the mid-1980s.[25] The hip-hop phenomenon in Brazil is essentially a social movement organized by Afro-Brazilian youth as a response to social disaffection, poverty, and racism. As in Cuba, young Brazilians, particularly those of predominantly African descent, immediately perceived the connection between their sociopolitical plight and that of blacks in North America. In response, they helped spawn a new wave of consciousness both politically and culturally. Niyi Afolabi explains that,

> The emergence of hip hop in Brazil dates back to the mid 80s, influenced by the North American Hip Hop movement of the seventies, and indeed a backlash of the Civil Rights movement of the sixties with such heroic figures as Martin Luther King, Malcolm X and even the Black Panthers. A parallel Civil Rights movement in Brazil is the *Movimiento Negro Unificado* (United Black Movement) which is responsible for various protest rallies, educational programs and from which some of the culturally and ideologically inclined carnivalesque groups such as Ile-Aye and Olodum evolved in the mid seventies.[26]

The confluence of the Movimiento Negro Unificado and Afrocentric *blocos afros* (emerging neighborhood-based black performing groups) during carnival set the stage for the next generation to adopt hip-hop as an increasingly global popular culture. These threads running through several decades of political and artistic organizing in Brazil reflect the connective marginalities of race, class, and the empowerment derived from embracing black culture. In the hip-hop movement, these resonances are particularly manifested through rap music and graffiti art.

Brazilian rap artists render connective marginalities of class and culture particularly clear. According to Afolabi, "major thematics of Brazilian Hip Hop artists range from police brutality, violence, poverty, life in the periphery, crime, self-esteem, revenge, transformation, survival, death, darkness and light, and the correction of negative images of Afro-Brazilians. . . . Brazilian rap must be seen as a national phenomenon that has come to stay and not a passing phase of juvenile delinquency."[27] Here, Brazil's plight, manifested in its notorious crime, abandoned children, and street people, separates it from socialist Cuba, where hip-hop youth may be poor, but have basic needs such as shelter, education, and health care guaranteed by the government.

Brazilian rap, like its underground American and Cuban counterparts, as Afolabi notes, serves an important counterhegemonic role, directly addressing local issues of crime, violence, continuing social inequalities, and negative portrayals of Afro-Brazilians. For example, according to Brazilian ethnographer Jennifer Roth Gordon, Brazilian rap artists give

> voice to hundreds of favelas and suburbs that often remain unnamed on maps and in the Brazilian political agenda. MVBill (MV stands for *Mesageiro de Verdade,* "Messenger of Truth") begins his song, "How to Survive in the Favela," with a list of favelas in Rio. . . . As MVBill likes to say, "We are marginalized, but we are not marginal."[28]

Indeed, from Brazil to the Caribbean to the United States, social commentary, situated within the vibrant polyrhythms and layered bricolage that emerged from poor communities, has been at the heart of the distinct creation of cultures throughout the Americas.

Yet, particularity within this context, broad-based struggle is crucial. Murray Forman argues this exact point in *The 'Hood Comes First.*

> The "where" of experience has a powerful influence over the social meanings derived from the experiences themselves, for just as our actions and mobilities bring space into cultural relief, so, too, does socially produced space bring meaning to our actions.[29]

Hence, the concept of particular spatial experience with attendant marginalities—*my* favela, barrio, hood—is central to hip-hop globally. Local manifestations of marginality that resonate with other particularized evidence of social injustice in a completely different part of the world demonstrate patterns of global hierarchies that are often connected by world systems of political economy. Rap is particularly poised to address these connective marginalities through imaginative metaphor and pumping base rhythms, artistically addressing how these patterns manifest themselves in different localities. Pleasure, play, and politics find a poignant relationship in global rap, as they have in Trinidadian calypso and U.S. soul music in the past. Yet rap, situated alongside hip-hop culture's other elements of break dance, graffiti art, and turntableism, becomes particularly dynamic in addressing continuing twenty-first-century social inequities.

Unlike the preponderant images of gangsters, thugs, and pimp-playas among commercial American rappers portrayed on MTV and BET, Brazilian emcees try to counter "the negative images constantly projected on national television about Afro-Brazilians as drug-users, gangsters, and criminals, with such positive images as creative producers of culture, respectable business owners, and musical intellectuals."[30] Jennifer Roth Gordon emphasizes Brazilian rappers' crucial delineation of commercial versus underground or conscious rap:

> They identify the American rap group Public Enemy as their primary source of inspiration, but express strong sentiments against the current (what they think of as commercialized) state of rap in the Untied States. MVBill's DJ, DJTR, criticizes not only American rap stars like 2Pac, Notorious B.I.G., and Coolio, but also Brazilian rappers who take their inspiration from these "misguided" role-models.[31]

Since MTV-oriented commercial rap, rather than the work of U.S. underground emcees, is hip-hop's main U.S. export, indigenous hip-hop cultures globally may very well be the primary source of continuing counter-hegemonic activism in the subculture.

Brazilian hip-hop street culture in the city of São Paulo has been documented in Francisco Cesar Filho's film short *Hip Hop SP* (1990). São Paulo has over nine million people, making it the largest urban center in Brazil—with several teeming favelas. The film demonstrates the city's full-blown street culture with B-boys and B-girls who oftentimes combine hip-hop dance with Brazilian capoeira, a dance-based martial art originating in Angola, *afoshe* (a Brazilian Afrocentric dance style evolving with the *bloco afro* movement), and the signature Brazilian dance, samba. Again, many world-famous rhythms and dances throughout the Americas, such as samba and capoeira, derived from the pervasive Africanist aesthetic, join with postmodern manifestations of the same aesthetic in hip-hop. The athleticism of capoeira, for example, resonates with break dance's acrobatic style, and many B-boy shows in the United States include traditional Brazilian capoeira. U.S. B-boy club events that include local capoeira groups, for example, demonstrate their explicit understanding of these cultural connections across the diaspora—connections that hip-hop has revitalized.

The connective marginality of culture is apparent in forms from Africa to South America to the United States and back again. *Hip Hop SP* situates the vibrant youth culture within the context of the São Paulo favela's poverty and police brutality as well as the youths' articulate critique of these social inequities. Yet along with obvious issues of class and historical oppression that hip-hop youth around the world address, the South American and Caribbean hip-hop cultures reflect a strong *cultural* connective marginality that resonates across time and space. Thus African-derived rhythms and dances inextricably connect the Americas aesthetically.

Several Brazilian rap groups and solo emcees, such as Thaide, have risen to national prominence, and use their newfound platform to articulate cultural connections with black American culture. Thaide, one of the first Brazilian rappers and who appears in *Hip Hop SP,* locates the historical development of Brazilian hip-hop within the cultural continuum from samba-rock and soul music of the seventies, as well as the Afro-Brazilian religion candomblé in his rap "Senhor Tempo Bom" (Mr. Good Times): "In the past, Samba-Rock and Black Power is Soul. Just like Hip Hop, it was our music. . . . I also know that I made many mistakes. But I never detached myself from my roots." Thaide's invocation of the U.S. black power movement and attendant sixties soul music forms a cultural resonance between black American and Afro-Brazilian cultures. Later in the lyrics he also alludes to Afro-Brazilian religion, capoeira, and samba, representing the African legacy in Brazil. His blending of African American and Afro-Brazilian sacred and secular music and dance maps the history and cultural memory of the black Atlantic that signifies ancestral roots to his generation of young Brazilians. Even if he personally has not always followed this cultural legacy, he reveals that he was never fully separated from these roots. Thaide's lyrics succinctly summarize the connective marginality of culture that proliferates throughout the African diaspora.

Racionais MC's (The Rationals) are one of the most popular of the contemporary rap crews in Brazil, having won the prestigious Brazilian MTV awards in the summer of 1998.[32] Their CD *Sobrevivendo no Inferno* (Surviving in Hell) has sold over a half million copies, a great achievement by Brazilian standards. Yet they are considered by the Brazilian mainstream to be a renegade group that emphasizes race consciousness and racial inequality. Even with their commercial success in Brazil, according to Gordon, they continue to be a voice from the favelas, criticizing other black rappers for selling out to "white" culture and trying to fit into white middle-class Brazilian lifestyles. As in Cuba (despite racial intermixing and the revolution's ideals that eschew social discourses of racial difference), racial and economic issues exist in Brazil. Gordon notes that racial discourses by Brazilian rap artists such as Racionais MC's are judged within a "context of 'racial democracy' where any discussion of race has historically been considered 'un-Brazilian,' [and thus Brazilian] rappers disrupt the desired silence around the issues of race."[33] Hip-hop culture in Brazil is indicative of all the connective marginalities, including class, race, historical oppression, culture, and youth that bind it to American hip-hop and the ghetto context out of which it first emerged.

Conclusions

Contrary to the typical American view of contemporary U.S. rap music as a commercial sellout to mass marketing, the "booty call" and the "bling bling" of the multi-billion-dollar U.S. rap music industry, global hip-hop promotes the social margins, still rampant with poverty and inequality for too many people, in too many parts of the world. Hip-hop culture, particularly when viewed from a global perspective, is a potentially subversive epistemology, affirming cultural connections across nation-states, as well as connective marginalities reflective of extant global social inequities. The language of the body politic of hip-hop is certainly part of what allows connections between African hip-hop advocates of the Pan-African website, the Brazilian hip-hop favela movement inspired by black American historical forms, and the specific Cuban connection to the underground U.S. Black August Collective. Young hip-hoppers, as products of the racialized legacy throughout the Americas, battle articulately within this contested terrain.

Hip-hop has benefited from systemic changes over time in various societies absorbing the African diaspora. But it also takes its place in the long history of social criticism through the arts that has created a critical difference in thinking, allowing such changes to take root. The kind of social critique possible today through rap could not have happened, for example, in the rhythm-and-blues era of the 1950s. There are now black voices who dare to enter the cacophony of identity representation in diaspora politics and claim space for their particularized hood.

The centrality of *ghettocentricity* in global hip-hop insures a shift in thinking about the world's social hierarchy, creating spaces where Ulf Hannerz's concept of new "symbolic constellations" of postmodernity may be realized.[34] As old-school rapper Run (Joseph Simmons) of Run-D.M.C. has said, "It's all about who's got the soul, who got the flavor, who got the raw freedom, the rebellious attitude in them."[35] In hip-hop, this becomes the major criterion for participation in the communally oriented Africanist aesthetic that has become international. Hip-hop's involvement in commodification, ironically enough, is simultaneously implicated in its potential as a globally democratizing pop subculture.

Young black hip-hop artists in the African diaspora have, in addition to the connective marginality of historical oppression, the added dimension of a connective cultural aesthetic that allows them to celebrate the moment even as they critique their respective social conditions. Hip-hop in the African Diaspora continues a powerful legacy of accessing the Africanist aesthetic through music and dance to reveal and critique the world's extant social inequalities. In so doing, the youth in Brazil and the Caribbean form crucial cultural and class links with black U.S. youth and hip-hop youth of all ethnicities. Even though these connections and their potentialities have been explored by previous generations, the hip-hop generation is situated in the twenty-first-century with a global interdependence and technology like no time in the past. Black cultural trafficking has existed since the Atlantic slave trade, but today's youth inherit a fast-paced global consciousness that continues to invoke past black cultural practices, making the African Diaspora fertile ground for potential new solutions to old problems through hip-hop culture.

NOTES

1. Tony Mitchell, "Another Root: Hip Hop outside the USA," in *Global Noise: Rap and Hip Hop outside the USA,* ed. Tony Mitchell (Middletown, Conn.: Wesleyan University Press, 2001), 11.

2. This era is not without its own contradictions. For an extensive exploration of those contradictions from the perspective of a previous generation see Ernest Allen, Jr.'s "Making the Strong Survive: The Contours and Contradictions of Message Rap," in *Droppin' Science: Critical Essays on Rap Music and Hip Hop Culture,* ed. William Eric Perkins (Philadelphia: Temple University Press, 1996), 158–91.

3. "Ladies First" was recorded on Latifah's debut album, *All Hail the Queen* (Tommy Boy Music, 1989). The Louisiana State University English and Women's Studies departments have included the video in an anthology of female pop singers' feminist statements.

4. Joe Austin and Michael Nevin Willard, "Introduction: Angels of History, Demons of Culture," in *Generations of Youth: Youth Cultures and History in Twentieth-Century America,* ed. Joe Austin and Michael Nevin Willard (New York: New York University Press, 1998), 1.

5. Eric Hobsbawm and Terence Ranger, eds., *The Invention of Tradition* (Cambridge: Cambridge University Press, 1993). The musical forms that I mention do not

fall under Hobsbawm's criterion of "a process of formalization and ritualization, characterized by references to the past" (4).

6. "Africa—Wake Up & Unify," July 1998, http://www.africaserver.nl/rumba-kali.

7. Manthia Diawara, "Toward a Regional Imaginary in Africa," in *The Cultures of Globalization*, ed. Frederic Jameson and Masao Miyoshi (Durham, N.C.: Duke University Press, 1998), 103.

8. Robert Farris Thompson, "Hip Hop 101," in Perkins, *Droppin' Science*, 214–15.

9. For further exploration of Jamaica's sound system culture in relation to hip-hop see S. H. Fernando, Jr.'s *The New Beats: Exploring the Music, Culture, and Attitudes of Hip-Hop* (New York: Doubleday, 1994), particularly his chapter "Rap's Raggamuffin Roots."

10. Rodrigo Salazar, "Cuba Libre," *Source*, March 2001, 203.

11. Salazar, "Cuba Libre," 203.

12. Tricia Rose, *Black Noise: Rap Music and Black Culture in Contemporary America* (Hanover, N.H.: Wesleyan University Press, 1994), 19.

13. Shawnee Smith, "Words and Deed," *Billboard*, http://afrocubaweb.com/rap/pabloherrera.htm, p. 2.

14. Annelise Wunderlich, "Underground Revolution," *ColorLines*, fall 2001, 37.

15. Smith, "Words and Deed," 3.

16. Wunderlich, "Underground Revolution," 37.

17. Wunderlich, "Underground Revolution," 35.

18. Wunderlich, "Underground Revolution," 37.

19. Alejandro de la Fuente and Laurence Glasco, "Are Blacks 'Getting Out of Control'? Racial Attitudes, Revolution, and Political Transition in Cuba," in *Toward a New Cuba: Legacies of a Revolution,* ed. Miguel Angel Centeno and Mauricio Font (Boulder, Colo.: Lynne Rienner, 1997), 63.

20. de la Fuente and Glasco, "Getting Out of Control," 69.

21. Wunderlich, "Underground Revolution," 35.

22. "AfroCubaWeb: Black August 2000," http://afrocubaweb.com/rap/blackaugustoo.html.

23. Wunderlich, "Underground Revolution," 36.

24. Ibid.

25. The first wave of global hip-hop culture was initiated by the recording of the Sugarhill Gang's "Rapper's Delight" in 1979 and continued with the early 1980s Hollywood break dance films, as well as a few underground hip-hop films and documentaries such as *Wild Style* (1982) and *Style Wars* (1983). Hip-hop culture, as the latest American pop culture export, came not coincidentally on the heels of the civil rights and black power movements in the United States. Martin Luther King's assassination in 1968 occurred right before the Poor People's March was scheduled to converge on Washington, attempting to connect class with race in a blaze of American solidarity and contestation. The hip-hop generation inherited these insidious dual marginalities in the poor Bronx, a product of both poverty and racism manifested as 1970s postindustrial neglect, gentrification, and defunding of social services in black and Latino neighborhoods. For a detailed description of postindustrial New York in relation to hip-hop see Rose, *Black Noise*, particularly pp. 27–34.

The hip-hop generation in New York used their evolving new, vibrant street culture to elevate their marginalized voice in an era of disco clubs and the downtown "beautiful people." The political and the cultural revolutions of the United States after the civil rights movement inspired Brazil's youth, and this inspiration has affected the nation through the current hip-hop generation.

26. Niyi Afolabi, "Brazilian New Wave: Hip Hop and the Politics of Intervention," paper presented at the Annual Meeting of the Modern Language Association, Washington, D.C., December 2000, 2.

27. Afolabi, "Brazilian New Wave," 4.

28. Jennifer Roth Gordon, "Hip Hop *Brasileiro:* Brazilian Youth and Alternative Black Consciousness Movements," *Black Arts Quarterly* 7 no. 1, 9.

29. Murray Forman, *The 'Hood Comes First: Race, Space, and Pace in Rap and Hip-Hop* (Middletown, Conn.: Wesleyan University Press, 2002), 23.

30. Afolabi, "Brazilian New Wave," 4.

31. Gordon, "Hip Hop Brasileiro," 9.

32. Ibid.

33. Ibid.

34. Ulf Hannerz, *Transnational Connections: Culture, People, Places* (London: Routledge, 1996), 21.

35. Quoted in Mandalit del Barco, "Rap's Latino Sabor," in Perkins, *Droppin' Science,* 67.

PAULLA A. EBRON

Continental Riffs
Praisesingers in Transnational Contexts

African music was and remains a music of encounters.
  —Manu Dibango

African music: the primordial sound of the global imagination. Yet "African music" is only as primordial as the history of intercontinental audiences and the transnational music industry. African music is particularly indebted, these days, to the music industry, which facilitates musicians' ability to record and thus to establish their reputations. At the same time, African music is spread through projects of nationalism that allow audiences to hear the music as authentic and significant. The nationalisms of the continent as well as the nationalisms of the diaspora call out to musicians to play the sounds of their cultural and political projects.

Nationalisms—whether continental or diasporic—both enliven and contain the music, inviting listeners to hear within certain political agendas. For its part, the music industry celebrates its own power to re-create all global diversity in its own image; even detractors, who see musicians as caught in the industry's shackles, imagine these producers as an all-powerful force. Still, the music itself manages to escape the grasp of both producers and meaning-makers. Musicians are able to negotiate a creative space of encounter that expands nationalisms and sometimes undermines them and that makes use of industry opportunities even as it opens up the industry in new directions. To say that African music is a music of encounters is to see the meeting of musicians, producers, and audiences across continental riffs as a primary means of understanding the music. That is the approach I take in this essay.

This essay considers a form of music that is much valued for its traditional valences: the music of West African praisesingers and, in particular, Mandinka *jalis*, the oral historians, poets, singers, and instrumentalists who trace their art to the thirteenth-century Malian Empire. Jali music may be traditional, but it is popular now because it has recently experienced a revival. In countries such as the Gambia, it is the music of the state as well as, to some promoters, the music of the people. In North America, it is the music of African roots. In the global music industry, it is woven in and out of varied folk and urban musics to inform the sound of cosmopolitanism. Contemporary jali music emerges from the encounters that take place within these various performative niches. Indeed, all internationally circulating "African music" emerges from such encounters, in which "imagined communities" of audience create the continental significance of the sound, while music industry entrepreneurship extends and multiplies these audiences.

In this essay I argue for the importance of three particular performative niches in the shaping of contemporary jali music created, respectively, by West African state-making, the African American search for roots, and the world-music industry. Each niche generates a characteristic "structure of feeling," to use Raymond Williams's evocative phrase.[1] Audiences are formed through a particular structure of feeling that makes it possible to appreciate the sound with more pleasure. As Williams defines it, a structure of feeling is a formation that has not achieved the status of hegemony—the taken-for-granted status of "commonsense" power—but that nevertheless asserts a hold on a community's imagination.[2] It makes sense out of ways of life. Such structures may not be supported by official pronouncements, but they create common attitudes and interpretations of public life; although they are sometimes in conflict with official ideologies, they are not exactly alternatives to them because they reside more in the interpretation of everyday practices than in declarations. Diverse structures of feeling may thus sit side by side, overlap, or blend without raising official comment.

The concept of structures of feeling is particularly relevant to the study of the popular arts. One understands how to participate in music, song, or dance only to the extent that the performance catches on to a structure of feeling. Only then does music, for example, move us; it does not itself offer automatic access to the interpretive frame in which audiences come to hear it. In the case of jali music, the music becomes "African" through structures of feeling; the musicians become "African"—in the sense of being representatives of the continent—through their engagement with the communities of listeners that each of these performative niches offers them. The music itself can stimulate more than one way of hearing, that is, more than one structure of feeling. African music, as an instrument of encounters, gains its power in many instances through distinct yet over-lapping structures of feeling, as these appeal to different audiences or, alternatively, mix and rearrange audiences.

While all three of the performative niches I describe in what follows are associated with structures of feeling, I privilege musicians' encounters with the third, the world-music industry, as the lens through which I examine the making of the music in the essay's second half. This is in part because, for the purposes of this essay, I examine the work of musicians who have recorded internationally, rather than, for example, describing local perfor-mances. These internationally recorded artists have the reputations to set standards for genres of music; they influence the possibilities for perfor-mance. In this essay I trace how musicians with stakes in the "imagined communities" of Mande and African American nationalism bring these commitments to their international recordings, extending and rewriting those commitments. The nationalisms come to life through this cos-mopolitan venue, but they can also be transformed.

The first half of this essay traces the imagined communities and struc-tures of feeling that give jali music a continental feeling. In the second half, I discuss particular examples of jali music to show how encounters among audiences and musicians have proven a generative zone for musical expression.

Mande Worlds

Jaliya is the art of jalis. Acquiring the skills to recite oral poetry and genealogical histories as well as learning to play the kora (a twenty-one string harp), the balafon (a wooden xylophone), and other more minor instruments is central to its practice. In addition, jaliya includes other oral arts, speech making, and negotiation—for powerful men are also a part of the tradition. Jalis are empowered artisans by birth, specialists who train from childhood.

Jaliya forms a part of everyday life in Mande regions in West Africa. Thus, jalis perform in naming ceremonies and weddings, serve as everyday negotiators, and are essential assistants for important people. Yet, because jaliya continually refers listeners back to the power of ancient kingdoms and their leaders, it has also become an idiom for contemporary political power. In their praisesongs, dedicated to great warriors and political figures such as Sunjata Keita, the founder of the Malian Empire, jali performers generate a sense of continuity between precolonial and contemporary polities. In the Gambia, where I conducted ethnographic research in the 1990s, jalis are tapped into contemporary politics both for and beyond the state. The Gambia is relatively new as a nation-state, achieving independence only in 1965. Surrounded on three sides by the much larger nation of Senegal, the Gambia is tiny and has few resources. In this context, nation making is not simple or taken for granted. Jaliya is considered by many as one of nationalism's most potent resources.

Benedict Anderson's influential work on nationalism popularized the notion of the nation as an "imagined community."[3] Anderson argues that people have had to learn to think of themselves as citizens of nations rather than of localities, regions, empires, or other kinds of polities. Newspapers facilitated this process in many national contexts, Anderson argues, by creating a readership focused on events within the emergent "nation." Newspaper readers thus created an "imagined community" of people who had never met face to face. Contemporary nations continue to use newspapers and other media to create imagined communities of nationalism.

Newspaper reading in the Gambia, however, is a small-time activity in which relatively few participate. A much larger audience is convened around performances, including jali performances. It is no surprise, then, that Gambian leaders have enlisted jaliya into their efforts to build popular support for the projects of the nation. Politicians surround themselves with jalis; jali performances support state programs, including literacy and development issues, as well as patriotism in general. Jalis tap their traditional abilities to praise leaders and promote polities in an effort to support popular appreciation of the nation.

Yet jaliya is not an automatic answer to the problems of building the Gambian nation-state. Jaliya traditionally refers to the world of ancient Mande kingdoms, a world that stretches far beyond the boundaries of the present Gambian nation. Indeed, the kind of polity jalis best praise does not correspond very well to the reality of the modern nation-state, with its obsession with boundaries, its bureaucracy, and its impersonal authority. In addition, jaliya is as easily tapped for transnational ethnic causes as it is for any state. Mande cultural nationalists look to jaliya to reconfigure the territorial boundaries created by European colonialism and bring Mali, Gambia, Senegal, and Guinea together; this aim can variously support or interfere with the plans of the Gambian state. Within the nation-state, the problem of incorporating people of different ethnic backgrounds is poorly addressed by reliance on a single ethnic tradition. Furthermore, jalis form part of a traditional system of stratification that fits poorly with the state's "modern" ideas about development and progress. And yet, during my research in the early 1990s, I found that jaliya was, despite challenges like these, strong in particular Gambian political circles. Jaliya attempts to tap the feelings of the populace and to move it into the polity.

Because the music is moving, even skeptics are ambivalently touched. Cultural critic Manthia Diawara, for example, has emerged in print as one of the harshest critics of the use of jaliya in the formation of contemporary identities:

> Laying in bed that night, after Toumani's concert, I thought about the griots' power to keep West Africans in a retrograde position, to make us respond to feelings that have not changed in seven hundred years. Despite our attempts to catch up with the modern world, they have trapped us in a narrative of return, a permanent identification with Sundiata, Mansa Musa, Samory Toure and other "Duga" and "Simbon."[4]

Yet even Diawara cannot fully resist the jali's charm. He admits to succumbing to the skill of a powerfully charismatic jali during a performance in Mali one evening: "[D]espite my resistance to embracing what I consider archaic aspects of tradition, he [the jali] brings back to life within me an unquestioned identification with Mande structures of feeling."[5] As Diawara explicitly notes, these Mande structures of feeling include the unequal play that characterizes relations between patron and jali, a performance that entails a reciprocal set of obligations and responsibilities. Jaliya draws one back into a world of heroism, of status hierarchies that reengage particular historical understandings of clan, gender, and caste relations— a world that Diawara finds antithetical to the modern democratic nation-state.

Yet jaliya, through the structures of feeling it generates, has also been rather successful in coalescing an imagined community of identification among Mande people. Through the performance repertoires of jalis, those living in the urban spaces of Europe and North America as well as those living on the continent are able to imagine a sense of connection and longing stimulated by the idea of Sunjata.

African American Roots

A second imagined "African" community, formed by African Americans, exists in diaspora across the Atlantic. To cultural nationalists of the early 1970s, the West African griot—including the jali—was a figure that could bridge the gap between Africa and African America. In the late 1970s, many more African Americans came to hear of jaliya through Alex Haley's book and subsequent television drama, *Roots.*[6] Haley's story features a jali who helped him discover and revive his ancestral connections in Africa. Academic critics whose research focuses on the Mande world are quick to note the fictional aspects of Haley's work; they argue that he did not know much about West Africa or the jaliya tradition.[7] Still, for many people throughout the diaspora, this was a moment of revitalization. Jalis became a model for connection between Africa and the New World. They were the oral historians who could recover history for those from whom it had been stolen by slavery. Jalis were imagined as masters of memory and the oral arts, skilled at oration and wordplay. Some imagined them as the quintessential "raptavists," the precursors of contemporary rap artists.[8]

Poets and musicians, in particular, started to look at jaliya as a source of African origins. Blues artists found jaliya inspirational. Scholars, such as Samuel Charters in *Roots of the Blues,* have explored the connection between African American music and the music of Senegambia jali.[9] Another imagined community of performance was in formation, yet this one, unlike its counterpart in West Africa, had none of the resources of the state. Performance in this instance supported an imagined community of cultural connections between Africa and its historical diaspora.

While the structures of feeling inspired by jali performances in West Africa on the one hand and among African Americans on the other are each born of nationalist sentiments, the contrasts between them are instructive. In West Africa, jaliya tells of greatness; it informs us of the conditions of power. The skill of the musician indicates the importance of competence to make power effective—it is worth employing experts. Among African Americans, jaliya, in contrast, is the art of African roots. It affords African American artists the opportunity to listen back to a time of origins, when the New World diaspora was still connected to the continent. The beauty and complexity of the music attests to the richness of that history. Of course, this was the time of kings; mastery and power are essential. But what one hears, while helped along by the CD liner notes as well as the tunes themselves, is the evidence of the past, the routes of memory made real in melodic lines and oral techniques. For the West African audience, too, history is there; the music of jalis stretches back across the centuries. But the complexity of the music and the mastery of memory the artists offer tell us of contemporary prowess; these kings are still with us today. The music stirs great men to action; it inspires the state. History works for power, rather than power for history.

These structures of feeling overlap as well as diverge. Both allow audiences an appreciation of music and wordplay, both signal the importance of beauty and complexity. But they lead down different paths. The power of jaliya today is its ability to inspire both these routes at once and, in their intersection, to forge new roads. The performative niches of West African and African American nationalisms have helped give rise to a third: the world-music scene. The world-music industry—including producers, agents, recording arrangements, and distributors—sets the parameters for spreading the reputations of many performing artists. Here another structure of feeling emerges as significant. World-music audiences are generally invested in neither the nationalism of West African state-making nor the pursuit of African American roots. Instead, they value a cosmopolitan appreciation of the arts. Expertise in music is valued as an example of the global creativity of humanity. Through it, one hears both the unity and diversity of humankind. The listener enjoys the ability to taste the variation and agility of traditional musics as well as the creativity of new juxtapositions and hybrids. Jaliya emerges, then, in the overlap among these three structures of feeling.

World Music and the Structure of Encounters

Jalis are able to perform internationally because of the rise of a new appreciation for what has been called "world music." Jalis have long had transnational sensibilities: they are travelers and carriers of news as well as being performers. Pan-African festivals on the continent, such as Festac, that began as part of a postcolonial enthusiasm in the 1960s only encouraged this predisposition, by bringing jali in touch with a number of other African musicians beyond the Mande sphere as well as with other cross-local traditions, thus stimulating new experiments in collaboration. These ongoing conversations and experiments in turn coincided with, and helped fuel, the period of Western interest in African music, providing an ongoing impetus for reworking traditional legacies.

In the 1960s and 1970s, the folk-music revival in Britain and North America drew new attention to traditional musics around the world. At the same time, "ethnomusicology," the study of traditional musics both within and beyond the West, became a scholarly discipline.[10] Scholars, producers, and performers mixed their roles and combined their talents in bringing new traditional musics into the public arena. Ethnomusicologists were particularly fascinated by "high" court musics that were found outside the West, for these exhibited a complexity and expertise that challenged musicological ethnocentrism. West African kora music and Indonesian gamelan were two early foci of ethnomusicological attention. But note: it was the mastery of the instruments and the complexity and the possibilities of the music itself—not the power of kingdoms or the materiality of roots—that drew these listeners.

International appreciation opened the door for a greater number of African musicians to perform in the West. Among the early jali musicians to venture abroad were well-known Gambian jalis Alhaji Bai Konte and Nyama Suso, as well as some lesser-known figures. The youthful yet talented Jali Yankuba Saho, for example, participated, by invitation, in the Smithsonian Folk Life Festival in the early 1970s.[11] The Manding festival in Britain in 1972 brought a range of jali to perform. During this period, the audiences for these musicians were relatively small and specialized. They were primarily folk-festival enthusiasts savoring the variety of global tradition or students of ethnomusicology skilled in interpreting musical traditions.

In the early 1980s, however, a shift began to occur, and the audience for world music broadened. "World music" became a popular performance category. Recording companies were interested. Performance genres generated new styles. Audiences as well as performers began to talk about collaborations, fusions, and hybridity. Foday Musa Suso, for example, moved to the United States in the late seventies and formed his own hybrid group, Mandingo Griot Society. Suso formed a collaborative connection with U.S. musician Don Cherry, as well as with Herbie Hancock and Philip Glass.

Other jalis, especially those who already had ties to international promoters, were quick to seize upon this opportunity. Many sought to expand their traditional base of patronage to include transcontinental sponsors. Certain jalis were able to make international performances an important part of their work. While some have earnestly taken on the task of explaining jaliya to foreign audiences, others choose to perform without providing any explanation of the music's traditions. This leaves the meaning of their music open to reinterpretation by their promoters and collaborators; it also creates an opportunity for the jalis themselves to learn the new global musics and incorporate them into their domestic as well as their foreign repertoires.

Audiences drawn to jali music as part of the world-music scene are not necessarily attuned to the political dimensions of jaliya or the extended significance of what is expected of jalis. Musicologists have worked diligently to explain the social and cultural context of jaliya. Yet many audience members at world-music concerts turn to universal frameworks for appreciating the music. For many, this is a chance to participate in a "global village." All kinds of tribal, ethnic, and folk musics, unmoored from their local significance, join in a syncretic mixture of cultural forms that cross genres and reform into a multiethnic fusion. The technical complexity or the rhythm is valued for itself, not for its ability to enliven a national community. The music, the aesthetic play of melody and rhythm, seems to signify only itself.

Despite its apparent independence, however, the world-music scene does not stand by itself; it both affects and is affected by the other encounters in which jaliya participates. Jalis use their performance and recording opportunities to make both old and new kinds of music. They bring forward disjunctive as well as hybrid agendas. The nationalisms of the postcolonial era in West Africa enliven a political culture that makes sense of their repertoire, at home and abroad. The African American enthusiasm for roots provides possibilities for collaboration and elaboration of the music. Furthermore, the world-music scene offers opportunities that stretch and contravene both these nationalisms. For example, women performers, who have difficulty speaking for the "brotherhood" of the nation, are sometimes able to travel and perform. Thus, new musical possibilities are explored.

In the next section I examine particular recorded performances and particular structures of feeling at work. To explain a little about how the music comes to mean and to entice readers to explore the music themselves, I avoid the use of musicological terminology in favor of offering a sense of the music's texture. I also introduce the communities that I imagine listening, and the audiences to whom an appeal is being made.

The performance encounters I offer below are recorded ones. This presents a certain limitation: the recorded form restricts the publicly interactive relationship of performers to audience. In live performances of jalis music it is common for musicians to call out to members of the audience, and members of the audience in turn can express their appreciation for being recognized. In recordings, obviously, musicians must interact primarily among themselves to create the performance. As audience participants listening to a CD, we find ourselves in a more reflexive pose, created by a temporal and spatial disjuncture; we are unable to negotiate the performance except after the fact. And yet, we can repeat the performance, enjoy it, work to understand it from different angles. Thus, even without the benefits of a live performance, it is possible to experience the rich texture of an encounter with jali music.

My process of selection will reveal a bit of a turnabout, as I include jalis from the Gambia who are not generally the popular icons that one associates with jali music. The regional dominance of Mali and Senegal has allowed certain performers from these countries to distinguish themselves. Although jalis from the Gambia are by no means bystanders in this traffic in culture, constraints on the means of production have greatly curtailed some of the promotional aspects of this commercial venture. The Gambian state at one point wanted to record and feature a number of its artists, yet in order to do so they had to rely on a recording studio in Senegal. The musicians featured here do speak to the diverse encounters discussed in the first section of the essay.

Performance Encounter I

The twenty-one string lute harp—the sound of the kora—awakens with the music of Mande jalis. Its melodic tone is cast along the higher register of the instrument's strings. The sound manages to transport listeners back centuries ago: to a time, as the lyrics attest, when royal kingdoms and elaborate patronage arrangements were the formal aspects of the social composition of the day. If you are a member of one of these lineages, the performance is even more significant to you because it is about you and your ancestors; it is their great deeds and accomplishments to which songs make testimony. Their deeds have been memorialized and returned as praisesong, the thematic focus of this genre. The melody forms the repetitive structure of a tune soon wrapped up in embellished ornamentation as the music weaves around its basic phases, contributing more and more complicated renditions.

The song (track 1, "Jimba Sengo," on the CD *Gambie, L'Art de la Kora*) begins with a melodic phase, a musical entry that introduces a tune providing the underlying melody to the lyrical phases and the praises to important patrons. Interludes in the progression of the song's journey, also framed by prophetic sayings, become messages to the living about their purpose in life. Of course, jali music is much more than this, but it may take some time and repeated listenings to catch some of the deeper significance. This opening signals one significant musical encounter, the one between instrument and musician, working their dialogue into a formal presentation.

Consider, as a preeminent example of such a musician, Jali Nyama Suso, a master kora player. His reputation brought the music of jalis to wide-ranging audiences and placed him in a world of international acclaim. Notable among his international exchanges were the students he attracted. Nyama Suso is able to move between different styles with the ease of a master, offering fast-moving repetitive passages that give way to the stop made on a single string, illustrating his command of the instrument. Yet this command is much more than a musician's dream or the result of hours of dedicated practice. Indeed, his accomplishment speaks to the social responsibility of jalis; it is a testament to the power embodied in jaliya and its ability to promote its patrons. Jali Nyama Suso's musical style also incorporates a wide range of musical influences. One of his devoted students, Roderick Knight, on the CD, notes that one of the tunes is in waltz time, a seemingly unusual rhythm for African music. Clearly, jalis move with ease between musical worlds; the particular agendas or wishes of some of their patrons cannot contain them.

Jali Nyama Suso's ability to generate a following that includes audiences on the continent and beyond makes him a strong example of the viability of jaliya in multiple arenas. Musicologists formed one potent collaborative encounter for Jali Nyama Suso. Many learned these instruments as they introduced their teachers to the world. With a jali-like zeal in mastering their craft, musicologists found their interests in dialogue with these jali professionals, and they helped promote the jali's presence in expanded circles. Musicologists, like Gambian audiences of jalis, appreciate the complexity of the music. When they hear a musician like Nyama Suso, they hear the mastery of music just as Gambian audiences do. Yet that appreciation leads each audience in a different direction. Mastery reminds the Gambian audience of the authority of ancient kingdoms and the necessity of caste hierarchy; it is music as power. In contrast, the Western musicological audience hears mastery as musical talent. This diversity is the power of jaliya. It juxtaposes and combines diverse filters through which music is given meaning, offering a doubled or tripled framework for listening.[12]

Jali Nyama Suso opens one tune with kora phases and hums along with the song, actually picking out a melody at the same time as he sings and recites poetic verse. Several rhythms are at work at the same time. Listening to it is like hearing a complex conversation, created not just between voice and instrument but also between right and left hand as the quick finger-work leads the listener to believe there are multiple instruments playing at once. Jali Nyama Suso makes the difficult sound simple, yet he also makes us aware that he is creating this effect. He is a master of mastery: the door to many audiences.

Jali Yankuba Saho performs more frequently in the Gambia than Jali Nyama Suso did at the height of his career—although he is equally cosmopolitan. On the CD *Yankuba: Kora Music from the Gambia,* Jali Yankuba Saho offers a selection of recently arranged praisesongs that are informed by classical notions of what jali music is supposed to include and, at the same time, reworked with his own elaborations. Jalis in the Gambia are no less interested in incorporating world-gathering influences into their musics than those who have gained a wider transnational reputation. A critical aspect of jalis cultural production is improvisation, the effort to make the songs speak to the particular audience for whom the musician is performing. Jali Yankuba Saho performs with his wife, Jali musa Binta Suso, who, in addition to singing along with her husband, taps the side of the kora to add another rhythmic accompaniment. Most of the songs on Yankuba Saho's CD celebrate his patrons and friends, noting their deeds and the places they are from. But the words are set within the traditional kora tunes, again reminding one of the link between present and past. Yankuba Saho's kora playing is particularly stunning when he shows off his mastery of the kora, frequently lapsing into exulted riffs with the melody. In both Nyama Suso's and Yankuba Saho's recordings musical encounters are in large part about the display of power and authority. The jali is able to use the performance as a medium through which to invoke a sense of mastery—his own as well as that of his patrons.

Jali musa Kandia Kouyate from Mali is one of the most successful women performers on the continent and beyond. She is known for her abilities as a singer in her own right rather than simply as the backup to her husband's performances. One of the striking aspects about her performance on the CD *Kita Kan* is that, in addition to the usual praisesongs to patrons and heroes laced with prophetic sayings, she includes a moving song in which a woman speaks regretfully about the practice of arranged marriage. She is forced to say good-bye to the one she loves because her parents have decided whom she will marry. Kandia Kouyate's commanding voice adroitly conveys the sense of sadness, keeping the audience under her sway even as her role as jali is to reinforce tradition. The instrumentation helps strengthen the mood. The kora is joined by a number of other instruments that offer a kind of mournful lament, creating the effects of a movie soundtrack. One can imagine the departure sorrowfully through the minor notes and the synthesizer's ability to mimic a sound of loneliness.

Even within the given conventions of nationalist dreams and the place of jalis in reinforcing these dreams, there are multiple alternative visions that the world-music scene has helped create. Women performers who become part of world-music promotions, small as their numbers may be, are able to expand the contours of public debate. The additional source of promotion has also afforded some jalis, both men and women, the possibility of moving beyond traditional lines of power and authority created through patron-client ties. Others continue to thrive within the powerful conventional arrangements that have long assured jalis an important symbolic place in the nation's memory. Heroic songs, prophetic sayings that frame important messages, and even the critique of certain practices become elements that help create a structure of feeling among Mande audiences and help to generate a public discourse both within and beyond the Mande world.

Performance Encounter II

This time you will hear the opening phase played by a steel body guitar whose steady tempo is kept alive by an alternating bass line. This opening provides an invitation to the kora to join the guitar. This time the musical dialogue is staged between Africa and the diaspora, where instruments and musicians try to fill the gap created by the Atlantic slave trade centuries ago. Both instruments attempt sonic recognition, recalling the elements long said to create the link between those on the continent and on the shores of the New World. Malian kora player Toumani Diabate and African American blues musician Taj Mahal perform on a CD entitled *Kulanjan,* a title taken from an important traditional tune within the jali repertoire. These two musicians are joined by others: Kassamady Diabate, Ramatou Diakite, Bassekou Kouyate, Dougouye Koulibaly, Lasana Diabate, and Ballake Sissoko, as well as Western-music enthusiasts and longtime students and promoters of Mande music, Lucy Duran on kora and Erye Banning on guitar. This musical collaboration took place in the southern United States, in Georgia, in 1999.

When you listen to the first selection on the CD—"Queen Bee," an old tune in the African American repertoire—you are immediately drawn into the self-conscious overlap between Mande music and acoustic blues. A double voice is created between guitar and kora as Taj Mahal links the alternating bass line and finger-picking style of African American blues/folk with that of the finger-picking styles of Malian instrumentalists. The guitar provides a steady frame while the kora strings embellish the main theme. The high strings play around the theme in a way that suggests the movement of a bee in a hive. On this first selection, Taj Mahal and singer Ramatou Diakite sing back and forth in their respective languages in a kind of musical dialogue.

The scale and syncopated rhythms of both instruments make this reunion seem natural. And yet the liner notes reveal more: Taj Mahal apparently learned of the kora in the 1970s and considers this meeting his chance to connect with Africa; thus, the musical encounter transports him home. In his celebration of being "home," Taj Mahal changes his name to Dadi Kouyate, the first jali family name. Images abound of a world that brings him closer to Africa through music. Important aspects that make this encounter work effectively are the repetitive frame of roots and authenticity, the resonances of the acoustic sounds of both instruments, and the playing of tunes that have significance in the traditional repertoires of each musician's respective musical heritages. But the gap between Africa and the United States is repeatedly made smaller as Mahal has discovered a sense of affiliation. Taj Mahal describes his goal for the recording session this way:

> To complete a cycle, to return to the intact original, to have been visited by very powerful visions of ancestors and their music, to realize the dream my Father and Mother had along with many other generations of Africans who now live outside of the Continent of Africa.[13]

The inspirational moment for this CD can also be linked to a larger folk-revival moment in which acoustic instruments are able to bring listeners back to a "pure" sound that is made to seem even more authentic in this case by the combination of other instruments associated with jalis. These include the ngoni and balafon and, from the diaspora side, the guitar and dobro.

Another example of jaliya's musical significance to the second imagined community of the diaspora is the encounter forged between guitarist Ernest Ranglin and several Senegalese musicians, among them well-known musician Baaba Maal. Promoted by the *New York Times* as "the patriarch of Jamaican music," Ranglin and friends are on a mutual quest. They claim a privileged place in turning to Africa in search of their roots, albeit in different ways than Taj Mahal. Ranglin's tour is through the improvisational possibilities offered by jazz. In contrast to Taj Mahal, whose agenda, in many ways, is explicitly dedicated to preserving a sense of Mande heritage via acoustic blues collaborations that celebrate ancient kingdoms, Ranglin's CD offers a different kind of musical intersection. The global traffic between Senegalese musicians and musicians from the Caribbean and North America was established several decades ago. Thus, these musicians read each other's music, exchanging elements of percussion and style stimulated by the jazz-inspired encounters of this earlier period. Senegalese musician Baaba Maal looks to Ranglin as a mentor. Ranglin then travels to Senegal to forge a collaborative production between his performance style and Senegalese music. As with Taj Mahal, the structure of feeling in this encounter is produced again through a sense of connection and reunion with Africa. Yet the music itself speaks of its hybrid and cosmopolitan style, of traditions made over through the mutual appreciation of the cultural worlds this imagined diasporic community has already produced.

Jane Cortez, a poet from the United States, uses kora players and West African drummers to accompany her jazz-inspired poetic form. Her CD *Taking the Blues Back Home* provides another example of the range of jali cultural production and the circulation of jalis in a diasporic imagination. Here the musicians form the background to her frequent poetic riffs. One performance on the opening cut provides a sample of a genre found throughout the CD. Cortez recites, "I'm taking the blues back home, I'm taking the blues back home. I taking the blues back home, I taking back home." The sounds of a number of electric instruments, drums, and harmonica accompany her verbal phase in a way that brings words and music together. The jali's significance on this CD draws primarily from the notion that jalis are oral poets as well as musicians and that we in the diaspora have inherited this ability to work as wordsmiths. As suggested earlier, oral skills tend to be the feature of jaliya held in highest regard by those in the diaspora.

Overall, the structures of feeling in these three diasporic encounters, while somewhat divergent, produce a similar kind of double voicing between the desires of those in the diaspora for reconnection and the jali who are willing to go along with these projects.

Performance Encounter III

In a final selection, once again you will hear the familiar opening of the kora, a prelude to the song's beginning. Soon a woman is heard singing what sounds similar to a phrase offered by the kora; she joins the introduction with "da dum de de dum," and the kora keeps pace. You will also hear faintly in the background a mouth bow, known as the do-do. Its subtlety shadows the kora's tune. Soon the jali and singer join in a song that alternates between verses celebrating Tiramakan, a Mande hero who lived during Sunjata's time, and "Eg Vippa Meg," a Norwegian lullaby. Kirsten Berg combines the lyrics from the lullaby with verses from the West African song, and the tune moves back and forth between the two worlds evoked. Thus begins the collaborative exchange between West Africa musicians from Senegal and Ivory Coast and Norwegian folk musicians on the CD *From Senegal to Stesdal*. The group members include Kirsten Braten Berg, Solo Cissokho, Kouame Sereba, and Bjorgulu Strame.

The adaptation of songs from both musical traditions effectively allows one to see the world produced by musical encounters in which the performers retain a musical identity at the same time they attempt to escape their respective traditions. They create an explicitly hybridized form in which songs, in content, are made to speak of similar events in Norwegian ballad and traditional jali compositions. The effort is to generate a musical dialogue through this meeting of their different folk/ethnic traditions. The structure of feeling inspired in the exchange of these ethnic musics moves listeners beyond the confines of an explicitly aimed imagined community as represented in the previous examples.

This musical encounter is an imaginative effort to take pieces out of their familiar contexts. The liner notes again become an important guide to understanding the aims of the collaboration, for the synchrony between traditions is not always apparent when listening, nor is it foreshadowed by the already-constituted set of political agendas one might find in the previously discussed encounters. Yet the cliché "the universal language of music" seems to frame the moment. In another cut, mouth bow and kora link up on "Jegerleik," a song about a hunter who is alone in the forest. In order to appreciate this song one must bring a sensibility, already cultivated in the ear, of the kora's ability to play multiple rhythms. Along with the kora, the mouth bow and the drum form a compelling trio, joined by the voices of all.

Consider one final example under the rubric of world music. The flamenco guitar and the kora appear to be unlikely companions. Yet on the CDs *Songhai* and *Songhai Two*, jali Toumani Diabate and Spanish musical group Ketema join together to offer a rhythmic competition between West Africa and Spanish stringed instruments. From the opening bars, the kora strings run alongside the pace set by the guitar. The liner notes again offer clues to what informs this encounter: "Like so many West Africa countries, Mali's musicians play almost as much Latin music as their own traditions." Ever circulating, jali music in this encounter produces a fusion that disrupts many of the familiar refrains offered in the previous sections. The balafon plays a much more dominant role here than in other recordings, and the most significant aspect I hear is the play of rhythms across cultural traditions. Another imaginative link, then, between the music of the Mande world and world music lies in the ability of these two musical traditions to speak the universal language of the arts and the ability of these musicians to reach across their respective traditions.

Conclusion

The theme "traffic in black culture" raises the question of how cultural products translate across audiences. In this essay I have considered a few of the performative niches in which jali music is currently produced, with the aim of exploring how the music comes to have significance in a number of different encounters. The listening communities described here cross and exchange in their expectations, and the musicians refuse to be bound by a single desire. I have also argued that the nationalist projects at work in these encounters are both extended and modified as listeners find themselves moved by performances while speaking to their political longings.

These nationalisms are not the same. A third niche is the world-music scene, which further helps produce and circulate the musical cultural products of jaliya.

The initial questions animating my discussion (though not explicitly discussed here) have to do with the ways performance becomes a racialized venue for the enactment of blackness. In particular, what is blackness as a performance? I revisit this question at the end of the essay, hoping that the first half of the paper illustrates the historically contingent ways performance has taken on a life within three different moments. The answer then, can only be appreciated within the particular ways race has come to have significance. To start with this question might appear to some—particularly those from the continent—as an awkward imposition inserted by those in the North American diaspora. Within the social fabric of the United States, race is a salient category and a frame in which most things are understood, but this is not the case on the continent, where many people maintain that race is not a significant category. Thus what is understood as blackness in one instance becomes less the prevailing icon of difference in another context.

To people found throughout the diaspora, particularly those in North America who link their histories to the Atlantic slave trade, the sense of Africa is kept alive through a set of contingent "remembrances." These images and feelings are continually invoked through the rubric of performance: style, presence, and performative genres that are spoken about over and over again as the links to Africa. The mutual figurings of performances in this instance—the world provoked by and through jalis and their audiences—provides an important conversation. Of course, performance "worlds"—to make of this word a verb—Africa not only in a variety of European and North American encounters but in overlapping and, at times, contradictory ways.

As I have shown here, different types of encounters with jali cultural productions generate divergent alliances. This fact, along with the efforts of international commercial producers who promote and circulate jaliya, both music promoters and artists—not to mention our own experiences as members of an audience—remind us of the ways the questions about cultural production and the traffic in Africa commingle at this historical juncture.

NOTES

1. Raymond Williams, *Marxism and Literature* (New York: Oxford University Press, 1977).

2. Williams, *Marxism and Literature*.

3. Benedict Anderson, *Imagined Communities: Reflections on the Origin and Spread of Nationalism* (New York: Verso, 1983).

4. Manthia Diawara, "Return Narratives," in *In Search of Africa* (Cambridge: Harvard University Press, 1998), 114.

5. Diawara, "Return Narratives," 96.

6. Alex Haley, *Roots* (Garden City, N.Y.: Doubleday, 1978).

7. See, for example, David Gamble, *Postmortem: A Study of the Gambian Section of Alex Haley's "Roots,"* Gambian Studies no. 39 (Brisbane, Calif.: D. P. Gamble, 2000); Thomas Hale, *Griots and Griotees* (Bloomington: Indiana University Press, 1998).

8. David Troop, *Rap Attack* (London: Pluto, 1983).

9. Samuel Charter, *Roots of the Blues* (Boston: M. Boyars, 1981).

10. For further discussion see Mark Slobin, *Subcultural Sounds: Micromusics of the West* (Hanover, N.H.: Wesleyan University Press, 1992).

11. Interview notes, Gambia, 1990.

12. It is important to note here that I am working with a nuanced idea about power. In places within West Africa, power is often figured in ways that go beyond a top-down hierarchy. For an extended discussion of power, see Bonnie Wright, "Power of Articulation," in *Creativity and Power,* ed. William Arens and Ivan Karp (Washington, D.C.: Smithsonian, 1989), 39–57. In keeping with certain poststructuralist interpretations, Wright suggests a more fluid notion of how power operates in social interactions than many Western theorists and texts propose.

13. Taj Mahal, *Kulanjan,* CD liner notes.

PART FOUR

Trafficking in Black Visual Images
Television, Film, and New Media

HERMAN GRAY

Where Have All the Black Shows Gone?

The members of various political and cultural communities whose job it is to monitor commercial network television seem constantly surprised by the episodic nature of black and minority representation in the commercial arena. Close monitoring of the performance of the commercial networks by media watchdog groups, television critics, and civil rights activists is often followed by public notice—in the form of a crisis of representation—about the diminution of the numbers of black and minority characters, shows, or themes on commercial network television. Such notice is then followed by a period of threatened political action—usually in the form of a boycott of the network—followed by negotiation between the networks and some advocacy group. Then comes a promise by the networks to do more, which is followed by a period of notable increase in the number of black (and minority) faces on television and in some token management positions. Several seasons later there is the announcement of yet another network lapse and the process begins once again.

I am interested in this cycle, especially the institutional conditions and cultural assumptions that structure this dance and set the terms in which it is repeatedly played out. Contained in this relationship are a number of instructive examples of theoretical and methodological commitments that confine, to earlier historical periods and analytic paradigms, the cultural analysis of race and, by extension, the cultural politics that flow from it within television studies. What persist are theoretical and political assumptions about commercial network television as a utopian site of possibility for racial and cultural diversity, the social responsibility of the networks as cultural producers to deliver this vision of possibility, and media activism as a political practice that aims to insure its realization.

I take the 1997 television season as a case example of these theoretical and structural dynamics because it anticipates if not precipitates the political struggles that would occur late in 1999 and early 2000 over diversity and representation. I also offer 1997 as a case because it points to the limits of prevailing theoretical and methodological categories that continue to stress networks, characters, programs, race, and certain forms of activism as the most salient units of analysis in the new social, financial, and representational conditions of production and circulation of network television. In other words, with the case example of the 1997 season I explore the operation of these dominant cultural assumptions about diversity and representation in network television—in today's cultural environment—with the aim of showing their limits for thinking about cultural media and the politics of representation. Although I do not remark directly on more recent contemporary television seasons or representations (i.e., after 1999), I present this case analysis in relationship to these more recent television offerings as a way to measure the distance that our critical understandings of media, race, and politics have, or more likely have not, traveled since the late 1990s.

Much about the world of American network television changed in the years since the close of the 1992 television season.[1] In subsequent seasons black-oriented shows like *The Cosby Show* and *It's a Different World* moved from premiere network schedules to the financially lucrative orbit of reruns and syndication. Although a perceptible shift in focus from middle class to urban youth appeared for a while, urban youth were replaced in the network schedule with black shows preoccupied with domestic families, parenting, and social relationships. For a while Fox Television continued its quest for legitimacy and financial profitability with black shows like *New York Undercover* and a stable of hip-hop youth and urban-oriented comedies. Inevitably, these offerings gave way to the cash cow of reality programming, old staples like feel-good comedies (aimed at white youth), and big-ticket items like sports.

Two new mini-networks—Warner Brothers (WB) and Paramount (UPN)—joined Fox in challenging the dominance of the three major networks. To wage this challenge, the new networks used black-oriented programming to anchor their fledgling evening schedule. Using such programming (especially situation comedies) to get a scheduling toehold in a network's formative years continues the strategy that the Fox News Corporation used in its nascent years. With a calculated financial risk and little to lose in terms of their reputation as a television network, Fox Television pursued urban and youth audiences interested in black-oriented programming.[2] Today mininetworks like WB and UPN operate in an environment transformed by cable and satellite delivery systems and niche marketing.[3]

By 1997 black-cast and black-theme-oriented shows were still confined largely to the genre of situation comedy and entertainment variety. That year the major networks scheduled a thin slate of nighttime drama(s) featuring black lead characters: *NYPD Blue, ER, Law and Order, Chicago Hope, Homicide: Life on the Street, Touched by an Angel, 413 Hope Street,* and *Players.* The network also scheduled the usual fare of black-oriented situation comedies with identifiable black actors like Bill Cosby, Gregory Hines, LL Cool J, and Jaleel White.

There was little news here. These developments were quite unremarkable. The network strategy of offering programs featuring all-black casts and themes, accompanied by a smaller number of shows with a sprinkling of black cast members, continued a pattern that began the early 1970s following the urban rebellions of the previous decades. Nevertheless, I am intrigued by the persistent preoccupation by journalists, some scholars, and media activists with the ebb and flow of black television representations from season to season.

According to a 1998 *New York Times* piece, the prospect for black television representations in the 1998 season seemed considerably more dismal than prior seasons.[4] Ironically, it seemed that the hour-long drama was finally about to deliver the goods, presenting programs with multiracial casts, developing story lines with complex depictions of black life, and locating such programs in integrated workplace settings. But again it should come as little surprise that this has not been the case for television's construction and representation of the intimate domestic spaces of home and family. For not only does the representation of blacks remain largely confined to the genre of situation comedy, but there seems to be a general apprehension (if not outright fear) on the business side about the financial risks involved in pursuing racial crossover dreams.

As interesting is the discursive frame through which journalists, critics, industry observers, network executives, and studio heads talk about television representations and race. The conventional wisdom seems to be that black, brown, Asian, and white television viewers watch different programs. Since white viewers remain the idealized subjects of television advertisers, studios, and networks, the culturally pressing question is whether or not they will watch shows about the lives of people different from them and whether or not networks and studios will take the financial risk of programming these shows.

American television audiences are migrating in record numbers to other forms and sites of service delivery.[5] In this context, the racial politics of audience composition, viewing preferences, and financial risks indicated by the consistency of data on the racial character of audience preferences may well be the cultural expression of a crisis. That is to say, the structural transformations in the global media and information industries are articulated culturally and so too is the racial logic that structures audience choices and preferences. Television, especially television news, remains a particular and important kind of public sphere; hence the problem of diversity in television representation is both cultural and structural.

Black television representations are shaped by shifting conditions of possibility that include new global markets, larger and more powerful interlocking structures of ownership, newer and more complex relations between products and means of distribution and circulation, and less and less regulation by local, national, and international governments. Among the most far-reaching and consequential transformations affecting American television are passage of the 1996 Telecommunications Act, the changes in corporate ownership of media conglomerates, the emerging structure and global reach of entertainment-media-information companies, and rapid advances in new technologies and program delivery.[6]

In the years since the close of the 1992 network television season (where the concluding episode of the season's most popular program, *The Cosby Show,* was broadcast opposite news coverage of the flames of the LA rebellion), a new industrial logic has taken shape. Within this logic, larger and often more nimble corporate entities have emerged, with the hope of insuring access to more profitable shares of the global market in entertainment, information, and communications. Through joint ventures, buyouts, mergers, and new investments, global companies like Fox, Warner, TCI, and Microsoft have solidified their positions as global players. These companies have acquired television stations, movie studios, cable operations, satellites, publishing houses, record companies, theme parks, communications infrastructure, and movie studios. While maintaining large complex bureaucratic organizations, these global media corporations are nevertheless organized into smaller administrative (and creative) units. This is all designed to strategically and efficiently identify markets, control distribution, generate products, and move them anywhere on the globe. In other words, larger and larger, yet more nimble and flexible, administrative and financial units are intended to generate and distribute a diverse range of entertainment and information products. The goal is to establish greater access to and control of global markets.

In this new mediascape, distinctive creative, technological, and financial entities and activities—computers and related information technologies, cinema, telephony, broadcasting, publishing, satellite, theme parks, cable, music, and electronics—are combined to form giant global media firms like TCI, Time-Warner, Fox News Corporations, Disney, Bertelsmann, and Seagram. While this kind of reconfiguration was anticipated in the late 1970s and early 1980s, one of the immediate political and legal factors that insured its realization was the passage of the 1996 Telecommunication Act.[7] The act restructured major aspects of the telecommunications industry. These included the scope of federal regulation and oversight; the size and composition of firms; the assignment of broadcast frequencies for television, radio, and cellular telephones; the upper limit on the operation and ownership of broadcast stations; the control of delivery systems; and the complementarity between various media technologies.

The Telecommunications Act sharply deregulated the telecommunications industry, essentially giving major American corporations like Time Warner, General Electric, Fox News Corporation, Disney, TCI, Microsoft, Seagram, and Disney the green light to pursue mergers, joint ventures, new research and development, and worldwide expansion with the blessings (and supposed oversight) of the United States Congress. So profound and far-reaching was the act that no aspect of American telecommunications was left unaffected.[8]

As the major corporate players acquire new properties, enter joint ventures, and otherwise pursue the globe as one giant market for media, information, and entertainment, newer, more powerful, and diverse corporate entities appear. Microsoft, the computer software giant, is suddenly in the television business; Fox News Corporation is in the sports and satellite business; General Electric is in the sports arena business; Time Warner and its competitors either own or are busy pursuing deals for news, cable, movie, publishing, and music entities.[9] Television production companies, television stations, television networks, and cable operations are all components of these global media giants.

In this global environment, media companies must maintain consistent sources of content or software that can be moved efficiently through multiple delivery systems (e.g., cable, wireless, terrestrial, satellite) to destinations (e.g., computers, television sets, CD players, or movie screens) across the globe. The technological distinctions, organizational partitions, and cultural meanings that once defined technologies, delivery systems, or media are no longer meaningful in any productive sense. Media content moves easily from novel to cinema screen to television to video to theme park.[10] With such a voracious demand for content and information to fill markets worldwide, telecommunications companies must contend with increasing production costs, greater consumer choices, and different systems—all the while trying to exert greater control over production, distribution, and markets.

Through joint ventures, multiple ownership (TCI, for instance, owns controlling interests in the black cable network operation Black Entertainment Television, which was purchased in 2000 by Viacom), and cooperative development agreements covering hardware and software, the major corporations extended their control.[11] As consumers, we experience these forms of control at the point of our most familiar, mundane, and ritualized encounters with the telephone receiver, the cable box, the computer screen, and the television set.

Where Have All the Black Shows Gone?

The summer of 1999 saw the twentieth century's final installment of the serial television game of "now you see us on TV, now you don't." For now, however, I want to focus attention on the two-year period prior to the call for a boycott of the television networks by black and Latino media activists and political organizations, for during this time the contours of the impending confrontation were already visible.[12] Because the 1997 fall season of American network television presents a telling pattern with regard to black television representation, it is worth recalling the network's programming choices. That fall, black television shows were still in the schedule; however, they were concentrated largely among the program offerings of the newest television networks. Of the six commercial television networks, WB, UPN, and Fox had a combined total of *sixteen shows* that could be identified as black or black-oriented prime-time programs. Of the traditional majors, CBS scheduled three and NBC one. ABC did not schedule a single black show that season.[13] Fox scheduled three shows (including the only nighttime drama), WB scheduled four, and UPN placed a total of five shows on its fall schedule. Most of the scheduled programs were returning from previous seasons; of these the most popular and well-known black show on Fox was *Living Single,* starring Queen Latifah. *Living Single* was initially cancelled, but was quickly revived by Fox after a successful letter-writing campaign by the show's fans. The often-controversial *Martin* and the popular *New York Undercover* were not renewed for the 1997 Fox season.

In addition to Queen Latifah, familiar stars like Bill Cosby, the members of the Wayans family, Jamie Foxx, Brandy (*Moesha*), Steve Harvey with the addition of Cedric the Entertainer, Jaleel White, and Malcolm Jamaal Warner all returned to the prime-time schedule that year. It should come as no surprise that situation comedy was still the dominant genre, and households and workplaces the preferred setting, for shows that season. Stories about adolescent maturation, relationships, friendships, and roommates provided continuing story lines and narrative action. The season's televisual black Americans were drawn largely from the middle and working class and included small children, students, and retirees. Characters could be found in various domestic arrangements including extended families, shared living spaces, marriages, and nuclear families. All of the shows stayed close to the predictable conventions of the genre—medium camera shots, lighthearted narrative dramas, familiar settings in which everyday difficulties and relationship tensions are the stock in trade. These genre conventions move characters through predictable experiences and situations that provide momentary transformation. The action and emotional cues are pumped up and pushed along with laughter provided by enthusiastic studio audiences and laugh tracks. Contemporary music, fashion, language, and information gave the shows the feel of being steeped in contemporary urban black popular culture and style that was made more explicit with regular guest appearances by a slate of entertainers and athletes. Recognizable figures—mostly athletes and musicians—regularly found their way to the small screen. Similarly, former television personalities like Will Smith (star of *Fresh Prince of Bel Air*) and Martin Lawrence *(Martin)* moved from the grind of sustaining a weekly series to the more lucrative world of film.

While not particularly remarkable aesthetically, these shows helped to sustain a black presence, albeit separate, in the mediascape of American network television. This stubborn separate (and not always equal) racial representation on American commercial network television remains the source of continuing frustration and concern, especially on the part of media activists, journalists, and scholars. Upon closer inspection it is evident that the most integrated casts and story lines in those years took place on hour-long dramatic programs like *ER, Homicide,* and *NYPD Blue.* Like their sitcom counterparts (and contemporary progeny), these shows were most often set in the public spaces of work. On the other hand, the situation comedy—long associated with intimacy, family, romance, and domesticity—is still the site of some of the most benign but persistent segregation in American public culture.

Furthermore, while the television industry continues to maintain a minimal commitment to black presence on commercial network television, the shows that do survive are located, structurally anyway, in the least risky part of the network schedule (and the low investment sector of corporation). Following the leads of cable, Warner Brothers, United Paramount Network, and Fox News Corporation—all among the newest networks—use the principle of narrow-casting and the strategy of niche marketing, with youth as their target audience. Even though ABC, NBC, and CBS still enjoy a considerable share of the commercial television market, when cable and the new networks are factored in, the traditional network share is below 50 percent. Traditional networks like NBC and CBS also adopted niche-marketing strategies by positioning shows like *Friends, Seinfeld, Fraser, Cybil, Susan, Third Rock from the Sun, ER,* and *NYPD Blue* as name brands that appeal to white middle-class professionals.[14] As with cable, the newest networks made the greatest inroads into the traditional network share by targeting youth and urban markets. That is, these new networks pursue such programming strategies until they establish a brand identity with advertisers and in key sectors of their market.[15]

From the culture of the television business and financial interests of media corporations, what appears on the social and political radar as segregation and containment of black shows may be the articulation of the new industry logic. Since the television environment is no longer dominated by three major networks, the force of various new delivery systems, global media operations, and marketing clutter is felt ever more immediately and directly. This means that in order to remain competitive, television programmers must be clear about their audiences or market niche, efficient in the production and scheduling of their programs, and strategic about cultivating their brand identities. To remain competitive—despite their claims to the contrary—networks long ago abandoned the strategy of aiming the least objectionable programs at the widest possible audiences. Cable operators, new networks, and old-line majors made explicit marketing decisions to use their programming to reach distinct demographics, including black urban markets.[16] Black shows, where they are developed at all, are selectively developed and deployed by networks as part of their overall marketing and branding strategy, a strategy and ideal demographic that in all likelihood does not include black people as a prime market.

These operations are after smaller, more sharply defined demographics, lifestyles, and disposable incomes. They schedule relatively inexpensive shows (including reruns, movies, game shows, and, most recently, reality programs) with identifiable stars and personalities.[17] They combine various forms of programming and service delivery including cable wire, the traditional broadcast signal, and satellite service. Accordingly, Fox, UPN, and WB have modeled their approach explicitly after cable.[18] This approach to marketing, scheduling, and program development of the new networks is helping to reshape American television.

The Cultural Politics of Black Representation

In light of the new technologies, sophisticated means of circulation, and reconfigured systems of production, the challenge is to consider how blackness means, what it means and where. Just what exactly is a black program and what does it signify? Discursively, the emphasis on the local politics, the conditions of production, the specific social circumstances in which programs are received and the particular investments in the cultural meaning that they express will continue to shape what such representations mean in the United States. I want to insist on the cultural significance and historical specificity of American black television programming. This significance rests with the fact that such images function as cultural sites for the articulation of specific desires, meanings, relations, histories, and struggles pertaining to black life in the United States. At the same time, the significance of this programming can no longer just be limited to local and specific meanings and American politics, since cultural encounters are neither just local nor specific to the United States. American network executives remain deeply unsure that black television programming can do any more than generate short-term profits in American television markets.[19] But can the new technologies of exhibition, circulation, and delivery broaden the field of play and the terms of the game?

It seems to me that black program makers and buyers can seriously consider how black television programming will play in the distant reaches of the markets increasingly made more accessible by satellite, cable, the

Internet, and other forms of service delivery, information circulation, and cultural travel. Given this circumstance, is a prerequisite for black television shows (and cinemas) simply that they travel well? That they speak in a universal language? And if so, what is that language and what is the embodied representation or representations through which it is expressed? Is it the naturalized (racialized) athletic and dancing black body? Perhaps it is the body endowed with musical prowess? Is it the black corporeal body of the liberal civil rights subject? Perhaps it is the neonationalist subject of hip-hop discourse?

The American television experience seems to suggest, historically, that blackness articulated in integrated, public work spaces is preferable to that which threatens the intimate spaces of the family and domesticity. This narrative is, of course, a very old story in the American racial imagination. Shows that finally do make it to a network or cable schedule (or a cineplex screen) now, more than ever, are required by the global structure of ownership, delivery, and markets to speak in a universal language. All of this means that black shows now signify in relation to a rapidly changing political and cultural field of finance, production, exhibition, and circulation of media content including sports, film, information, music, games, fashion, and style. The meanings, pleasures, and identifications generated from black television representations, no matter where and how they travel, still bear the perceptible traces of the specifically American circumstance in which African American blackness is constructed and operates. This means that the global journey of media images of blackness is also an occasion to consider the role of media and television in the cultural production of the United States as a structured racial and national formation.

Black Representation and the Post-Civil-Rights Public Sphere

While liberal journalistic discourses about segregation and integration, crossover, and separation persist in the United States, the shifting global media environment provides the occasion for asking a different kind of question about the racial politics of American network television and its programming practices, in particular for making sense of racial patterns in audience reception as the breakdown of a public sphere organized by the media and defined (on questions of race) by civil rights discourse. The persistence of racialized programming patterns and viewing preference may well suggest the presence of a post-civil-rights public sphere.[20]

The new logic of television broadcasting—the logic of the neonet-work—in the United States may well have two seemingly contradictory social implications for television representations of blackness. In purely economic and marketing terms, television shows about blacks will continue to appeal to networks to the extent that they can compliment and add value to the product identification of their programmer networks. As traditional network identities—expressed through their logos and stable of programs on a given evening, across the schedule, and throughout the season—become more focused and explicit, the defining market characteristics (regardless of regional or national location) and aesthetic parameters of a network will drive the demand for programs. The genre, star power, program conventions, and scheduling strategies cannot help but constrain studios and networks even as they continue to guide their decisions. While it may well fulfill demand within identifiable genres designed to attract a particular market niche, this strategy, developed to reduce market uncertainty, means that the program offerings that do manage to find their way to a network's program schedule will remain safe and conventional. As buyers and schedulers of programs, network executives continue, indirectly at least, to shape the range, look, content, and style of a show that it seeks to program. All of this with the explicit aim of matching advertisers with the ears and eyes of those guaranteed by the networks.

At the same time, despite their domination by Western corporations, a broader range of service delivery options and the rising importance of television programs as sources of product identity for global media companies may well mean greater possibilities for black and minority representations to circulate more widely within and across various market niches. Take, for example, the persistent finding that in the United States, blacks and whites like and view different programs. Black-oriented programming, which enjoys a wide reception in black households, seldom if ever registers with white viewers.[21] Rather than interpret this finding as a failure of the integrationist ideal of the post-civil-rights public sphere, I take the finding as an expression of black tastes, interests, and pleasures. For me the real question is whether or not program makers and buyers will respond to these expressions of tastes and preferences in terms of their strategies of brand identity and marketing or continue to see them as minor, and hence of little consequence, because of their lack of crossover. In terms of cultural politics, this expression of black interests may require a different take on the post-civil-rights public sphere and the role of television in the production and organization of that public.

This expression of black cultural tastes, the production of a new black public, together with the logic of the neonetwork focus on niche markets and flexible production may well mean the production of programming driven by the demand to reach such publics and less by the demand for intelligibility and relevance by broad audiences who may speak a given language or know the intimacies of a particular cultural experience.[22] Though small and marginal, but with increasing implication for global corporations, the success of ethnic programming on cable stations; Internet developments with file sharing, downloads; radio in music production and circulation, and the production of film for the Internet are all examples of this intimacy. Politically, these possibilities make for interesting opportunities for new cultural articulations: for engaging memories, histories, and stories that are particular and specific at the same time that they require information and understandings rooted in identifications, loyalties, and interests that transcend specificity and particularity.

If this is to occur at the level of global media and not just below their radar, then it assumes that global corporate entities remain open to identifying and serving such niches (and that they are profitable). Although American television broadcasting continues to slip, in terms of audience share and innovative programming, relative to cable, it nevertheless remains hegemonic. Giant entertainment-information-media companies control libraries, film holdings, book lists, and software around the world. With their vast financial resources and through their control of telephone lines, satellites, broadcast stations, publishing houses, and software, there is little doubt that they are the major purchasers and schedulers of programming content around the world.

No matter how hegemonic, the logic that drives this global structure still must respond to and organize the uncertainty that still exists at the local level. Even as the global structure continues to structure identifications and alliances that can be realized through the new technologies of communication, it can never completely discipline nor absolutely control such possibilities. Thus, we might ask: where is it possible for blacks, Asians, Latinos, gays, and lesbians to get a small toehold into an industry whose hallmark is packaging our desires and identifications? Several models are on offer—the cable route illustrated by BET and Univision, the small cable operations of ethnic television, the niche strategy of mininetworks.[23]

The immediate problem for makers of black programs may no longer be just making these programs—though widely dispersed and often wildly erratic, they are nevertheless available—but how to make a greater variety of programs and get them to desirable audiences. In addition, negotiating the logic of the market as a terrain on which forms of community, identification, and association are constructed and structured is as tricky as it is potentially productive—or hollow. Program makers will face the onerous task of generating programs that speak to the specific concerns of particular and local markets. Spike Lee, Walter Mosley, Oprah Winfrey, and other filmmakers, novelists, and entertainment figures have recognized this challenge and tried to respond with television programming aimed at specific segments of blacks. Latinos have also recognized the opportunities presented by the shifting structure of the television industry and have responded with, for example, children's programming aimed at multicultural and bilingual audiences.[24] Some of these efforts involve traditional networks, while others are aimed at cable channels and networks; among the most responsive and innovative has been Home Box Office (HBO). By the same token, since these programs must travel to distant markets and audiences with different histories, traditions, languages, and experiences, the meanings (and politics) of culture, including blackness, will have to be negotiated within the terms of these competing aesthetic and economic demands.

How does one speak with confidence about what such shows mean and how, when the audiences and the markets they organize do not always share particular histories, identifications, and experiences? To be sure, in a global media world, neither immediate experience nor shared identification is required for a given program to produce meaning and pleasure. (Indeed, one might argue that our modern global mediascape itself—whether the Internet, cinema, music, or the satellite—constructs identifications and shared histories through its very existence.) On the other hand, representations, no matter where they circulate or how they are generated, are more than free-floating signifiers cut loose from the social and historical moorings that make them intelligible in the first place. Though media representations do obviously signify at multiple levels and in different times and places, they continue to bear the traces of their conditions of production and the historicity of their time and place.

NOTES

A different version of this chapter appeared as "Cultural Identity and American Television in the Post Network, Post Civil Rights Era" and was published in *Race, Racism, and the Mass Media,* ed. Simon Cottle (Buckingham: Open University Press, 2000) and as Chapter 4 in Herman Gray, *Cultural Moves: African American and the Politics of Representation* (Berkeley: University of California Press, 2005).

1. Herman Gray, *Watching Race: Television and the Struggle for Blackness* (Minneapolis: University of Minnesota Press, 1995).

2. Gray, *Watching Race.* See also Craig S. Watkins, *Representing Hip-Hop Culture and the Production of Black Cinema* (Chicago: University of Chicago Press, 1998); and Kristal Brent Zook, "How I Became the Prince of a Town Called Bel Air: Nationalist Desire in Black Television," Ph.D. diss., University California, Santa Cruz, 1994.

3. Byran Burrough and Kim Masters, "Cable Guy," *Vanity Fair,* January 1997, 76–79, 126–31. Also James Sterngold, "A Racial Divide Widens on Network TV," *New York Times,* December 29, 1998, National Desk, P1.

4. Sterngold, "Racial Divide."

5. Burrough and Masters, "Cable Guy," as well as "Hollywood's Fading Charms," *Economist,* March 22, 1997, 81–89.

6. Edmund L. Andrews, "Congress Votes to Reshape Communications Industry, Ending a Four-Year Struggle," *New York Times,* February 2, 1996, A1, C4.

7. Robert W. McChesney, *Rich Media, Poor Democracy: Communication Politics in Dubious Times* (Urbana: University of Illinois Press, 1999).

8. McChesney, *Rich Media, Poor Democracy.*

9. Ken Auletta, "American Keiretsu," *New Yorker,* October 20 and 27, 1997, 225–28.

10. Susan G. Davis, *Spectacular Nature: Corporate Culture and the Sea World Experience* (Berkeley and Los Angeles: University of California Press, 1997).

11. Auletta, "American Keiretsu."

12. It was evident as early as the spring of 1997, when the networks announced their fall season, the same season that I wrote the original draft of this chapter.

13. This is a telling observation; by the 2001 season, ABC began to enjoy considerable success with the Damon Wayons vehicle *My Wife and Kids.*

14. Victoria Johnson, "Welcome Home: CBS, PAX-TV, and 'Heartland' Values in a Neo-Network Era," *Velvet Light Trap,* fall 2000, http://www.utexas.edu/utpress/journals/javlt.html#46; see also John Caldwell, *Televisuality: Style, Crisis, and Authority in American Television* (New Brunswick, N.J.: Rutgers University Press, 1995).

15. Fox is the obvious example here.

16. Todd Gitlin, *Inside Prime Time* (Berkeley and Los Angeles: University of California Press, 2000).

17. The runaway success of MTV's *The Osbournes* and reality failures like *The Chair* make a point about the volatility of this environment.

18. Bill Carter, "A Wiley Upstart That Did a Lot of Things Right," *New York Times,* January 4, 1998, Arts and Leisure Section, 34–35. See also "Now What? The Dawn of the Post Network, Post Broadcast, Post Mass Television Age," *New York Times Magazine,* September 20, 1998.

19. This ambivalence is not just specific to black-oriented television programming, but is true more generally of television programming, regardless of genre, audience or schedule. The force of this logic seems to impact black-oriented programming more directly since there is so little programming to begin with and the shows that do make it to the network schedules are pressured to produce the requisite ratings in a very short time.

20. George Lipsitz, *Dangerous Cross Roads* (London: Verso, 1994).

21. James Sterngold, "How Cable Captured the Mini Series and the High Ground," *New York Times Magazine*, September 20, 1998, 86–87.

22. Though the range of difference within a given market niche will perhaps be reduced, the proliferation of niches—the five-hundred-channel model touted for digital television—could mean more programming outlets for black film, video, and television makers. (The hegemony of corporate control of television means that even with the proliferation of channels and new delivery systems, this proliferation may well mean that these five hundred–plus channels will look more alike than different.)

23. Both BET and Univision began as small, specialized cable networks and were subsequently purchased by major media companies, Viacom in the case of BET and General Electric in the case of Univision.

24. In an ironic illustration of precisely my point here, I came across a story about similar concerns in a local English-language newspaper published in Mexico City while working on this chapter in San Miguel de Allende, Mexico: David Bauder, "Latina Heroine Wins over US Toddlers," *The News,* July 15, 2001, 15.

NICOLE R. FLEETWOOD

Hip-Hop Fashion, Masculine Anxiety, and the Discourse of Americana

From leather Louis Vuitton suits to fat-laced or no-laced Adidas athletic shoes, to tight spandex shorts, African medallions, baggy Tommy Hilfiger jeans and oversized hooded sweatshirts, hip-hop fashion has provided the visual markers for a larger cultural movement that has transformed popular music and international youth cultures in recent times. Since the 1970s, hip-hop music has been associated with a broader set of cultural practices, including dance trends, graffiti art, and fashion. Aside from the music itself, fashion continues to be the most profitable and recognized of the practices affiliated with hip-hop culture.

While studies of hip-hop culture have mentioned the significance of fashion and some have described trends of particular artists or "moments," scholars have paid very little detailed analytical attention to hip-hop's fashion system and the rapidly growing industry that promotes the fashion. When fashion is discussed in the context of earlier studies of the music form, it is quite often through the lens of subculture theory; thus fashion is relegated to one of many practices that mark (and oftentimes romanticize) the cultural movement as distinct from normative American culture.[1] Yet hip-hop fashion's success in recent times deserves focused attention. Furthermore, examining the significance of urban male fashion and the iconic, racialized, adorned male body of hip-hop's material and visual culture offers insight into the relationship between materiality, representation, and consumption in black popular culture. Embedded in representations of the fashioned black male body of hip-hop is the interplay between a highly stylized and reproducible racial alterity, nationalism, and consumption.

Applying Roland Barthes's analysis of the fashion system, this study examines the recent attempts through hip-hop fashion to frame the black male figure of hip-hop as possessor of a new American dream and inheritor of the legacy of Americana.[2] I reorient fashion studies away from (white) women's wear and femininity to analyze black male fashion, the industry that supports it, and the interplay of masculinity, desire, and national identity. Dorinne Kondo's influential study of male Japanese business fashion is useful here for her analysis of the relationship between masculinity, race, and nationalism in fashion codes.[3] Kondo argues that "[c]lothing can have a political edge as signifiers of subcultural style and as components of ethnic/racial pride," while simultaneously reinscribing problematic codes of nationalism and essentialism.[4] In considering the racialization and masculine construction of hip-hop clothing, I also critique notions of subcultural authenticity by focusing on the strategic production and performance of racial authenticity through hip-hop fashion wear. Authenticity is a highly racialized and complex term in American culture. In the context of race and masculinity, authenticity imbues the subject with a mythic sense of virility, danger, and physicality; in representations of hip-hop, authenticity most often manifests itself through the body of the young black male who stands in for "the urban real." In looking at the production of racialized and gendered wear in hip-hop fashion, I offer a brief overview of the development of this particular fashion industry. I then choose the advertising campaign for the hip-hop fashion company Phat Farm as a case study for examining how racial authenticity, masculinity, and nationalism are retooled and addressed through black masculine street fashion.

Hip-hop fashion, like the music, flourishes through the "mixing" of elements as diverse as high-end couture, found artifacts, tagging (or brand-naming), and sports apparel. For over a decade, journalists, cultural critics, and scholars alike have launched criticisms of the commercialism of the art form and related practices as a move away from core values and attitudes of the early movement.[5] Yet, as Tricia Rose has examined, hip-hop, as a style based in referentiality and reflexivity, thrives on appropriation and redefinition, which is the essence of "mixing"—the musical technique that is at the root of the cultural movement.[6] Hip-hop fashion also regenerates itself through the same process. The ever-changing trends, many of which appropriate white upper-class status symbols, such as luxury car insignias and European fashion designers, are the equivalent of the musical practice of sampling. In *Hip Hop America*, journalist Nelson George cites an example of a Harlem entrepreneur who in the 1980s made knock-off designer clothes with a hip-hop flair for many of the first successful rappers.[7] Kobena Mercer argues that this process of mixing is fundamental to the development of black diasporic practices in his analysis of black hairstyle: "Diaspora practices of black stylization are intelligible at one 'functional' level as dialogic responses to the racism of the dominant culture, but at another level involve acts of appropriation from that same 'master' culture through which 'syncretic' forms of cultural expression have evolved."[8] Hip-hop fashion and music—and black cultural practices in general—complicate simplistic cultural models that posit authenticity against appropriation, or originality against commercialism.

Hip-hop culture, particularly fashion and the referencing of fashion in lyrics, often defies the pejorative paradigm of appropriation described in much of subculture studies in which commercialism and commodification destroy or disempower the authenticity of the cultural practice studied. Noel McLaughlin, in his study of rock music, masculinity, and fashion, argues that authenticity is also a much-bandied term in discussion of popular music and intensifies in discussions of music and blackness:

> Indeed, the performative possibilities of black performers have been overlooked by a more general rock discourse that has validated black music as the authentic expression of racial "essence," and a key aspect of this has been the longstanding "necessary connection" forged between black people, black culture (clothes and performance styles) and music-making: between blackness, the body, rhythm and sexuality.[9]

The significance of appropriation, the performance of success/excess, and the preoccupation with "looking good" that are performative enactments at the heart of the hip-hop fashion system challenge the aura of authenticity that cloaks much of hip-hop's earliest musical and clothing styles and grassroots cultural practices. The "syncretic" process by which an aesthetic of racialized alterity blends with the quest for material wealth and financial success are most clearly evidenced in the more recent material invocation of Americana (and its aesthetic of red, white, and blue) by contemporary hip-hop fashion designers. These visual symbols of patriotism merged with consumer fashion goods interplay with notions of urban, black masculine alterity reproduced through hip-hop music and culture to create a character who is at once an ultrastylish thug and the ultimate American citizen.

The Development of an Industry

The relationship between hip-hop music, specifically its lyrics, and fashion is mimetic. Clothing acts as the visual identifier of the sound. At the same time, clothing, specifically brand names, is cited frequently in hip-hop lyrics. One of the most notable and documented examples of the exchange between the music and the clothing style—the visual and auditory signs— is Run-D.M.C.'s popular 1986 song "My Adidas," along with the wearing of the sports shoes in the rappers' music video, concerts, and public appearances. Nelson George relays how Russell Simmons, then manager of Run-D.M.C., negotiated a deal with the owners of the German-based company Adidas. "Within a year, Adidas and Rush Management had negotiated a $1.5 million deal with the rappers to market Run-D.M.C. sneakers and various accessories."[10] Run-D.M.C., it is important to note, is considered the first major crossover rap group to win large audiences of young white people in addition to core urban black fans.[11] George sees this deal between Adidas, Run-D.M.C., and Rush Management as a defining moment when hip-hop fashion moved from the incorporation and redefinition of existing trends to actually designing and marketing products as hip-hop fashion. The affiliation between the product and the rap group is significant because it set the stage for other rappers to endorse retail products. It marked a significant transition of the localized cultural practices associated with hip-hop into a culture industry.

By the early 1990s, the relationship between hip-hop musicians, their lyrics, and major apparel companies had grown more intermingled, as large retail companies realized the economic potential of tapping into hip-hop culture. According to journalist Marc Spiegler, Tommy Hilfiger was the first major fashion designer who actively courted rappers as a way of promoting his street wear. Spiegler writes, "Over the past few years, [Biggie] Smalls [now deceased] and other hip-hop stars have become a crucial part of Hilfiger's open attempt to tap into the urban youth market. In exchange for giving artists free wardrobes, Hilfiger found its name mentioned in both the rhyming verses of rap songs and their 'shout-out' lyrics, in which rap artists chant out thanks to friends and sponsors for their support."[12] Hilfiger's success convinced other large mainstream American fashion design companies, like Ralph Lauren and Calvin Klein, to tailor lines to the lucrative market comprised of hip-hop artists and fans.

The 1990s also saw another crucial shift in hip-hop fashion production, as the market continued to expand through the popularity of the music and the visibility of the artists in music videos and other venues. Black designers, many having created locally for black urban communities throughout the 1980s, acquired success and recognition nationally for urban gear targeted at hip-hop communities. As stated earlier, much of hip-hop's early fashion trends (like Run-D.M.C.'s Adidas and LL Cool J's Kangol hat) began as appropriations of cultural products intended for mass audiences, but with the growth of hip-hop designers and entrepreneurs, fashion trends were now specifically created for hip-hop markets. One of the first black designers to gain national attention and success in this market was Karl Kani, who has received significant recognition and praise from the fashion industry and business magazines like *Black Enterprise*.[13] Kani's success is a result of the appeal of his clothes beyond urban black hip-hop fans, a shift that brought profit to many hip-hop clothing companies. Journalist Tariq K. Muhammad writes, "His trademark style, which includes baggy jeans and oversized casual knits, found an unexpected white suburban audience eager to mimic black urban fashion."[14] In examining the roots of Kani's popularity, Muhammad employs a typical schema used to analyze hip-hop that reinforces notions of authenticity about black cultural practices in which blacks create and whites consume. The success of Karl Kani opened the door for several other black designers and marked the expansion of a lucrative market.[15] For example, the fashion company Fubu (For Us, By Us), founded by four young black male designers, made $350 million in sales in 1998.[16]

One of the most notable aspects of the growth in the hip-hop fashion industry has been the emergence of the hip-hop musician/producer turned fashion designer. This phenomenon further complicates the relationship between commodification, materialism, and the art form. With the creation of the hip-hop clothing company Phat Farm in 1992 by Def Jam Records cofounder and producer Russell Simmons (the same businessman who negotiated the deal between Adidas and Run-D.M.C. mentioned earlier), the production of the music and the creation of its fashion trends were inextricably linked. Simmons, one of the most successful entrepreneurs of hip-hop culture, opened up the possibility for the cultural producers of the music to become producers of its fashion trends as well.[17] The number of rappers and hip-hop groups who have their own clothing line continues to grow; the Wu-Tang Clan, Lil' Kim, Outkast, and Busta Rhymes are just a few. The companies are so numerous currently that in many respects a clothing line is just another venue of celebrity promotion and is an extension of the rapper's lyrics and public image. Hip-hop cultural industries, like multinational retail companies in the mid-nineties (GAP and Abercrombie and Fitch, for example), have turned profits on branding a lifestyle.

Phat Farm apparel invokes the discourse of Americana while playing with and remaining bound by the trope of black male as public threat, the menacing, "hoodie"-wearing black thug of postindustrial American visual culture. Russell Simmons's company and Bad Boy Records producer Sean "P. Diddy" Combs's Sean John clothing line are among the most successful apparel companies directly connected to the hip-hop music industry. Simmons's Phat Farm line makes for an interesting case study of how fashion becomes a venue for branding and marketing the hip-hop lifestyle and demonstrates the reproducibility and desirability of the hip-hop B-boy as a commercially viable marker of the cultural movement. Part of the company's success rests in Phat Farm's ability to market its line as mainstream American culture, while simultaneously incorporating notions of subcultural authenticity. Simmons, who is closely involved with the development of Phat Farm's fashion products, was quoted as proclaiming that T-shirts "are gonna make me richer than records ever did."[18] Influenced by the successful marketing and design of fashion moguls Tommy Hilfiger and Ralph Lauren in hip-hop communities, Phat Farm employs the red, white, and blue of the American flag in clothing patterns and the company's logo. In the selective advertising campaigns—geared toward hip-hop and young adult magazines and billboards in urban settings—Phat Farm, as representative of many hip-hop fashion companies, seeks new sites of coolness through a reappropriation of the aesthetics of Americana. These campaigns exploit cultural nostalgia for a mythic national past while reenvisioning urban B-boys and those who want to be such hipsters as the native-born sons and inheritors of "the America" of myth.

While the urban black male who represents hip-hop fashion stands for alterity and difference from mainstream fashion and society, he is bound by the restrictive visual codes of this particular fashion system and the normative ideology of American capitalism and nostalgia. Fred Davis argues that fashion distinguishes itself from style and custom through its compulsion for change; he also argues that change in fashion is necessarily cyclical. Davis adds that the cycle of fashion moves from cultural producer (such as fashion houses or independent designers) to elite consumers or small-group-identified populations to mass markets to the death of the trend.[19] According to him, while change is essential to fashion, originality and creativity are subjugated to familiarity with styles for retailers and consumers.[20] Diana Crane, in her study of the sociology of clothes and gender, expands this analysis to examine how social norms discipline fashion and the fashioned body.[21] Hip-hop's fashion trends exemplify the normative and commercial prerogative toward modesty as they also define themselves by their visibility and distinction from other fashion styles. For instance, a simple, quite mundane, item produces much of the wealth in hip-hop fashion: baggy, oversized jeans. Tommy Hilfiger built his fashion empire on this seemingly understated article of clothing. New lines by emerging designers often test the market by branding jeans (often competing lines are manufactured by the same sweatshops) and selling them selectively at street markets, in regional boutiques, or showrooms. Like most styles produced by the fashion industry, hip-hop clothing trends change each season; yet oversized designer jeans, hooded sweatshirts known as "hoodies," athletic shoes, and boots have remained staples throughout the past decade. In this same period and through these conservative trends, the hip-hop fashion industry has secured itself as a force to be reckoned with. As the industry grows, the market moves toward a level of homogenization exemplified by the popularity of hip-hop-styled jeans. Apart from denim and seasonal colors, the more popular hip-hop fashion styles are based on reproducing the three colors of the American flag in patterns and fabrics that both reference and redefine the nation and patriotism. What distinguishes the articles of clothing is the company's label placed strategically on the products. Wearing a hip-hop fashion line is a method of demonstrating whose line one supports as a customer, similar to supporting a favorite athlete by wearing the jersey of the sports star.

Like popular sports and the music itself, hip-hop clothing style is virulently masculine, and designers cater to male teenagers and young adults. This is not to say that women do not exist in hip-hop fashion or music, but that the industry promulgates itself on the fetishized body of the black young male. Until recently with the creation of Baby Phat (the feminized division of Phat Farm), Lil' Kim's clothing line, and Jennifer Lopez's fashion company, hip-hop designers almost solely made clothing for males or created unisex articles and accessories, in part because female fashion is a much more difficult and risky industry to penetrate. More significant, though, is the emphasis on the racialized and masculine body in hip-hop culture. When hip-hop fashion companies like Phat Farm create apparel for females, the line is branded as something distinct from its trademark male line. In Phat Farm's case, Baby Phat has as its logo a silhouette of a stationary domestic cat with a curvy tail. This clothing line is highly sexualized, consisting of club clothing such as tight-fitting body suits, miniskirts, and revealing lingerie. Russell Simmons's wife, model Kimora Lee, actually promotes the line, further demonstrating that Baby Phat products construct young women as accessories to the hip-hop-fashioned thug. Phat Farm, with its relaxed style of baggy jeans, oversized sweaters, and head gear can be seen as an extension of Simmons's fashion style and personality (he is known for his casual dress that always includes a Phat Farm baseball cap or hat), while Baby Phat embodies Simmons's wife, the iconic, biracial (Asian and black) runway model, whom Simmons describes as his trophy. In Phat Farm's recent line, Kimora's face actually appears on a series of T-shirts targeted at men, further highlighting the role of the female body as accessory to that of the male.

The performance of a racialized masculinity and the performance of success (material and sexual) are linked inextricably through hip-hop fashion. The declaration of success/excess is reiterated in the lyrical play of rappers. For example, Notorious B.I.G.'s "Big Poppa" analyzes and romanticizes the decadence of this condition: "Money, hoes and clothes all a nigga knows / A foolish pleasure, whatever / I had to find the buried treasure / So grams I had to measure / However living better now / Gucci sweaters now." The growth in the hip-hop fashion market is evidence of the seemingly unlimited possibilities of capitalism to make a profit off of cultural movements, no matter how dissident.[22] The diversification of hip-hop culture into various successful industries can also be seen as a maturation of the cultural movement after more than two decades of growing from the local to the national to the transnational. The hip-hop fashion industry's success in mass marketing is, as Fred Davis argues, the natural course of fashion trends that begin as identity-specific styles—often connected with urban subcultures—and then spread to mass audiences through absorption and commercialism.

Marketing Hip-Hop Americana

The growth of the hip-hop fashion industry and the spectacle induced by this latest hip-hop gold mine are clearly evidenced in the coverage and advertising in hip-hop magazines, most notably Quincy Jones's *Vibe*. Nelson George writes that in the August 1997 edition of the magazine,

twenty-six of its ninety-three full-page advertisements were for clothing.[23] In the October 2001 edition, however, forty-five of the magazines
ninety-four full-page advertisements were for clothing and shoe apparel.
Out of these pages, fifteen advertised apparel from young hip-hop fashion
companies.[24] As the hip-hop fashion industry has grown, *Vibe* magazine
has moved to incorporate more fashion into its content, not just through
advertisements. The "V Style" and "V Fashion" sections of the magazine—consisting of theme-based fashion shoots that often include top
models, musicians, and other celebrities—take up a significant portion of
the magazine's pages. In this same issue, the two sections occupied twelve
pages and showcased designers as diverse as Gucci, Ralph Lauren, Helmut
Lang, and Mecca USA. In *The Fashion System,* Roland Barthes outlines
the relationship between "real" (my quotation marks)—or material—
clothing, image clothing as in photographs and illustrations in magazines,
and written clothing, or the language used to describe articles of fashion.
"V Style" and "V Fashion" are particularly interesting because of their
incorporation of narrative into fashion; the sections produce written
clothing that, according to Barthes, "endows the garment with a system of
functional oppositions (for example, fantasy/classic), which the real or
photographed garment is not able to manifest in as clear a manner."[25]
Vibe's fashion spreads place the body of hip-hop in a state of constant
leisure and play. The highly stylized fashion photography in the magazine
often reinterprets music videos and rap lyrics. These "functional oppositions" arise in *Vibe*'s fashion sections, in part because of the inaccessibil-
ity of realizing these fantasies for most of its audience—teenagers who are
in some way bound by parental, financial, and legal constraints. Dorinne
Kondo analyzes the relationship between desire, identity, and fashion
advertising:

> Within our regime of commodity capitalism, it is hardly surprising to
> find powerful articulations of identity in a domain whose business is
> the figuration of idealized objects of desire: advertising. Designed
> specifically to promote identification and provoke object lust, con-
> sciously deploying techniques to pull on issues resonant for their audi-
> ence, ads—particularly fashion ads—become privileged sites for the
> examination of subject formation.[26]

Accordingly, the magazine is a central site, along with music videos, for
transmitting messages of the fashioned, and predominantly masculine,

Fig. 1. Phat Farm suburbia. (Courtesy Phat Fashions, LLC.)

body of hip-hop (often through visual fantasies of material wealth and sexual excess).

A Phat Farm advertisement in the October 2001 issue of *Vibe* occupies two of the most expensive pages in the front of the magazine. The advertisement is seemingly simple. In close focus is a young dark-skinned black male in a gray sweat suit. In the center of his chest and on his left thigh is the "Phat Farm" logo in red-and-white block letters. His hands are in his pockets and the hood of the sweatshirt covers his head. The "hoodie" frames his features and the photographic lighting emphasizes his high cheekbones, bald scalp, polished skin, broad nose, forehead, and slightly puckered full lips. The model does not meet the spectator's gaze. Instead, he looks down and off to the side, outside of the spectator's line of vision. Behind him, an olive-skinned young male with wavy hair walks toward him with his hands in his pockets; he looks off to the side, in the same direction as the other model's gaze. His head is angled upward, while the black male's head is slightly tilted down. The approaching model wears the ubiquitous baggy blue jeans and a plaid blue shirt with "Phat Farm" scripted above the breast pocket. He also wears a large, blue casual jacket with the company's name again above its breast pocket. While he is clean-cut and carefully groomed, his clothes are referential of the uniform of the Crips gang, particularly the uniformity of the color blue by which the gang is identified. The two models are on a picturesque autumn lawn replete with auburn leaves. They both have anticipatory glances on their faces as they look outside of the spectator's line of vision. A large two-story brown shingled home serves as the backdrop with a peaceful sky above. Next to the olive-skinned model is a graphic of the Phat Farm logo—a large letter *P* encapsulated by two slightly curved lines on each side. The ubiquitous motto of the company, "Classic American Flava," resides underneath the *P*. In the corner of the advertisement, as a small graphic, is the Phat Farm *P* again, but this time in a layout reminiscent of the American flag with red-and-white stripes.

The Phat Farm advertisement invokes an aesthetic of suburban sublime oddly in harmony with the markers of an urban, youthful, and racialized code. The suburban house with its colorful leaves on the lawn is not foreign territory for the urban young men in the photograph; instead, they exist in this space as its normative occupants. They *belong*. The black male model in the hoodie references the trope of the urban black menace so clearly visualized in the ghetto action films of the early 1990s as well as in contemporary music videos.[27] Yet here in this setting of suburban bliss, he is clearly not a threat. He stands reflectively—at peace—with hands in pocket, looking at that which is unknown to the spectator. His gang-identified companion no longer evokes fear or intimidation; instead he walks with his body open toward the camera and a wistful gaze on his face. Although they employ the racialized and youth-based codes of visual threat in contemporary U.S. culture, here, on the lawn in peaceful suburbia, they occupy a place of tranquility and belonging. They are *together* here in this American dream. Their clothed bodies that in certain contexts allude to alterity and disidentification with normative cultural systems here have become incorporated into the American sublime—the pastoral—the belief in mythic destiny and unlimited success. The Phat Farm tag line "Classic American Flava" is crucial to the *refashioning* of their bodies in the advertisement. Applying Barthes's concept of written clothing, the words produce meaning that

conveys a choice and imposes it, it requires the perception of this dress to stop here (i.e., neither before nor beyond), it arrests the level of reading at its fabric, at its belt, at the accessory which adorns it. Thus, every written word has a function of authority insofar as *it* chooses—by proxy, so to speak—instead of the eye. The image freezes an endless number of possibilities; words determine a single certainty.[28]

"Classic American Flava" reinforces the image and the positioning of the two young males as inheritors of American wealth and manifest destiny. At the same time, the use of "flava" in exchange for *flavor* implies a racial and stylistic rewriting of the American dream. Thus, the tag line invokes American privilege and dominance while subverting the normative whiteness and history of exclusion that these concepts connote.

Fred Davis's notion of ambivalence in contemporary fashion is useful here for analyzing the merger of normative icons of Americana with non-normative or underrepresented (in the realm of fashion) bodies. For Davis, ambivalence—like change—is the basis of the regenerative nature of fashion styles. He writes: "As for fashion specifically, while it must of necessity work within the broad parameters of a relatively well established and familiar clothing code, it turns for fresh inspiration to tensions generated by identity ambivalences, particularly those that, by virtue of cultural scripting and historical experience, are collective in character."[29] The role of ambivalence is central to the success of hip-hop fashion marketing campaigns and is what makes the Phat Farm advertisement readable. As has been widely acknowledged and discussed (possibly overemphasized), white young males make up the largest demographic of consumers of hip-hop cultural products. Thus Phat Farm, in appealing to an audience beyond urban racialized fans, reframes the B-boy and gang-identified tropes of visual culture and domesticates them by setting the models in the milieu of hip-hop fashion's expanding consumer base—middle America, the suburbs. In an article geared toward marketing executives, Spiegler analyzes this consumer trend: "But to take advantage of this phenomenon, you have to dig into how hip-hop culture spreads from housing projects to rural environs, understand why hip-hop is so attractive to suburban whites, and discern the process by which hip-hoppers embrace products."[30] Hip-hop fashion routinely gets constructed as a manifestation of the creativity and originality of urban black men who then influence legions of nonblacks and audiences of all ages. This oversimplification is faulty in many respects. Most importantly, it does not acknowledge the significant number of women and nonblacks who work as cultural producers in hip-hop; it also constructs black hip-hop audiences as poor and insignificant consumers. At the same time, the hip-hop fashion industry is represented as a passing trend or another gimmick for greedy hip-hop entrepreneurs to capitalize on the contemporary cultural obsession with young urban black masculinity.

The media coverage of one of the most public and successful hip-hop entrepreneurs, Sean Combs, demonstrates this ambivalence. Combs and his highly publicized personal life, including trials for criminal wrongdoing and romantic involvement with Puerto Rican superstar Jennifer Lopez, come to stand in for his clothing line. His representation as an above-the-law, resourceful, and refined thug overshadows the industry recognition that he has received for his clothing company. Most notably, Sean Combs was the first black designer to be nominated for the prestigious Perry Ellis Award for Menswear at the American Fashion Awards.[31] Yet in a February 2002 series covering New York's fashion week, the *New York Times* featured Sean Combs and his well-received clothing line Sean John with a headline reading "A Fashion Statement: Hip-Hop on the Runway."[32] The journalist Guy Trebay writes:

> A clue to Mr. Combs' ambitions came Thursday, when he appeared, along with Terry Lundgren, the president of Federated Department Stores, to ring the opening bell at the New York Stock Exchange. Some on hand remembered that the last time Mr. Combs appeared publicly downtown was to hear his acquittal in criminal court on charges of carrying a concealed weapon in a nightclub. He was wearing a suit on that occasion last year, and he wore an even nattier one of chalk stripes from Versace this week, as he spoke about the importance of giving New York economic support.[33]

Trebay's comments invoke the language and imagery of black criminality and illegitimacy; in doing so, they overshadow the success of Combs's entrepreneurial venture. For Trebay, Combs's fashion line is only newsworthy in how it reflects upon normative ideas about black masculinity, specifically the specter of the black deviant thug who is always already criminalized.[34]

The role of ambivalence in hip-hop fashion does not stop at the product itself, the marketing campaign, the possible desires and fantasies of its consumer, or the media coverage of the industry and its figureheads, but also plays out in the struggle of hip-hop fashion producers to signify racialized alterity through their products and to be embraced by mainstream American culture. Spiegler discusses this dilemma for fashion producers without questioning the polemics of his conceptual framework (which employs authenticity as natural and tangible): "core hip-hoppers display an almost fanatical obsession with authenticity. Sanitizing any element of hip-hop culture to make it more palatable for middle-class suburban whites is likely to result in failure, because the core hip-hop audience will reject it."[35] Hip-hop entrepreneur Russell Simmons aligns his fashion company with American cultural and national symbols while at the same time promoting his clothing as based in the realness or authenticity of the urban streets. Moreover, Simmons performs the authenticity of his clothing as B-boy gear by wearing Phat Farm fashion routinely in public. Yet, Simmons self-consciously articulates his desire to make Phat Farm clothing mainstream. Nancy Jo Sales's "Hip-Hop Goes Universal" bubbles in giggly fascination with the ambitions and excesses of Russell Simmons as a rich black cultural icon who wants to be accepted by mainstream American consumer culture. She blatantly places herself as a voyeur in Simmons's world, a world that is representative of urban cool, American capitalistic success/excess, and anxiety about belonging. Sales uses the metaphor of being in high school and sitting at the cool table with Simmons and his entourage ("If Moomba, the inaccessible downtown lounge, is currently the high-school cafeteria for famous people, then Simmons and [Andre] Harrell are at the cool table").[36] The tone of the article makes a spectacle of black wealth and business success and insinuates an air of illegitimacy, in ways similar to those journalist Guy Trebay uses to place Sean Combs's success under scrutiny. Underlying this critique is a dialectic that places authenticity in hip-hop cultural production at odds with the pursuit of capitalism—a dialectic that has existed as long as the art form itself. Sales portrays Simmons as sensitive to how whites might read him as illegitimate or as an imposter. She quotes Simmons's reaction to a buyer from a major department store who shows little interest in carrying Phat Farm apparel:

> "I'm talking to that [name deleted] who does the buying for [name of shopping mall chain deleted]," he sputters, "and she says, 'Oh'"—he makes his voice high and phony—"'we just don't want any *jeans stores* in our shopping center.' Now, what does *that* mean?" He's frowning, waiting.

"Means she doesn't want a lot of little ghetto niggas runnin' up in there," he says.[37] This exchange, as reported by Sales, brings to the fore what Simmons must do in order for T-shirts to make him richer than records, his previously stated ambition. Simmons's response to the buyer articulates the anxiety of hip-hop fashion producers who, having capitalized on a niche market, find themselves bound by the niche that they helped to create. In constantly calling attention to Simmons's ambition and anxiety, Sales, through her voyeuristic eye, demonstrates the polemics of visibility in hip-hop commercial industries. The drive to turn a profit from hip-hop cultural production and the desire to create the visual markers of urban coolness in turn bring questions of credibility and an interrogation of the authenticity of the product and producer. In this paradigm, critics and skeptics frame hip-hop within the realm of subcultural authenticity in which profit is incompatible with cultural practices.

"'What Russell really wants to be,' says Andre, 'is the hip-hop Ralph Lauren.'"[38] Quoting Andre Harrell, music producer and Simmons's best friend, Sales continues her pursuit to document Simmons's struggle with this dialectic. This framing of Simmons's pursuit is interesting in light of the predominant understanding of the relationship between designer fashion and urban black culture. The concept of "the cool hunter," who stalks the streets of Harlem for the latest sign of cool, posits the originality of fashion as existent essentially in black culture practice, specifically black youth culture. Yet, Sales rewrites this narrative so that Simmons's ambition is not one of reclaiming "the cool" inherent in black culture, but of brokering "the cool" as mainstream Americana.[39] Along these lines, the journalist quotes Harrell self-importantly expounding on the impact of the hip-hop industry on American culture and its economy: "'This is not about a moment. . . . This is way past a moment. This is Americana; this is a cultural change.'"[40] Harrell's grandiose statement to Sales, presented as such in her article, implies an awareness of his audience and her fascination with their success and hypervisibility. He performs for her to her expectation. He announces to a larger public who fears a change in power from white male hands to black male hands that change has already occurred. Harrell explicitly claims American myth and legacy for the hip-hop community, specifically its black male entrepreneurial leaders, as he actively constructs a new narrative for "Americana." They are the new "forefathers" in Harrell's framework for understanding hip-hop's impact. We are to understand his proclamation as continuing, while reinventing, the legacy and "greatness" of America. Harrell's statement can be read within what Hazel Carby calls the legacy of "race men" who consider the work of race and nation building in the United States as (black) men's business.[41]

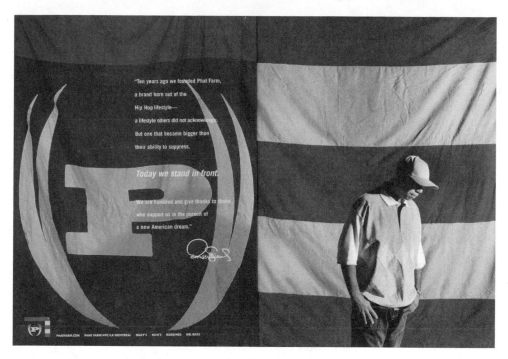

FIG. 2. Phat Farm Flag. (Courtesy Phat Fashions, LLC.)

This high level of self-consciousness about evoking the rhetoric of Americana, while reinventing "the nation," emerges explicitly in Phat Farm's advertising campaign after September 11, 2001. In the April 2002 issue of *Vibe,* Russell Simmons addresses his customers and his mythic hip-hop nation directly through a full two-page advertisement that consists of Simmons, dressed in Phat Farm clothing, standing in front of the Phat Farm rendition of the American flag. Text with his signature accompanies the image; the quote reads:

Ten years ago we founded Phat Farm,
a brand born out of the
Hip-hop lifestyle—
a lifestyle others did not acknowledge.
But one that became bigger than
their ability to suppress.
Today we stand in front. [In larger, bold and italicized font]

> We are humbled and give thanks to those
> who support us in the pursuit of
> a new American dream.

In the post–September 11 era, Simmons even more explicitly invokes patriotism, possessing the symbols of Americana, and framing consumerism in nationalist terms.

The anxiety of being marginalized (as "ethnic" rather than "American" designers) has led to a shift in marketing and labeling for many fashion companies. In an article about hip-hop fashion, Leslie E. Royal writes, "To further widen their appeal many urban designers are moving away from using the label 'urbanwear' and moving toward 'contemporary' or 'metropolitan' says Ellzy of the Fashion Association."[42] This further demonstrates the tension between reaching out to nonblack audiences and at the same time marketing cultural products as the authentic. Herman Gray writes of this tension that exists throughout black masculine visual and material cultures: "Self representations of black masculinity in the United States are historically structured by and against dominant (and dominating) discourses of masculinity and race, specifically whiteness."[43] Simmons's response to the complexity of negotiating this terrain is to "niggerize"— that is, imbue with a sense of urban grit and authenticity—white consumers who purchase his products:

> You know what the *Jerry Springer Show* proves? . . . That white people
> are niggers, too. It's important. People don't realize it when they live in
> a different world, but a lot of those people are uneducated, they have
> the same set of experiences, they have the same lifestyle, and now,
> because of hip-hop, they're all dressing the same and they're using the
> same language.[44]

Embedded in Simmons's statement are layered assumptions about not only whites who purchase his products, but black urban youth. Most obvious is Simmons's implication that black consumers are poor, uneducated, and always already "niggers." Furthermore, he reinforces the invisibility of various other ethnic and national consumers who participate in hip-hop culture by reproducing the racial dichotomy of black and white. His words also point to the instability of authenticity or "realness" in hip-hop music and visual culture. In other words, Simmons constructs race as a performative engagement with social and symbolic signs and participation in certain practices as a consumer. Beyond the intentionally provocative language, Simmons argues that hip-hop fashion becomes a shared language for the imagined nation as envisioned by hip-hop entrepreneurs.

The tension and ambivalence of promoting hip-hop fashion as "the urban real" while mass-marketing the items as a new reading of "America" fuel the success of these companies. While the popularity and success of hip-hop fashion companies is in every way a manifestation of advanced capitalistic processes in which the development of niche markets and the marketing of lifestyle brands continually fuel capital's expansion, the phenomenon is also an example of the rich and complex history and practices of hip-hop culture. Throughout much of the cultural movement's history, its cultural producers have courted capitalism and promoted consumption through the marketing of difference. The more recent trend to refashion "Americana" as cool and racialized through hip-hop clothing evidences black masculine investment in the legacy, wealth, and myth of America. These recent strategies to reclaim "America" have increasing significance given hip-hop's growing transnational marketability. The refashioning and promotion of the new and cool America performed through the black male B-boy and produced by the hip-hop entrepreneur begs to be analyzed in light of studies of globalization and the marketing of youthful alterity as a stylized and reproducible commodity.

NOTES

1. For more on subculture studies, see Dick Hebdige, *Subculture: The Meaning of Style* (London: Routledge, 1979); Stuart Hall and Tony Jefferson, *Resistance through Rituals: Youth Subcultures in Post-war Britain* (London: Hutchinson, 1976); and Ken Gelder and Sarah Thornton, *The Subcultures Reader* (London: Routledge, 1997).

2. Roland Barthes, *The Fashion System,* trans. Matthew Ward and Richard Howard (Berkeley and Los Angeles: University of California Press, 1983).

3. See Dorinne Kondo, "Fabricating Masculinity: Gender, Race, and Nation in the Transnational Circuit," in *About Face: Performing Race in Fashion and Theater* (New York: Routledge, 1997).

4. Kondo, "Fabricating Masculinity," 16.

5. For more on debates and critiques of racial authenticity in black popular culture, see Kendall Thomas, "'Ain't Nothin' Like the Real Thing': Black Masculinity, Gay Sexuality, and the Jargon of Authenticity," in *The House That Race Built: Black Americans, U.S. Terrain,* ed. Wahneema Lubiano (New York: Pantheon, 1997), 116–35; Philip Brian Harper, *Are We Not Men? Masculine Anxiety and the Problem of African-American Identity* (New York: Oxford University Press, 1996); and Michael Eric Dyson, *Between God and Gangsta Rap: Bearing Witness to Black Culture* (New York: Oxford University Press, 1996).

6. See Tricia Rose, *Black Noise: Rap Music and Black Culture in Contemporary America* (Hanover, N.H.: Wesleyan University Press, 1994).

7. Nelson George, *Hip Hop America* (New York: Penguin, 1998), 158.

8. Kobena Mercer, "Black Hair/Style Politics," in Gelder and Thornton, *The Subcultures Reader,* 430.

9. Noel McLaughlin, "Rock, Fashion, and Performativity," in *Fashion Cultures: Theories, Explorations, and Analysis,* ed. Stella Bruzzi and Pamela Church Gibson (London: Routledge, 2000), 269.

10. McLaughlin, "Rock, Fashion, and Performativity," 158–59.

11. See William Eric Perkins, "Rap Attack: An Introduction," in *Droppin' Science: Critical Essays on Rap Music and Hip-Hop Culture,* ed. William Eric Perkins (Philadelphia: Temple University Press, 1996).

12. Marc Spiegler, "Marketing Street Culture: Bringing Hip-Hop Style to the Mainstream," *American Demographics,* November 1996, 29.

13. The magazine has featured the designer in at least four articles in four years; in 1996, the magazine labeled his company "BE Company of the Year."

14. Tariq K. Muhammad, "From Here to Infinity: A Hip-Hop Clothier with Mainstream Appeal, Karl Kani is Poised to Become the Fashion World's New Wunderkind," *Black Enterprise,* June 1996, 141.

15. See Muhammad, "From Here to Infinity"; and Leslie E. Royal, "Hip-Hop on Top: We Look at the Elements and Top Designers That Have Helped Urban Fashion Skyrocket, and Predict Where the Industry Is Headed," *Black Enterprise,* July 2000, 91–94.

16. Royal, "Hip-Hop on Top," 93.

17. As a part of a larger trend toward the increasing visibility of black male figures in American popular culture, this transition of rappers to designers runs parallel with a number of rap stars becoming film actors and directors.

18. Nancy Jo Sales, "Hip-Hop Goes Universal," *New York,* May 10, 1999, 25.

19. Davis enumerates the fashion process as (1) invention, (2) introduction, (3) fashion leadership, (4) increasing social visibility, and (5) waning. See *Fashion, Culture, and Identity* (Chicago: University of Chicago Press, 1992).

20. Davis, *Fashion, Culture, and Identity,* 137.

21. Diana Crane, *Fashion and Its Social Agendas: Class, Gender, and Identity in Clothing* (Chicago: University of Chicago Press, 2000).

22. See Thomas Frank, *The Conquest of Cool: Business Culture, Counterculture, and the Rise of Hip Consumerism* (Chicago: University of Chicago Press, 1997); and Thomas Frank and Matt Weiland's *Commodify Your Dissent: Salvos from the Baffler* (New York: Norton, 1997).

23. George, *Hip Hop America,* 156.

24. The companies are Enyce, Mecca USA, Phat Farm, Fubu, Roca Wear, Akademiks, Ecko, Sean John, and Bloomingdales, which has a three-page advertisement for its Phat Farm, Sean John, and Enyce lines.

25. Barthes, *The Fashion System,* 14.

26. Kondo, *About Face,* 158.

27. For more on the ghetto action film and its relationship to hip-hop, see S. Craig Watkins, *Representing: Hip-Hop Culture and the Production of Black Cinema* (Chicago: University of Chicago Press, 1998).

28. Barthes, *The Fashion System,* 13.

29. Davis, *Fashion, Culture, and Identity,* 26.

30. Spiegler, "Marketing Street Culture," 30.

31. Royal, "Hip-Hop on Top," 94.

32. Guy Trebay, "A Fashion Statement: Hip-Hop on the Runway," *New York Times,* February 9, 2002, front page, B4.

33. Trebay, "A Fashion Statement," front page.

34. For a more detailed profile on Combs's impact on mainstream fashion and his ambivalent embrace by the fashion industry, see Michael Specter's profile, "I Am Fashion: Guess Who Puff Daddy Wants to Be?" *New Yorker,* September 9, 2002, 117–27.

35. Spiegler, "Marketing Street Culture," 31.

36. Sales, "Hip-Hop Goes Universal," 23.

37. Sales, "Hip-Hop Goes Universal," 28.

38. Sales, "Hip-Hop Goes Universal," 25.

39. See Malcolm Gladwell, "Annals of Style: The Coolhunt," *New Yorker,* March 17, 1997, 78–88.

40. Sales, "Hip-Hop Goes Universal," 24.

41. Hazel V. Carby, *Race Men* (Cambridge: Harvard University Press, 1998).

42. Royal, "Hip-Hop on Top," 94.

43. Herman Gray, "Black Masculinity and Visual Culture" *Callaloo* 18, no. 2 (1995): 401.

44. Sales, "Hip-Hop Goes Universal," 29.

HARRY J. ELAM, JR.

Spike Lee's *Bamboozled*

In an early scene from Spike Lee's film *Bamboozled,* the fictitious group, the Mau Maus, expand on the meanings of blackness as their rap song, "black is black," from their "black album," blares in the background. This filmic moment serves as a signifying revision of the prologue that begins Ralph Ellison's classic novel, *The Invisible Man.* As the Invisible Man drinks sloe gin, smokes reefer, and listens to Louis Armstrong sing "Why Do I Have to Be So Black and Blue," he envisions himself in the midst of a black church service where the preacher delivers a sermon on the meaning of blackness. The minister famously intones, "my text this morning is the 'Blackness of Blackness,'" and the amen corner chimes in with verbal agreement and support, "That blackness is most black, brother, most black."[1] Similarly, in *Bamboozled,* the new self-proclaimed ministers of culture and prophets of rap, the Mau Maus, smoke blunts, guzzle cognac, and pass around forty-ounce bottles of malt liquor as they discuss the ways in which blackness operates. Musing on the connotations and denotations of blackness, the Mau Maus proclaim that they from now on will spell the word sans the *c,* "B-L-A-K." This linguistic resistance, both profound and absurd, underscores the potential power of language and reaffirms the contradictory meanings and meaninglessness inherent in constructions of blackness. The Mau Maus imagine this new spelling as a strike against white hegemony, a step toward "blak" self-definition and determination. At the same time, this commission by omission of the *c* has no real material force and, in fact, only evidences the vapid black revolutionary politics of the Mau Maus. This parodic first glimpse of the Mau Maus, like the preacher's speech in the prologue to *Invisible Man,* points out that blackness in its representation is always contingent, subject to the context and cultural and political codings of its use. For as the preacher in *Invisible Man* remarks, "Now Black is . . . an' black ain't."[2]

Spike Lee's highly intertextual, intellectually and politically provocative and commercially unsuccessful film profoundly questions historical and contemporary traffic in blackness within the American popular imagination. Lee argues that with *Bamboozled* he wanted to "show from birth these two great mediums, film and television, have promoted negative racial images" and that "racism is woven into the very fabric of American society."[3] In a satirical critique of the American commercial media, Pierre Delacroix, a black Harvard-educated television executive besieged and beset by his white boss to create a new black hit television show, masterminds a project that he believes in its racial excess will reveal to the white writers and producers their own racism. Delacroix's boss Dunwitty (Michael Rappaport) demands that Delacroix, or Dela, develop a fresh idea that is authentically black. Dunwitty maintains that blacks are always at the cutting edge of fashion and commercialism. And clearly today with the global influence of hip-hop, as white suburban youth dress in baggy jeans, sport tattoos, and listen to rap music, blackness remains critical to the popular. In fact, black innovation fuels the popular. To Dela's surprise, the project he creates, entitled the *New Millennium Minstrel Show,* a return to blacks in blackface smiling, singing, and dancing on the plantation, becomes a smash hit. Through detailing the rise and fall of this new black television show and its creator, Lee's comedy condemns the culture industry and the white media establishment for its ability to co-opt the potency of blackness in popular culture, and its willingness to repeatedly portray blacks within stereotypical imagery.

Yet this is not just a white thing. Lee castigates blacks who find themselves seduced and engulfed within this system and justify and rationalize their own relation to stereotypes. Dela is himself a stereotype. With his perfect posture, his affected gestures, his accent that borders on British but is a thing all to itself, Dela sends up the black middle class and their disaffection from the masses in a way that even E. Franklin Frazier could not imagine. In fact, Dela is so much a stereotype that few blacks in the audience can connect with him and his depiction. Thus, Lee's critique of the black middle class through this figure threatens to miss its mark because Dela engenders no empathy. Dela too becomes caught up in the fame and success he accrues through his complicity in promoting pejorative black stereotypes on the *New Millennium Minstrel Show.* The film explores the interconnections between the politics of race and the seductive and corrosive power of American commodity capitalism. As *Bamboozled* critiques how blackness has historically circulated, it also examines the complex interactions between art, politics, and race within the public sphere.

Lee himself has a particularly interesting and potentially contradictory position with the system of American commercial capitalism, for he both rails against the politics of the system and deftly profits from them. Mark Anthony Neal writes in *Soul Babies: Black Popular Culture and the Post-soul Aesthetic,* "virtually every Spike Lee film from *She's Gotta Have It* to *Malcolm X,* is conscious of its own value in the markets where popular perceptions and popular commodities are exchanged."[4] Rap group Public Enemy's rebellious black anthem "Fight the Power" from the film *Do the Right Thing* with video filmed by Lee, became a pop hit. Black "X" hats sold on the street at the time of the film *Malcolm X* became a symbol of unity with this black icon as well as a successful marketing ploy by Lee. Thus, Lee's black nationalism is, as Neal states "deeply embedded with forms of corporate capitalism."[5] With *Bamboozled*'s explicit self-referentiality, this productive tension between black resistance and American commercialism is not just the conversation around the film but the very subject and content.

Lee critiques African Americans' historical lack of control over their own representation and their continued, naive willingness to function as critically disengaged consumers. In two commercial interludes that appear during the initial broadcast of the *New Millennium Minstrel Show* he attacks black complicity in a culture of consumption. The critical intervention of these satirical commercials repeats and revises a structure employed by the 1969 film *Putney Swope,* a satirical critique of blaxploitation, in which a black executive becomes the new head of a major white advertising agency and then produces a series of bitingly humorous Afrocentric commercials. In *Bamboozled* the commercials directed at a black clientele appeal to base material and prurient interests—sex, clothing, alcohol—that are too often racialized. An ad for The Bomb, a new malt liquor, riffs on the popularity of forty-ounce malt liquors within the black urban community. With a bottle shaped like a phallus and a "weapon of mass destruction" the bomb ad promotes its product as an African American aphrodisiac, a "black man's Viagra" that helps you "get your freak on." The other ad for Timi Hilnigger clothing parodies the popularity of Tommy Hilfiger's all-American clothing line in the hip-hop black urban market. Whereas Tommy Hilfiger features the Americana colors of red, white, and blue, the backdrop in this ad for Timi Hilnigger is the Republic of New Africa colors of red, black, and green. Hilfiger at various times has tried to distance himself from his black consumers even as he has taken advantage of their business. At one point, an urban legend circulated over the Internet proclaiming that Hilfiger had declared his racism on the Oprah Winfrey show; this email message now demanded a national boycott of the Hilfiger clothing line.[6] In this *Bamboozled* ad, Danny Hoch, a white hip-hop theater artist, plays Timi Hilnigger, and as he sings an explicitly patronizing rap, he discusses his desire to exploit black people through their obsession with consumerism. "If you want to keep it really real, never get out of the ghetto, stay broke, and continue to add to my million dollar corporation, then keep buying my gear . . . we keep it so real we give you the bullet holes." These ads with their ridicule of cultural authenticity and urban realness, much as the film as a whole, call for more critical awareness of the politics of representation and the possible impacts of the commercial trafficking in blackness.

The central action of *Bamboozled* marks Manray's (Savion Glover) evolution and name change from Manray, street dancer, to Mantan, star of the *New Millennium Minstrel Show* (his renaming is an homage to the black comedian Mantan Moorland). Lee thereby explores the intersecting histories of a functional African American art and American commercialism. At first Manray and his partner, Womack (Tommy Davidson), appear as street hustlers dancing for change on the sidewalks on New York City. Evident even within this crude mode of performance is an aesthetic functionalism. Their art operates as a means of survival. Later, when the Mau Maus force Manray to dance for his life as they spray gunfire at his feet, his artistry again shows an even more explicit functionalism as it also reveals the sheer power of his dancing rhythms, the magnificence of his beat. Now he literally dances for his life. At the outset of the film, on the sidewalks of New York, Manray dances with a flare of hip-hop style, rather than the upright body position, the animated hand movements, the constantly smiling visages that marked such earlier black tap masters such as Bill "Bojangles" Robinson. Manray's upper body is limp, his face cool and emotionless, his feet dazzling. Still, his dancing is a form of cultural history that even as it ties him to the movement styles of today's urban environs also connects him back to the early "hoofers" of legend. Historically, tap dance has embodied the confluence and complexity of fetishization, of virtuosity and ingenuity commonly associated with black cultural expression within the American social mainstream. The Nicholas Brothers' exhilarating tap routine in *Stormy Weather,* which includes amazing leaps and splits down a long white staircase, is both a site of wonder and fetishized moment of black entertainment. Manray's street solo in front of a gathered audience of passersby and his subsequent dance atop Dela's office table and before the white media boss Dunwitty—a sort of racialized lap ·dance—are equally multilayered performances that are once fodder for black exploitation and evidence of black cultural expression and artistic endurance. Later, when Manray dons blackface, white gloves, and stardom as Mantan in the *New Millennium Minstrel Show,* his dance is still one that conjoins art and politics, function and aesthetics. This new dance cannot be separated from the history of tap and minstrelsy or from Mantan's own history as a traveling "minstrel" street performer. He is still a virtuoso dancer. His feet still sparkle. But at what expense?

If Manray and his partner Womack hustling on the street are in effect another form of minstrelsy, when is black art within the popular cultural sphere, with its dependence on patronage and support from the dominant hegemonic culture, not minstrelsy? Is *Bamboozled* itself then not always and already a minstrel show? Michael Rogin writes, "Employing minstrelsy to attack it, Spike Lee leaves no black face in the world of white entertainment unmarked by cork."[7] Within the film Lee examines the compromises that black artists are willing to make in order to achieve success within the white-dominated entertainment industry. When Dela auditions actors for his new minstrel show, he discovers how desperate black actors are for any work and how willing these performers are to demean themselves for the opportunity to appear on film or stage and be compensated for it. With the earlier film *Hollywood Shuffle,* Robert Townsend looks satirically at the same problem: the lack of available roles for blacks within the white-controlled media industry can cause black actors to take on condescending and stereotypical roles because they afford the too-little-realized chance to practice their craft.

In *Bamboozled,* Lee complicates this dilemma of the black artists through the film's intertextuality. The band that wins the audition and becomes the house band for the *New Millennium Minstrel Show,* the Alabama Porch Monkeys, is in fact the Roots, a socially conscious contemporary hip-hop band that preaches black activism and unity through their music. Lee may have cast the Roots because of their appeal to the young hip-hop generation clientele that he hoped his film would attract. More importantly, such an audience would have recognized the Roots and the explicit contradictions between their true politics and the roles as Porch Monkeys. In this way the Roots are not easily subsumed by the happy darky stereotype since their "Porch Monkeyness" is not totalizing. Rather,

Fig. 1. *Bamboozled;* Savion Glover as Manray and Tommy Davidson as Womack in "Mantan: The New Millennium Minstrel Show." (© MM, New Line Productions, Inc. All rights reserved. Photo by David Lee, Courtesy of New Line Productions, Inc.)

through this clash of real and stage personas—or more accurately, between these two stage personae—Lee makes apparent the satirical thrust of *Bamboozled* to subvert racist stereotypes. This satirical strategy that Dela originally intended when he conceived of his new minstrelsy but that is purposefully lost on the audiences for the *New Millennium Minstrel Show* within the film. In this way, Lee presumes and constructs at a minimum two audiences—one within the film, one without—that are in tension just as are the two kinds of black stage performances (the Roots and the Porch Monkeys). Josephine Lee argues in "The Seduction of the Stereotype" that

> The Other invoked in stereotype might turn the tables by accentuating the stereotype's anxiety, its implicit instability. Although stereotypes cannot be reappropriated without invoking their racist history, they can nonetheless reveal in their performances the inner dynamics of this history, which already suggest the potential for disruption.[8]

Accordingly, the casting of the Roots as Alabama Porch Monkeys disrupts the minstrel stereotype through its invocation not only of the racist history of black minstrelsy but through the Roots' own history as activist band.

Lee's satirical reappropriation of blackface in the film also purposefully invokes a racist and racial history. When Manray and Womack first apply blackface, Lee shoots the scene in extreme close-ups as Sloan (Jada Pinkett) describes the process of administering the mask. For both audience and performers engaged in this application the scene is unsettling, as it is powerfully loaded with historical and current signification. Spike Lee notes, "The reality of putting this stuff on their face was devastating for Tommy Davidson and Savion Glover. It took away part of their soul, it took away a part of their manhood, and it made us think of Bert Williams. Tommy and Savion did it for a couple of weeks but Williams had to do that his entire career."[9] They literally must undertake their own self-hatred and dehumanization as they don the blackface makeup. While the mask represents a character outside of themselves, a figure on stage, it also represents the historical misrepresentation and diminution of black lives. Manray and Womack, while black in real life, must become black, applying a burnt cork darker than any black skin in order to authentically represent blackness on stage. Thus blacking up always entails an application or an acceptance of an already established code of blackness and behaviors associated with it. Lee's reiteration of the process of blacking up in discomfiting hyperreal close-ups produces a destabilizing anxiety that disrupts the notion of the happy darky as it reveals the face behind the mask.

Historically as in *Bamboozled,* the blackface mask has both limited and enabled black artistry. Manray and Womack in blackface as Mantan and Sleep-n-Eat respectively perform classic routines from the history of minstrelsy as their audience laughs. At one point Lee even cuts to an image of one of the militant Mau Maus laughing at a minstrel routine. Chastised by his fellow Mau Maus, the offender replies, "That shit seemed funny to me." Lee maintains that "some of this stuff—despite how much hatred is behind it, and despite how painful it can be—*is* funny, and the reason it's funny is because of the genius of the artists, of the performers who are able to make it funny even within that context."[10] Bert Williams, the comic legend referenced repeatedly in *Bamboozled,* excelled as a comic with physical grace, miming skills, and mastery of timing, even as the conventions of race and performance at that time required him to perform in blackface. W. C. Fields called him "the funniest man he ever knew" and "the saddest man he ever knew." Williams was constrained by the white entertainment system but also able through it to reach a new level of stardom. Williams was the first black performer to tour with the Ziegfeld Follies and one of, if not the, most successful and popular comics of his time. Yet racial conventions compelled him to wear blackface and prevented him from staying in the same hotels or eating in the same restaurants as his white compatriots in the Ziegfeld Follies. When black performers such as Williams donned blackface, they wrested representations of blackness from white minstrel exaggerations, and yet, at the same time, the new black performers had to fit into, as Eric Lott notes, "the ideological forms that the minstrel show had itself helped to generate."[11] Mantan and Sleep-n-Eat, despite their skills honed in a different arena, must subscribe to and embody a demeaning minstrel image and replicate existing racial ideologies. And yet, like Williams, it is the very blackface that brings them newfound wealth and fame. The question here is reiterated for black performers within the public sphere: "at what price success?"

Powerfully, not only the performers, but the spectators as well are complicit as they too put on blackface. Black, white, Asian, Latino, they all apply burnt cork and proudly proclaim, "We are niggers!" Here then the legacy of minstrelsy is at once summoned and surpassed. Michael Rogin writes in *Blackface, White Noise,*

> Minstrelsy was the first and most popular form of mass culture in the nineteenth-century United States. Blackface provided the new country

with a distinctive national identity in the age of slavery and presided over the melting pot culture in the period of mass European immigration. While blackface was hardly the only distinctive American cultural form, even in black-white relations and especially for African Americans, it was a dominant practice and it infected others. . . . Minstrelsy claimed to speak for both races [black and white] through the blacking up of one.[12]

Rogin argues that in the nineteenth century new European immigrants, most specifically Jews, symbolically became white through the application of blackface. Here in the *New Millennium Minstrel* an audience of all races apply burnt cork and become niggers. Blackface as racial equalizer points to the resiliency of blackness as object of desire in popular culture and to the continued American obsession with the politics of race. Eric Lott maintains that at its inception, the "phenomenon of minstrelsy itself was an admission of fascination with blacks and black culture." The politics of the minstrel show reflected the fact that "for a period of more than one hundred years white people were so politically, historically, emotionally, and sexually bound up with black culture that they directly mimicked and displayed it for their own enjoyment."[13] Negrophilia and negrophobia were in no way antithetical in the nineteenth century. Today, with the rise of hip-hop and the globalization of African American culture, with the dominance of blacks in sports, it remains possible to love black people's cool but to deny any love for black people. Blackface in *Bamboozled* comments on the enduring embrace of blackness within the popular media. The popular produces blackness as a commodity that can be packaged and sold on the global marketplace. The willingness of the multicultural audience of the *New Millennium Minstrel Show* to don blackface in this postmulticultural moment indicts society for its willing, if naive, complicity in the seductive power of representations. Lee suggests that given the politics of the present that enable the lasting attraction of blackness both as cultural icon and cultural scapegoat for crime, nihilism, and antiestablishment behaviors, such an adoption of blackface by a television studio audience is not so far-fetched.

Most significantly, not only are the spectators sporting blackface, they are also announcing their new social status as "niggers." The audience for the *New Millennium Minstrel Show,* who sit in highly raked bleachers, a hierarchy of sorts that stretches up from the stage toward the rafters—the spectators were previously marked by their diversity of race and dress—

are now all in black clothing, white gloves, and blackface. Blackface becomes the great leveler; everyone is a nigger. Honeycut, the emcee, enters dressed as a blackface Abe Lincoln—an interesting riff on Suzan-Lori Parks's *The America Play*—and announces that "400 years ago white folks was kicking our ass, but now it's a new Millennium." The new millennium brings a new appreciation of niggerness not as resistance but collective embrace. Moreover, much like the Pet Rock or Pokémon fads that have captivated commercialized America, Dela declares that blackface has become a craze that sweeps the nation. Everyone now has access to blackness and the urge to be a nigger. Television in *Bamboozled* fuels a perverse racial desire, a latent racism, and the showing and viewing of blackface on television makes it fashionable, desirable, acceptable, cool. Thus Lee's film satirically asserts that the medium of television not only produces new fads, but also makes those fads palatable.

The communal act of blacking up enables the performance of niggerness and enables us to understand it as performance with profound political consequence and meanings. For those of different ethnicities who can leave the theater and wash off their faces, and remove the mask, niggerness is portable and adaptable. W. T. Lhamon points out in *Raising Cain* that white immigrant and working-class youth in the 1830s blackened up and even identified themselves as "New York Niggers" in order to revolt against conventions of social control and authority at that time. Lhamon notes that these early-nineteenth-century whites employed the device of blackness "to shock and confound the [white] middle-class proprieties." They blackened up not simply to ridicule and pejoratively stereotype blacks but "to bring themselves together and to explain to themselves how others disdain them."[14] Now in our postmulticultural moment the audience for the *New Millennium Minstrel Show*, Asians, whites, blacks, Latinos, all sit together as niggers. Significantly, they are not black people but niggers. Once a pejorative racial slur, the term now signifies in *Bamboozled* a particularly American politics of belonging, a democratic appeal to a specifically racial, uniquely American denominator. Here in the *New Millennium Minstrel Show*, Lee has Honeycut as blackface Abe Lincoln entice the audience to join him in shouting "Niggers is a beautiful thing." Not simply a cultural nationalistic appellation of brotherhood, niggerness has been transformed into a nationalistic declaration: "Niggers is a beautiful thing."

The audience's appropriation of blackface niggerness raises questions of racial authority: Who has the right to use the term *nigger*? A Sicilian man rises and proclaims that he is more authentic than any other nigger, that "Sicilians are darker and bigger than any nigger" and then performs a blackface rap. His performance of race functions as a signifying revision of moments from Quentin Tarantino's *Pulp Fiction* and Lee's own *Jungle Fever,* where Sicilian Americans profess the most profound hatred of niggers. A black woman in blackface stands and announces that she is "keeping it real" as the only real niggress and even sings a bit of gospel, asserting her right to niggerness through black cultural expression. Dela's studio boss, Dunwitty, claims he has the right to use the term *nigger* because he has a black wife and two biracial children and knows more about black culture than Dela. Dunwitty chastises Dela for disparaging his use of the N-word and remarks that he agrees with Tarantino that "the word means nothing." While in a manner not unlike the conservative black critic Stanley Crouch, who often uses the term *Negro* rather than *Black,* Dela only refers to black people as Negroes, his father, the comedian Junebug (Paul Mooney) constantly uses the term *nigger.* His embrace of the term is one of affinity, of affirmation and even defiance. His usage of the term contrasts with that of Dunwitty. Junebug's racy black humor and vernacular repartee subverts the negative and demeaning connotations ascribed by the dominant culture. And yet, the word remains problematic within as well as outside of African American linguistic usage because of its potentially negative connotations. History has told us that the word means nothing and everything as it has been culturally appropriated and excessively employed; it still carries historical baggage and loaded meanings. When Dunwitty fires Manray and has him dragged from the stage, he tells Manray, "Niggers like you are a dime a dozen." He forcibly removes Manray for acts of sedition. For Manray, now enlightened and devoid of blackface, had entered the stage and, in another moment of intertextuality that harkens back to the insanely aware Peter Finch as Howard Beale in Paddy Chayevsky's classic *Network* (1976), asked the audience to "go to their windows and shout they are sick and tired of being niggers."

Evident in the use of the word *nigger* in *Bamboozled* are its contradictory valences that mirror its evolution in our contemporary society as an expression that has been reimagined even as it remains historically charged. Increasingly with the popularity of hip-hop music and the saturation of rap videos, youth from different ethnic groups in addition to those of the black inner city have embraced the term *nigga* as an expression of their own antiauthoritarian, masculinist bravado and group solidarity. Historian Robin D. G. Kelley in *Race Rebels* differentiates the negative term *nigger* from the appellation *nigga.* He argues that black gangsta rappers and urban black youth use the term "'Nigga' to describe a condition rather than a skin color or culture. Above all, Nigga speaks to a collective identity shaped by class consciousness, the character of inner-city space, political repression, poverty, and the constant threat of intraracial violence."[15] Thus for Kelley, the concept of "nigga" symbolically represents a new collective identity as it also linguistically reflects a reworking of the pejorative term *nigger.* Discussing rap artist DMX, Todd Boyd in *The New H.N.I.C.* maintains that even as the racism implied by the term forms the backdrop for the word's usage, DMX by embracing the term *nigga* "realizes a certain freedom and libratory potential in his use of language."[16] In *Bamboozled,* however, the libratory possibilities are always contestatory; sometimes the use of the term comes at great cost. The rap group the Mau Maus wear various scarves rapped around their heads and address each other with the appellation "nigga," but they differentiate themselves from the minstrel Manray, whom they berate as a "handkerchief head Uncle Tom nigger." They imagine their freedom yoked to constraining and silencing of the nigger Manray.

The Mau Maus in their desire to censure minstrelsy raise a question that is reiterated in *Bamboozled:* who has the right to perform blackness and to determine how it is performed? The Mau Maus argue that Manray has no right to his blackface performance and that his display of blackness is "fucking it up for everybody." Junebug, Dela's father, plays in small black clubs and disdains Hollywood because he refuses to conform to their demeaning representations of blackness.[17] His humor in its social criticism of black-white relations contrasts sharply with the humor of the *New Millennium Minstrel Show* that laughs at black people's imbecility even as it laughs with them. Mel Watkins in *On the Real Side* defines black American humor as "often assertive and openly critical of mainstream society" and notes that its "in-group ridicule was often coupled with a broad range of outwardly directed satire."[18] This definition contrasts "real" black humor with minstrel buffoonery, and accordingly, Junebug's humor bitingly satirizes the racial status quo. Yet his comedy, like any other comedy, is always a product of hybridity and cultural crossings, always in its physicality bordering on buffoonery. Spike Lee's 2000 concert film *The Original Kings of Comedy* displays equal doses of self-deprecation and social critique. That film and Junebug's menial existence as a comic entertainer as well as Manray's desire to make money as a hoofer all stress the problem for the black artist within the white-controlled capitalist marketplace: how do you maintain the integrity of your art, uplift the race, and yet make a living? As a black artist do you have a responsibility to the mythical "black community?" Dela decides to disdain his father's choices and to work within the system, to make money within its rules. With the success of and controversy around the *New Millennium Minstrel Show,* he appears on a black radio talk show and defends his right as a black artist to create such a show. He asks, "Who is to judge, who is to stand and say this is right and this is not?" He uses the defense that art is art and should be accepted as such. He speaks out against the past politics of victimization, the slave mentality, the ressentiment of identity politics that limit black advancement. Myrna Goldfarb, the white Afro American Studies Ph.D. from Yale, the niggerologist—as Dela calls her—a media consultant brought in by Dunwitty to mount an offensive campaign in defense of the *New Millennium Minstrel Show,* equally asks, "Who determines what is black?" She challenges any form of black cultural policing. Her point is that Manray has a right to his own form of cultural expression and that his minstrelsy should not be taken as representative of all black people.

Yet *Bamboozled,* through its satire, challenges the positions of both Goldfarb and Dela. The film argues that because of America's racial history, black representation is always and already highly politicized and these politics must be taken seriously. In a clever send-up of their own theatricalized politics of racial agitation, Lee has the real Johnny Cochran and Al Sharpton protest the demeaning images of blacks on the *New Millennium Minstrel Show* outside the show's corporate headquarters. The self-conscious presence of these two publicity-conscious, media-savvy figures troubles the relationship of the real to the representational. For if the *New Millennium Minstrel Show* were real, certainly Cochran and Sharpton would use the power of the media to demonstrate against it. More importantly, it is through such representations as this that we understand the "real" force of the racial imagery. How blackness is constructed and employed on film and television continues to have profound and actual impact on lived experience.

The end of *Bamboozled* escalates in a cacophony of violent, disturbing images that testify to the interconnections and interactions of race and representation. The Mau Maus kidnap Manray and execute him during a live broadcast across the Internet. The Mau Maus believe that Manray must be killed for his degradation of black people. Yet in their willingness to take another black life and in their lack of any real revolutionary agenda—"What are you rebelling against?" Sloan asks—they represent a vacuous activism, an oppositionality gone awry. Named for the legendary Kenyan Mau Mau that led a dramatic rebellion in 1952 against British colonialism, the rap group does not appear actively engaged with this history. Boyd argues that "Hip Hop has always placed a great worth on making connections to a larger historical sense of culture, thus the lofty status accorded to the idea of an 'old school.'"[19] Here in *Bamboozled,* the Mau Maus seem to connect with the cultural style of their namesakes but not with the ideological substance. In a parody of contemporary rap and the performativity of rap names, the Mau Maus all have taken on Afrocentric names, such as "Big Black African," that express their commitment to the black revolutionary effort. In another move of intertextuality, socially conscious rapper turned actor Mos Def plays Big Black African, the leader of the Mau Maus. The Mau Maus' names, in their excess, comment on the process of rap naming as well as the rhetoric of Afrocentricity. Like so much of gangsta rap, the Mau Maus attack conventional capital and consumption even as they affirm the primacy of production and consumption. They envy the fact that Manray is a star on television with a billboard on Times Square and even audition for the *New Millennium Minstrel Show* themselves. As Michael Rogin points out, the Mau Maus "condemn minstrelsy even as they embody its stereotypes."[20] The Mau Maus misdirect their racial fervor onto Mantan as the symbol of black degradation rather than the white producer (Michael Rappaport) or the white-owned corporate structures that control the politics of his representation.

The Mau Maus murder of Mantan represents a public lynching, a new escalation of reality television. It becomes a new phenomenon in popular culture. Within reality television the audience peers in as Peeping Toms while others embarrass themselves or push the edges of decency or the bounds of human life and will. The distance and privacy of the television screen provide sanction and safety for the audience. One can safely surrender to the seductiveness of personal failure with little cost to oneself. Moreover, the audience function is one of impotency, unable to change the events even in this day of interactivity. The passivity of the idiot box is well documented, and reality shows test the passive, vicarious pleasure of someone else's pain and humiliation. *Survivor* in fact gained some of its highest ratings in an episode where one of the participants almost died. Idea of Internet execution is now all the more real as radical insurgents in Iraq and Saudi Arabia have beheaded kidnapped American prisoners live on the Internet in the spring of 2004. Closer to home, much debate occurred in 2001 around the execution of Oklahoma City bomber Timothy McVeigh and whether his execution would be broadcast live back to families back in Oklahoma. Within such broadcast executions, whether that proposed for McVeigh or actually carried out in Iraq, prurient interests and moralistic retribution perversely commix. Horrifyingly, the equally dangerous and decisive interconnections of the real and the representational become manifest.

With Manray in *Bamboozled* the element of blackness and its historical use in the field of representation adds another factor to the spectacle. Junebug comments that "every nigger is an entertainer." Like the televised trials of O. J. Simpson, the daily hearings of Clarence Thomas and Anita Hill, the black body becomes the site of public spectacle and entertainment. Orlando Patterson in *Rituals of Blood* theorizes that lynching in all its inhumanity constituted an act of ritualized human blood sacrifice, a rite of segregation that served to redress the crisis of postslavery transition and uncertainty for white America. By figuratively and actually removing the threatening "black beast," these acts affirmed the baseness of blackness and valorized the privileges and sanctity of whiteness. The lynching of Manray by black hands ritualistically removes the offending Uncle Tom but does not reify a new power of blackness, which like the act of blacking up is disturbingly painful to watch. Yet the murder of Mantan does not change or rebel against the material system but sadly and painfully affirms the power of representation and the ultimate power of the dominant hegemony. This is a performance of blackness heavily layered. Manray's final exhilarating "dance of death," like any good reality show, blurs the lines between fiction and reality. He dances for his life before the Mau Maus, before a television audience within the film impotent to act, and ultimately before us, the viewing audience for the film.

As the self-satisfied Mau Maus exit the site of the execution, all but one are gunned down in a hail of bullets in another excessive display of brutality toward people of color by Mayor Giuliani (prior to his post–September 11, 2001, redemption as a national hero) and New York's finest, who of course arrive at the scene too late. The one Mau Mau not killed appears to be white, despite his dress and his verbal dexterity with black urban vernacular. Thus, in this moment, the question of "who is really black" is not a question of semantics. The white Mau Mau claims blackness as the police handcuff him. He shouts "I'm black: one-sixteenth, one drop of black blood is all that's required. Why didn't you kill me?" His rap name with the Mau Maus is in fact "One-Sixteenth Black," so his call-out to the police is at once reciting his name, outing his unmarked racial history, and calling for their recognition of his identity. The real reflects ironically on the representational as DJ Surge, a white rapper from the all-white early 1980s rap group 3rd Base, portrays this character. The group 3rd Base preceded a wave of commercially successful white rappers such as Eminem in troubling the racialization of rap music, and raising the question of whether others can legitimately perform this music that arose from the black urban environs and whose "realness" in performance depends on one's representational proximity to that hood. His invocation of the one-drop rule takes us back to an earlier time of racial performances and a history of passing. Yet his declaration of blackness must be seen in relation to the Sicilian's earlier satirical proclamation of niggerness and placed within today's racial context in which mixed racial status and hybridity have new political and cultural consequences. His claim is an insane or unreal claim; he actually weeps because he is not martyred with the others. Through this action, the film suggests that in the lived world "blackness" is often simply how one looks; it's straightforwardly physical, not theoretical or "constructed," at the moment the cops decide whom to shoot. Even as blackness's meaning is constructed, it is not negotiable in all places at all times.

Dela too is murdered, killed accidentally by the hysterical Sloan. She succumbs to another stereotype of the hysterical woman even as Lee sees her as a particularly strong black woman. Dela's narration from beyond the grave provides a repetition and revision of such films as *Menace to Society* that feature a dead narrator whose death ends the story. In death the show for Dela still must go on, a telling comment on the powers of representation. Dela dies surrounded by black memorabilia. The excess of these images emphasizes that blackness in its representation cannot be contained or simply controlled. Dela's "Jolly Nigger Bank" takes on a life of its own. Symbolically it represents and indicts black artists and a society willing to perform for a little payment, despite the dehumanization.

As Dela bleeds to death from his wounds, a montage of demeaning black and blackface representations flashes across the screen. These include cartoon images of smiling darkies, famous white actors such as Bing Crosby and Mickey Rooney blacking up, and stereotypical comic black actors such as Steppin Fechit, Mantan Moreland, and Butterfly McQueen. The horror of the images underscored by soft cool jazz music has and needs no dialogue. Rather, the music in its understatement moves spectators to meditate on a shameful legacy that has passed as mainstream entertainment. The litany of images of mammies, coons, and pickaninnies in its excess and accumulation is often painful to watch. Through this disturbing imagery, Lee rubs history against the grain and raises his audience's awareness of the ways in which blackness has functioned within American popular culture. The juxtaposition of this documentation with the *New Millennium Minstrel Show* and the dying, now blackfaced, Dela once again troubles the relationship of the real to the representational, for all these racial representations have had and do have real effects. Dela dies, but the shadow, residue, and scars of minstrelsy remain. Such trafficking in blackness to satisfy the expectations and desires of the viewing public has shaped the national consciousness and the enduring conditions of race in America.

NOTES

1. Ralph Ellison, "Prologue," *Invisible Man* (New York: Vintage, 1995), 9.

2. Ibid.

3. Spike Lee, interview by Gary Crowdus and Dan Georgakas, "Thinking about the Power of Images," *Cineaste* 26, no. 2 (2001): 4–5.

4. Mark Anthony Neal, *Soul Babies: Black Popular Culture and the Post-Soul Aesthetic* (New York: Routledge, 2002), 112.

5. Neal, *Soul Babies,* 113.

6. More recently, with the growth of black hip-hop fashion lines, Hilfiger has lost his stronghold in the urban market place and has sought to reinvent himself and his advertising. See the discussion of hip-hop fashion by Nicole Fleetwood in this volume.

7. Michael Rogin, "Nowhere Left to Stand: The Burnt Cork Roots of Popular Culture," *Cineaste* 26, no. 2 (2001): 15.

8. Josephine Lee, "The Seduction of the Stereotype," in *Performing Asian America* (Philadelphia: Temple University Press, 1997), 96.

9. Spike Lee, interview, 6.

10. Ibid.

11. Eric Lott, *Love and Theft: Blackface Minstrelsy and the American Working Class* (New York: Oxford University Press, 1995), 104.

12. Michael Rogin, *Blackface, White Noise* (Berkeley and Los Angeles: University of California Press, 1998), 5.

13. Lott, *Love and Theft,* 97, 101.

14. W. T. Lhamon, Jr., *Raising Cain: Blackface Performance from Jim Crow to Hip Hop* (Cambridge: Harvard University Press, 1998), 51.

15. Robin D. G. Kelly, *Race Rebels* (New York: Free Press, 1994), 210.

16. Todd Boyd, *The New H.N.I.C.* (New York: New York University Press, 2003), 39.

17. Here again the casting is self-reflexive, as Paul Mooney's own career has been like that of Junebug, marked by his nonconformity and angry black humor.

18. Mel Watkins, *On the Real Side: Laughing, Lying, and Signifying—the Underground Tradition of African-American Humor* (New York: Simon and Schuster, 1994), 39.

19. Boyd, *The New H.N.I.C.,* 124.

20. Rogin, "Nowhere Left to Stand," 15.

JENNIFER DEVERE BRODY

Moving Violations
Performing Globalization and Feminism in *Set It Off*

No Parking, Baby, No Parking on the Dance Floor!
Well a moving violation is easy to fix, just tell the DJ to fix it in
the mix.
   —Midnight Star

Keep on moving, Don't Stop, Don't stop the hands of time
   —Soul II Soul

Shadowed in my title, "Moving Violations," is the movie violence portrayed in the film *Set It Off* (1996). Each of the terms in my subtitle may be
read as moving violations, as acts subject to policing policies because they
are mobile. They may also be cited as "enabling violations"—to borrow
Gayatri Spivak's term—for the violence that is constitutive of identity. The
terms under which we/I labor—globalization and feminism—drive my
desire to analyze *Set It Off*. These namings occlude as much as they reveal;
it is the obscuring oscillations that I map and track in the following essay.
More specifically, I read this film because it is an antiromantic idyll that
shifts the terms and subjectivities represented in more conventional "black
nationalist" neoblaxploitation films.

Having paid the proverbial "price of the ticket" to view all but one of
the film's provisionally victorious black female victims come to a vicious
end, I wondered about the events relayed in and by the film. I believe that
the film merits the attention of black cultural critics for its ability to revoke
and revitalize performance scripts that continue to govern representations
of black women in filmic discourse. Indeed, *Set It Off* "complicates the
portrait of black women as merely objectified—as completely under the
power of the gaze—by detailing the lure and function of underground tactics of power like crime."[1] In thinking about how to contextualize the film,

I was reminded of a discussion of Chicana gang members' bodies performing on the "bronze" screen written by Rosa Linda Fregosa.[2] Fregosa argues that the Chicana gang members' "comportment registers the outer boundaries of Chicana femininity; her body marks the limit of *la familia;* her masquerade accentuates her deviance from the culture's normative domestic place for women. And perhaps the production of pachuca-chola-homegirl subjectivities has not been celebrated by many of us [feminists] precisely because her body [real and discursive] defies, provokes challenges as it interrogates the traditional familial basis of our constructions of the Chicano nation."[3] In many ways, *Set It Off*'s four black female protagonists (who are also from Los Angeles) can code as "pachuca-chola-homegirlz." They too use various strategies of masquerade to accentuate their deviance (as well as their spatiotemporal differences) from a "cultural normative domestic place." I wish to take liberties with Fregosa's phrasing, shifting slightly her understanding of the domestic to include national rather than merely familial space. Thus, if we think of the four women in the film as a family, the one who deviates from its own cultural norm is the "escaped" figure, Stony.

The following essay reads the performances of these "typed" products packaged for screen productions—the single mother/welfare queen, the butch lesbian, sapphire, and jezebel—with an eye toward elucidating how they perform their own fractured feminist praxis in the course of their work. Moreover, I take the "performativity of space seriously . . . meaning that I understand that categories such as gender, race, and sexuality are not only discursively constructed but spatially enacted and created. . . . While these categories are often considered to be mobile, spatially independent, or even merely discursive, they emerge in part through the production and sedimentation of space."[4] Acting intersubjectively within the spaces they inhabit (which simultaneously inhibit and empower them), the women exercise agency, as well as affect and effect change. The film's foregrounding of the "setting" sets off the characters literally and figuratively. In other words, the film engages with "the spatial turn" in cultural studies requiring us to think critically about the subjectivity of space and the space of subjectivity.[5] For space, no less than subjectivity, is a figure of, and in, perpetual motion. Finally, I hope to think about what Francesca Royster highlights as the film's "*diversification* of black women's desire" (8, emphasis added) in the context of capital's ability to manage/market such diversity.

The Midlife Crisis of the 1990s

The year of *Set It Off*'s national and then international release was 1996, a propitious year for changes to the "welfare" of women worldwide. It was the year in which Justice for Janitors marched in Quebec, the year that the Aid to Families with Dependent Children was reconstituted in the Personal Responsibility and Work Opportunity Reconciliation Act, and the year in which debates about the North American Free Trade Agreement (NAFTA) raged. Such coincidental sociopolitical events helped to transform the film into a timely, contemporary endeavor able to address and thematize current events. Within the film's purview is an understanding that

> new spatial and social relations of our time have important conse-
> quences for knowledge. . . . The shake up in spatial and social relations
> in our time does nothing to dislodge long-standing forms of white
> supremacy. Instead, structural-adjustment policies, mass migrations,
> and attacks on the social institutions traditionally responsible for creat-
> ing greater equality all function together in our time to make "white-
> ness" a global as well as a national project, to insure the permanent
> supremacy of the largely "white" global north over the largely "non-
> white" global south.[6]

The film also addresses the increased power and presence of the California police state, whose local LAPD force (which, under the Patriot Act, is increasingly a branch of a global policing force whose license to kill is managed by the battle cry "democracy") is a military unit that can mobilize and command SWAT teams, helicopters, and armies of soldiers.[7] In response to these larger structural changes, numerous acts of resistance—in favor of abolishing the prison-industrial complex and the death penalty, against genetically altered food, the war in Iraq, and the consolidation of wealth—have been performed.

In 1999 mass demonstrations in Seattle during the World Trade Organization (WTO) meetings dramatized the impact of the rapid spread of capital through corporate mergers. Resistance to such events came also in the form of the high-tech highway of the Internet. It is now commonplace to proclaim that we are living in an era of globalization epitomized by the consolidation of media infotainment conglomerates, the rise of a single superpower, and "the loosening of the hyphen between nation and state"[8] that necessarily bears upon our understanding of black cultural traffic. Invoking "globalization"—that buzzkill of a buzzword—may be seen as a kind of moving violation, heralding multiple, multinational phases and phrases and, according to the statistics in *Global Hollywood,* movie screens as well.[9] I write this essay in what might be seen as an apocalyptic moment: California burns in the wake of an historic recall vote in which Governor Gray Davis was terminated, and has been replaced by the new governor Arnold Schwarzenegger, himself a product of a global Hollywood.

Globalization has been read as being concomitant with, if not responsible for, what David Harvey (followed by Doreen Massey, Edward Soja, and others) discusses as "time-space compression," an attribute of post-Fordist, procapital postmodernity in which "investment boundaries change constantly because the dynamics of international capital are fast moving."[10] In short (for time is nothing but today), I read globalization as a set of practices and resistances that push at formerly formally bounded barriers such as the nation-state, *norte y sud,* overemployed and underemployed, home and homeless, masculine and feminine. Moreover, I believe that globalization had its roots in an earlier manifestation of international trade that we can map along the perimeter of the Atlantic. Over some four hundred years, this route made the exchange of flesh and gold routine. Indeed, it is important to remember that among the first international movements was the organization to abolish the slave trade. These ideas come to bear on my analysis of the critical representation of globality in the film with particular reference to black women, crime, and consumerism in the (new) border zone between the United States and Mexico (both of which were at one time Mexico). Ultimately, I suggest that the film, a material artifact with a star cast and a platinum-selling hip-hop soundtrack, is itself part and parcel of the processes of globalization that it diegetically seeks to critique. On this last point, I would concur with Saidiya Hartman, who argues that the very politico-aesthetic assets we now claim as sites of modern black production, having been forged in the crucible of captivity, are always already subject to the limits of freedom as opposed to signs of an unfettered liberation.[11]

Old (Country) Genres, New (City) Ethnicities (Propositions 187 & 209)

The film *Set It Off,* directed by former hip-hop videographer F. Gary Gray and written by Takashi Bufford (who also wrote the screenplay for Kid and Play's *House Party*) and Kate Lanier (who wrote the film *What's Love Got to Do with It*), follows a quartet of young black urban women from South Central Los Angeles to different final destinations: three of the four die for their "choice" to become bank robbers, leaving one to survive, albeit beyond U.S. borders. The growth of the global entertainment media industry can be seen in the "collateral merchandising" of multiple materials tied to a single product or brand name. Thus, there is no longer a divide between the film, the stars, and the soundtrack CD, nor between hip-hop music and an industry-supported film. The cross-referencing of products provides a link to sell more merchandise. Films are one of this country's major exports: 70 percent of films consumed in France were made in Hollywood, and the Academy Awards have hundreds of millions of viewers worldwide. That the sole survivor is reluctant to continue as a career criminal; that she dreams of a future; that she accepts the rights afforded by the rights of private property; in short, that she desires to live the liberal romance of bourgeois subjectivity, allows her to live in a New World Economy. Marginalized subjects desire rights (such as the right to marry) and recognition by the state; such privileges, we must recall, are problematic by their very exclusionary practices. So, too, as Mary Pat Brady reminds us, the

> production of the "Americas" coincided with the solidification of the Cartesian subject as a subject of the state, as holder of property, as "cogito ergo sum" and its unspoken corollary, "I conquer." The emergence of the Cartesian subject resulted in a process that "de-spaced" people depriving them of access to their means of subsistence, repressing the Cartesian subject's topophilia (the centrality of property to subjectivity); at the same time that it turned some people into subjects or citizens and other people into slaves, juridically nonexistent.[12]

Stony's miraculous escape beyond the U.S. national, if not economic, border is meant to be a progressive aspect of a film that also has an openly "lesbian" character (thus catering to the newest market), a black male bank officer, and a black female police officer. Nevertheless, the film's soul survivor, Stony, who departs to Mexico on a tourist bus in the penultimate scene, depends singularly on the largesse and noblesse oblige (like the extension of civil rights?) on a singular kinder, gentler, compassionate white male LAPD detective named Lieutenant Strode. In other words, I wish to caution against seeing Stony's getaway as singularly triumphant.

Elvis Mitchell, an L.A. film critic now writing for the *New York Times,* reviewed the film on National Public Radio, contextualizing it in terms of its roots in nineteenth-century realism; he compared it explicitly to Victor Hugo's classic *Les Misérables* and Dickensian social realism. Unlike those who saw the film as "Thelma and Louise Riding Shotgun in the Hood While Waiting to Exhale," Mitchell labeled it a B picture and defended it from detractors who were concerned with the problem of representing and glorifying violence. Reporters like Mitchell indirectly suggest that the film's meaning lies with a sociological currency that too many critics and viewers have interpreted as its glorification of gangsta lifestyle. I read the film in two rather contradictory registers: as, first, a critique of buck-wild styles of black masculinity that traffic in misogyny and, given that Stony does get the man but simultaneously attempts to stay married to her all-girl crew, as an indictment of forms of bourgeois black femininity.

Actually, I would agree with such readers but in an entirely different way. Where most would see the picture as "making tragic heroes [note gender] of the cast of black female characters"; I read the film as glorifying the violence of bourgeois subjectivity itself. For when Stony is allowed to escape (as the beneficiary of white benevolence in the form of the white male cop who has the power to let her go by looking the other way), she mimics the dominant strategy of earlier imperial subjects who depart with capital "stolen" from the labor of black (female) bodies and lights out for new territories that she can conquer with material wealth. So too, the film makes affirmative action appear as something that is in the hands of a few good (white) men as well as something that already has worked. Yet, there are contradictions.

What kind of feminist vision is presented in this popular fiction? For all her "newness" as a black woman with means, Stony is also the only one of the four women we see engaging in the oldest profession of trafficking in her body, in a scene with Nate, the owner of a car dealership. In the scene, Stony asks upfront for her check. When Nate refuses, she can only swear: "You gonna wait an' see if you like it? Jesus!" In the next shot, in a cheap hotel, Nate continues to defer paying Stony. She pleads, "You said only an hour." Nate replies: "I didn't know we was punching a time clock." Stony, rising, says, "Deal's a deal." Nate kisses her neck and pushes her shoulders down, forcing her back into the bed. He whispers, "You want your check? . . . let me hit it one more time."

The subtext of the actions and dialogue is concerned with value, which is to say, with politics. The film seeks to transform such forms through a focus on the various vehicles of transportation to new modes of knowledge, if not existence. As a certain kind of (radical, curmudgeonly?) black feminist reader, I am neither happy to have Stony leave the "girlz" in the ghetto, nor happy to have her remain with them in L.A. What I would wish for these characters (a project that I have begun to articulate in other work) would be for them to enact justice within the confines of the celluloid adventure. In the original screenplay, Stony leaves the money from the final robbery for the Mexican maids and sends the rest to Tisean's son, Jujuan—with Stony's own destination unknown. As an action film, in the Hollywood-meets-hip-hop version distributed by New Line Cinema, *Set It Off* circulates in a wide market. Like earlier blaxploitation films that drew upon conventional action genres such as Westerns, gangster and martial arts films, as well as pornography, the film downplays dialogue. The film's overt intertextuality, its postmodern pastiche remind us that Gray began his feature career by honing his skills in music videos; he made the classic video for Ice Cube's song "Today Is a Good Day" and TLC's "Waterfalls," both of which have broad appeal as pure film spectacle. Even within such confines of the neoblaxploitation action film genre, *Set It Off* opens up certain boundaries of representation.

The film requires its viewers to think about the women's encounters with a biased state system that removes children from their mother's custody and condones racist police violence, as well as the misogyny of the masters whom these modern maids serve. In a collective effort to leave their low-paying jobs as janitorial custodians, the heroines decide to rob a bank. Let me set the scene: The female leads, Stony Dorsey (played by middle-class, pretty Jada Pinkett-Smith), Cleopatra Sims (feminist rapper Queen Latifah), Tisean Williams (Kimberly Elise, making her film debut; she went on to star as daughter Denver in *Beloved*), and Frankie (Vivica Fox, Will Smith's wife in *Independence Day* and the middle-class mother of three in *Soul Food*),[13] are motivated by revenge. Stony's brother, Stevie, who has just graduated from high school at the start of the film, has his dreams to attend UCLA dashed because he is rejected. He keeps this information from Stony, who is obsessed with getting the money she thinks he needs to attend college. All of her machinations (and her humiliation) are moot, because Stevie dies an untimely, unjust death at the trigger-happy hands of the LAPD in a tragic case of mistaken identity and guilt by association. Tisean's son, Jujuan, is removed by Child Protective Services because she cannot afford child care and he ingests toxins at her cleaning job. Frankie is fired from her quasi-respectable post as a bank teller when, in the harrowing opening sequence, a homey-from-around-the-way, with whom she has some acquaintance, robs the bank where she works. She subsequently becomes a suspect in another instance of guilt by association (for these black women, to reverse the dictum, it's where you are from, not where you are going). Part of my argument is to demonstrate how black women become redundant, in the Malthusian sense, and ultimately obsolete. The film suggests, simplistically perhaps, to exist in the hood is to be perpetually in the wrong place at the wrong time. Following a formula set in the first wave of 1970s blaxploitation films featuring female leads (Pam Grier's career epitomizes the genre), the women's violent action is a last resort motivated in part by being "screwed over" by a patriarchal figure.

The exception in *Set It Off* is Queen Latifah's character, Cleo, who is already an outlaw: literally, because she has a prior conviction, and figuratively, because she is a lesbian. One early scene in the movie serves as an introduction to the characters and their mise-en-scène. We see a dimly lit parking lot, a mountain of dumpster garbage, and Cleo, Stony, and Tisean with their black male boss, Luther. The dialogue makes interesting references to human, nonhuman, male, and female (Cleo is called a "Mighty Morphin Power Ranger"—a term that befits Stony's metamorphic character as well). Cleo and Stony argue with the boss so that he won't dock their pay for being late. They are being paid under the table and therefore have no recourse or clout with their employer.

Cleo and Stony are the dominant (butch/femme) pair played, not coincidentally by the movie's most famous stars, Queen Latifah and Jada Pinkett-Smith. This leaves Tisean and Frankie, accomplished lead-quality actresses themselves, to take a back seat to the main stars. The hierarchy among the four is reinforced by the movie poster for the film in which Pinkett-Smith's Stony occupies the top left corner of a diagonal line that descends from her to Cleo to Frankie and ends in the bottom right corner with Tisean. The actresses' names are written to correspond to the hierarchy of images. The women in the film are collaborators and friends but not a collective in the political sense of the term. In the film, there is an elegiac scene—a kind of still life, in that all the women are still alive—in which thick smog lends a surreal glow to the low-setting Los Angeles sun as the soon-to-be outlawed crew sits on a slanted rooftop smoking chronic and shooting the breeze. This scene contrasts with the shots taken of the women by the undetected detective, Strode, who puts together the women's perp profiles. Strode oversees the "telematic postmodern terrain of information command," to quote Spivak. With the women lined up as

in a police lineup, camera work here calls attention to the double apparatus through which the women are shot (motion and still pictures), an
apparatus noted in Chon Noriega's *Shot in L.A.*

As Kathleen McHugh points out in "Women in Traffic," still photos are
not close-ups that break the diegesis to create the desired spectacle of
beauty (think Marlene Dietrich). Rather, they are "mug shots, surveillance
photos"[14] or, in my words, freeze-frame memories that become memento
mori. All the singularly hood-identified women, namely, Cleo, Tisean, and
Frankie, die; they become frozen in the photos the sole survivor, Stony,
fingers nostalgically at the end of the film. Stony's feminine versatility
assures her vitality. She can accompany the banker played by Blair Underwood to a swanky party as well as rob the bank where he works. In short,
she excels at female impersonation. Stony hones her skills at deal making
when she decides to sleep with the car dealer "for one hour," only to have
him extort her time.[15]

Moving Venues: Vintage/(Ad)vantage

When buying arms for the first bank heist in the film, Cleo goes to Black
Sam (played by rapper Dr. Dre). It is in this scene that Cleo deploys the
film's title by exclaiming, "We're not robbing stage coaches, we want to set
it off." This mention of the Old West also signals the idea of a new west
that is part and parcel of the film's mise-en-scène (the film pans Jameson's
icon of postmodernity, the Bonaventure Hotel, a site that, given the proliferation and standardization of hotels crucial to the growing travel industry, also signifies globalization). Part of the problem here is that Cleo's way
of being in the world, while appearing "new" in the context of blaxploitation, is also paradoxically outmoded. For example, she drives a 1962 Chevy
Impala, signifying upon the fact that her chosen vehicle of mobility, while
"bumping," is impractical and passé. Throughout the film, the car functions as an appendage of her body. Indeed, she ends her life impaled on the
Impala's open door. In contrast, Stony drives away at the end of the film in
a brand-new red Jeep Wrangler. In Southern California, cars are famously
an extension of one's identity; Ann Friedberg's book, *Window Shopping:
Cinema and the Postmodern*,[16] shows that the gaze of the car windshield has
a corollary with the gaze of the big screen.

A discussion of the characters' modes of transportation signals the
importance of what McHugh terms the concept of "automobility."

McHugh includes *Set It Off* in a list of films that feature women for whom driving through the diegesis is a significant act. Contextualizing the concomitant developments of both the film and auto industries, she reads *Set It Off* as a film fundamentally about "mobility and opportunity [that] elicits and alters the generic elements of the road/outlaw movie, as well as those of the gangster film, the female friendship film, and the 'hood flick'" (405) by explicitly or implicitly referencing classics of those genres such as *Thelma and Louise, Bonnie and Clyde, Body Heat, Point Break,* and *Boyz in the Hood.*[17]

The film fits Stuart Hall's paradigm, explicated in his oft-cited essay "New Ethnicities," of "a new cultural politics which engages rather than suppresses differences, decoupling ethnicity from the violence of the state and shows the black experience as a diaspora experience."[18] Stony reverses the outmoded, dated paradigm of "bank robbery" that hearkens back to the days of the Wild West, when traders were only "robber barons" and not yet raiders.[19] Stony understands that money is not housed in banks alone; her last resort after her comrades have been killed is literally a resort on the Baja Coast. As also happens in Ken Loach's film *Bread and Roses* (2001), Stony trades her body for money. In each film, women prostitute themselves as a means to survive for the sake of their kin. As the primary caretakers of (male) descendents, the women in the film feel the need to take responsibility for the family line. Stony is willing to be made over in a man's image of what a woman should be; consequently, she is transported to the transnational at the end of the film. It is she who becomes a carrier of new mobile global capital, particularly when compared with her compatriots, who are stuck behind in the death grip of manifest destiny in the Old West. At the party where Stony meets Keith's associates, these captains of industry are described as being from (and therefore "representing") multinational corporations rather than geographical places such as a city or town state or province; rather, they hail from Sanwa, Citibank, Chase—global corporations whose locations are dispersed.

While we might be tempted to read the ending of the film—woman leaves man to try her luck alone in a new land—as a liberal (black) feminist statement, the film also may be interpreted as showing that black women's sacrifices allow black men to succeed. Indeed, such feminist readings are undercut by the film's careful attention to class, region, and gender—and provide us with a lesson about the limits of liberal feminism in the age of capital. Cleo's female masculinity (to use Judith Halberstam's term) is an interesting case in point. As Halberstam asserts, "the black female masculinity that Latifah portrays is convincing precisely because it is infused with racial and class dynamics that render the masculinity . . . making clear the multiple markers that construct all forms of masculinity."[20] Thus, Blair Underwood's Keith, a Harvard-educated, upwardly mobile buppie bank manager, also has a particular masculinity to perform. He takes Stony as his pretty woman (with reference to Julia Roberts in *Pretty Woman*). In exchange, Stony gets a demure black Armani dress as an update to her garish ghetto-fabulous style and trots off in a black limo to a black-tie event for his bank, where she charms the bosses with her improvised knowledge of stocks and bonds.

The second half of the film cuts between Cleo's home—a garage—and Keith's house, a high-priced loft downtown (we no longer have the 1950s suburban dream house in the valley). The new urban settlers return to recolonize the urban jungle; urban renewal or urban removal—depending on income—is tied to work and living in different ways: Cleo occupies a garage loft, Keith's apartment is merely loftlike—a simulacrum and transformation of working place/space. The film also juxtaposes the evacuated lot of a former manufacturing plant with the crystal stair and oversize table of the boardroom where the women clean. In its ability to depict the glories of globalization and mobility for some in the same diegetic space as the withering ghetto, the film counters "the mainstream account of economic globalization [that] operates like a narrative of eviction because it excludes a whole range of workers, firms, and sectors that do not fit the prevalent images of globalization."[21] The film makes visible connections between the eviction of populations and vacated geopolitical spaces of the nation-state (e.g., inhabited by the poor, the homeless, the residents of the reservation, some African Americans) with the increase in vacuous vacations for beneficiaries of the new globality, wealthy tourists who travel easily to formerly remote reaches of the globe. The other significant change in venue occurs between the original screenplay and the film itself. Initially the film took place on the mean streets of San Francisco (perhaps giving a clearer context, if not a spatial logic for Cleo's queer character) and Oakland, a black background with a violent Black Panther past, and concluded not in Mexico but in Arizona. The shift in venue from the Bay Area and the Southwest to the South Central Los Angeles and Mexico nexus changes the film's narrative of globalization.[22]

Commenting on the film, Jewelle Gomez points out that with the exception of Cleo's silent partner, her girlfriend Ursula (she is rendered literally as a dumb blonde, never uttering a word), "the lesbian community is invisible." In my opinion, this is one of the progressive aspects of the film; Cleo's community is composed of a (lesbian) continuum, a feminist community giving primacy to female love and ritual. The conflict is actually between different ways in which diversity is figured and represented. On the one hand, the film does not marginalize or ghettoize Cleo by segregating her into an already segregated gay ghetto; on the other hand, it contains her in the clichéd, ravaged space of the savage black hood. Both Kara Keeling and Francesca Royster tease out the implications of Cleo's butch performance. Keeling writes, "Cleo's characterization seeks to expand ghettocentric black masculinity to include her, it also challenges the erotic economy that ghettocentric black masculinity currently facilitates."[23]

In an homage to her homme homies, Cleo occupies the occupied territory in U.S. culture that Sharon Holland, following Taussig, names the black space of death in the U.S. Imaginary.[24] The most moving scene in the film is the moment of Cleo's mortal end, the moment of gravitas and veritas that reads as if it were a kind of cinema verité, seen live on TV. Cleo's death is shot as macabre masculine dance and underscored by a haunting funeral dirge sung by Lori Perri entitled "Up Against the Wind." The execution is witnessed by a diverse sector of the economy/population—by Keith in his plush bedroom, by Black Sam in a basement, and by Ursula, alone. All watch the event on live TV in real time. For all its ideology of liveness, it may be death that forms the point of televisual intrigue. I would add as well that these televisual scenes place the film in the context of America's spectacle of (racial) death bearing unwitting witness (it is never deliberate) to Los Angeles as the home of the televised trial of the century and the war zone of the Uprisings of the late 1960s and early 1990s. Such a space is by no means natural—although it is portrayed as the outcome of "nigga [sic] authenticity."

Ad-venture Capital Idea: Blue Chip, Red Light

Stony's sampling of difference begins with Keith's suggestion that they have dinner at a restaurant on their first date, made after Stony has met him under false pretenses—she posed as a potential "client" while she actually was casing the joint in preparation for a robbery. Consuming difference in his many travels, Keith names food according to already homogenized ethnic categories. While the couple decides that they are more comfortable choosing soul food for their first date, Keith cajoles,

"Next time, I'll cook Mexican and then we can go for Italian," invoking not only a future for the duo, but an anthropological hierarchy of cultural consumption (black, Mexican, Italian). This first date is Stony's first taste of freedom and allows her to cook up the plan to migrate to Mexico at the film's end. Once she begins dating Keith, she quickly "ventriloquizes [his] philosophy of embourgeoisment," to quote Bob Miklitsch's essay on suture and *Set It Off*'s soundtrack as audiovisuality. Miklitsch notes that Keith's eclectic musical tastes signal his superior socioeconomic status. I extend this idea and suggest that the singular ability to consume and represent diverse styles is a mark not just of sophistication but, ultimately, survival in cosmopolitan elite as well as subaltern spaces. When Stony escapes the otherwise long arm and eye of the law (she is let go by the LAPD), she gets away on a tourist bus bound for the Hotel Playa Blanca—white beach—on the Baja coast. She puts on a straw "Mexican peasant hat" she has purchased at a gift shop and blends in with the white tourists on the bus. In the penultimate shot, Stony calls Keith on a pay phone to thank him for showing her the way up, out, and away from the now "pathologized" matriarchal world she had lived in with girlfriends who sacrificed their lives to give her the money. Rejecting the female world of love and ritual, of shared pasts and experiences, she also rejects the stereotypes portrayed in the Moynihan report: dysfunctional female-headed households that the report contended caused the emasculation of black men and poverty of black families. Stony takes the money and keeps moving, final destination unknown. We suspect, however, that wherever she goes, Visa (and therefore a visa) will be with her. So, unlike the screenplay in which Stony divests herself of the money she has stolen and sends most of it to Tisean's son Jujuan, leaving the rest for the maids in the Mexican hotel, in this version she is outfitted in a flannel shirt and Calvin Klein underwear worn above the waistline. Is her new look just commodity lesbian—the rough rider—or is she reviving Cleo's look (but not her lifestyle)? Is it meant to be a ritual of mourning, a memory of Cleo and the crew? Reminding us of Pierre Nora's term *lieux de mémoire,* she fingers each photo carefully while the film shows flashbacks.

What puzzles me about the end of the film is whether or not it can be read as a "feminist" statement. In rejecting Keith's offer to be his, and setting out on her own, does she become a queer postmodern subject? Thinking globally, is that a good thing? Does she leave her class status and politics, whatever they might have been, behind in such a transformation? In the Hollywood filmed version, Stony "gets hers." The final words in the film are exchanged between Stony and Keith, the globalized survivors. Although Keith is guilty of the exact, "guilty by association" crime that Frankie was at the beginning of the film—each happened to know the perpetrator of the bank robbery but did not have premature knowledge of the event—Keith keeps his job, whereas Frankie loses her livelihood and, in short order, her life as well. This speaks to the difference in gender—black women often lose to black men at the upper echelons. In this version, the bourgeois subjects get away with capital murder.

Postpartum Dis-location: Va va va voom . . . Transgendernational Movements

Imagine this unseen, off-screen scene: Stony (who wanted to be the stone butch all along) takes hormones on her way to transforming her body into a gender outlaw staying in character by buying, rather than building, her body anew. She sends the saved stack of stashed cash not to baby Jujuan but to baby Ursula, the ultimate hood ornament, in preparation for the couple's flight to fantasy island. On arrival, Tatoo bellows, "De plane, de plane" to strategize with Justice for Janitors. They meet Rosa, the refugee organizer from Bread and Roses returning on the bus from the United States. Finally, Ursula utters her first words: "She de man," said in a sultry West Indian whisper. This fantastic scenario returns us to the vexed victories inherent in the itinerant movements of globality, ethnicity, gender/sexuality, named here as black cultural traffic.

NOTES

1. I conceived this paper before the publication of Francesca Royster's wonderful chapter "Queering Cleo: *Set It Off* and Queen Latifah's 'Butch in the Hood'" in her superb book, *Becoming Cleopatra: The Shifting Image of an Icon* (New York: Palgrave Macmillan, 2003). Her discussion of the ways in which the characters in the film control the gaze is compelling and convincing. She too has noted the significance of a film that "levies a metacritique of representation and criminalization of black women by the police and in the media at the same time that it attempts to diversify the image of black female desire" (173).

2. *The Bronze Screen* is the title of Chon Noriega's study of Chicano film.

3. Rosa Linda Fregoso, "Re-imagining Chicana Urban Identities in the Public Sphere, Cool Chuca Style" in *Between Woman and Nation: Nationalisms, Transnational Feminisms, and the State,* ed. Caren Kaplan, Norma Alarcón, and Minoo

Moallem (Durham, N.C.: Duke University Press, 1999), 90. See also David Harvey's *The Condition of Postmodernity* (London: Blackwell, 1991) and *Spaces of Capital: Towards a Critical Geography* (London: Routledge, 2001), 124–25.

4. Mary Pat Brady, *Extinct Lands, Temporal Geographies: Chicana Literature and the Urgency of Space* (Durham, N.C.: Duke University Press, 2002), 9.

5. "The Spatial Turn in Cultural Studies" is the title of the Annual Cultural Studies Conference at Indiana University in 2003 at which I was a guest speaker. I thank Tom Foster and his colleagues for organizing the event.

6. George Lipsitz, *American Studies in a Moment of Danger* (Minneapolis: University of Minnesota Press, 2001), 9.

7. For more on this topic, see Ruth Wilson Gilmore, "Globalization and U.S. Prison Growth: From Military Keynesianism to Post-Keynesian Militarism," *Race & Class* 40, no. 3 (1998–99): 171–88.

8. Gayatri Spivak, *Outside in the Teaching Machine* (New York: Routledge, 1993), 33.

9. Toby Miller, Nitin Govil, John McMurria, and Richard Maxwell, eds., *Global Hollywood* (London: BFI Publishing, 2001).

10. Spivak, *Outside,* 33.

11. Saidiya Hartman, *Scenes of Subjection* (Oxford: Oxford University Press, 1996).

12. Brady, *Extinct Lands,* 9.

13. I follow the convention here of identifying actors (like directors and authors) by their works—a strategy used to sell the film and video as well. This marketing tool keeps earlier work in circulation and helps to show that "we are what we do."

14. Kathleen McHugh, "Women in Traffic: L.A. Autobiography," in "Psycho-Marxism: Marxism and Psychoanalysis/Late in the Twentieth Century," special issue ed. Robert Miklitsch, *South Atlantic Quarterly* 97, no. 2 (1998): 407.

15. In the same way my recent trip to Menard's yielded testimony from a worker who said that though his shift was to end at ten, he worked often until one or two in the morning without overtime pay, at the discretion/whim of management. See also Barbara Ehrenreich's eminently readable book, *Nickel and Dimed: On (Not) Getting by in America* (New York: Metropolitan Books, 2001), which chronicles the author's time working for a cleaning service, for Wal-mart, and as a waitress.

16. Ann Friedberg, *Window Shopping: Cinema and the Postmodern* (Berkeley and Los Angeles: University of California Press, 1993).

17. McHugh, "Women in Traffic," 405.

18. Stuart Hall, "New Ethnicities," reprinted in David Morley and Kuan-Hsing Chen, eds., *Stuart Hall: Critical Dialogues in Cultural Studies* (New York and London: Routledge Press, 1996), 446.

19. In the HBO documentary *Born Rich,* by Jamie Johnson, a conversation with the director leads one of the descendants of the 1890s "robber barons" to claim that "they were all crooks back then."

20. Judith Halberstam, *Female Masculinity* (Durham, N.C.: Duke University Press, 1998), 229.

21. Saskia Sassen, *Globalization and Its Discontents* (New York: New Press, 1998), 82.

22. For an excellent reading of the geographical significance of Arizona, see the first chapter in Mary Pat Brady, *Extinct Lands, Temporal Geographies.*

23. Kara Keeling, "'Ghetto Heaven': *Set It Off* and the Valorization of Black Lesbian Butch-Femme Sociality," *The Black Scholar* 33, no. 1: 39.

24. See Sharon Holland, *Raising the Dead: Readings of Death and (Black) Subjectivity* (Durham, N.C.: Duke University Press); and Michael Taussig, *Mimesis and Alterity* (New York: Routledge, 1990). See also Joseph Roach, *Cities of the Dead: Circum-Atlantic Performance* (New York: Columbia University Press, 1996).

HARRY J. ELAM, JR.

Change Clothes and Go
A Postscript to Postblackness

In August 2001, artist and composer Keith Townsend Obadike put his blackness up for sale via the online auction house eBay with bidding open from August 8 though 18, 2001. Listed under Collectibles/Culture/Black Americana, Obadike offered buyers "an heirloom" that had been "in the seller's possession for twenty-eight years," along with a certificate of authenticity, but warned that he could not guarantee its operation outside of the United States.[1] This project, the latest installment in Obadike's Internet installations entitled *Black.net.art,* extends his online explorations of blackness and its meanings. As "cyber" performance or conceptual art, Obadike's work constitutes a further example of black cultural traffic. In addition, its content and form raise significant issues for our consideration as we end this collection. For Obadike's auction foregrounds not only an impending avenue for the travel of blackness through the circuits of cyberspace but highlights the very portability of blackness. Rife with cultural and political implications, Obadike's cyber action asks: What happens as the connection between black bodies and black cultural expression becomes not only more diverse but more disconnected, when blackness travels on its own, separate and distinct from black people?

Most certainly, Obadike's trafficking in blackness holds historic resonance as well as contemporary significance. It conjures images of the auction block and black bodies sold to the highest white bidder. In the arena of slavery, the auction block compelled restricted, distorted performances of blackness where any display of black agency raised concerns, and blackness became understood only in terms of white desire and black economic utility. Saidiya Hartman terms the auction block a "scene of subjection" in which terror and pleasure converged. She maintains that performative moments of blacks singing on the way to the auction blocks were "envisioned fundamentally as vehicles for white enjoyment" and that black bodies were "the purveyors of pleasure."[2] During the strange institution of slavery, blackness circulated as commodity, as a figurative product only equal to three-fifths of a man. Hortense Spillers has recognized in slavery a particularly American "grammar" that placed humans and inanimate objects in one "grammatical series" and collapsed through congruity these disparate and unrelated items within the "same text of realism."[3] Reimagining Spillers and equally re-creating a unique "American Grammar," Obadike's posits his blackness for sale on eBay as a black collectible, next to black lawn jockeys, ceramic smiling mammy cookie jars, and Black Sambo dolls, and through this alignment constructs a "simultaneity of disparate items in a grammatical series."[4] Such an arrangement highlights the absurdity of Obadike's sale as well as its historical legitimacy. With Obadike as with slavery, blackness circulates as object, as commodity, for blackness repeatedly has been the subject of commercial traffic, bought, sold, used, and abused.

Yet present in Obadike's sale of blackness, in spite of its invocation of black historical commodification, auction blacks, and chattel slavery, are tones of irreverence. For Obadike pursues this auction with humor and satire, without the seriousness or veneration expected when one discusses or even artistically engages in the sale of black bodies. Such artistic license with history reflects perhaps what Mark Anthony Neal terms a "postsoul aesthetic." Delineating the political, social, and cultural experiences of the African American community since the end of the civil rights and Black Power movements as "postsoul," Neal sees within the postsoul aesthetic a seemingly sacrilegious approach by contemporary African American artists to sacred icons of the African American past.[5] Discussing the treatment of Rosa Parks in the hip-hop duo Outkast's song "Rosa Parks," Neal theorizes that "one of the post-soul strategies is to willingly 'bastardize' black history and culture to create alternative meanings."[6] These tactics emerge from and within the current conditions of black cultural traffic in which a wariness about the burdens of blackness often exists in tandem with a nostalgia for sounds, figures, clothing from that past; in which historical images, music, politics are interrogated, repeated, and revised in ways that acknowledge the different modalities, exigencies, needs, and desires of today. Neal maintains that the postsoul aesthetic functions as a "radical reimagining of the contemporary African-American experience, attempting to liberate contemporary interpretations of that experience from sensibilities that were formalized and institutionalized during earlier social paradigms."[7]

The fact that Obadike himself, not a white slave trader, brokers the sale subverts the historical record and offers a contemporary revision of past traffickings in blackness. For Obadike functions as his own agent, a free man of color, willing to determine the worth of his blackness on the open market, unyoked by previous historical constraints even as he invokes history. His position parallels that of other contemporary black artists as they consider the currency of their own black cultural products. Divorced from the pain and pressures of the past, black artists need no longer conform to previous conventions that demanded they address the current state of black politics through their art. As the articles contained within this collection confirm, no longer must blackness be imagined within essentialized dimensions that confined and defined black expression in times gone by; rather, black performance and popular culture can now more freely express the multiple hues and proportions of blackness. Art curator Thelma Golden, as noted by Kennell Jackson in his introduction to this volume, has christened this "exciting moment" in artistic production "postblack." For Golden, the postblack is "characterized by artists who were adamant about not being labeled as 'black' artists, though their work was steeped, in fact deeply interested, in redefining complex notions of blackness."[8] According to Golden, then, the notion of postblack does not entail moving past any connection to race or racialized meanings, but rather traveling beyond past definitions of blackness that delimit creation or that necessitate certain artistic expectations. As a result, the postblack artist putatively experiences a new creative license, previously not possible in black artistic production. Golden writes that postblack artists' "work, in all its various forms, speaks to an individual freedom that is the result of this transitional moment in the quest to define ongoing changes in the African-American art and ultimately to ongoing redefinition of blackness in contemporary culture."[9] Thus, the postblack responds to the changing political climate but rejects the programmatic ties of black art to politics as in the 1970s Black Arts Movement. The postblack paradoxically invokes the power of race and racism and, at the same time, refutes their authority. The dynamism of the postblack emerges in this racial paradox. Liberated from racial exigencies, it explores new racial meanings. Blackness travels outside of existent boundaries. Golden proclaims that postblack is "the new black."[10]

This paradoxical proclamation presents a blackness that is simultaneously free from, and yet connected to and perhaps even haunted by, the legacies of the past in the present. Recognizing the heritage of black prejudicial treatment, Obadike does not recommend that his "Blackness be used while demanding fairness" or "be used while voting in the United States or Florida" or "while demanding justice."[11] Can blackness ever travel light—free from the baggage of the past—or is black cultural travel always accompanied, or burdened, or even weighed down, by its history? Among the ten benefits Obadike lists for his product in his online sale of blackness is that it "may be used for creating black art." Among the ten warnings Obadike lists is this: "Seller does not recommend that this Blackness be used in the process of making or selling 'serious' art."[12] The inference is simple, yet historically significant: black art has never been understood as "high" or "serious" art. Thus, a battle that black artists have faced and still encounter, even in this postblack moment, is that while they may resist pejorative racial labels, others may place such determinations upon them. Artistic merit and achievement can be negatively colorized and black arts diminished in the critical standards of the mainstream white art world. At such times, the history of black struggle shadows contemporary cultural production, and the legacy of black struggle and white hegemony certainly has an impact on black cultural expression and reception.

Yet, the realm of "serious" art has always been held in distinction from that of the popular. Within the realm of popular culture, as evidenced by the discussions within this anthology, blackness has reached new heights or "lows," as blackness has become almost synonymous with the popular. And this expanding dynamic profoundly evidences the portability and commercial utility of blackness. Blackness in the form of urban rap sounds has been packaged to sell everything from hamburgers and sneakers to dog food. Through the ever-growing reach of technology, black singers, musicians, and sports stars now play to global audiences. Black rap performers tour the world with concert dates in such places as Latvia, Poland, and Japan. The dynamic expansion in the scope of blackness in the popular realm has served to disarticulate the embedded connections of blackness to black bodies in the public arena and, equally significantly, to the history and politics of black struggle. And so, as direct consequence of blackness engulfing the sphere of the popular, it has become increasingly possible, perhaps, to have blackness or performances of blackness without black people.

Certainly the prime symbol of this new disjuncture is the rapper Eminem, whom *Source* magazine rightly named as the most powerful force in hip-hop music as of 2004. Significantly, Eminem gained entrance into the once overwhelmingly black world of rap through introduction and promotion by star rapper and producer Dr. Dre. In other words, he needed the endorsement of black hip-hoppers to provide him with legitimacy. The sanction of black bodies carried him into the arena. And yet, as evidenced by his precipitous rise to worldwide superstardom, black bodies can take you only so far. The disassociation of blackness from its black embodiment, the re-presentation of rap tropes in the skilled lyrical flow of this white rapper, have proved a commercial juggernaut. Although the *Source* has uncovered early recordings of Eminem that profess a racist attitude and disdain for black people, this has not served to diminish his popularity. Rather, Eminem's reign has helped to distance hip-hop from its original history, its colored roots.

As evidenced by his semiautobiographical debut film, *8 Mile*, Eminem emphasizes knowledge, not of black experience, but of lower-class, "white trash" experience. Within the particular hip-hop politics of location, roots or "realness" and authenticity are explicitly connected to the hood. A "hardness" learned and earned in these streets has been a crucial component in the rap milieu and its aesthetic. Importantly, the hood for Eminem and other white rappers such as Kid Rock is the trailer park. He is still working class. Suburbia and a middle-class, bourgeois background of any race have no legitimacy in rap. During a climactic rap battle in *8 Mile*, Eminem exposes a black rapper who tried to hide his bourgeois background and affirms his own white trash–ness, taking pride in this cultural identity and class location. Within the film and within hip-hop's politics of location, there is little recognition of the history of racial tensions that has existed between the white working class and the black urban masses. For historically, even from Reconstruction, the white working class has been resistant to political coalitions with blacks. Despite their shared socioeconomic position, they have seen black advancement as a threat to their own status. Significantly, *8 Mile* is set on the Eight Mile Road that separates Detroit from its suburbs, and Detroit has been the site of repeated black-white racial and class conflict. In 1943 after years of seething urban unrest between black and white working-class youth, riots erupted in which thirty-four people—twenty-five black—died, and over eighteen hundred were arrested. Although Eminem sports black friends in *8 Mile* and associates with black hip-hop luminaries in real life, this interaction with black bodies does not necessarily represent the possibility of new cross-racial politics but perhaps a new, complex form of black cultural traffic. For Eminem is not a wigger; his transaction with black bodies is not about miscegenation nor racial mimesis. Rather, with his verbal dexterity Eminem makes rap his own, and his success grants license for white working-class entrée and participation in hip-hop. Showing that rap is far from just a "black thing," 8 Mile provides an explicit critique of rap's previous racial orientation as he uncouples hip-hop cultural expression from black people.

Yet even as Eminem's hip-hop flava indicts black essentialism, he still asserts a new racial authenticity. Through his actions during the climactic moment of 8 Mile, when Eminem accepts his white trash identity and calls the black bourgeois perpetrator out on grounds of inauthenticity, he becomes the arbiter of rap realness, positing himself as more authentic than his black opponent. He now becomes the legislator of hip-hop credentials—verbal skills and working-class roots—and seemingly reracializes them as white. Still, his white body requires the sanction of blacks, for he competes against the bourgeois rapper before a crowd consisting overwhelmingly of black youth. And where they had booed him once before, they now embrace him as the new hip-hop king. Crucially, he gains their cultural approval at the expense of the black middle-class representative. Thus, the politics he creates with the black masses is not coalitional but hierarchical and intraracially divisive. By trafficking in blackness, Eminem gains ascendancy to the throne. Todd Boyd argues that "Hip hop transcends the boundaries of culture, race. and history, while being uniquely informed by all three."[13] Yet rather than racial transcendence, what the emergence and prominence of Eminem and the "battle royal" climax to 8 Mile suggest is a complex and disturbing recirculation of race.

Perhaps one of the more intriguing importers of blackness is Japan, documented by Joe Wood in his 1997 article "Yellow Negro." Wood discusses traveling to Tokyo to study "Jiggers," Japanese youth who openly assimilate the black rap scene and lifestyle. According to Wood, "'Jiggers' come in several flavors. The most curious are undoubtedly the blackfacers, b-boys and girls who darken their skin with ultraviolet rays."[14] Wood observes that the blackfacers are "proud of their assumed skin color," that "they wear blackface in order to embrace black people."[15] Yet this "embrace" of blackness reveals more about Japanese desire and the portability of blackness than it does about black people. For through the performance of skin darkening, through crimping and curling their hair, through wearing baggy pants and the other sartorial accoutrements of hip-hop, through gesture and pose, these blackfacers perform blackness and appropriate tropes of racial authenticity to their own self-interest.

The work of African American artist iona rozeal brown performs an interesting bit of "signifying" on the contemporary uses of blackness in Japanese culture and offers a further riff on the ever-widening possibilities of black cultural travel. Intrigued by Japanese appropriations of hip-hop, brown, a Washington, D.C.–based artist, began a series of works that juxtaposed contemporary African American cultural signifiers—cornrows, Afros, hip-hop chains, insignia, and clothing—with the figures and techniques of nineteenth-century Japanese printmaking. In her 2004 solo exhibit, "a3 . . . black on both sides," her geisha figures sport Afro hairdos. Black face makeup embellishes Japanese faces. Ghetto fabulous wear peaks out from beneath kimonos. What is evident in her work is her inversion of the more conventional directions of black cultural traffic. Rather than representing the images of Japanese co-optations of hip-hop that she encountered, in brown's art symbols and representations from Japanese tradition are appropriated and become black. The notion of "black on both sides" in the title of her exhibit riffs on the transatlantic voyages of blackness as well as the notion of how blackness can reach below the surface level of the skin. Iona rozeal brown's work explodes in "cultural paradoxes and contradictions" and serves, as Phil Auslander points out, as an "extraordinary cultural encounter."[16] Her prints express the notion that no culture is pure, that cultural identity is always about mixing, about positioning, about exchange and interchange.

Correspondingly, Joe Wood in "Yellow Negro" identifies an anxiety, a sense of both pleasure and panic, within the Japanese culture past and present, around the representation of blackness. For Japan is a society in which "a profound attraction to black music" has existed alongside the sale of black Sambo images on toothpaste tubes. Like the minstrel mask, these performances serve as an example of what Eric Lott terms "love and theft." Lott writes, "It was cross-racial desire that coupled a nearly insupportable fascination and a self-protective derision with respect to black people and their cultural practices, and made blackface minstrelsy less a sign of white power and control than of panic anxiety, terror and pleasure."[17] According to Wood, "The uneasy response to blackness and black culture—the combined attraction and repulsion, the 'affirmation of the barbarian'" links "contemporary blackfacers to an earlier moment in Japanese culture and American culture as well."[18] What Wood observes in

Japan, as in America, is a complex and contradictory relationship of the dominant culture to blackness, the site of both fear and desire. With the blackfacers as with white American minstrels in nineteenth century, blackness functions as something that you can apply, put on, wear, that you use to assuage social anxiety and perceived threat: the desire to be included without the necessity of including black folk. When Wood asked one blackfaced girl of nineteen, "Why do you choose to look like me?," she responded, "Because it's cool." Cool then serves as the ultimate aspiration of social belonging, and blackness is just a means to this end.

To be sure, it remains exceedingly attractive and possible in this postblack, postsoul age of black cultural traffic to love black cool and not love black people. Such black love operates on the affective level where style is much more important than political substance. Thus, even in the seeming multicultural mix, the cross-cultural embrace that such love of black cool engenders, these conditions do not necessarily produce any sort of progressive politics or promote avenues for social change and black liberation. There is often no investment in black struggle nor commitment to the particular causes and histories of black advancement. Accordingly, in James Toback's 1999 film *Black and White*—a film in which a dreadlocked Brooke Shields as the character "Sam" makes a documentary on wiggers, young affluent white kids invested in black rap culture—one of the subjects of her documentary, Charlie (Bijou Phillips) turns to the camera, as the light glistens on her gold tooth, and explains, "Look, we're into this black thing now 'cause it's hip. That doesn't mean we'll always be into it. Ten years from now we'll probably be into something else."[19] These lines tellingly reveal the luxury of white privilege, the power of normative whiteness as well as the potentially exploitative nature of cultural appropriations. Because of their subject position, the rich white teenagers in *Black and White* can act as cultural tourists and enjoy the enticement and liberating sensuality of blackness. All the while, they maintain the ability to return to their vanilla suburbs and escape the inherent dangers of blackness in contemporary America.

For black subjects, the allure of a portable blackness that one can apply or remove at will creates both anxiety as well as an appeal. In George C. Wolfe's 1984 satirical play *The Colored Museum*, the "Man" character in an exhibit entitled "Symbiosis" laments as he throws away all the material remnants of his black past, R & B albums, Afro comb and pick, "Free Huey" buttons: "Being black is too emotionally taxing, therefore I will be black only on weekends and holidays."[20] Wolfe's comically perplexed bourgeois figure riffs on the inescapability of blackness for black people but also the pleasures of black cool. The urge to be "black only on weekends and holidays" augurs signal moments when the richness of black culture finds expression, on weekends and holidays when you can be black among black people and enjoy the communal, cultural exchange. One of the benefits of buying his blackness, according to Obadike on eBay, is that it "can be used by blacks as a spare." This "benefit" implies that blacks experience a genuine need for their blackness, and it also underscores the connection of blackness to travel and traffic. Like a spare tire, blackness can help you to reach your next destination. And yet there is also anxiety, for what if you do not in fact have a spare? Do you then surrender your ability to travel, or even lose your blackness and forfeit your certificate of authenticity?

In today's increasingly globalized world, the possibilities and performances of blackness have proliferated, and one can delve into a variety of different expressions of blackness, postblack or not. Perhaps with blackness it is not as simple as what Jay-Z in his 2003 *Black Album* offers on the hit song "Change Clothes": one can't simply "change clothes and go." And yet as we have discussed within this volume and here in this epilogue, blackness does function as a commodity for good or bad, and tests of black authenticity often do rely on what adorns the body rather than what is within it. In some ways, both black commodification and black authenticity are mythical sites for black cultural traffic. Paul Gilroy argues that black cultural forms have been "joyously rediscovered and reinvented repeatedly."[21] Uneasiness can arise with this process of reinvention, because with the emergence of diverse representations of blackness, questions remain as to who is the arbiter of blackness and how we define black art. Moreover, if there is now more access to a portable blackness, then there is more potential for it to be used, mined for value, discarded, exploited by others, and even bought and sold on eBay.

NOTES

1. <http://www.blackradicalcongress.org> Friday, 10 August 2001 22:04:46–0400.
2. Saidiya Hartman, *Scenes of Subjection* (New York: Oxford University Press, 1997), 23–24.
3. Hortense J. Spillers, "Mama's Baby, Papa's Maybe: An American Grammar Book," *Diacritics* (Summer 1987): 79.
4. Spillers, "Mama's Baby," 78.

5. Mark Anthony Neal, *Soul Babies: Black Popular Culture and the Post-soul Aesthetic* (New York: Routledge, 2002), 8.

6. Mark Anthony Neal, *Soul Babies,* 22.

7. Neal, *Soul Babies,* 3.

8. Thelma Golden, "Post-Black" from the Exhibition Catalogue to Freestyle Exhibition Studio Museum of Harlem, 2001, 1.

9. Thelma Golden, "Post-Black," 2.

10. Thelma Golden, "Post-Black."

11. <http://www.blackradicalcongress.org> Friday, 10 August 2001 22:04:46–0400.

12. Ibid.

13. Todd Boyd, *The New H.N.I.C: The Death of Civil Rights and the Reign of Hip Hop* (New York: NYU Press, 2002), 18.

14. Joe Wood, "Yellow Negro," *Transition,* 73 (1997): 43.

15. Ibid.

16. Philip Auslander, "Mixing the Colors," *Art Papers* (May/June 2004): 4.

17. Eric Lott, *Love and Theft: Blackface Minstrelsy and the American Working Class* (New York: Oxford University Press, 1993), 6.

18. Wood, 47.

19. James Toback, *Black and White,* Columbia Pictures, 1999.

20. George C. Wolfe, *The Colored Museum.*

21. Paul Gilroy, "'. . . to be real': the dissident forms of black expressive culture," *Let's Get It On,* ed. Catherine Ugwu (Seattle: Bay Press, 1995), 12.

Contributors

Jennifer Devere Brody is Associate Professor of English, Performance Studies, and African American Studies at Northwestern University. She is the author of *Impossible Purities: Blackness, Femininity, and Victorian Culture* (Duke University Press, 1998); her book in progress is entitled *The Style of Elements: Politically Performing Punctuation.* It will be published by Duke University Press. She has been a Ford Postdoctoral Fellow, and a recipient of the Monette/Horwitz Prize for independent research against homophobia. She has written articles and reviews in such venues as *Genders, Signs, Callaloo, American Literary History, American Quarterly, Theatre Journal,* and *Screen.*

Donald Byrd since 1976 has created over eighty works for his own company, Donald Byrd/The Group, as well as for modern dance repertory companies including the Alvin Ailey American Dance Theater, Dayton Contemporary Dance Company, Philadelphia Dance Company (Philadanco), Cleo Parker Robinson, Dallas Black Dance Theater, and Phoenix Dance in Leeds, England. He served on the faculty of the California Institute for the Arts for six years, and has taught at Wesleyan University, the School of Visual Arts, Harvard Summer Dance Center, California State University Long Beach, the University of California at Santa Cruz, and Ohio University. He was recently appointed Artistic Director of Spectrum Dance Theater in Seattle, and currently serves on the Board of Trustees for Dance Theater Workshop.

Catherine M. Cole is Associate Professor of Dramatic Art at the University of California, Santa Barbara. She is author of *Ghana's Concert Party Theatre* (Indiana University Press, 2001), which won an honorable mention for the Barnard Hewitt Award from the American Society for Theatre Research. A practicing theatre artist, Cole is a co-creator of *Five Foot Feat,* a dance theatre piece that toured North America in 2003–4. Her work has received funding from the National Endowment for the Humanities, the American Association for University Women, and the Fund for U.S. Artists. She is currently serving as the Associate Director for Special

Projects at UCSB's Interdisciplinary Humanities Center. Her next book, *Stages of Transition,* analyzes the performative dimensions of South Africa's Truth Commission.

Manthia Diawara teaches at New York University, where he is University Professor in Comparative Literature and Africana Studies. He is the author of *In Search of Africa,* and director of *Bamako Sigi Kan.*

Paulla A. Ebron is an Associate Professor in the Department of Cultural and Social Anthropology at Stanford University. An extended discussion of her research among jalis can be found in her book *Performing Africa* (Princeton University Press, 2002). Her current research is on the making of tropical Africa in the U.S. South.

Harry J. Elam, Jr. is the Olive H. Palmer Professor in the Humanities of Stanford University. He is author of *Taking It to the Streets: The Social Protest Theater of Luis Valdez and Amiri Baraka* (University of Michigan Press, 1997), and *The Past as Present in the Drama of August Wilson* (University of Michigan Press, 2004), coeditor of *African American Performance and Theater History: A Critical Reader* (Oxford University Press, 2001), *Colored Contradictions: An Anthology of Contemporary African American Drama* (Penguin, 1996), and *The Fire This Time: African American Plays for the New Millennium* (TCG Press, 2004). He is the current editor of *Theatre Journal.*

Nicole R. Fleetwood is Assistant Professor of American Studies at Rutgers University. She researches and teaches in the areas of visual culture, technology studies, gender theory, and race and representation. Her articles appear in *Signs, Social Text, TDR,* and in edited anthologies. Currently she is completing a manuscript on visuality, discources of blackness, and gender relations.

Michael Franti is a musician, spoken word artist, and political activist. His group Spearhead is reinventing hip-hop, drawing on influences from funk and soul music. In 1990 he formed a band called Disposable Heroes of Hiphoprisy. The band established itself among rap's foremost proponents of multiculturalism and liberalism, pointedly attacking hip-hop tenets like homophobia, misogyny, and racism. In 1994 he formed Spearhead, whose albums include *Home* and *Chocolate Supa Highway;* his latest venture is *Stay Human.* His works raise questions about issues as wide ranging as capital punishment, AIDS, gay rights, homelessness, drug addiction, and suicide.

Herman Gray is Chair of the Department of Sociology at University of California, Santa Cruz. He is the author of *Watching Race: Television and* *the Sign of Blackness* (University of Minnesota Press, 1995) and *Cultural Moves: African Americans and the Politics of Representation* (Berkeley: University of California Press, 2005).

Rennie Harris is the founder of Puremovement, a hip-hop dance company to preserve and disseminate hip-hop couture through workshops, classes, mentoring programs, and public performances. Drawing upon Shakespeare's *Romeo and Juliet* as well as *West Side Story,* Harris created, choreographed, and directed *Rome & Jewels;* the piece garnered significant acclaim, picking up three Bessie Awards and two Black Theater Alvin Ailey Awards as well as nominations for Herb Alpert and Lawrence Olivier awards. Other important pieces include *Legends of Hip-Hop, Students of the Asphalt Jungle,* and *Facing Mekka.* His company is currently implementing an after-school mentoring program for children in Philadelphia, to provide structured, constructive, and creative activities for at-risk youth.

Kennell Jackson is Associate Professor of History at Stanford, specializing in the study of cultural history, particularly mass culture phenomena such as black hair's global impact. He has written a popular history of African Americans, *America Is Me,* and has contributed to the history of East Africa through scholarship on oral traditions and the 1950s Mau Mau uprising. Currently, he is pursuing research on Kenyan cultural history.

E. Patrick Johnson is Associate Professor of Performance Studies and Director of Graduate Studies at Northwestern University. A scholar/artist, his essays have appeared in *Callaloo, Text and Performance Quarterly, TDR,* and the *Journal of Homosexuality.* He is the author of *Appropriating Blackness: Performance and the Politics of Authenticity* (Duke University Press, 2003) and winner of several awards, including the Errol Hill Award from the American Society of Theatre Research and the Lillian A. Heston Award. He has co-authored, with Mae G. Henderson, *Black Queer Studies,* (Duke University Press). He is currently working on a book manuscript entitled *Sweet Tea: An Oral History of Black Gay Men in the South* for University of North Carolina Press.

Rhodessa Jones is a director, actress, dancer, singer, writer, and teacher. She is Co-Artistic Director of the San Francisco–based performance company Cultural Odyssey and founder-director of the Medea Project: Theatre for Incarcerated Women, for which she was honored with the Community Bridge Builder Award from the San Francisco Foundation in December 2000. Her new show, *Hot Flashes, Power Surges, and Private Summers,* premiered at the Working Women's Theater Festival. She teaches art for social change in diverse venues, including Lowell Prison for Women in Florida, Yale, University of California, Berkeley, and LaMama's directors' symposium in Spoleto, Italy. Jones recently directed Will Power's solo piece *The Gathering* and the 1999 nationally acclaimed world premiere of Erin Cressida Wilson's *Trail of Her Inner Thigh* for Campo Santo at Intersection for the Arts in San Francisco.

W. T. Lhamon, Jr. teaches English and American Studies at Florida State University. He is the author of *Raising Cain: Blackface Performance from Jim Crow to Hip Hop* (Harvard University Press, 1998); *Deliberate Speed: The Origin of a Cultural Style in the American 1950s* (Harvard University Press, 2002); and *Jump Jim Crow: Plays, Lyrics, and Street Prose of the First Atlantic Popular Culture* (Harvard University Press, 2003). His next book, *Fetish and Flow: Secret Histories of Emergence and Survival,* will be on the flow of cultural transmission across borders, eras, and forms.

Christian McBride graduated from the High School for the Creative and Performing Arts in Philadelphia in 1989. He attended the Juilliard School of Music and was hired by Bobby Watson to play with his band at Birdland. McBride has performed on more than seventy albums with the likes of Joe Henderson, Etta Jones, Betty Carter, Wynton Marsalis, Bruce Hornsby, Pat Metheny, Cyrus Chestnut, Freddie Hubbard, Kathleen Battle, Joey DeFrancesco, Benny Green, and Joshua Redman, among others. In 1992, McBride was named *Rolling Stone* magazine's "Hot Jazz Artist." In 1995, he made his debut as a leader with his album *Gettin' to It,* one of the biggest-selling jazz records of 1995. *Family Affair* came next in 1998, followed by his most ambitious project, *Sci-Fi* in 2000.

Keith Antar Mason is Artistic Director and cofounding member of the Hittite Empire. In addition to its own highly acclaimed repertory of work, the Hittite Empire has collaborated with communities around the United States and in the United Kingdom to create works that grow from the experiences of young members of the African diaspora. Their work, including *Anatomy of Deep Blue, The Harsh Reality of Toys,* and *Man in the Belly of a Slaveship,* has been seen in venues throughout America. Mason's writings have been published nationally and in 1974 he was awarded the Harvard Book Award for Poetry for "Gunge Tomorrows." He is the founder of blackmadrid, a black poetry-jazz-rap-griot recording collective that has created works for New American Radio, BarKubCo Music, and New Alliance Records. Mason also founded the Los Angeles Black Repertory Company, a nonprofit umbrella organization.

Kobena Mercer is a cultural worker-critic whose varied work on the politics of representation in African diasporic visual arts has inaugurated an important line of inquiry into postidentitarian cultural politics. His first book was *Welcome to the Jungle: New Positions in Black Cultural Studies* (Routledge, 1994). He has taught at University of California, Santa Cruz in the History of Consciousness Program and the Africana Studies department at New York University as well as the Humanitus Research Institute at University of California, Irvine. In addition to monographs on Keith Piper (1997) and James van Der Zee (2003), he has contributed exhibition catalogue essays to *Adrian Piper: A Retrospective* and *Looking Both Ways: Art of the Contemporary African Diaspora*. As the series editor of Annotating Art's Histories, his next book is the edited collection *Cosmopolitan Modernisms* (2005). He is currently senior Research Fellow in Visual Culture and Media at Middlesex University, London.

Robert Moses is a dancer and the Artistic Director of *Robert Moses Kin* (1995), for which he has choreographed over forty works. He has performed with American Ballet, Los Angeles Opera, Twyla Tharp Dance, ODC/San Francisco, Long Beach Ballet, Walt Disney World Productions, and Gloria Newman Dance Theater as well as in numerous film and television productions. His work ranges from the specific oral histories in African American culture and the work of author James Baldwin to the more universal themes of solitude, love, and the darkness of urban living. Moses has collaborated with many other notable artists including Julia Adam, Margaret Jenkins, Alonzo King, Sara Shelton Mann, SoVoSo, Marcus Shelby, Keith Terry, and Frank Boehm. He has taught at numerous universities including Stanford, University of California, Berkeley, University of California, Davis, University of Texas, University of Nevada, and Mills College.

Chike C. Nwoffiah is Cofounder and Artistic Director of Oriki Theater, a nonprofit community theater that brings to audiences a shared experience of the real Africa, its people and their way of life through dance, drama, music, folk stories, song, chants, and the drum. At the Oriki, Nwoffiah has written and directed ten major stage productions, including *Wake Up Africa, Bridges, Pulse of Life, Buwa,* and *Echoes of the Drum.* He is also a filmmaker whose children's television program of African folk stories *Ago! Amee!* won 1998 Cinema in Industry "Cindy" Gold and Black Filmmakers Hall of Fame awards. Nwoffiah is also Director of the California Black Arts Alliance, a statewide advocacy coalition representing black artists and arts organizations across the state. In April 2003, the Silicon Valley Chapter of the NAACP awarded him the NAACP Freedom Fighter award.

Halifu Osumare is an Assistant Professor of African American and African Studies at the University of California, Davis. She holds an M.A. in Dance Ethnology from San Francisco State University and a Ph.D. in American Studies from the University of Hawaii. She has published extensively on the globalization of hip-hop culture. Her forthcoming book, *Power Moves: The Africanist Aesthetic in the Hip Hop Globe* is currently under contract with Wesleyan University Press.

Euzhan Palcy, born in Martinique, is the first woman of African descent to ever direct a Hollywood studio movie. She directed her first film, *The Messenger,* at age seventeen. *Sugar Cane Alley* (1983) won over seventeen international prizes including the Silver Lion and the Cesar Award for Best First Feature Film. *A Dry White Season* (1989) picked up an Academy Award nomination for best supporting actor, and Palcy received the "Orson Welles" Prize for Special Cinematic Achievement. Her three-part portrait *Aimé Césaire: A Voice for History* (1995), on the Martinique poet, playwright, and philosopher, garnered international critical and popular acclaim. In 1994, French president François Mitterand honored her as the Chevalier Dans L'ordre National du Merite. In 2001 she won the Sojourner Truth Award at the Cannes Film Festival.

Will Power, a pioneer in the emerging genre of hip-hop theater, has been featured in publications such as *Vibe, Source,* and *American Theatre,* as well as on Fox, NBC, CBS, and ABC. His performances, workshops, and lectures have been seen in twenty-five states and over fifty-five cities abroad including Paris, Amsterdam, Strasbourg, Vienna, London, Glasgow, Cologne, Toronto, Montreal, and Vancouver. His play, *2017,* is a hip-hop musical about AIDS in the black community. His solo show, *The Gathering,* directed by Rhodessa Jones, marked the beginnings of hip-hop theater. From 1997 to 2000, Will Power was the lead vocalist of the Omar Sosa Sextet, an internationally recognized band known for innovatively fusing jazz with Latin rhythms and hip-hop. He cofounded, with Mohammed Bilal, the hip-hop band Midnight Voices. As a cultural and community activist, Power conducts workshops in schools, community centers, colleges, and universities.

Danzy Senna grew up in Boston, where her parents, who are both writers, were active in the civil rights movement. After graduating from Stanford, she received her M.F.A. in creative writing from University of California, Irvine. Senna has worked as a journalist for several major magazines, and her critical writings on race and gender have been anthologized. Her first novel, *Caucasia,* was published in 1998. She currently lives in Brooklyn.

Tyler Stovall is Professor of History at the University of California, Berkeley. He is the author of *The Rise of the Paris Red Belt* and *Paris Noir: African Americans in the City of Light,* as well as numerous articles and book reviews in scholarly journals. He is currently working on a historical study of migration from the French Caribbean to France.

Caroline A. Streeter is Assistant Professor in the Department of English and the Center for African American Studies at UCLA. She holds a Ph.D. in Ethnic Studies with a Designation in Women, Gender, and Sexuality from the University of California, Berkeley. Her research focuses on representations of "race" and "mixed race" in post-civil-rights era U.S. American literature, film, and popular culture.

Tim'm T. West, an educator, scholar, journalist, poet, and rapper, received his B.A. at Duke University in Philosophy with a focus in Women's Studies. In 1998, he received an M.A. in Liberal Studies/Philosophy from the New School for Social Research and, in January 2002, a M.A. in Modern Thought and Literature from Stanford. In 1999, he cofounded and began recording and touring nationally with Deep Dickollective (D/DC). The former Department Chair of English and Creative Writing at the Oakland School for the Arts in Oakland, California, Tim'm currently works as an activist in Washington D.C. He is the author of *Red Dirt Revival:* a poetic memoir in Six Breaths. In 2004 Tim'm released a musical complement to this memoir on Cellular Records entitled, "Songs from Red Dirt."

Index

3rd Base, 178, 361
50 Cent, 178

Abiodun, Nehanda, 280
Achebe, Chinua, 145, 255
Afolabi, Niyi, 281
African American modernisms, 148–60
African art and cubism, 21, 150
African diaspora spirituality: candomblé in Brazil, vodun in Haiti, Santeria in Cuba, Yoruba, 157
African theater: critical studies of African popular theater, 45–46; indigenous African performance, 44; in Kenya, 24, 43; the Kumapin Royals in Ghana, 45; in London, 31; in Nigeria, 24; Pan-African Historical Theatre Festival, 48; *Woza Albert!* in South Africa, 43. *See also* concert party theater in Ghana and Jaguar Jokers
Africobra: Ben Jones, Jeff Donaldson, and Wandsworth Jarrell, 152
Afro hairstyle, 15, 23, 197, 199, 246, 248, 263, 386
Aggrey, Dr. James Emman Kwegyir ("Aggrey of Africa"), 51, 52
Ali, Muhammad, 251, 252
Amos 'n' Andy, 134
Anderson, Benedict, 175, 177, 292
apartheid and postapartheid in South Africa, 44
Appollinaire, Guillaume, 227
Armstrong, Louis, xx, 18, 95, 102, 346
Ashanti, 147
Auslander, Philip, 385
Austin, Joe, 268
Avedon, Richard, 262

Baby Phat, 332, 333
Badu, Erykah, 88, 170, 173, 189, 197
Bahamadiya, 267
Baker, Houston, 255
Baker, Josephine, 128, 135, 222, 230–37
Balibar, Étienne, 169, 179
Bamako, 242
Bannister, Edward Mitchell, 151
Banton, Buju, 181
Baraka, Amiri (LeRoi Jones), 152, 255
Barber, Karin, 24
Barkley, Charles, 92, 93
Barr, Alfred, 150
Barthes, Roland, 89, 93, 103, 326, 334, 336
Basquiat, Jean-Michel, 156
Beale, Howard, 356
Bearden, Romare, 148–50, 155, 156
Beastie Boys, The, 178
Beatles, The, 104, 242, 244, 250
Beenie Man, 181
Bell, Clive, 150
Bennett, Gwendolyn, 228, 229, 236
Berger, John, 198
Berkeley, Busby, 235
Bernhard, Sandra, 135, 193–94
Berry, Halle, 203
B.G. (Baby Gangsta), 11
Bhabha, Homi K., 46, 131, 186, 223
Big Punisher (Chris Rios), 27, 134–36
Black Arts Movement (BAM), 149, 152, 153, 173, 381
Black August Hip Hop Collective, 279, 280
blackface performance: Harriet Beecher Stowe, 127; influence on Ghana concert party theater, 44–53; Japanese, 128, 131–35, 223, 235, 266, 347, 350–62, 384–85; Jim Crow, 120–24; and

Black Cultural Traffic traces how blackness travels globally in performance, including television, hip-hop, R&B, gospel, film, theater, fashion, and pop music. The contributors are an international and interdisciplinary mix of scholars, critics, and practicing artists who provide nuanced and complex perspectives on black culture—not as a static set of shared beliefs and customs but as something that is contingent and dynamic. The book's engaging combination of scholarship and artists' statements will appeal to anyone interested in understanding the circulation and multi-directional movements of black culture.

Harry J. Elam, Jr., is Olive H. Palmer Professor in Humanities and Professor of Drama at Stanford University. He is author of *The Past as Present in the Drama of August Wilson* and *Taking It to the Streets: The Social Protest Theater of Luis Valdez and Amiri Baraka.*

Kennell Jackson is Associate Professor of History at Stanford and author of *America Is Me: 170 Fresh Questions and Answers on Black American History.*